The Journals and
Miscellaneous Notebooks
of
RALPH WALDO EMERSON

GENERAL EDITORS

WILLIAM H. GILMAN   ALFRED R. FERGUSON

MERRELL R. DAVIS

MERTON M. SEALTS, JR.   HARRISON HAYFORD

The Journals and Miscellaneous Notebooks

of

RALPH WALDO EMERSON

VOLUME II

1822–1826

EDITED BY

WILLIAM H. GILMAN   ALFRED R. FERGUSON

MERRELL R. DAVIS

THE BELKNAP PRESS

OF HARVARD UNIVERSITY PRESS

Cambridge, Massachusetts

1961

Distributed in Great Britain by Oxford University Press, London

Typography by Burton J Jones

Printed in the U.S.A. by the Harvard University Printing Office

Bound by Stanhope Bindery, Inc., Boston, Massachusetts

Library of Congress Catalog Card Number: 60–11554

Preface

As this edition of Emerson's journals and miscellaneous notebooks grows, the debts it owes to individuals, institutions, and foundations must necessarily expand. Although these acknowledgments will fall far short of discharging the obligations, the editors are happy to make them in the hope that they will be received as at least a minimum expression of their gratitude.

The Ralph Waldo Emerson Association has continued to provide regular annual grants-in-aid which have been indispensable to the progress of the edition, and Edward Waldo Forbes, its president, and David Emerson, its treasurer, have supplemented this with many personal kindnesses.

The John Simon Guggenheim Memorial Foundation has graciously granted a research fellowship. The Universities of Washington and Rochester have generously provided sabbatical leaves and Ohio Wesleyan University and the University of Rochester have made grants for research assistance, travel, and freedom from summer teaching.

Professor William A. Jackson, Director of the Houghton Library, has continued to ease the burdens of the editors, and Miss Carolyn Jakeman, also of the Houghton Library, has shown her usual thoughtfulness and prompt cooperation, in crises as in normal times.

Mrs. Linda Gallasch prepared the original text from microfilm and paved the way for research on the notes with such accuracy and insight into the problems of editing as to shorten by several months the period of gestation. Mr. Ralph H. Orth, of the University of Vermont, through precise and imaginative research in his doctoral dissertation on Emerson's Encyclopedia, saved many a week of hunting for the sources of Emerson's quotations. A diligent group of research assistants have given patiently of their minds and physical energies in the laborious exercises of source-hunting and checking

v

notes — Messrs. Donald Adams and David Porter, and Mrs. John A. Leermakers, who has served with exceeding industry and without compensation. Mary A. Koethen, Millicent Kalaf, Mrs. Leermakers, Mrs. Charles Rob, Mrs. Stephen M. Tucker, Mrs. Merrell R. Davis, and Mrs. William H. Gilman have rendered careful aid in the exacting task of reading proof.

Professors Elmer Suhr, Virginia Moscrip, Alfreda Hill, and John H. Whittemore, all of the University of Rochester, have helped with knotty problems in Latin and in French literature and language. The editors' immediate colleagues have answered their queries with patience and sympathy or given other effective support to their cause, particularly Professors Robert B. Heilman and Andrew R. Hilen, Jr., of the University of Washington and Wilbur D. Dunkel and Glyndon G. Van Deusen of the University of Rochester. Professors in other universities have also contributed valuable aid to the editors — Leon Howard of the University of California at Los Angeles, Kenneth B. Murdock, Perry Miller, Howard Mumford Jones, and Mark DeWolfe Howe of Harvard University, and Lewis Leary of Columbia University.

Mr. William H. Bond of Houghton Library has provided some acute detective work on the manuscripts, and Mr. Robert H. Haynes has courteously made the use of Widener Library a more than ordinary privilege. The staffs of the libraries of the University of Washington, the University of Rochester, Harvard University, and Ohio Wesleyan University have been steadily helpful.

Unless otherwise noted, translations from Greek and Latin are from the Loeb Classical Library and are reprinted by permission of the Harvard University Press and the Loeb Classical Library.

The variation of the title and half-title pages of this volume from those of volume I reflects a change of editors. Those designated on the title page of volume II have been primarily responsible for its preparation; all the General Editors have actively contributed in various ways.

The title page of each subsequent volume will designate those primarily responsible for its preparation.

W.H.G. M.M.S.
A.R.F. H.H.
M.R.D.

Merrell Rees Davis

1912–1961

Merrell R. Davis died on March 21, 1961. For nearly a year he had known that he was seriously ill, but he chose to go ahead quietly with his teaching and his work on this edition. With what resolution and bravery he did so, most of his friends and colleagues did not realize, for with his characteristic selflessness he had not asked them to share his burden of knowledge. He had endured other misfortunes, and he was equal to this final adversity.

The son of teachers, he was a born and devoted teacher. He graduated from Whitman College in 1935. He took his higher degrees at Tufts (M.A., 1937) and at Yale (Ph.D., 1948). He was Teaching Fellow at Tufts College (1935–1937); Instructor at Evanston Collegiate Institute, now Kendall College (1937–1939); Tutorial Fellow at Northwestern University (1939–1940) and Instructor (1940–1944); University Scholar at Yale University (1945–1946); Assistant Professor of English at the University of Washington (1947–1953), Associate Professor (1953–1961), and Professor (1961). As a teacher he was at once demanding and sympathetic; he sought the highest quality of work, but he was extraordinarily kind to students beset by academic and personal problems.

At Northwestern, under Professor Leon Howard, he began the studies in Melville and in Emerson which he continued at Yale under Professor Stanley T. Williams, and which became the foundation for his articles and books. His major publications were *Melville's* MARDI: *A Chartless Voyage*, his edition (with William H. Gilman) of *The Letters of Herman Melville*, and this edition of Emerson's *Journals and Miscellaneous Notebooks*. The high caliber of his scholarship has been affirmed by critics in both America and Europe.

His contributions to this edition were abundant and vital.

vii

Much of the preliminary work of surveying all the manuscript journals and notebooks and of drawing up the Editorial Title List was his. For volume I, he collated galleys with manuscript, and solved, in his shrewd and painstaking way, many textual problems; he wrote the textual notes and many of the headnotes and bibliographical notes; he planned the Index; and he worked out innumerable problems of printing. Though in failing health, he did a substantial share of the same work for volume II. The standards he set and the techniques he devised or refined constitute a permanent endowment for the whole edition.

His associate editors in this edition were his friends and fellow scholars of many years, from graduate-school days at Yale, and even earlier. They enjoyed with him the happy rigor of mutual criticism; they best know his qualities as a scholar. To this edition as to all his work he brought his immense respect for the truth: that is what his precision, his patient skill, his infinite scruple meant; that is what his curiosity, his learning, and his wisdom were devoted to. He was modest, humorous, and magnanimous; he was never solemn. He thought it mattered to do a job right, and he spared himself nothing to make it so.

No one who knew much of Merrell Davis, and of mankind, could hesitate to apply to him what Hawthorne wrote of Melville, that he was of "a very high and noble nature, and better worth immortality than most of us."

Contents

ix

Illustrations

Foreword to Volume II

The journals and notebooks from 1822 to 1826 begin on the same note of enthusiasm for exploration of the wide world of mind which Emerson struck in his first regular journals in 1820. It is true that the exuberance later becomes tempered and the tone of self-reliance sometimes sounds hollow. Inevitably the sense of exalted purpose and the youthfully self-conscious excitement evaporate. In June, 1823, Emerson stops dedicating his journals to some ideal aim, and in 1824 he finally drops the title Wide World and uses mute, impersonal letters and numbers for the journals, including four previously called Wide World. Still, the major purpose of the journals continues. Emerson carried on the effort to translate experience into living thought, to endow the passing show of life and of intellectual perceptions with permanence. Much of the experience, perhaps too much, was bookish. Emerson continued his wide reading, at least until the late winter of 1825. By then he had read or dipped into some hundreds of books and periodicals. Characteristically, the reading challenged him, gave him ideas, or stimulated creative thinking, and in various ways it affected his style. The discerning reader will detect the influence on Emerson of Bacon, Johnson, Hume, Thomas Brown, Madame de Staël, writers for *The Edinburgh Review*, and others. That Emerson still aspired to the company of illustrious essayists, particularly those concerned with moral problems, cannot be doubted. The journals have "essays" on final causes, on God and his attributes — Omniscience, Omnipotence, Benevolence — on moral civilization, moral obligation, the moral sense, and moral beauty; on slavery, on taste, on greatness and fame, on friendship, solitude, and apathy, and on compensation. The representative list is taken from Emerson's index headings to his journal pages. The outlines of the later, formal essay-writing are vividly clear. Yet the impulse to write for publication, to achieve immediate fame, is not so strong as in the more expectant journals of the college years. Emerson's probing of ideas and issues was virtually private. There is little matter addressed to some imaginary editor or audience — no "Idol No. 1," only a few pages in the manner of *The Spectator,* and mere driblets of Gothic or other romance like those Emerson wrote earlier, with a secret hope, perhaps, of publication. Later, he did publish a few poems and sketches written in the period, but his ambition to "shine in . . . *theme, poem,* or *review*" not only cools but gives way at times to a defensive and perhaps compensatory scorn for a fame which was still far from his grasp.

Both the reading and the writing were in part a flight from or a substitute for life. For most of these years, Emerson could find no formal occupation except teaching adolescent girls, and he loathed it. "O fortunate nimium!" — "O too fortunate one!" — he exclaimed in 1823 about a friend who had managed to escape from "his pedagogical career." Emerson's escape lay mostly in his journals, his "ancient friend & consoler," as he called them. And his reading, diffused over so many authors and subjects, also has the air of escape, of a restless search for some elusive elixir which would finally distill all truths, resolve all moral and metaphysical anomalies, and supply the satisfaction which everyday existence sorely lacked. His habits were bad enough to evoke sharp self-condemnation: "My cardinal vice of intellectual dissipation — sinful strolling from book to book[,] from care to idleness[,] is my cardinal vice still; is a malady that belongs to the Chapter of Incurables." Bedeviled periodically by skepticism and depression, and trying repeatedly to schematize affirmations of his old beliefs and new intuitions — about the origin and nature of evil, the nature and existence of God, the fundamental unity of man and God and of history, time, and the universe, the universality of the moral law, and the dependence of matter upon mind — he repeatedly failed. The journals of 1822 to 1826 show him wrestling again and again with the angel of truth.

Biographically, the journals are illuminating. These were the years of a growing sense of diffidence and isolation, of recurrent self-analyses, exhaustive and painful, and of critical decision about his career. One side of Emerson demanded total freedom, with a self-reliance that rejected all demands not originating in the ego. The tone was Byronic, aggressively defiant (see plate I). The other side pressed him to heed the obligations of his moral and intellectual self, to answer the plain call of duty, and resulted in the dedication of his whole being to the service of God. He gave up both school-teaching and his independent self without a sigh and prepared for the ministry. Disaster shortly befell him; his overworked eyes gave out and he could study hardly at all, or write in his journals, except to scrawl a note or two (see plate IV). But here was at least one experience that was not from books but from life. Typically, he put the experience to literary use, in the eloquent passage of January 8, 1826 (see plate III). Reckoning up the value of long sickness, he concluded in an eleven-page essay that there was compensation in all things. He re-affirmed the ancient tenet, sorely tried, that faith and an unflinching will are the masters of all circumstance.

Besides the journals of the period there are five miscellaneous notebooks, two consisting largely of quotations and one remainder of a journal containing an uncompleted theme or essay on the Unity of God. The first is given over mostly to copies of letters which passed between Emerson and his aunt, Mary Moody Emerson. It is the record of an intellectual correspondence in which the would-be teacher, who had told her pupil that he was perfectly capable of thinking for himself, found with increasing anxiety that she was right. The second notebook is a small grab-bag of notes, original poems from as late as 1828(?), and quotations. The third notebook is, in a way, a fitting terminus to this volume. In the "Unity of God" Emerson had the temerity to oppose his largely intuited convictions and his faulty reasoning capacity to the sternly logical skepticism of Hume's analyses of natural religion. The unfinished and perhaps abortive little work is virtually a symbol of Emerson's history during the period — a history of the effort to counter empirically derived perceptions with a faith that what he felt *must* be true *was* true.

Two notebooks of the period are not included. "Collectanea," though dated 1825, it has seemed preferable to publish in a later volume together with other notebooks of quotations. Notebook "NP (New Poetry)," also dated 1825, contains mostly matter from several subsequent years, and like other poetry notebooks it is not included (see *JMN,* I, xxxvi).

Dating. The second volume centers around those journals and miscellaneous notebooks which Emerson kept regularly from July 11, 1822, through February, 1825, and irregularly, because of the eye trouble and other illness until January 8, 1826. The manuscripts also contain a few pages written not later than 1821, when Emerson graduated from Harvard, and a scattering of entries, mostly letters, which run to 1829. The dates of this volume, however, are determined not by the earliest and latest entries in all of the manuscripts printed but, more reasonably, by the period to which the overwhelming bulk of the regular entries belong. They are printed not in the order of their numbering, but in order of the dates when they begin.

Editorial techniques. The editorial process described in volume I has been followed, with two minor modifications. Emerson's dates have been normalized by the silent insertion of commas and periods. The policy of eliminating materials where there is maximum certainty that they have neither meaning nor significance has been more rigorously applied.

CHRONOLOGY 1822–1826

1822: Emerson lives at 26 Federal Street, Boston, and continues to teach in his brother William's school for young ladies; July, he begins essay on "The Religion of the Middle Ages" (published in January, 1823, in *The Christian Disciple* for November and December, 1822); December, he attends Edward Everett's lectures "upon Antiquities."

1823: Emerson continues to teach in William's school; May, he and William sign the "declaration of Faith subscribed by the members of the First Church of Christ in Boston"; May 24, the Emerson family moves to the Canterbury district of Roxbury; August 22–September 4, Emerson goes on walking trip to the Connecticut Valley; December 5, William goes to Germany to study theology and Emerson runs the school alone.

1824: Emerson continues the school, re-establishing it in May near Trinity Church; April 18, he dedicates himself to the Church and informally begins his "professional studies" (of divinity); August 25, he attends the Harvard Commencement, where La Fayette is honored, and hears his brother Edward deliver an oration.

1825: January, Emerson closes the school for young ladies; February 16, he is admitted to the middle class of the Harvard Divinity School; March, he loses the use of one eye for study; April, Emerson's mother moves to Cambridge; September, Emerson begins teaching in a boys' school in Chelmsford and William returns from Germany; fall, Emerson undergoes an eye operation and gradually regains the full use of his eyes; December 31, he closes the Chelmsford school.

1826: Emerson suffers the miseries of rheumatism; January–March 28, he conducts the school in Roxbury which Edward had given up.

SYMBOLS AND ABBREVIATIONS

⟨　⟩	Cancellation
↑　↓	Insertion
/　/	Variant
‖ … ‖	Unrecoverable matter, normally unannotated. Three dots, one to five words; four dots, six to fifteen words; five dots, sixteen to thirty words. Matter lost by accidental mutilation but recovered conjecturally is inserted between the parallels.
⟨‖ … ‖⟩	Unrecoverable cancelled matter
‖msm‖	Manuscript accidentally mutilated
[　]	Editorial insertion
[...]	Editorial omission
[　]	Emerson's square brackets
⌊　⌋	Marginal matter inserted in text
[　]	Page numbers of original manuscript

ⁿ   See Textual Notes

☞

⌐   Hands pointing

凶

∧   Emerson's symbol for intended insertion

[R.W.E.]   Editorial substitution for Emerson's symbol of original authorship. See volume I, plate vii.

* [or] **   Emerson's note

ABBREVIATIONS AND SHORT TITLES IN FOOTNOTES

E t E   Kenneth W. Cameron. *Emerson the Essayist.* Raleigh, N.C.: The Thistle Press, 1945. 2 vols.

J   *Journals of Ralph Waldo Emerson.* Edited by Edward Waldo Emerson and Waldo Emerson Forbes. Boston and New York: Houghton Mifflin Co., 1909–1914. 10 vols.

JMN   *The Journals and Miscellaneous Notebooks of Ralph Waldo Emerson.* Edited by William H. Gilman, Alfred R. Ferguson, George P. Clark, and Merrell R. Davis. Cambridge: Harvard University Press, 1960–

L   *The Letters of Ralph Waldo Emerson.* Edited by Ralph L. Rusk. New York: Columbia University Press, 1939. 6 vols.

Lectures   *The Early Lectures of Ralph Waldo Emerson.* Edited by Stephen E. Whicher and Robert E. Spiller. Cambridge: Harvard University Press, 1959.

Life   Ralph L. Rusk. *The Life of Ralph Waldo Emerson.* New York: Charles Scribner's Sons, 1949.

W   *The Complete Works of Ralph Waldo Emerson.* With a Biographical Introduction and Notes, by Edward Waldo Emerson. Centenary Edition. Boston and New York: Houghton Mifflin Co., 1903–1904. 12 vols.

"Books Borrowed." Kenneth W. Cameron, "Books Borrowed from the Boston Library Society by Ralph Waldo Emerson and His Mother (1815–1845)," in *Emerson the Essayist*, II, 149–186.

"Early Reading List." Kenneth W. Cameron, "Emerson's Early Reading List (1819–1824)," *Bulletin of the New York Public Library*, LV, 315–324 (July 1951), reprinted with additions in *Transcendentalists and Minerva* (Hartford, 1958), pp. 415–424.

"Emerson's Reading." Kenneth W. Cameron, *Ralph Waldo Emerson's Reading.* Raleigh, N.C.: The Thistle Press, 1941.

PART ONE

The Journals

Wide World 7

1822

Wide World 7 continues the series of regular journals Emerson began at Harvard. The dated entries, following without interruption from Wide World 6, cover the period from July 11 to November 4, 1822, with only a break in sequence for a vacation in August.

The manuscript is composed of a single gathering of thirteen folded sheets, hand-stitched together with white thread into a booklet of twenty-six leaves. The leaves are numbered from 1 through 52. As in Wide World 6, the folded sheets are of two sizes so that fourteen leaves measure approximately 17 x 20.5 cm and twelve leaves measure 15 x 19.2 cm.

[1] R. Waldo Emerson.

Wideworld.[1]   No 7.

"Ζητῶ γαρ την αλεθειαν, ὑφ᾽ ἡς ὀυδεις πωποτε εβλαβη." [2]
MARC. ANTONINUS [*Meditations*, Bk. VI, 21]

Boston, July 11, 1822.

Dedication.

I dedicate my book to the Spirit of America. I dedicate it to that living soul, which *doth* exist somewhere beyond the Fancy, to whom the Divinity hath assigned the care of this bright corner of the Universe. I bring my little offering, in this month, which covers the continent with matchless beauty, to the shrine, which distant generations

[1] "Wideworld." is enclosed in a partially shaded oval with a scroll at the left side. A decorative arrow appears in the upper right corner of the page.
[2] "For I seek the truth, whereby no one was ever harmed."

shall load with sacrifice, and distant ages shall admire afar off. With a spark of prophetic devotion, I hasten to hail the Genius, who yet counts the tardy years of childhood, but who is increasing unawares in the twilight, and swelling into strength, until the hour, when he shall break the cloud, to shew his colossal youth, and cover the firmament with the shadow of his wings.

Evening.

It is a slow patriotism which forgets to love till all the world have set the example. If the nations of Europe can find anything to idolize in their ruinous & enslaved [2] institutions, we are content, though we are astonished at their satisfaction. But let them not ignorantly mock at the pride of an American, as if it were misplaced or unfounded, when that freeman is giving an imperfect expression ⟨of⟩to his sense of his condition. He rejoices in the birthright of a country where the freedom of opinion & action is so perfect that every man enjoys exactly that consideration to which he is entitled, and each mind, as in the bosom of a family, institutes & settles a comparison of its powers with those of its fellow, & quietly takes that stand which nature intended for it. He points to his native land as the only ⟨w⟩one where freedom has not degenerated to licentiousness; . . ⟨as⟩[n] ↑in↓ whose well ordered districts education & intelligence dwell with good morals; whose rich estates peacefully descend from sire to son, without the shadow of an interference from private violence or public tyranny; whose offices of trust and seats of science ⟨with⟩ ↑are filled by↓ minds of republican strength & elegant accomplishments.* Xenophon and Thucydides would have thought it a theme, better worthy of their powers, than Persia or Greece; and her Revolution would furnish Plutarch with a list of heroes. If the Constitution of the United States outlives a century, it will be matter of deep congratulation to the human race; for the Utopian dreams which visionaries have pursued and sages exploded, will find their beautiful

* Such an one died yesterday — Professor Frisbie will hardly be supplied by any man in the community.[3]

[3] Levi Frisbie (1783–1822), under whom Emerson studied at Harvard, was Alford Professor of Natural Religion, Moral Philosophy, and Civil Polity from 1817 until his death on July 9, 1822.

the[3]⁴ories rivalled & outdoneⁿ by the reality, which it has pleased
God to bestow upon United America.

                                    Saturday Ev.g., July 13th.
            Continued from Wideworld No. 6, p.⁵
    I have proposed to attempt the consideration of those different
aspects, under which we are accustomed to view the Divinity. I shall
endeavour first to give some account of his relation to us as the
⟨f⟩Founder of the Moral law.
    It is not necessary to describe that law, otherwise than by saying
that it is the sovereign necessity which commands every mind to abide
by one mode of conduct, & to reject another, by ⟨recommending one⟩
joining to the one a perfect satisfaction, while it pursues the other with
indefinite apprehensions.
    Its divine origin is fully shewn by its superiority to all the other
principles of our nature. It seems to be more essential to our constitution, than any other feeling whatever. It dwells so deeply in the
human nature that we feel it to be implied in consciousness. Other
faculties fail, — Memory sleeps; Judgement is impaired or ruined;
Imagination droops; — but the moral sense abides there still. In our
very dreams, it wakes & judges amid the Chaos of the rest. The
depth of its foundations in the heart & the subtilty of its nature in
eluding investigations into its causes & character distinguish it eminently above other principles. If you compare it for example with
the phenomena of taste which also appear to be universal, we shall
readily discern a considerable distinction [4]⁶ withdrawing from the
one its transient resemblance. The judgement which determines a
circle to be more beautiful than a square, or a rose to be fairer than
a clod, is not founded upon aught existing in the mind independent
of the senses, but is manifestly derived from the humble sources of
the material world. It is nothing but a power to decide upon the
pleasures of sense. If this be not the limit of the province of taste, if
it ever rise to the judgement of questions which seem to involve
moral beauty, it is only where it begins to blend with the moral

    ⁴ "GOD" is centered beneath "discern" at the bottom of the page.
    ⁵ See *JMN*, I, 153.
    ⁶ "GOD" is centered beneath "vice," at the bottom of the page.

sense & becomes ennobled by its connection. But that sovereign sense whereof we speak, leaves the material world, & its subordinate knowledge to subordinate faculties, and marshals before its divine tribunal the motives of action, the secrets of character, & the interests of the universe. It has no taint of mortality in the purity & unity of its intelligence; it is perfectly spiritual. It ↑sometimes↓ seems to sanction that Platonic dream, that the soul of the individual was but an emanation from the Abyss of Deity, ↑and about to return ⟨thither⟩↓ whence it flowed. So it seems to predict, on *supreme authority*, that fate which is to be declared, when Time shall cease. It seems to be the only ⟨fact⟩ ↑human thought↓ which is admitted to partake of the counsels of the eternal world, and to give note already to man,[n] of the event & the sentence to which he is doomed. It may be observed that it is never deficient as ⟨is true of⟩ other powers in many instances ↑are↓; and if, in some cases, it becomes actually deadened and, ↑by an accustomed hardihood to crime,↓ confounds those distinctions of virtue & vice, which it is its office to define, [5][7] it will be found that this never takes place but in the wreck of the character.

Of this superior faculty we regard God as the Author. Wherever it acts, its action implies his existence, for it refers directly to Him. But in viewing the eternity of its obligation the question may occur to our minds whether it be as universal through all possible orders of created intelligence as to be exclusive of any other mode. We certainly can concieve that the Divinity may govern a being by some law which we have no faculties to understand — differing entirely from our system but not contradicting it; just as our senses differ from, but do not exclude each other. But these questions are above our sphere; we[n] are afraid to meddle with Omniscience & Omnipotence; the mind traverses with sufficient firmness its appointed paths, but totters on the brink of such m⟨g⟩agnificent scenes which grow infinite under its eye. Still we ⟨seem to have⟩ ↑venture↓ some faint objection to oppose to this. God is *essentially* a moral being, — for such is the information respecting him which we derive from all our conceptions; and it seems to violate his eternal Unity & ↑to↓ introduce confusion into the Principle of universal order, ⟨to⟩ ↑if we↓ attribute to him two natures of Godhead, in two parts of his universe.

[7] "GOD" is centered beneath "this question" at the bottom of the page.

If this do not satisfy our reason we must be content to leave[.]

Upon this question depends another, which [6] may also be above our capacity to decide; namely, whether they have been eternal; whether time was not when as yet they had not been framed, but in the mind of Omniscience, as future things? We look back to God as subsisting alone in the Universe. In that solitude *relations* did not yet exist; Creator & creature, power & weakness, good & bad could not be said to have being since there were no objects whereto they might be affixed. It was his ↑good↓ pleasure to fill the illimitable void with thinking beings in his own likeness, thereby to make happiness abound in his presence & to add to his glory.

(Continued on page 10)[8]

⟨By Wisdom's shrine the silent Muses weep
        And sad-eyed Sorrow ⟨veils⟩ ↑worships↓ at her Urn
The pulse of Joy, the ⟨toil⟩ zeal of Virtue sleep⟩

Hark! from their holy mount, the Muses send
        On loaded gales the piercing voice of wo
See round what URN the sacred sisters bend
        Whose faded wreaths a dying perfume throw.

I see proud Genius 'mid the circling band
        ⟨Though⟩ ↑But↓ his bright torch ⟨be⟩ ↑lies↓
                quenched in darkness /now/there/
And his wild eye whose godlike beams command
        Now rests on Death in comfortless Despair

[7][9]   A mighty tenant of inferior clay
        Whom awful *Virtue* clad with wings for Heaven
        Has left their haunts to climb the realms of Day
        Congenial soil to young Archangels given

        Oh let them weep whom Fate's unsparing arm
        Has robbed, in darkness, of their crowned son

---

[8] See below, p. 10.
[9] "DRAMA" is centered beneath "for dark" at the bottom of the page.

Their fervent grief can wake no Orphean charm
To win him back from Glory that's begun,

The saints aye singing by the gates of Light
Have stooped to bid his towering spirit hail
Beneath the Throne he feeds his ardent sight
And mid that triumph hears our lowly wail.

The value of public institutions is chiefly founded in the powerful effect they produce by means of human sympathy. A sentiment
felt at once by a thousand men, is expressed with tenfold ↑the↓
strength that attends it when it pervades solitary minds in distant
quarters; and this is not confined in its effects to a popular ebullition,
but penetrates the ↑mind's↓ inmost principles and inspires remarkable energy. The dark Ages are peculiarly noted for ⟨the⟩ great exertions of popular spirit, for the foundation of innumerable sects, for
dark seasons of public alarm, [8][10] for impending calamity & the
destruction of the world; for the Crusades; and the enormous processions of penitents; but no period certainly in the annals of the
world exhibits examples of deeper devotion to the vows taken upon
these occasions of universal excitement. The Crusading Host who
propagated that cry "It is the will of God" from village to village
& state to state along the fields of Italy persevered to the death in the
cause of the Cross.[10a] The zealous monks, who united under the eloquence of a priest, and in the panick of remorse bound themselves
to the fierce austerity of chastisement, hunger & cold languished till
their life's end in the stony cell and inhuman mortification which a
moment's enthusiasm had ⟨prescribed⟩ ↑imposed↓. ⟨And to this day

[10] "DRAMA" is centered beneath "object of" at the bottom of the page.
[10a] Emerson is thinking of the popular response to the preaching of the First
Crusade by Peter the Hermit. In Hallam's words, " 'It is the will of God!' was the
tumultuous cry that broke from the breast and lips of the assembly at Clermont. . . ."
See *View of the State of Europe during the Middle Ages*, 2 vols. (New York, 1882),
I, 46. Emerson had withdrawn all four volumes of the Philadelphia edition of 1821
from the Boston Library Society October 20, 1821, and renewed them December 15
for five weeks. See also David Hume, *The History of England*, 6 vols. (New York,
1850), I, 228, for a shorter version of the story. Emerson had borrowed volume 1
of an unidentified edition from the Boston Library Society September 1–8, 1821 (see
EtE, II, 158 and 177).

many⟩ ↑Some of those↓ institutions have survived ↑to this day with-
standing↓ through so many centuries ⟨withstanding⟩ the temptation
of prosperity and adhering to the agonies of martyrdom. These instances shew the stupendous power of *Sympathy,* and to what uses
it may be applied as a political instrument; they ⟨shew the⟩ suggest
vast advantages to be gained or lost by the skill or neglect with which
it is made to serve ⟨an⟩ ↑the↓ important needs of society. If it impart
its impulse to a virtuous principle human improvement reaps the reward; if it add darker corruptions to national vice — how great will
be that darkness!   And a nation should be careful to guard those
instit. which &c[.]

Now the grand object of the Drama is to chain [9][11] the affections
by awakening this sympathy. It represents an accumulation of human
wo ⟨under⟩ ↑with↓ gorgeous pomp to move the pity and indignation of
a susceptible audience. Its triumph is complete, when the passions of
the multitude which naturally move in unison, at last aid each other
to some general utterance, & consent to the weakness of feelings,
which in an individual would be ridiculous. From the Theatre, then,
drive out the buyers & sellers of corruption who ⟨profane⟩ have made
it a den of vice and make it an Oracle of those opinions & sentiments
which ⟨are fitted to sustain the world.⟩ multiply and strengthen the
bonds of society.

The more we reflect upon the subject the more thoroughly we
shall be convinced, how practicable it is to produce a Theatre of an
actively useful character. It is a mistake to suppose that only ⟨the⟩
vicious gratification can raise sufficient excitement to draw men together around a stage. On the contrary, what an inextinguishable
thirst for *eloquence* however rude, exists in every breast! It is historical fact, that when Demosthenes was about to plead in a cause,
multitudes flocked from the remotest corners of Greece to the Forum
at Athens. It is natural that we pant to feel those thrilling sensations
of a most agreeable character which passionate & powerful declamation never fails to move. They are akin to the emotions produced
by *the sublime,* in sense or thought. And for these, the ficti⟨c⟩tious
distresses of exalted personages, amid the passage of wonderful events,
such as a *pure* play will freely admit, seem to afford every desirable

---

[11] "⟨DRAMA⟩" is centered beneath "Indeed it is" at the bottom of the page.

facility. Indeed it is remarkable how many instances [10][12] are met with of dramatic orators, while the senate, the pulpit, & the bar deplore their deficiency in just eloquence. The reason is, that there is no comparison between the efforts necessary for excellence in the one & the other. To be an able reciter of another's sentiments, needs no more than a happy talent; which is, by no means, the sole requisite to a solid fame in a liberal profession. — Besides we have direct testimony of the certainty of success, in the instance of the Greek Tragedy, which, without impurity was universally popular at Athens.

(Continued from p. 6)   Saturday Evening, July 20th.
When this new event had taken place in the Universe, and another being had been caused, which could never end, — certain great connections also began, to unite this new existence to the already infinite substances to which it was associated. — To the Deity, to space, to duration. I do not apprehend that there is any necessity for vindicating the eternity of morals before the Creation of finite beings, for moral laws are relative, and therefore do not subsist prior to the *relation*. Indeed we cannot concieve of the solitude of Divinity, antecedent to his creating action; and ⟨though⟩ ↑if↓ in the ambition of man, our thoughts sometimes strive with the subject, yet language sinks beneath it and leaves us to indefinite notions, though from their nature ↑they be↓ sublime. We ⟨admit the⟩ ↑see a↓ necessity of giving a character to the new mind, and a path of action, — by binding it under [11][13] a law; and therefore the mind was made to understand the meaning of Truth, of Virtue, of God. Still we have one remarkable evidence to the character, from eternity, of that ⟨b⟩Being, in the divine determination to make man *in the image of God*. In all the insignificance and imperfection of our nature, in the guilt to which we are liable, and the calamity which guilt has accumulated, — man triumphs to remember that he bears about him a spark which all beings /acknowledge/venerate/ to be the emblem of God, — which may be violated, but which cannot be extinguished. And we remark with delight the confirmations of this belief in the opening features of human

---

[12] Two sketches in ink appear between the paragraphs on the page — one a group of buildings on a steep cliff, the other what appears to be a quill pen and oak leaf. "GOD" is centered beneath "a path" at the bottom of the page.

[13] "GOD" is centered beneath "p. 32)" at the bottom of the page.

character. And the ↑little joy of the↓ child who ⟨with joy⟩ plants ⟨the⟩ ↑a↓ seed ⟨to⟩& sees himself instrumental in the creation of a flower, forcibly reminds us of that beneficence which ⟨cr⟩built the heavens & the earth, and saw that it was good.

[I have spoken more desultorily than I intended upon this difficult topic; what has been said thus far, amounts to this; — that^n the ⟨divine⟩ moral sense has a divine origin, if any thing in man is divine; — because it has a distinct superiority over every other faculty; because it constitutes more of one's self than any other attribute, that is[,] enters more intimately into our constitution; because it seems to anticipate the future Judgement. That there can be no other system in the universe, than our moral law. That it is eternal in its existence, though perhaps not from its beginning; although some proof of it seems to be gained from Man as the Image of God.]
(Continued on p. 32)

[12] Fort Grenoble.   (Continued from Wideworld 6.)[14]
Time does not pass tediously to an unprotected man travelling an enemy's country; at least he commonly finds occupation for his thoughts. Claude Bashan, rude in speech and manner, was yet a scholar, to whom Cicero & Seneca, no less than Boethius, had imparted the consolations of philosophy. Hopes of greatness in his native land had given place to the new and ardent hope which animated the fathers of N. England. The entire change of circumstances which the founders of a colony meet in their new world, must give a spring to the mind and developement to the faculties which can be expected from no common event. Each bosom feels that its own character is of unusual importance to the history of man, as the inventor of institutions whose influence and extent will be indefinitely great. No man in the colony felt these sentiments with more force than Mr Bashan. He had transplanted his affections from a soil where they were withering to the mighty continent upon whose margin his countrymen had sat down to worship God in peace. At this time as he strode over the ground which gave such marks of rank vegetation

[14] What follows appears to be a continuation of the paragraph on "America" in *JMN*, I, 146–147. Since no historical Claude Bashan has been identified, it would seem that Emerson is making another abortive experiment in fiction.

beneath his feet, he indulged himself fully in his favourite reflections.

"Judgement is like a clock or watch where the most ordinary machine is sufficient to tell the hours; but the most elaborate alone can point out the minutes & seconds and distinguish the smallest differences of time."

Fontenelle.[15]

Sunday, July 28th, 1822.

Religion has been a powerful agent in augmenting the bonds of connection among [16] men, by its supreme appeal to their reason, which, when properly felt, no heart, no sophistry, no prejudice can withstand. We all know, that, in cases of duty, where many friends plead with us for the cause, [13][17] where the expediency of the thing, true honour, and even our own interest — combine in vain to vanquish our reluctance, — we know that there *is* a *plea* which will shake our obstinacy and reduce us, proud as we are, to offices of equality and kindness with the humblest solicitor. It does not always act, and hence our propensity to sin; but when ↑it↓ *is urged*, in moments of religious excitement, at the stroke of sickness, or in the hopeless death bed, we know how the sweat of that Fear damps the warmth of passions and affections, of fancy & pride; how it quells in a moment the strength of habits which were rooted with life, and, in fine, how that fear marches on with portentous rapidity, as if to anticipate the speed of Death, to obliterate in succession every stain, which years of indulgence have contracted and to root out the seeds of guilt. How well is this known by the worldly and impious policy of the Roman Church who take advantage of man's terror before his Maker, to win away his earthly riches to the service of their sinister institutions. But what is it that has made the miser thus prodigally good? what hath thus marvellously converted the riot of the bac⟨h⟩chanal and the rebellion of the fiend, into prayer, reformation, and remorse? Is there aught of positive infliction in Death beyond what we can see?

[15] From *Pluralité des Mondes*, Soir 6. Quoted in English by Hume in "Of the Delicacy of Taste and Passion," *Philosophical Essays*, 2 vols. (Phila., 1817), I, 38. Emerson quotes from the same essay in Journal XVIII (see *JMN*, I, 342–343).

[16] What appears to be the abbreviation "Nov" is written over the word "among" in the manuscript, perhaps when Emerson was reviewing this passage early in November.

[17] "DEATH." is centered beneath "infliction in" at the bottom of the page.

I 2

[14][18] Is there any mysterious evil besides the approach of a Change? No; the dying have told us of none. There is nothing but our ordinary sense of God's presence which by its common operation keeps crime from growing to outrage — now brought forcibly home to us by the expectation of an Account, and it presents to us the turpitude of every degree of transgression in its full amount. This very violence of the impression at that moment, demonstrates the sin of that life, and of our lives, which have dared to disregard or undervalue that law whereon our eternal fates must necessarily depend.

VACATION . . here [19]

Sunday, Sept. 7[8], 1822.

In the rancorous controversies to which the improvements of criticism in theology have given birth, men undoubtedl⟨e⟩y say in the heat of dispute many things which neither ⟨o⟩public op[i]nion nor their own sober judgement will warrant. These must not be unfairly [n] assumed as the doctrines of a party or as the proper fruits of the system in whose support they were adduced. But if a⟨n⟩ sentiment be by various writers expressed, and still oftener implied and if the other party be often arraigned from different quarters for holding an opposite belief it is perfectly ⟨to⟩ just to regard that sentiment as the [15][20] result or at least the attendant of the system of belief and to regard it as a part of the ⟨c⟩field of controver↑s↓y. And if such sentiment be at war with any partisan's primal notions of good sense and good reasoning and seem to involve important mischiefs in its consequences, it is his manifest duty to attack it at once and to use every means which he can compass to subvert the obnoxious principle. Such a principle, it seems to me is that hoary-headed error which considers Reason as opposed to Scripture and which frequently & loudly condemns Reason as an adversary and a seducer, as unbelieving and profane. To a man whose mind has not been darkened by party prejudices and little distinctions ↑of terms↓, such an opinion will appear, to say the least, irrational & absurd. Instead of placing ideots in his Universe, capable only of sensual gratification, able only to obey instincts, and requiring every moment a new direction from

[18] "REASON" is centered beneath "just to" at the bottom of the page.
[19] This phrase is enclosed in a box at the right of the page.
[20] "REASON" is centered beneath "*him*, and" at the bottom of the page.

heaven to prevent ⟨us⟩ ↑them↓ from grovelling in the dirt or being destroyed by the beasts — God has peopled it with images of himself, and kindled within them the light of his own understanding — a portion of that ray which illuminates as it formed the Creation. He has communicated to them an intelligence by which they are enabled to see their way in a universe where other beings are blind; to behold *him,* and their relations to him; to [16]²¹ read and understand ⟨his⟩ all those communications which in past or future time he is pleased to make; it ⁿ is an intelligence by which they find themselves distinguished from his other creations. There are about and amidst them a thousand beautiful forms with a thousand different properties; there are hills and waters, trees and flowers, the living forms of nature and the stars of the firmament; — but they are still & brutish — there is ↑no↓ eye and voice within them to detect and declare the stupendous glory which surrounds them; they lack that living spirit which opens the eyes of man and without which the Universe is as if it were not, and the glory of Deity is darkness. It is an intelligence which soars above these charms of the material world and can contemn them in the comparison with the objects which it is capable of enjoying. In fine, it is an intelligence which reveals to man another condition of existence and a nearer approach to the Supreme Being. This intelligence is *Reason.*

Yet some there are who tell you, as if it involved no inconsistency, and certainly no sin, to avoid profaning the revelations of God by submitting them to the tribunal of man's reason, — who seek to walk implicitly by a law which they do not and will not understand, because they refuse to apply to its explanation that light ↑with↓ which their maker has furnished them. It is not only a wilful perversion and abuse of a priceless gift; but it is [17]²² a most ungrateful neglect of divine mercy and a neglect which incurs a tremendous responsibility.

But it will be said that no one can be guilty of such a manifest and outrageous abuse of God's blessings and that there is some other light under which the subject may be viewed, and, that, Reason does not denote in their use of the term this plain and common use of our

²¹ "REASON" is centered beneath "priceless" at the bottom of the page.
²² "REASON" is centered beneath "see its object" at the bottom of the page.

faculties which all must acknowledge obligatory. Let us then gather from their own language its true meaning.

And first it is true that this light and intelligence which we have recieved from the Almighty ⟨b⟩may be considered as divided into different parts, and that none cast it all away, — but reserve to themselves the merit of a part. Thus we have a moral sense, by which, from infancy, we discriminate right & wrong; this,ⁿ it may be said, we do not call Reason; this we hold indispensable in its exercise and most rigidly would we conform to its dictates. We have ↑also↓ sympathies, affections and powers; we can attend, we can compare, we can remember, we can believe, we can judge; allⁿ these faculties we enjoy and are grateful for their exercise. But we feel that it is possible for us to act without giving an adequate reason for such action, and merely in obedience to command. God has ⟨given⟩ ↑issued↓ a command to us which we do not think ought to be studied by finite faculties in order to see its object or to fathom its obscu[18]²³rities. We confess that much is to appearance obscure and even contradictory to our human judgements; but because it has an infinite Being for its author we do not think that those faculties ought to be applied to develope its mysteries which should be applied to develope the mystery of human systems. And this is what we mean when we condemn the use of Reason. (Continued on the next page.)

> I   Among the bulrushes I ⟨sit⟩ lay
>   Which deck the river's murmuring tide
>   Upon those banks no men abide
>   But swans come sailing in their pride
>   And ⟨are not wondered at⟩ ↑graceful float into
>   the quiet bay↓

> II Fast sailed the golden fishes by
>   And some leaped out to see the sky
>   Nor saw the bird that stooped from high
>   Until he ⟨plunged below the wave⟩ ↑broke the
>   wave's white crest↓
>   And bore the ↑flapping↓ fish aloft unto his nest.

²³ "RIVER" is centered beneath "insects flew" at the bottom of the page.

15

III   An April cloud blew o'er the stream
      And cast its big drops down
      They oped the lilies' covering brown
      And shed its steaming perfumes round
      ⟨And the hoarse croaking frogs awoke my dream⟩
      And golden insects flew unto that flower supreme.

[Then I,]

[19][24]   (Continued)

Let us consider, for a space, this doctrine, which as it at first denies *reason*, seems to admit no judge but one, and that is experience. We can at least apply to such examples as the history of nations may furnish to discover what has been the condition of light ⟨in⟩& knowledge in those periods when this opinion which I have stated has been held.

⟨While the world was yet young, a⟩In[n] those primitive pagan nations where all the little treasury of knowledge was jealously hoarded by a few priests, it was a politic and lucrative doctrine which necessarily arose ⟨from⟩ ↑out of↓ the infancy of science, that religious knowledge, into which they wove all other learning, was a mystery ⟨into⟩ whereinto it was both sinful & perilous to pry. They were ignorant; for knowledge consists in stores, which nobody had yet accumulated. When therefore the disciple inquired upon topics which were still new and doubtful to his master, the ready reply which silenced his importunity without diminishing his respect, was that the subject was beyond the reach of his faculties. This sentiment, we know to have been sedulously inculcated by the bearded sages of Egypt and the East. We know that this doctrine and the consequences of this doctrine constrained the youthful genius of those laborious nations; that this learned aristocracy chained the minds of the million in an unworthy and unprofitable existence; that all their celebrated acquisitions were but a drop in the bucket, and that their views of God were most base & confused. Except that there was something consoling in the awe which would cover the Deity with obscurity ⟨and which thus⟩ ↑because it↓ prevented [20][25] them from

[24] "REASON" is centered beneath "with obscurity" at the bottom of the page.
[25] "REASON" is centered beneath "apply it with" at the bottom of the page.

exposing their ridiculous views at full length, there was nought in the system of theology of the earliest times (after the deluge) which was not disgusting. Afterwards Zoroaster appeared and tearing asunder this useless veil shewed his disciples simple and sublime truths which Reason taught concerning God. In Greece, where speculation also was more free, and the priests, from various circumstances, never obtained that sway, which ⟨had⟩ ↑⟨they⟩↓ they had in the East, the philosophers, advancing each on his master conceived just and stupendous notions of Divine Providence which have been the groundwork of even Christian creeds.

After the Apostolic age which succeeded the Christian Revelation, this fatal opinion began to be introduced into the Church. Its influence was soon seen in the production of a state of society very analogous to that elder ignorance to which the priest condemned the people. ⟨It was the characteristic⟩ The curse which is landed on the Roman Church records that she substituted *authority* for *reason,* that she took the Bible from the hands of men and commanded them to believe. This bondage was so crafty and so strong that it was long ere the mind was hardy enough to break it. But it was finally broken, and thenceforward the true Age of Reason commenced. I use a term which has been perverted and abused, but I apply it with propriety to the era of [21][26] Luther and Calvin, with still more propriety to the advanced reason of Clarke ↑&↓ Newton and with still more perfect propriety to this latter day when there is such an immense diffusion of knowledge and our eyes read with all the added splendour of those great and various lights.

And it would indeed be a criminal and infatuated relapse to the darkness of pagan night, if we, rich as we are in the privileges of heaven and the wisdom of a thousand years, should wilfully cast away that great auxiliary which has collected or disclosed to us this moral wealth; and with the magnificence of Paradise and heaven in view, should condemn ourselves[n] to eternal poverty. They who condemn Reason, have not used it aright, and do not know its value. They will find it impossible to shew in ↑the↓ Annals of the world a period when it was assumed for a guide in matters sacred or profane

[26] "REASON" is centered beneath "approaches the Infinite" at the bottom of the page.

without advantage. If man needs its assistance in his daily walk and first exigencies of nature and is betrayed to inconsi↑s↓tency & danger the first moment that he trusts to fortune or fancy, surely he needs the aid of ⟨every faculty⟩ ↑it,↓ when he approaches the Infinite & unsearchable Being.

Boston, Sept. 23d, 1822.

[22]²⁷ ⟨I desire to make a plan for my View of the Religion of the Middle Ages.²⁸ Such a plan should comprise a description of the peculiarities of the Roman church; a theoretical account of the influence of those peculiarities; an inquiry whether it subserved the purposes of a religion, and what rank we are to give it in the institutions which have benefitted Europe. — Because a system is best described by its characteristics which distinguish it from others, and a theoretic account of the same enables us to form a distinct view of its influence. A comparison of this influence with the desirable influence which a religious system should exert naturally follows; ⟨this⟩ after ⁿ a patient discussion of these branches of the subject we ⟨co⟩ shall be able to form a judgement of its proper merits considered as an instrument in the advancement of human mind.⟩

Friday Ev.g., Sept. [27.]

Man is a being the most inconsistent with himself of all the creatures of God. We are always pleased with those images, which the sacred writers abundantly use, of man's condition in his youth and strength drawn from the beauty and budding time of nature. We extend their application from his physical to his moral youth, and can find nothing so nearly allied [23]²⁹ to the ⟨bright⟩ ↑rich↓ promise of ⟨that⟩ ↑a↓ mind which is developing itself, as the magnificen⟨t⟩ce of opening nature. When the ↑sweet↓ southwind has scattered the wrecks of winter and the forests resume their ancient /honours/ array/, when the time of the singing of the birds is come, and the voice of the turtle is heard in the land; when the foot of the enthusiast who goes forth to behold this beauty, presses upon vines and

²⁷ "MAN" is centered beneath "can find" at the bottom of the page.
²⁸ See *JMN*, I, 304, n. 67.
²⁹ "MAN" is centered beneath "them for" at the bottom of the page.

flowers, and his eye is caught by gaudy blossoms and by unclouded skies, he feels, as he stands worshipping in the temple of Nature, that ⟨this⟩ ↑it↓ is ⟨the⟩ ↑no unfit↓ emblem of his own soul and that this majesty must yield to the majesty of that intelligence. For how can this glory, which is fleeting and without mind, vie with that, whose infancy is just begun, but which, while moons ↑wax &↓ wane, and suns ↑burn &↓ are quenched, can never die; whose powers instead of rotting and decaying at ⟨the⟩ ↑a↓ summer's end, shall be daily renewed and augmented forever, until they can compass immeasurable things, and enter into the heaven of heavens? [n] But there is another representation of man equally faithful, from a different class of natural objects. ↑Who is he that tortures truth to puff the vanity of man↓? He is the weed which withereth, the chaff which is cast into the oven; he saith to Corruption thou art my father; to the worm, thou art my mother, and my sister; there is darkness in his paths, and he is a worm. The sacred poets sometimes search for yet darker fancies to express their emphatic idea of the pitiable [n] condition of man. And who that has beheld the species will accuse them for having exaggerated one tittle[?]

[24][30] Who is he /that has never felt a sentiment of the deepest/ whose heart was never wrung with self condemning/ humili⟨ation⟩↑ty↓ at ⟨contemplating his lot?⟩ ↑the study of himself↓, that has not traced an ugly ⟨frightful⟩ affinity between the character of his fellows and that of the beasts wh⟨o⟩ich perish, and trembled lest an affinity should also prevail in their several destinies? This is a subject which may be dilated ad libitum.

The sacred writers abound in descriptions of a period of calamity which transcends all common measures of human misery. They lend their inspiration to an account of distress which language labours under and cannot adequately tell. Its severity absorbs all other terrors, all other thoughts; like a wasting plague it ⟨annihilates⟩ suspends all the kind offices which are due from man to man, and almost annihilates the affections themselves. Brothers are sundered and mother forgets her child in the selfishness of that overwhelming suffering. Pangs and sorrows shall take hold of them; they shall be amazed one at another; their faces shall be as flames; they shall fret themselves and curse

[30] "CURSES" is centered beneath "water of the" at the bottom of the page.

their King and their God, and shall look upward; and they shall look unto the earth, and behold trouble and darkness, dimness of anguish; and they shall be driven to darkness. The Hebrew prophet elevated by his sacred revelation sits upon the mountain and descries this magnificent dream of desolation extending far and wide around him. He sees the forests cut down and the flowers fade until no green thing is left alive; the water of the fountains is turned into blood; [25][31] the ⁿ whirlwind passed out from the desart; Babylon, Persia, and Egypt pour out their hosts upon the devoted land; from afar is heard a confused noise of chariots and horsemen like the noise of many waters. The Sun and the Moon withdraw their light. The clouds pour down curses as dew; beneath ⁿ this ⟨mighty⟩ ↑overshadowing↓ night of darkness the people are withered; the gardens and vineyards are trampled and forsaken; the defenced city is left desolate; the graves cast out their dead ⁿ ⟨into the streets⟩. There is a crying for wine in the streets; all joy is darkened; the mirth of the land is gone. They are gathered together as prisoners ⟨are⟩ gathered in a pit, mourning and howling for the desolation of the land. They gnash their teeth every man at his brother and bite the dust of the ground. On their faces is written ⟨a⟩Accursed, and the worms cover them. The prophet from his mount surveys the frightful wilderness and seeks in vain amid this ghastly abode of the dragon and the owl for the pleasant places of his childhood and the city of his country. And can this be Jerusalem? the beloved[,] the glorious city — the holy city of David. She that was the light of the earth whither the tribes went upward to worship. She that opened her gates to the morning star, and within whose walls the harp and tabret ceased not all the day long; whose children were the honourable of the earth, and whose glory was a Crown of rejoicing. Where be the shining towers of her temple? Where ⁿ are her feasts and solemn processions? Where are her priests and her young men? Where are the daughters of Jerusalem that were like roes upon the mountains. Behold! ⟨t⟩The displeasure of God hath broken down the towers of her strength, [26][32] the vail of her Temple is rent in twain; Death has come in among her

---

[31] "CURSES" is centered beneath "broken down" at the bottom of the page.

[32] "CURSES" is centered beneath "quenched;" at the bottom of the page. To the left of "Oct. 1, 1822" is a pen-and-ink sketch — two concentric circles, the outer one divided into quadrants.

banquets, — the wild beasts of the desart into her bridal processions; priest and prophet have failed from among men, the seer and the ancient of days; her youths and virgins wail for the ↑sore↓ plagues of the land and hide themselves in ↑lion's↓ dens. The scorpion crawls in her vineyards; the dragon and the wolf couch in her courts, instead of the horsemen ↑&↓ the chariots of strength; poisonous weeds and bulrushes grow instead of palm trees and pomegranates.* The darkness of hell is ↑round↓ about her. Her days are numbered and finished.[n]

This was the hideous retribution for the scarlet iniquities of Jerusalem, which God revealed to his prophets. They lifted up their voices in their generation and foretold these impending horrors with faithful energy. Incredulity mocked at their predictions but could not avert the tremendous accomplishment. Time passed on, and still the sackcloth of penitence was put off, until the cup of their abominations was full and the Curses long ago pronounced fell down (at length) ↑amain↓ and crushed the devoted nation.

Oct. 1, 1822.

[27][33] "And what is this galling burden which they cannot shoulder? It is a revelation of mercy which drags them up from the pit of darkness & death in which they are swallowed and lifts them up to a seat of light & joy amid the glorious world of God's Universe." [R. W. E.]

It is a curious question to ask what connection ↑exists between↓ the men of one generation, and those of another at a long and remote interval. Myriads of men have lived, and unnumbered events transpired before our names were written in this world's book of life; and these, as they passed, have involved an immense interest to the actors and spectators; they have also been the causes of other events in untold numbers and have given a character to the world.

*Insert, at the star, the following sentence. — O it was not thus ⟨when⟩ ↑in↓ the day when the Candle of the Lord was upon her tabernacle, when his glory shone upon her and the nations from afar ⟨off⟩ were glad when they saw the light; that[n] light is quenched; the[n] darkness of hell, &c. —

[33] "EVENTS" is centered beneath "tide in events," at the bottom of the page.

But to us, the existence of those beings and changes in affairs are of mean importance or have altogether passed away; and from all this multitude of grand occurrences we select a few points as worthy of note, and choose a few characters from the generations of mankind which we regard as representatives of the countless crowds from which we took them. And this is that boasted knowledge of the past which we call History. Our clouded eyes can distinctly trace an event but a little way. But we fully know that one event generates another, which produces a third, and so on, to an infinite extent. We are affected today by the characters of those persons who issued from the ark ↑after the flood↓ and replenished the world. Whether there be a *chance* in the changes of circumstances, or whether there be an order — we know not. Perhaps there is a tide in events, and the revolution of an age [28]³⁴ may restore the scene which the preceding age presented. ⟨Assyria⟩ ↑Egypt↓ was enlightened and then barbarized. When the dark period had passed the light reappeared in Greece; Mankind began to be darkened again but the glory returned in Rome; Night came in its turn, till the Sun arose in Arabia. It sunk once more, but the reign of light returned in France & England. But theories may be multiplied forever. This is certain; that, the remotest periods of human ⟨life⟩ history are fatally and forever connected by the consequences of its infant guilt; for the *first* man sinned, — and the last man shall die.

October, 1822.

In proposing schemes of reformation in so important a matter as the Drama, one should be cautious to avoid running into systems too visionary for popular understanding. The scholar in his closet must beware lest his poetical imaginations of the beauty of Tragedy lead him ⟨out of⟩ ↑into fields beyond↓ the track of common opinion and so render his speculations of no use. Nevertheless, it appears to me that the bold and beautiful personification in Milton's Penseroso is not an unapt description of the true drama —

> Sometime let gorgeous Tragedy
> With sceptred pall come sweeping by
> Presenting Thebes and Pelops' line
> And the tale of Troy divine [ll. 97–100]

³⁴ "DRAMA" is centered beneath "the emblems" at the bottom of the page.

For we wish that Tragedy should take advantage of that weakness or perhaps virtue in our nature which bears such an idolat(o)rous love for the emblems of royalty and that its [29]³⁵ moral lessons should be couched in the grand and pathetic fables which antiquity affords. Owing to the identity of human Character, in all ages, there is as much instruction in the tale of Troy as in the Annals of the French Revolution. The fable of its foundation clearly asserts the dependence of human upon divine power, and the judgements following upon ingratitude to celestial benefactors. Its subsequent history is the history of the growth of a flourishing nation from obvious causes but which are less interesting than the individual characters. The choice of Paris and the consequences which flowed therefrom are as perfect an exhibition as the moralist can wish of the influence of voluptuous love producing by its rapid excitement a display of dangerous but winning accomplishments which flattered the pride of the possessor and advanced the triumph of his vices but which could not long seduce the insulted reason of his countrymen. They proved his ultimate ruin in his day and generation, and in the distant view of the man which we take at the present hour they fade into infamy. (and curse the memory of his name.) The virtues of Hector, placed in strong contrast with the vices of his brother, teach the patriot the character and value of true fame, and the brawling factions of the Greeks, the impetuous bravery of the invaders and the timorous prudence of the beseiged together with the display of individual character and chiefly the constant reference and [30]³⁶ frequent interference of divine agents crowd that most remote and insignificant course of events with immense interest and instruction for every age. Let me not be thought to be wandering from my subject into a vague panegyric of the genius of Homer; I am only desirous of making clear by this statement the propriety with which these old but unforgotten events may be introduced into an useful drama. The (exhibition of the)ⁿ fall of a nation strikes the imagination with awe, and a thousand sublime ideas spring up from its ruins. But with whatever nicety we adjust our theories, the ultimate appeal must be (to)made to the vulgar; if they graciously recieve our pageant,

---

[35] "DRAMA" is centered beneath "and chiefly" at the bottom of the page.
[36] "DRAMA" is centered beneath "are" at the bottom of the page.

be sure, it is safely founded in good sense; if they do not, — ⟨their⟩ ↑its↓ virtues and embellishments are unphilosophically contrived, and failing now, must fail forever. But it seems to me that you may secure success by crowding sufficient interest into your narrative. Taste and education[n] cannot set the heart above curiosity, and if you say in room of company, that a man is killing his father in the street, I think you will find the philosophers excited as ⟨rapidly⟩ ↑soon↓ as the mechanic, and that all will run to the window with equal precipitation. ⟨What man⟩ ↑Who ever↓ yawned at the exhortation of a dying man? It is plain that there are occurrences in human society [31][37] which break over[n] the pride of the great, and the stupidity of the dull, and which bend the necks of all beneath the yoke of omnipotent sympathy. I grant that the representation of the same events which moved our tears, may be so languid or absurd as to move our laughter; but this danger must be otherwise provided for. We have discovered a stable and eternal foundation, when we have learned the secret to whose magic sway we may calculate upon the homage of the human heart. You must compensate for the coldness of fictitious suffering by additional interest and if you can weave a tale of ghastly distress, of overflowing pity or of love, rejoice, for you have achieved a triumph of the mind which ⟨shall⟩will always endure.

There is an embellishment ⟨to⟩ which I would recommend, though out of place here. I mean the introduction of prophecies. The author of Guy Mannering and the Bride of Lammermoor knew the value of the charm and has made fine use of the fascination. It is the most beautiful use of supernatural machinery in fiction.

[32][38] I shall attempt to resume the subject which was left upon page 11.

All the attributes of the Deity are attributes of human nature; when these miniature qualities are extended to infinity, they are applied to Him, and are called Perfections. Since they are all ⟨indispensable⟩ essential to the idea of God, there is no natural classification of them which puts one above another, in a description of them. I begin with Wisdom or Omniscience. We notice first that it is alto-

---

[37] "DRAMA" is centered beneath "use" at the bottom of the page.

[38] "OMNISCIENCE" is centered beneath "more, we are ourselves" at the bottom of the page.

gether inconceivable, and that our best notions ↑concerning it↓ are arrived at by gradual ascents from the lowest ⟨order⟩ degrees of intelligence which we can discern in ↑animated↓ nature, to the highest, in man; hence, we ascertain steps of proportion in intellect which give us an approximation to the notion of infinite wisdom. Moreover we can so easily concieve of knowledge superior[n] to our own, that we are less perplexed by this idea than by others. The contrast, also, of great known attainments, with brute ignorance, helps us. A simple addition of facts and classes of facts which we can easily make will soon amount to a superhuman accumulation of knowledge which yet does not surpass our conception; because we readily imagine, that, if our time were longer, and our opportunities more, we are ourselves capable of such [33][39] acquisitions; and that in another state we shall be. Our views of Supreme Wisdom may be rendered more forcible by reverting to our modes of acquiring information. The senses, as the philosophers say, are our ⟨organs⟩ sole sources of thought; so[n] when we have opened our little page, for the energies of the Universe, to write their lines upon, and have thus gained, one after another the results of our ↑humble↓ experience in the changes of events, and the borrowed experience of others, Death comes apace to interrupt our labour, and we are obliged to shut up again our little book, with the reputation of learning, to garnish our gravestones. And why? — because we can walk but a step at a time, and can therefore see but a small part of the little ball we inhabit; and because our eyes are small, and can take in but a little at a glance; and because our minds can consider but one idea in the same moment, and so ⟨can coun⟩ out of innumerable events can count but few. — Therefore it is that our knowledge is so exceedingly little & imperfect. But the God, who, by his attributes of omnipresence and omnipotence, acts, at all moments, throughout the Universe — God, adds not grains to a heap, descends not to gather portions of knowledge, — but embraces all immensity in ⟨a glance⟩ his eye. *We* find it painful to advance a few steps in geometry and ascertain a few indisputable properties of some little lines, — before we die. But His mind sees the depths of space; the countless tribes of worms and men,

[39] "OMNISCIENCE" is centered beneath "relations which connect" at the bottom of the page.

of angels and archangels and unknown orders of being; the thousand moral affinities and relations which connect intelligent beings and [34][40] the moral world; the changes and progress of Nature, that is, — of his Universe; the stupendous story of all the past; and the coming events which lie dark in the bosom of Eternity; — all, pass before Him in one solitary Conception.

But I am asked — why this must be as I have represented it? Let us cast about for an answer.

The argument *a priori*, it is plain, should depend upon the proof of the attributes of Omnipresence↑,↓ ⟨&⟩omnipotence & eternity, which united in ⟨a⟩ ↑an intelligent↓ being, ⟨must⟩ of necessity make him omniscient. These attributes should therefore have been considered first. The other argument which is deduced from the exquisite wi⟨d⟩sdom evinced in Nature, is unfolded by the discoveries of human science; and, what is chiefly remarkable with regard to it, is, that, this evidence daily grows stronger from age to age. For, as Clarke ⟨obser⟩ notices, if Plato and Tully, with the limited light which Natural History in their age, threw upon the subject considered a man, to the last degree brutish & stupid, who was not convinced by the marvellous art and design, seen in the Universe; [41] — what must be that blindness which still remains ↑unconvinced,↓ when the progress of ages has accumulated wonders on wonders, in the stupendous exhibitions of contrivance and uniformity that our better acquaintance with nature affords[?] The student who dissected the human eye and successively examined its intricate and manifold parts, and considered their[n] exact adjustment, rose from his interesting scrutiny with a cer[35][42]tain conviction that he had found proof of a God. As he ⟨bowed to⟩ ↑went up to↓ worship, he met the Anatomist, who had

[40] "OMNISCIENCE" is centered beneath "his interesting" at the bottom of the page.

[41] Emerson is evidently recalling Dr. Samuel Clarke's observation that because of carelessness and inattention some men fail to understand religious truths, "seem to have . . . hardly any Notion of God," are guilty of "the *grossest and most stupid Ignorance* imaginable," and are "like Brute Beasts." He supports his indictment with remarks from Plato and Cicero. See *A Discourse Concerning the Being and Attributes of God* and *A Discourse Concerning . . . Natural Religion, and . . . The Christian Revelation,* 3 vols. in 1 (London, 1716), II, 155, 157, and *passim.*

[42] "OMNISCIENCE" is centered beneath "Christian Philosopher," at the bottom of the page.

explored the vessels and the Arteries of blood, and detected the dark-
est secrets of the animal economy and he had found in this curious
investigation ⟨a⟩ triumphant evidence of a wise Author. But here also
was one, who had searched the bosom of the earth, and seen how the
plants suck up their nourishment; who had studied the causes of their
decay and of their renovation; — and he came rejoicing in a final
discovery of the transcendant wisdom of a Creator. Next the Student
found the philosopher[,] who had looked through the whole history of Animated Nature[,] who had observed the beasts of the
field, and the birds, and the fishes of the Ocean, and the Worms
and Moles in the secret chambers of the Earth; he described their
mysterious instincts; their modes of protection or escape from the
cold; the provision for preserving them upon the earth, and their
common subjection to the service of man. He also had come to reveal his wonderful results which attested an intelligent Providence.
The Astronomer put away his telescope in amazement & joy; for he
had looked out from this world to see an hundred thousand others,
wheeling their vast revolutions, without interruption, & without end.
From his little observatory, the Divine Architect had shewn him a
plan of his Universe, and his soul was enraptured with the godlike
proportions of the Fabric. He also had come to bear witness to the
incontestable truth of Supreme Wisdom in the order of things. Last
of all, came the Christian Philosopher, who, from the history [36][43]
of man, and from the internal and external evidences of Revelation, — had convinced himself, & was come to convince the world,
that, there was a God, & that he was Wise. Then he that came first,
communed with himself; if[n] I, he said, from mine own pursuits
discovered incontestably that the Maker of the human Eye must
be an intelligent & wise Being; and all these have likewise, independently o⟨n⟩f me, and of each other, from their own peculiar
studies of different portions of his works, in and out of this world,
arrived at the same conclusion — must I not then believe that the
being whom I knew to be wise in *one thing*, is actually wise in *all
things*; at least in all things of which we have any cognizance; and
since every new inquiry adds new strength to the same fact, I am

[43] "OMNISCIENCE" is centered beneath "by its accumulated" at the bottom of
the page.

forced to acknowledge that all the Analogies of the Universe establish the belief that he is *Infinitely Wise*. Now when we consider that
this conclusion was arrived at ages ago, and that the inquiries which
then led to it have been continued and enlarged, and the industry
of Man has been adding ⟨to the⟩ ↑to the number of scientific↓ results, every day, for a thousand years; and when we examine these
results, and find that every individual one, without exception, affords
the selfsame inference [with the former] by shewing new instances
of order & design or explaining the true causes of seeming disorder;
— when we consider this, the Conclusion grows irresistible by its
accumulated weight.

(Continued p. 42)

[37]⁴⁴   Thursday Morng.
   Among the very first differences which strike us in society are
↑the two orders↓ those who from the nature of their pursuits devote
all their thoughts to matter, and those who are thinkers and inquirers
about better & brighter things. Although we are intelligent beings,
and our bodies were designed only to be vehicles to our minds —
yet ⟨you se⟩ there are hundreds of thousands now living and acting
in the world, and of mature age, who would be unable to answer
you, with any degree of propriety, the simplest questions about intellectual things. This is one of the first and broadest distinctions
which you can draw between men. And until the fact be explained
why so ⟨small⟩ ↑insignificant↓ a portion of men are thinkers, we should
confess that the purposes of our existence are very much concealed
from our knowledge. But when the inquirer who has recently made
this observation advances to a more minute examination and directs his
attention to the character and ⟨t⟩ results of the thinking part, he is
equally surprised to find instead of a united band of philosophers,
⟨to⟩ a multitude, separated into a thousand parties, by distinctions as
broad, as that which divides them all, from the rest of the world.
He rapidly discovers that men do not any where act unanimously
for any long period of time, that they do not pursue under any circumstances the same invariable course of conduct, or preserve the
same [38] set of opinions. So that a uniformity in the history of all

⁴⁴ "VARIETY" is centered beneath "course of" at the bottom of the page.

these minds in the after ages of their existence is not to be expected from ↑the analogy of↓ the elemental history of their minds in this world — which is the world of their education. Nevertheless it cannot be contested that there subsist among these manifold ⟨dif⟩ varieties certain grand and universal features of similarity, which spring from the common notion of *a God* and from their condition as moral agents. And the consideration of these instantly becomes supremely important to that inquirer. He feels that it is a sublime spectacle to see the creatures of the Deity wandering in a thousand paths far and wide asunder in their pursuit of truth, and yet all meeting in one consenting congregation in their first notions of ⟨h⟩Himself.

(I have altogether lost the design I had formed
for this piece at its commencement.)

Il faut que les idées dans l'esprit de Tout Puissant seroient toutes presentes a la fois, et sans la succession. Car s'il y a une succession, donc, *dans un moment* il[n] ne sait pas toutes choses dans l'Univers, ou, qui est la meme chose, ne comprend pas toutes possibles idées. Mais cela ⟨est⟩ dans notre conception ⟨non⟩ ↑n'est↓ pas vraisemblable que le Grand Auteur de l'Infinité, et des infinites idees, seroit toujours contente avec une idie quoique ce soit que vaste et transcendante. Mais cette idee est l'Univers. Vraiment le sujet s'eleve audessus de nos facultés, et nous avons tort pour parler ainsi [39][45] d'une Existence dont le pouvoir la gloire et la mystere sont inconcevables. x x x Il y a quelque chose de l'absurdite de tenter ecrire sur sujets inexprimables, dans une langue que je n'entends pas. Fauxpas. —

[46] When I was a lad — said the bearded islander — we had commonly a kind of vast musical apparatus in the Pacific islands which must appear as fabulous to you as it proved fatal to us. On the banks of the rivers there were abundance of Siphar Trees which consist of vast trunks perforated by a multitude of natural tubes without having any external verdure. When ⟨these were⟩ the roots

[45] "ORGAN" is centered beneath "charmed congregation." at the bottom of the page.
[46] The following story was printed with an introduction and some revisions in *The Offering for 1829*, ed. Andrews Norton (Cambridge, 1829), pp. 8–10.

of these were connected with the waters of the river the water was instantly sucked up by some of the tubes and discharged again by others and ↑when properly echoed↓ the operation attended by the most beautiful musical sounds in the world. My countrymen built their churches to the Great Zoa upon the margin of the water and enclosed a suitable number of these trees, hoping to entertain the ears of the god with this sweet harmony. Finding however by experience that the more water the pipes drew the more rich and various were the sounds of the Organ, they constructed a very large temple with high walls of clay and stone to make the echoes very complete, and enclosed a ⟨very large number of⟩ ↑hundred↓ Siphars. When the edifice was complete six thousand people assembled to hear the long expected song. After they had waited a long time and the waters of the river ⟨began⟩ ↑were beginning↓ to rise↑,↓ the Instrument suddenly began to emit the finest notes imaginable. Through some of the broader pipes the water rushed with the voice of thunder, and through others with the sweetness of one of your lutes. In a short time the effect of the music was such that it seemed to have made all the hearers mad. They laughed and wept alternately and began to dance and such was their delight that they did not percieve the disaster which had befallen their Organ. Owing to the unusual swell of the River and to some unaccountable irregularity in the ducts the pipes began to discharge their ⟨water⟩ contents within the chapel. In a short time the evil became but too apparent, for the water rose in spouts from the top of the larger ducts and fell upon the multitudes within. Meantime the Music swelled louder and louder, and every note was more ravishing than the last. The inconvenience of the falling water which drenched them, was entirely forgotten until finally the whole host of pipes discharged every one a volume of water upon the charmed congregation. The faster poured the water [40][47] the sweeter grew the music and the floor being covered with the torrent the people began to float upon it with intolerable extacies. ⟨f⟩Finally the whole Multitude swam ↑about↓ in this deluge holding up their heads with open mouths and ears as if to swallow the melody[n] whereby they swallowed much water. Many hundreds were immediately drowned and the enormous

---

[47] "NOT" is centered beneath "such ⟨are⟩ is" at the bottom of the page.

pipes as they emptied the river swelled their harmony to such perfection that the ear could no longer bear it and they who escaped
the drowning died of the exquisite music. Thenceforward there was
no more use of the Siphar trees in the Pacific islands.

                                                        Thursday Evg.

            Preface to Travels in the Land of Not.
    The author of the following sheets submits to the public the
question whether any inordinate modesty be required of him in his
first appearance as a candidate for their favour. In support of his own
opinion upon the subject which he is not anxious to communicate he
offers the following considerations. His ⟨many years'⟩ ↑long↓ residence in the country he describes and his familiar acquaintance with
its customs & the tone of feeling prevalent there, will justify him in
any remarks he may think proper to hazard. With regard likewise
to these manners & customs, one thing is noticeable that they are not
of a subtle & delicate nature such as might elude ↑the↓ examination
and analysis of an ordinary traveller, but are, on the contrary, enormous and gross to the last degree.
    An important distinction also between this book and others, is
that ⟨that there is⟩ no ⟨demand for any⟩ apology ↑need be made↓ for
introducing the subject to the notice of the public. For though it does
not pretend to be the ⟨th⟩ first account ever published of that interesting country, but rather the thousandth, yet such ⟨are⟩ ↑is↓ the in-
exhaustible store of its manners [41][48] and history that I can assure
the public they will not find[n] an individual fact, in my whole Journal,
which they have met with before. That I may not seem to want courtesy, I would recommend as the best book of travels in that Country
which I have ever seen, "The Arabian Night's Entertainments;"[49]
for the author of this work has seized with admirable precision and
described with singular accuracy the most striking features of that

[48] "NOT" is centered beneath "as in" at the bottom of the page.
[49] Emerson had reread volumes 2,3, and 4 between August 8 and September 19.
For this and other information about Emerson's reading, the editors have consulted
the studies by Kenneth W. Cameron, making corrections and additions where necessary: EtE; "Books Borrowed"; "Early Reading List"; and "Emerson's Reading."
See the table of abbreviations for the full bibliographical facts.

remarkable region. And I cannot sufficiently praise the discernment of the public, if they shall judge my volume, the supplement to that of my Arabian Friend.

It is now nineteen years since I left the land of Not. And I may safely say that in the countries in which I have passed my time since that period it ⟨w⟩ has been invariably true that there is more crime, misery, and vexation in every one of them in the course of a single year than transpires in the ↑peaceful↓ land of Not in the lapse of many centur⟨y⟩ies. Except for the ↑existence↓ [of] one single institution which has been established from time immemorial, there is no question that a vast tide of emigration would rapidly flow into that country. This institution is a rigorous Alien act which ordains that no man who leaves the limits of the country shall ever be permitted to set foot within it again. But to my knowledge many who have left it have often afterwards looked back to its pleasant abodes, and desired in vain to return.

Before I leave my book in the hands of the public I would make one more remark which may serve to set my character for candour in a ⟨good⟩ ↑favourable↓ light. I said just now that this was the thousandth volume which has been offered upon the subject; and this is true; but[n] a deception has been ⟨practised⟩ put upon society and ⟨Under⟩ the books which have been published under a thousand imposing names were in fact nothing more than merely travels in Not. This imposition has been detected in many instances as in an Octavo called Fearing's Travels [42][50] in America;[51] in some Folios, called Kant's Philosophy; and in many others of various sizes and various ornamental names but there are innumerable others still in circulation which have never been detected. For myself, I disdain dishonesty; ⟨and⟩ ↑I↓ have written my book's name on the title page, and have a just claim upon the attention of the learned world. ⟨If⟩ ⟨s⟩Should my hopes[n] be disappointed and my labours be

[50] Emerson canceled "NOT" and revised it to "OMNISCIENCE" beneath "and you have" at the bottom of the page.

[51] Undoubtedly Henry Bradshaw Fearon's *Sketches of America*, of which three editions had been published in London by 1819. In April 1820, *The North American Review* had called attention to the approval which both *The Edinburgh Review* and *The Quarterly Review* had given to Fearon's calumniously false story of his travels in America (X, 342), and in July 1821 had attacked Fearon again (XIII, 27, 30).

treated with neglect, I shall abandon forever an ungrateful age, and publish my Second Edition in the land of my idolatry.

(Continued from p. 36)   Saturday Evg., Oct. 22.

The sublime belief, to the consideration of which I have devoted a few pages, is a source of confidence and liberal views which doth not fail. He who believes that Chance created the Universe, and may shortly demolish it, ⟨and⟩ that he is himself here only by a lucky accident, and that no unseen Mind has measured his progress or appointed his end, must often, in his dark hours of weariness or distress feel that he is ⟨solitary⟩ ↑alone↓ and sink under the disgust of his uncomfortable solitude. It is a desolate belief which converts into a wilderness the great and blooming garden of nature; which, by depriving things & beings of object & utility, deprives them of the very principle of beauty. If I am shewn a machine constructed of the choicest materials and finished with exquisite art, but am also told that [it] is made without an object, and can serve no purpose under the sun, the pleasure which I felt at first would be lessened at once and almost forgotten. But such a machine is the Universe except that it fell by chance into its present divine form. But add to this Universe an Omniscient Governor and you have infused a soul into the [43][52] mighty mass. Instead of the dreary monotony of eternal matter you have around and above you an omnipresent spirit who understands all and cannot therefore do wrong. You feel at once *secure*. Events will be ordered for the good of all without a moment's interference of weak or adverse agents. You feel that you are known; that not a high thought worthy of your condition, not a sentiment of exalted devotion breathes unregarded from your soul; that you converse immediately with Heaven and are never forgotten in the conduct of God's Providence. He that established Nature, and adjusted the moral relations of his creatures, can surely appreciate the good and the evil of the life of a man. The march of events which was loose and fortuitous, becomes dignified & divine; the commerce of minds and the advancement of your own — things of which the importance was doubtful, — call out your wonder as soon as you

---

[52] "OMNISCIENCE" is centered beneath "secret & omnipotent" at the bottom of the page.

begin to discern the perfections of God walking amid these events and his Omniscient mind communicating with yours. You had sometimes felt an extraordinary kindling of thoughts within you, which burned with greater purity and expanded to a wider benevolence than you were wont. But you had never suspected that it might be the influence of a Mighty Spirit upon yours. But now that you have found yourself enveloped by this pervading Soul of Knowledge & Power can you not believe your education is in part conducted and your heaven soaring thoughts originated from this foreign but secret & omnipotent source?

[44]⁵³   Saturday Evening, Nov. 2, 1822.

My adventurous and superficial pen has not hesitated to advance thus far upon these old but sublime foundations of our faith; and thus without adding a straw to the weight of evidence or making the smallest discovery, it has still served to elevate somewhat my own notions by bringing me within prospect of the labours of the sages. After the primitive apostles, I apprehend that Christianity is indebted to those who have established the grounds upon which it rests; to Clarke, Butler, and Paley; to Sherlock, and to the incomparable Newton. And when it shall please my wayward imagination to suffer me to go drink of these chrystal fountains; or when my better judgement shall have at last triumphed over the daemon Imagination, and shall itself conduct me thither, — I shall be proud and glad of the privilege. For the present, I must be content to make myself wiser as I may, by the same loose speculations upon divine themes.

I must confine myself at present to the consideration of Omnipotence, which seems indeed to have a claim to be noticed first in the circle of Attributes.

The world is constituted we know not how, and every able inquiry ends in a new limitation of man's researches. [45]⁵⁴ There is a chain of events subsisting, a wide variety of changes, in con-

⁵³ "OMNIPOTENCE" is centered beneath "new limitation" at the bottom of the page.
⁵⁴ "OMNIPOTENCE" is centered beneath "a shadow of this" at the bottom of the page.

stant activity and eternal reproduction; this[n] great mass of things, we call the Universe. A little part of this we ourselves have seen; of a little greater part we have heard tidings; but of far the greater portion, we have very imperfect intelligence, and have had to form just notions of its value and importance, from *reasonings* that we have been able to make. Because we cannot concieve that this magnificent fabric could have been one moment out of existence, and a blank, and anon, spreading its splendours into infinit⟨i⟩y — existing and annihilated, — like transient dreams, without any reason for the one state or the other, but are constrained by certain tendencies within us, to think that if it so appeared starting out of the darkness and hush of nothing into this transcendant glory, there was a Cause; for this reason the human mind has been obliged to believe in the existence of God. And, because that by reason of this same tendency we cannot discover why this Being should have begun to be, we are constrained to believe that he existed eternally. Here Philosophy stops, and does not go further to inquire why such an existence should have been from eternity, at all, or why things *are,* instead of *not being*; but overmastered, she leaves these incomprehensible doubts to minds of gods. Let it not be imagined that the fond idea of Antiquity can remove a shadow of this last darkness; that [46][55] a great Fate or Necessity controuls all existence and binds the actions alike of human and divine Beings. This explains nothing; for *this Fate* is the God whom we worship and the misnamed *gods* of Olympus have been dead for Ages. But this is wandering from the subject. It is as difficult to account for the activity which we observe in all things which have being as ⟨it is to⟩ for their mere existence. God therefore is again the Source of their activity and the source of changes and this quality which we believe him to possess of creating and changing substances — we call *power*.

We likewise know him to possess this quality in a supreme degree, and to an universal extent; — and this enlargement of the attribute, we term — Omnipotence. We find this to be necessary to Him, because all the changes that take place must be accounted for; and these changes are *infinite*.

[55] "OMNIPOTENCE" is centered beneath "an infinite number" at the bottom of the page.

It is not a question of much moment in this connexion, if in any, whether, as some have supposed, the Deity is the immediate Author of every change which takes place in matter, or whether he has, in a manner, delegated a portion of his power to the material world. For to impart certain virtues under inviolable laws in such a manner as that no time shall alter and no circumstances prevent one and the same invariable event, and this to an infinite number of substances [47][56] will require, it seems to me, a potency as perfect as Omnipotence. And when we consider the insignificance of our own faculties, and that ⟨in the stupendous⟩ we do not so much as lift a finger to act in the stupendous whirl of events which takes place under our eye in the economy of the Universe; that the seasons change, ⟨a⟩the tides sink and rise, the earth is darkened by storms or shaken by Earthquakes, the stars pursue their orbits or are cast down from heaven, unmoved by the little fortunes or wishes of man; and that though man meddles with nature and seeks to fashion its dross to his service yet he is totally incapable of creating or destroying a hair; — when this is considered I think we should not be loth to admit the notion that to create is the special distinction of Deity and that it requires infinite power ⟨to⟩for any creation whatever so that it will not be at all necessary to prove any thing more than that God can create, in order to prove him Omnipotent.

Power, as manifested in the world, ⟨⟨(for be as novel and convincing as Brown may, he cannot deprive us of a strong and distinct feeling affixed to that word,⟩⟩[57] engages, more than aught else, our daily admiration. [For the conclusion of this paragraph see p. 22 Wide-world No 3 — beginning — "We have loosely" &c.][58] [48][59] It is in this manner that a strong incidental testimony to the character of the Deity is drawn, ⟨from this;⟩ that whatever there is in the human mind which most forcibly arrests the imagination, — *that* is

[56] "OMNIPOTENCE" is centered beneath "No 3 — beginning" at the bottom of the page.

[57] Emerson had withdrawn volume 1 of Thomas Brown's *Lectures on the Philosophy of the Human Mind*, ed. M. Newman, 3 vols. (Andover, 1822), from the Boston Library Society on September 26 and returned it October 10. Lectures six, seven, and nine include discussions of power.

[58] See *JMN*, I, 76.

[59] "OMNIPOTENCE" is centered beneath "benevolence and justice" at the bottom of the page.

found to be a special attribute of the Divine Character. When we had
extended to the utmost our conceptions of duration and had still
found the existence of the everlasting God stretching far ⟨b⟩far behind the remotest time and tasking and baffling our most extravagant
imaginations, that approached no nearer to its beginning, we have
to bestow upon this Being brooding upon space throughout ⟨t⟩his
vast eternity — a new principle quite as inconceivable and as perfect
as the last; a principle which takes away ⟨his⟩ the selfishness of his
existence by enabling him to impart the mysterious gift; for the
moment that this Being is invested with *power*, he has become the
Creator of other beings. To our feeble powers it is perhaps a more
distinct description of this sublime subject, to represent the Divinity
as merely existing, and then to add successively to this idea, the several attributes composing his Character; to add power to ⟨wisdom⟩
eternity and wisdom to power, and benevolence and justice to ⟨p⟩
wisdom, [49][60] until you discern his Matchless Arm lifted up amid
the Infinite night to open the morning of Creation — and lo! the
light hath broke, and instead of the silence of darkness and the
void, are seen the revolutions of a brilliant Universe wherein the
morning stars sing together and the sons of God shout for joy.

I believe we fight against phantoms when we laboriously contend for the surpassing power of God. It is that attribute, the proofs
of which are most gross and undeniable, in the view of every being
to whom that Power has communicated the organs of sense. Does the
man wake who doubts it? Hath he an eye and an ear, touch and
smell? I recommend to him to turn his face to the East and see the
sun; to look at the light, what it is? to climb the everlasting hills;
to go where Deep calleth unto Deep and find the fountains of the
sea; to open his ears to the thunder, and his eye to the fire of the
cloud; and if his fastidious soul find amid these, instances rather of
decay & weakness than of power, why I will bid this over-proud worm
estimate the force which is here required in these ordinary phe-

[60] "OMNIPOTENCE" is centered beneath "valley of A⟨v⟩jal⟨ion⟩on" at the
bottom of the page. Beside it is "V. Brown / Lect. XCIII" written in pencil. The
lecture occurs in volume 3 of *Lectures* . . . , which Emerson borrowed from the
Boston Library Society December 26 — January, 1823, and is entitled "On the
Existence, — The Unity, — The Omniscience, — The Omnipotence, — and The
Goodness of The Deity."

nomena; I will bid him make trial of his strength and compare it if he durst with Omnipotence. Put forth now thine arm and arrest the fierce comet in his journey to the sun. Like Joshua bid the sun stand still in Gideon & the Moon in the valley of A⟨v⟩jal⟨ion⟩on.[n] Pluck out a world [50][61] from yon wilderness of stars, and extinguish its light forever. In vain. They all move serenely on, ⟨at their⟩ looking down from their immeasurable height with pity upon the insolent reptile. Let the hand that sustains the Universe for a moment be withdrawn — wilt thou put thy shoulder to the Centre and support the falling worlds? No they stand and move by higher forces which thy little will is ⟨un⟩↑not↓ able to hinder or supply; no, not to conceive. Creep into thy grave, for the Universe hath no need of thee; Omnipotence is planted for its preservation.

Although we are surrounded by these proofs of the Omnipotence of God, yet, owing to the peculiar character of the Divine government, it is a fact that we are very blind to the forceful exhibitions of it which a purged eye can see. For when we diligently reflect, we feel that every motion of our bodies, every moment of life, is a new act of power; because preservation is nothing but a continual action of restraining power. As the atmosphere surrounds us, so are we surrounded by the Power of God. As mind is compounded with our frame, and enters intimately into its economy so does this all pervading *power* make it impossible to point to the place or the time where it is not. Since it is thus omni⟨sc⟩present it would appear natural to us [51][62] that it should oftener make itself signally felt by some extraordinary display befitting the present grandeur of a God. When frail man in hours of ungoverned rage, invokes curses upon himself or blasphemes the name of the Holiest, why should not then this present Power burst out in terrors ⟨and⟩ to assert its justice and strike him dead? The reason is manifest. It is because the Divine Being is not actuated by the motives of men, and is incapable of the malignity of revenge. It is because his law is a moral one, addressed to men's reason, and not their sense, and he chooses to leave the "good and

[61] "OMNIPOTENCE" is centered beneath "omni⟨sc⟩present" at the bottom of the page.
[62] "OMNIPOTENCE" is centered beneath "Genius of America," at the bottom of the page. Emerson continues his discussion of omnipotence in Wide World 8, beginning at p. 44 below.

evil of eternity" [63] to the choice of the soul not to the compulsion of an active terror. But that Omnipotence nevertheless envelopes you still. Fear to awake its wrath; for though its chastisement sleeps in this life, it is surely reserved for that which is to come. The Power which so quietly rests in the serenity of a preserved and upholden Universe, may shake or annihilate the whole in its fury, or exercise with untold anguish the intelligent beings which have provoked its displeasure.

November 3d —

———————

I have come to the close of the sheets which I dedicated to the Genius of America, and notice that [52][64] I have devoted nothing in my book to any peculiar topics which concern my country. But is not every effort that her sons make to advance the intellectual interests of the world, and every new thought which is struck out from the mines of religion & morality — a forward step in the path of her greatness? Peace be with her progressing greatness, — and prosperity crown her giant minds. A victory is achieved today for one,* whose name perchance is written highest in the volume of futurity. Boston, ⟨S⟩ November 4th, 1822.

CONCLUSION [65]

* Webster was chosen representative to Congress by a majority of 1078 votes this morning.

[63] From Samuel Johnson, *Life of Milton.* See *Lives of the English Poets,* ed. G. B. Hill, 3 vols. (Oxford, 1905), I, 182.

[64] The words "Wideworld" (encircled) and "No 7" are written upside down at the bottom of the page and are canceled; the word "Corinthian" (also upside down) has not been canceled.

[65] A sketch of a moon-shaped face is related to "CONCLUSION" by a flourish.

Wide World 8

1 8 2 2

Except for one entry in 1823, the regular dated entries in Wide World 8 follow without interruption from Wide World 7 and cover the period from November 6 through December 21, 1822.

The manuscript is made from twelve folded sheets, hand-stitched together into a single gathering to form an uncovered booklet of twenty-four leaves (forty-eight numbered pages). The sheets are of different sizes so that the leaves vary in width from 16.4 to 16.8 cm and in length from 19.8 to 21 cm.

[1][1] R. Waldo Emerson.

Wideworld.   No. 8.

Boston, November 6, 1822.

DEDICATION.

To glory which is departed, to majesty which hath ceased, to intellect which is quenched — I bring no homage, — no, not a grain of gold. For why seek to contradict the voice of Nature and of God, which saith over them, "It is finished," by wasting our imaginations upon the deaf ear of the dead? Turn rather to the mighty multitude, the thunder of whose footsteps shakes now the earth; ⟨their⟩ ↑whose↓ faces are flushed by the blood of life; ⟨and⟩ ↑whose eye is enlightened by↓ a living soul↑.↓ ⟨flashes in their eyes.⟩ Is there none in this countless assembly who hath a claim on the reverence of the sons of Minerva?

I have chosen one from the throng. Upon his brow have the Muses hung no garland. His name hath never been named in the

---

[1] "Wideworld." is circled. In the left margin beneath "R. Waldo" is a sketch of a young man's head, with curly hair, and possibly wings.

halls of Fashion, or the palaces of State; but I saw Prophecy drop the knee before him, and I hastened to pay the tribute of a page.

In my dreams, I departed to distant climes and to ⟨many⟩ ↑different↓ periods and my fancy presented before me many ⟨period⟩ extraordinary societies, and many old and curious institutions. I sat on the margin of [2]² the river of ⟨g⟩Golden Sands when the thirsty leopard came thither to drink. It was just ⟨daylight⟩ ↑dawn↓, and the shades were chased rapidly from the Eastern firmament by the golden magnificence of day. As I contemplated the brilliant spectacle of an African morning I thought on those sages of this storied land who instructed the infancy of the world. Meanwhile the sun arose and cast a full light over a vast and remarkable landscape. About the river, the country was green and its bed reflected the sunbeams from pebbles and gold. Far around was an ample plain with a soil of yellow sand, glittering everywhere with dew and interspersed with portions of forest, which extended into the plain, from the mountains which surrounded this wide Amphitheatre. The distant roar of lions ceased to be heard, and I saw the leopard bathing his spotted limbs and swimming towards the woods which skirted the water. But his course was stopped; an arrow from the wood pierced his head, and he floated lifeless ashore. I looked then to see whence the slayer should have come, and beheld not far off a little village of huts built of canes. Presently I saw a ⟨na⟩ band of families come out from their habitations; and these naked [3]³ men, women, and children sung a hymn to the sun and came merrily down to the river with nets in their hands to fish. And a crimson bird with a yellow crest flew over their heads as they went, and lighted on a rock in the midst of the river and sung pleasantly to the savages while he brushed his feathers in the stream. The boys plunged into the river and swam toward the rock. But upon a sudden I saw many men dressed in foreign garb run out from the wood where the leopard had been killed; and these surrounded the fishers, and bound them with cords, and hastily carried them to their boats, which lay concealed behind the trees. So they sailed down the stream, talking aloud an[d] laughing as they went; but they that were bound, gnashed their teeth and uttered

---

² "VISION" is centered beneath "their habitations;" at the bottom of the page.
³ "VISION" is centered beneath "day long" at the bottom of the page.

so piteous a howl that I thought it were a mercy if the river had swallowed them.

In my dream, I launched my skiff to follow the boats and redeem the captives. They went in ships to other lands and I could never reach them albeit I came near enough to hear the piercing cry of the chained victims, which was louder than the noise of the Ocean. In the nations to which they were brought they were sold for a price and compelled to labour all the day long and scourged with whips [4][4] until they fell dead in the fields, and found rest in the grave.

Canst thou ponder the vision, and shew why Providence suffers the land of its richest productions to be thus defiled? Do human bodies lodge immortal souls, — and is this tortured life of bondage and tears a fit education for the bright ages of heaven and the commerce of angels? Is man the Image of his Maker, — and shall this fettered & broken frame, this marred and brutalized soul become perfect as ⟨h⟩He is perfect? This slave hath eat the bread of captivity and drank the waters of bitterness and cursed the light of the Sun as it dawned on his bed of straw, and worked hard and suffered long while never an idea of God hath kindled in his mind from the hour of ↑this↓ birth to the hour of his death; and yet thou sayest that a merciful Lord made man in his benevolence to live and enjoy; to take pleasure in His works and worship him forever. Confess that there are secrets in that Providence, which no human eye can penetrate, which darken the prospect of Faith, and teach us the weakness of our Philosophy.

[5][5] Nov. 8.

At least we may look farther than to the simple fact and perhaps aid our faith by freer speculation. I believe that nobody now regards the maxim 'that all men are born equal,' as any thing more than a convenient hypothesis or an extravagant declamation. For ⟨all⟩ the reverse is true, — that[n] all men are born unequal in personal powers

---

[4] "Paradis" is centered beneath "fields, and" between the paragraphs. "SLAVERY" is centered beneath "Philosophy." at the bottom of the page, and to the right of this index heading is a tiny sketch of a man, apparently at labor.

[5] "SLAVERY." is centered beneath "of our own" at the bottom of the page.

and in those essential circumstances, of time, parentage, country, fortune. The least knowledge of the natural history of man adds another important particular to these; namely, ⟨of⟩ what class of men he belongs to — European, Moor, Tartar, African? Because Nature has plainly assigned different degrees of intellect to these different races,[n] and the barriers between are insurmountable.

This inequality is an indication of the design of Providence that some should lead, and some should serve. For when an effect invariably takes place from causes which Heaven established, we surely say with safety, that Providence designed that result.

Throughout Society there is therefore not only the direct and acknowledged relation of king & subject, master & servant, but a secret dependence quite as universal, of one man upon another, which sways habits, opinions, conduct. This prevails to an infinite extent and however humbling the analogy, it is nevertheless true, that the same pleasure and confidence which the dog and horse feel when they rely upon the superior intelligence of man is felt by the lower parts of our own species with reference to the higher.

[6][6] Now with these concessions the question comes to this: whether this known and admitted assumption of power by one part of mankind over the other, can ever be pushed to the extent of total possession, and that, without the will of the slave?

It can hardly be said that the whole difference of *the will*, divides the *natural* servitude of which we have spoken from the forced servitude of 'Slavery.' For it is not voluntary, on my part, that I am born a subject; contrariwise, if my opinion had been consulted, it is ten to one I should have been the Great Mogul. The circumstances in which every man finds himself he owes to fortune and not to himself. And those men who happen to be born in the lowest caste in India, suffer ↑much↓ more perhaps than the kidnapped African with no other difference in their lot than this, that God made the one ↑wretched↓ and man, the other. Except that there is a dignity in suffering from the ordinances of Supreme power, which is not at all common to the other class — one lot is as little enviable as the other.

When all this is admitted, the question may still remain en-

[6] "SLAVERY." is centered beneath "a right" at the bottom of the page.

tirely independent and untouched — apart from the consideration of slavery as agreeable or contradictory to the analogies of nature — whether any individual has a right to deprive any other [7][7] individual of freedom without his consent; or whether ⟨when⟩ he may continue to withold the freedom which another hath taken away?

Upon the first question 'whether one man may forcibly take away the freedom of another,' the weakness and incapacity of Africans ⟨has⟩ ↑would seem to have↓ no bearing; though it may affect the second. Still it may be advanced that the beasts of the field are all evidently subjected to the dominion of man, and, with the single restriction of the laws of humanity, are left entirely at his will. And why are they, and how do we acquire this declaration of heaven? Manifestly from a view of the perfect adaptation of these animals to the necessities of man and of the advantage which many of them find in leaving the forest for the barnyard. If they had *reason,* their strength would be so far superior to ours, that, besides our inability to use them, it would be inconsistent with nature. So that these three circumstances are the foundation of our dominion; viz. their want of reason; their adaptation to our wants; and their own advantage, (when domesticated.) But these three circumstances may very well apply to the condition of the Blacks and it may be hard to tell exactly where the difference lies. Is it in *Reason?* If we speak in general of the two classes Man and Beast, we say that they are ⟨|| ... ||⟩separated by the dis[8][8]tinction of Reason, and the want of it; and the line of this distinction is very broad. But if we abandon this generalization, and compare the classes of one with the ⟨g⟩classes of the other we shall find ⟨that⟩ our boundary line growing ⟨mor⟩narrower and narrower and individuals of one species approaching individuals of the other, until the limits become finally lost in the mingling of the classes. (Continued p. 12)

(Continued from Wideworld No 7.)[9]   Saturday Evg., Nov. 9th.
I have alluded more than once to that attraction by which *power*

[7] "SLAVERY" is centered beneath "that they" at the bottom of the page.
[8] "SLAVERY" is centered beneath "of time;" at the bottom of the page.
[9] Emerson's discussion of omnipotence in Wide World 7 begins on p. [44]. There are frequent references to *"power"* from p. [46] to the end of the journal. See above, pp. 34–39.

engages the human mind, above any other quality which we conceive
to exist. I do not know that any argument of the Divine Omnipotence
can be drawn from this singular fact, unless it may seem to enter
somewhat more intimately into our idea of God than any other
attribute. Hence the poetical tradition that Power is the darling,
Perfection, of the Supreme. It ⟨is⟩ ↑may be↓ altogether unnecessary
to add that our sublimest images will always be found to be those
⟨referrin⟩ involving this principle; the fall of empires; the mastery
of a mind over an age; the antiquity which survives the storm of
circumstances and the lapse of time; the pictures, which [9]¹⁰ astronomy presents, of the Universe — all possess the highest order of
sublimity, and borrow it from their intrinsic *power*. But the mind
which has been long absorbed in great conceptions of God learns
gradually to contemn the deficiency and lowness which appear in
the noblest forms of matter by comparison with what is purely
divine. The sublimest scene which ever opened on the thought of
man, is the Judgement of the World, in the partial representations of
the sacred writers. We are daily pointed to the majesty of the everlasting Universe whose suns and systems fulfill their immeasurable
rounds not without a pitying influence upon the little world which
man inhabits. But on ↑the arrival of↓ this tremendous event, a mournful grandeur is thrown over the unbounded whole in the ↑growing↓
expectation of its ruin. Instead of the ordinary picture of benevolence
and joy which arises from the contemplation of the heavenly host,
ten thousand ghastly spirits start up in the distant worlds, ten thousand melancholy portents of downfall and death. Nature is dismayed
within herself, and her thousand refulgent centres of light are fast
growing dim; Annihilation waits in silence the moment of Fate when
he shall stretch a hideous blank where Creation shone, and all its
strength and greatness and beauty shall be swallowed up forever.
[10]¹¹ The sun is quenched; the moon is turned to blood; the stars
fall down from heaven; and amid the general dissolution, nothing
remains firm, but the Throne of God. About it are assembled all the

¹⁰ "OMNIPOTENCE" is centered beneath "and beauty" at the bottom of the
page.
¹¹ "OMNIPOTENCE" is centered beneath "topic. The" at the bottom of the
page.

creatures of his hand, all intelligences that ⟨he hath made⟩↑live↓. And the judgement is set, and the books are opened.

[Growing somewhat verbose upon too good subjects for verbiage.]

10th Nov.

Abernethy thinks that the best way of concieving of the divine attributes, is not to attempt to grasp an abstract idea of immensity or omnipotence, but to consider God as present and active in all parts of his works. We can easily imagine intelligent beings of such diminutive proportions as to think it wonderful how a soul can animate at the same moment so large a bulk as the human body. And, in like manner, we can stretch our conceptions to the existence of beings, to whose frame the human body were but a point of ⟨space⟩ magnitude. So also we may concieve of the whole Universe as being but the body of a being who is its soul. Let this be believed with one essential restriction, that, the Supreme Soul created its own body, if such a parallel may be admitted.[12] Pope hath the same idea.

> "All are but parts of one stupendous whole,
> Whose body, Nature is, and God, the soul."
> [Pope, *Essay on Man*, ll. 66–67]

There is an important remark to be made before we quit this topic. The preservation and renewal of the [11][13] Universe is a constant and immediate exertion of Omnipotent power. We commonly say that God ordained the laws of Nature and that by that ordination they have remained. ⟨But⟩ As man contrives a machine which when once wound up performs its part without ↑human↓ interference for a certain length of time so hath God adjusted a vast system of Nature which has within itself, independent sources of motion. But there is a fallacy in this statement, because it neglects a fundamental difference between the works of God and the works of men. The machines of man depend for their operation upon the continuance of certain laws of nature, as, upon the continuance of elas-

---

[12] See John Abernethy (1680–1740), *Discourses Concerning the Being and Natural Perfections of God*, 3rd ed., 2 vols. (London, 1757), I, 222, 232–233, and *passim*.

[13] "OMNIPOTENCE" is centered beneath "is not the" at the bottom of the page.

ticity or gravitation, and would cease to act were these laws once broken. Now upon what law do the revolutions of the Universe depend? That is; what causes the ⟨co⟩operation of gravitation which is thus constant? We plainly have no other principle, but must answer directly — the Power of God. And therefore the art of man hangs directly upon the same cause. For when the Artist has wound up a clock, what causes its motion? Gravitation. And what causes Gravitation? — The power of God.

Besides this, there is another illustration of the same remark. Why, I ask, does the seed produce the plant? Because God ordained that when the seed should be lodged in the earth the same effect should always follow. But it is perfectly plain that unless ⟨the⟩ a Command were attended ⟨like the⟩ with power the substances would remain together as they were left and would produce no more effect than two wheels of a watch which the artist laid carelessly together. Such is not the manner of God's operation. [12][14] His power perpetuates his command; and thus,

> "His word leaps forth to its effect
> He calls for things that are not, and they come." [15]

We have considered those attributes which belong to the rudest ideas of Deity in every nation. His perfect power, wisdom, and eternity constitute him *a God*, before a happier faith hath found reason to rejoice in the discovery of yet greater titles to the Throne of the Universe. We are introduced to another class of qualities, the knowledge of which gives us an insight into new principles of human nature, and makes an immediate division of all intelligent beings into two great companies, the good, and the bad. It inspires us with a feeling of delight hitherto unknown, at a view of some actions, and with an indignant loathing of others. It blesses Virtue, and ⟨execrates⟩ ↑hates↓ Vice.

The qualities of the divine character which excite these emotions

---

[14] "SLAVERY" is centered beneath "true that" at the bottom of the page.

[15] Perhaps a reminiscence of

> "Whose word leaps forth at once to its effect;
> Who calls for things that are not, — and they come."

These lines are quoted without identification in Thomas Brown, *Inquiry into the Relation of Cause and Effect* (Andover, 1822), p. 63.

are ⟨his⟩ Justice ↑&↓ Benevolence, and these comprise all that we mean, when we speak of his *moral character*.

Nov. 10.   Continued p. 14

Continued from p. 8 —

It can hardly be true I think that the difference lies in the attribute of Reason; I saw ten, twenty, a hundred large lipped, lowbrowed black men in the streets who, except in the mere matter of language, did not exceed the sagacity of the elephant. Now is it true that these were created supe[13][16]rior to this wise animal, and designed to controul it? And in comparison with the ⟨ord⟩ highest orders of men, the Africans will stand so low as to make the difference which subsists between themselves & the sagacious beasts inconsiderable. It follows from this, that this is a distinction which cannot be much insisted on.

And if not this, what is the preeminence? Is it in the upright form, and countenance raised to heaven, — fitted for command? But in this respect also the African fails. The Monkey resembles Man, and the African degenerates to a likeness of the beast. And here likewise I apprehend we shall find as much difference between the head of Plato & the head of the lowest African, as between this last and the highest species of Ape.

If therefore the distinction between the beasts and the Africans is found neither in Reason nor in figure i.e. neither in mind or body — where then is the ground of that distinction? is it not rather a mere name & prejudice and are not they an uppe[r] order of inferior animals?

Moreover if we pursue a revolting subject to its greatest lengths we should find that in all those three circumstances which are the foundations of our dominion over the beasts, very much may be said to apply them to the African species; even in the last, viz. the advantage which they derive from our care; for the slaveholders violently assert, that their slaves are happier than the [14][17] freedmen of their class; and the slaves refuse oftentimes the offer of their freedom. Nor is this owing merely to the barbarity which has placed

---

[16] "SLAVERY" is centered beneath "their slaves" at the bottom of the page.

[17] "MORAL LAW" is centered beneath "nature, so" at the bottom of the page.

them out of the ⟨reach⟩ power of attaining a competence by themselves. For it is true that many a slave under the warm roof of a
humane master with easy labours and regular subsistence enjoys
more happiness than his naked brethren parched with thirst on a
burning sand or endangered in the crying wildernesses of their
native land.

This is all that is offered *in behalf* of slavery; we shall next attempt to knock down the hydra. ↑[See page 25]↓[18] Nov. 14.

Continued from p. 12

Saturday Evg., Nov. 16.

The child who refuses to pollute its little life with a lie, and the
archangel who refuses with indignation to rebel in the armies of
heaven against the Most High, act alike in obedience to a law which
pervades all intelligent beings. This law is the Moral Sense; a rule
coextensive and coeval with Mind. It derives its existence from the
eternal character of the Deity — of which we spoke above; — and
seems of itself to imply and therefore to prove his Existence. For
since nothing can exist without a cause, — whence comes this strong
universal feeling that approves or abhors actions? Manifestly not
from *matter*, which is altogether unmoved by it and the connection
of which with it, is a thing absurd — but from a *Mind*, of which it
is the essence. That Mind is God.

This Sentiment which we bear within us, is so subtle ⟨in it[?]⟩and
unearthly in its nature, so entirely distinct from [15][19] all sense and
matter, and thence so difficult to be examined, and withal so decisive
and invariable in its dictates — that it clearly partakes of another
world than this and looks forward to it in the end. It is further to be
observed of it, that its dictates are never blind, are never capricious,
but however they may seem to differ, are always discovered on a
close and profound examination to point to a faultless and unattainable perfection. They seem to refer to a sublime course of life and
action which nowhere exists or to which we are not privy; and to
be an index of the Creator's character lent to mankind in vindication

[18] See below, p. 57.
[19] "MORAL LAW" is centered beneath "know why" at the bottom of the page.

or illustration of the command — "Be Ye perfect as He is perfect." [20]

This Sentiment differs from the affections of the heart and ⟨the⟩from the faculties of the mind. The affections are undiscriminating and capricious. The Moral Sense is not. The powers of the intellect are sometimes wakefull and sometimes dull, alive with interest to one subject, and dead to the charm of another. There are no ebbs and flows, no change, no contradiction in *this*. Its lively approbation never loses its pleasure; its aversion never loses its sting. Its oracular answers might be sounded through the world, for they are always the same. Motives and characters are amenable to it; and the golden rules which are the foundation of its judgements we feel and acknowledge, but do not understand. That is we do not pretend to know why Truth is amiable and [16][21] not falsehood; why justice and mercy are better than injustice and revenge. The cause must be traced up to the character of God, and we must answer as before — it is because Justice & Benevolence are his nature.

God is infinitely just. To have an origin in us, the virtue or the sense of Justice must have ↑previously↓ existed in Him. The law itself implies a sanction and consequences which are infinite in their extent and duration. He is the Sanctioner and the Cause, and must therefore be infinitely just.

Add to this, the inference arising from the history of the world. One event is appointed to justice and another to its violation. In all the instances which have passed beneath the eye of man, pain and misery follow every individual outrage upon this primal law. And if every action done in society were perfectly just, society would cease to be miserable. Now we are obliged to learn the will of God by observing where he sets the reward, and where, the punishment. If therefore we invariably find that Justice is recompensed, and injustice suffers, we discover the one to be agreeable to the divine character.

A still nicer scrutiny of God's Providence establishes the fact, that, not only pain is affixed to the commission of crime, but, that, it is proportioned to the offence; that is, ⟨that⟩ it is administered in accordance with the principles of Justice. He who has long been an inmate of this world, who has ⟨lived⟩ ↑treasured up the observations

[20] Cf. Matt. 5:48.
[21] "JUSTICE" is centered beneath "a long" at the bottom of the page.

of↓ sixty or seventy years has lived long enough to verify this remark. He must have discerned the progress of divine Retribution in
public and domestic affairs and in watching a long line of events must
have [17]²² sometimes seen the ⟨secret⟩ fire which was smothered
at one point stealing secretly along until it broke out at a distant
interval and made amends ↑to destruction↓ for its delay. He distinctly beholds the Character of one generation sowing the seed of
events to the next; when he has lost the view of those who opened
the ground, he watches the approach of the fated reaper of the harvest and can satisfy himself why it belongs to *him* & not to another.
Events that to the idle eye of the world, are fortuitous, are bound
and ordered by an adamantine chain which his clearer vision can
easily distinguish. That bond is the divine Justice, which inseparably
connects character to its rewards. The pain which Vice plotted for
another, redounds to its own destruction; and the terrible Agent who
walks in darkness among the homes and societies of men, never errs
or falters in his stroke.

> "Even handed Justice
> Commends the ingredients of our poisoned chalice
> To our own lips."
>   [Shakespeare, *Macbeth*, I, vii, 10–12]

With this condition of things established in the world, there is
a madness in crime which was not manifest before. The bold misdoer
who transgresses the law of Justice, grapples with he knows not what.
He has offended against an essential attribute of the Divinity which
will plead against him inexorably, until it be avenged. His ⟨hand dis⟩
rash hand has disordered a part of the moral machinery of the Universe and ↑he↓ is in peril of being crushed by the mischief he has
caused. Heaven and earth may pass away, but this law shall not pass
away [18]²³ until all be fulfilled.

Upon this elementary truth depends the whole hope and impulse
of virtuous action. Unless God be just, human virtue is null. If the
Highest disregards rectitude and leans favourably to the side of impiety and wrong, the Meanest may throw down their altars, and
curse Heaven for oppression. For this reason man comes with anxious

²² "JUSTICE" is centered beneath "pass away, but" at the bottom of the page.
²³ "JUSTICE" is centered beneath "*benevolence* and" at the bottom of the page.

eye to the books of Natural and Revealed Religion to seek an explanation of those dark problems which ⟨the⟩ his first views of the Universe sometimes offer to bewilder his understanding. How shall he reconcile his freedom with that eternal necessary chain of cause and consequence which binds him and Nature down to an irreversible decree? How shall he reconcile his freedom with that prophetic omniscience which beheld his end long before the infant entered on the world? Perhaps he is a slave—and men have worn his limbs with irons, and his soul with suffering; the name of virtue and the smile of kindness never have stooped to alleviate his hard and bitter bondage; but ere his little day of apathy and distress was done, he cursed God and died;—hath he descended into hell? Or how dost thou reconcile the creation and destiny of this being with that Infinite and benevolent Justice that would not abuse its Omnipotence and would not create a mind to be miserable?

⟨Tell not that man of those feelings and thoughts which give a joy to *your* existence and warm your heart to the world; for it will be but to mock his wretchedness. Tell him not of the dignity of human nature, of its *benevolence* and *philanthropy*,—he will clank [19]²⁴ his chains at the word. He scoffs bitterly at your pictures of the golden gates of Heaven, for they are closed ⟨to⟩ ↑on↓ him.⟩

The man is bold who undertakes to answer beyond a doubt these perplexing ⟨doubts⟩ questions. ⟨Still⟩ ↑But↓ theology would be a vain science, unworthy of our attention if it left them all in their full force, without notice or solution.

If an ignorant man were carried from his Closet to the prisons and penitentiaries of a vast kingdom and shewn a multitude of men confined and scourged and forced to labour, and informed that this was the act of the government, if he knew nothing more of that state and perhaps foolishly concieved that its limits extended no further than ⟨over⟩ the walls wherein he stood, it would be a very ⟨natural⟩ ↑plain↓ Conclusion that this government was a savage and outrageous tyranny; while perhaps at that very moment the government was the most perfect and beneficent in the world. Our rash conclusions

²⁴ "JUSTICE" is centered beneath "discussion" at the bottom of the page. The text is written over one pen and ink sketch of a man's head in profile and at least thirteen or fourteen pencil sketches of heads in front view or profile.

from the dark side of human affairs are analogous to these, and like these are to be corrected by broader views of the system which we misunderstand.

The questions we have named, are incidental to the subject, but of such importance, that we shall digress from the main topic to attempt to answer them. The endeavour is always laudable to ⟨end⟩ clear up the darkness which settles around portions of the system. God in heaven is answerable for his works, to those principles which he hath set within us to judge of them. To the discussion of some of them, our nature is incompetent.

[20] It is admitted I believe, by all philosophy, that every change which takes place in the world, succeeds some former change, without the existence of which, it would not itself have transpired. This fact is true of mind as well as matter; in those trains of thought, which do not depend upon the will, each idea is suggested by the last, and itself suggests another; and in voluntary action, every determination of the will results from a view of motives presented from within or from without. No event therefore in mind or matter starts up into an independent existence, but all have an immediate dependence upon what went before. This is the foundation of the doctrine of human necessity.

1   I love thy music mellow bell [25]
1823   I love thine iron chime
     To life or death, to heaven or hell
     Which calls the Sons of Time

2   Thy voice upon the deep
     The homebound seaboy hails
     It charms his cares to sleep
     It cheers him as he sails

     To merry ⟨feast —⟩ hall or house of God
3   Thy summons called our sires
     And good men thought thy awful voice
     Disarmed the thunder's fires.

[25] For an earlier version, see *JMN*, I, 301–302.

4   And soon thy music sad, Deathbell!
Shall sing its dirge once more
And mix my requiem with the gale
Which sweeps my native shore.

[21]²⁶   ⟨Thy iron song our sires believed⟩
⟨Disarmed the thunder's fiery ball⟩
⟨3⟩   ⟨To merry feast or holy church⟩
⟨Thy well known ⟨accent⟩ ↑summons↓ called our sires⟩
⟨And oft they thought thy honoured voice⟩
⟨Disarmed the winged thunder's fires.⟩
⟨And soon old bell the notes I love⟩
⟨Will wail one weary deathnote more⟩
⟨And roll my passing requiem⟩
⟨Upon the⟩
⟨To mingle with the Atlantic roar⟩
⟨And soon thy music sad Death bell⟩
⟨Shall strike one peal of kindness more⟩
⟨And mix my requiem with the ⟨winds⟩ ↑gale↓⟩
That sing

("Law," said Plutarch, "is Queen of
all the mortals & the immortals.") ²⁷

One of the best satires upon women is the popular opinion of
the 3d Century, that they who took wives were of all others the
most subject to the influence of evil demons. X X Men's minds visit
heaven as they visit earth, & hence the Turkish heaven is a Harem;
the Scandinavian, a hunting field; the Arabian, a place of wheaten
cakes & murmuring fountains. [R. W. E.] We've supple understandings & so it comes that a new religion ever suits itself to the state in
which 'tis born whether despotism or democracy,ⁿ as Montesquieu
has remarked.²⁸

²⁶ The fourteen lines from "⟨Thy iron" to "the ⟨winds⟩ gale⟩" below have been
canceled by wavy lines running at angles across the page.
²⁷ Cf. "Law, the king of all,
Both mortals and immortals." *Moralia*, 780C.
²⁸ Cf. "Lorsqu'une religion naît et se forme dans un État, elle suit ordinairement
le plan du gouvernement òu elle est établie. . ." in the chapter headed "Que la reli-

[22]²⁹   (Four daughters make the family of Time,
          But rosy Summer is the darling child.)
                                        Saturday Evening, Nov. 23d.
    The hours of social intercourse, of gratified hope, of the festive
board, have just now yielded to quieter pleasures of the closet and
the pen. This tender flesh is warmly clad, the blood leaps in the
vessels of life, Health and Hope write their results on the passing
moment, — and these things make the *pleasure* of a mortal bodily
mental being. There are in the world at this moment an hundred
million men whose history today may match with mine, not counting
the numberless ones whose day was happier; there ⁿ are also in existence here a countless crowd of inferior animals who have had their
lesser cup filled full with pleasure. The sunny lakes reflect the noon-
day beams from the glittering tribes which cover its bottom, rapid
as thought in their buoyant motions, leaping with the elasticity and
gladness of life. The boundless Ocean supports in its noisy ⟨whales⟩
waves its own great population, — the beautiful dolphin, the enormous whale and huge sea-monsters of a thousand families and a
thousand uncouth gambols dash through its mighty domain in the
fulness of sensual enjoyment. The air is fanned by innumerable
wings, the ⟨wo⟩green woods are vocal with the song, of the insect
and the bird; the beasts of the field fill all the lands untenanted by
man, and beneath the sod the mole and the worm take their pleasure.
All this vast mass of animated matter is moving and basking under
the broad orb of the Sun, — is drinking in the sweetness of the air,
ʼtis feeding on the fruits of nature,↓ — is pleased with life, and loth
to lose it. All this pleasure ⟨below⟩ flows from a source. That source
is the Benevolence of God.
    This is the first superficial glance at the economy of the world
and necessarily leaves out a thousand circum[23]³⁰stances. Let us take
a closer view, and begin with the human mind. I find within me a

gion Catholique convient mieux à une monarchie, et que la Protestante s'accommode
mieux d'une république." *L'Esprit des Lois*, in *Oeuvres Complètes de Montesquieu*,
ed. Édouard Laboulaye, 7 vols. (Paris, 1875–1879), V, 123.
    ²⁹ "BENEVOLENCE" is centered beneath "necessarily leaves out" at the bottom
of the page. The couplet is crowded in the top margin to the left of the date.
    ³⁰ "BENEVOLENCE" is centered beneath "why are any" at the bottom of the
page.

motley array of feelings that have no connection with my clayey frame and I call them my *mind*. Every day of my life, this mind draws a thousand ↑curious↓ conclusions from the different things which it beholds. With a wanton variety which tires of sameness it throws all its thoughts into innumerable lights and changes the fantastic scene by varying its own operations upon it; by combining & separating, by comparing and judging, by remembering and inventing all things. Every one of these little changes within, produces a pleasure; the pleasure of power or of sight. But besides the mere fact that the mind acts, there is a most rich variety in thought, and I grossly undervalue the gift I possess if I limit its capacity to the puny round of every day's sensations. It is a ticket of admission to another world of ineffable grandeur — to unknown orders of things which are as *real* as they are stupendous. ⟨It⟩ As soon as it has advanced a little in life it opens its eye to thoughts which tax its whole power, and delight it by their greatness and novelty. These suggest kindred conceptions which give birth to others and thus draw the mind on in a path which it percieves is interminable, and is of interminable joy. To this high favoured intellect is added an intuition that it can never end and that with its choice it can ↑go↓ ⟨advance⟩ forward to take the boon of immortal Happiness. These are causes and states of pleasure which no reason can deny. But this is the true history of all the individuals of the mighty nations that breathe today. These point also to a Source — which is the Benevolence of God.

But a groan of the dying, a cry of torture from the diseased, the sob of the mourner, answer to this thanksgiving of human nature and produce a discord in our Anthem of praise. If God is good, why are any of his creatures unhappy?

[24]³¹   Sunday Evening.
It seems to me that a liberal view of the subject should reconcile the mourner to his transient affliction, and his affliction to the benevolence of God. Those who consider the foundations of human happiness, find that it is a contrasted and comparative thing. It is never

³¹ "BENEVOLENCE" is centered beneath "weaning man away" at the bottom of the page. The text is written over a pencil sketch of a man's head and shoulders in profile in the center of the page.

↑so↓ absolute but a lurking ambition can indicate a higher degree; nor so poor, but ⟨its⟩ ↑man's↓ fears or experience can concieve a lower. And the idea of *Comparison* is always involved in our notions of mundane happiness. For this reason, high and multiplied sources of pleasure are often in our possession, without being enjoyed, for they never were lacking; God disturbs or removes them for a time; and he is dull, who sees no wisdom in this mode of giving them value and sharpening the blunted edge of appetite. Thus Health and Peace are insipid goods, until you have been able to compare them with the torments of Pain and the visitation of War. And after this Comparison has ↑once↓ been made, man runs riot in holding them.

Next, it should be remembered that we ↑wisely↓ assume the righteousness of the Creator in placing man in a probationary state. We do not seek with vain ambition to question the abstruse and un-searchable grounds of this ordination, because it is plain matter of fact that we are incompetent to the discussion. This being assumed, there is no longer any doubt of the Divine Benevolence arising from the existence of evil. Evil is the rough and stony foundation of human Virtue; weaning man away from the seductive [25][32] dangers of vicious transient destructive pleasures to a hold and security of Paradise where they are perpetual and perfect.

Continued on p. 28

Of Professor N.[33] Shakespeare long ago wrote the good and bad character

> "Oh it is excellent
> To have a giant's strength, but it is tyrannous
> To use it like a giant."
> [*Measure for Measure*, II, ii, 107–109]

¶ [34] To establish by whatever specious argumentation the perfect expediency of the worst institution on earth is ⟨an⟩*prima facie* an assault upon Reason and Common sense. No ingenious sophistry can ever reconcile the unperverted mind to the pardon of *Slavery*; nothing but tremendous familiarity, and the bias of private *interest*.

[32] "SLAVERY" is centered beneath "the same liberty" at the bottom of the page.
[33] Possibly Andrews Norton (1786–1853), professor of Sacred Literature at Harvard Divinity School, 1819–1830.
[34] Continued from page 49.

Under the influence of better arguments than[n] can be offered in support of Slavery, we should sustain our tranquillity by the confidence that no surrender of our opinion is ever demanded and that we are only required to discover the lurking fallacy which the disputant acknowledges to exist. It is an old dispute which is not now and never will be totally at rest, whether the human mind be or be not a free agent. And the assertor of either side must be scandalized by the bare naming of the theory that man may impose servitude on his ⟨fellow.⟩ ↑brother.↓ For if he is himself free, and it offends the attributes of God to have him otherwise, it is manifestly a bold stroke of impiety to wrest the same liberty from his fellow. [26][35] And if he is not free, then this inhuman barbarity ascends to derive its origin from the author of all necessity.

⟨T⟩A creature who is bound by his hopes of salvation to imitate the benevolence of better beings, and to do all the kindness in his power, fastens manacles on his fellow with an ill grace.

A creature who holds a little lease of life upon the arbitrary tenure of God's good pleasure improves his moment strangely by abusing God's best works, his own peers.

> Rich in the playful joys of solitude
> The peaceful muse begins her jubilee
> When Night's black car, sprinkled with golden stars,
> Has chased the Sun's magnificence away.
> Pleased with the closet's motley furniture,
> And broken shadows, where the elves and Gnomes
> Fight with the rats for noise or victory,
> The muse roves boldly on her vagrant wing.
> Disdains the recent times and days of dwarfs
> And this cold land Apollo never knew;
> Abandons with proud plumes, the passing hour,
> And follows Fancy through a thousand worlds.
>
> It is a curious spectacle, to see
> The panorama of unnumbered hues

[35] "MUSE" is centered beneath "wonders loudly" at the bottom of the page. In the left margin opposite the first stanza is a pen and ink sketch of a man seated at a desk before a window, with a picture on the wall; opposite the second stanza is a pen and ink sketch of a man's head and shoulders in half-profile.

That her wild journey marshals round her eye.
⟨And⟩But icy Reason scowls upon the shew, —
And its gay battlements, and beaming towers,
And shining forms, all vanish at his frown.
Yet I, who never bowed obedient neck
To Reason's iron yoke, will still rebel
And vex the tyrant in his ancient halls.
I'll ponder pleasantly the changing scenes
23   And tell their wonders loudly on the lyre.

[27][36] The ardour of my college friendship for ⟨Gay⟩ is nearly extinct, and it is with difficulty that I can now recall those sensations of vivid pleasure which his presence was wont to waken spontaneously, for a period of more than two years. To be so agreeably excited by the features of an individual personally unknown to me, and for so long a time, was surely a curious incident in the history of so cold a being, and well worth a second thought. At the very beginning of our singular acquaintance, I noticed the circumstance in my Wide-world,[37] with an expression of curiosity with regard to the effect which time would have upon those feelings. To this day, our glance at meeting, is not that of indifferent persons, and were he not so thoroughly buried in his martial cares, I might still entertain the hope of departed hours. Probably the abatement of my solitary enthusiasm is owing to the discouraging reports which I have gathered of ⟨p⟩his pursuits and character, so entirely inconsistent with the indications of his face. But it were much better that our connexion should stop, and pass off, as it now will, than to have had it formed, and ↑then↓ broken by the late discovery of insurmountable barriers to friendship. From the first, I preferred to preserve the terms which kept alive so much sentiment ⟨to⟩ ↑rather than↓ a more familiar intercourse which I feared would end in indifference. Nov. 29th, 1822.
                                                                Pish

[28₁][38]   (From p. 25)   Saturday Evening, Nov. 30th.
    Heraclitus was a fool, who wept always for the miseries of

[36] The page is struck through with a single wavy, diagonal line.
[37] See *JMN*, I, 22.
[38] "BENEVOLENCE" is centered beneath "bias of any instinct" at the bottom of the page. See n. 39.

human life. Or was he blind and deaf to beauty and melody? In his day, was the sky black, and were snakes instead of flowers coiled in his path? Was his mind reversed in its organization; — had he Despair for Hope, and Remorse for Memory? Could his disordered eye discern a *savage* Power sitting in this splendid Universe, thwarting the *good* chances of Fortune and promoting the *bad*, sowing seeds of *sorrow* for *glory*, turning grace and tranquillity to desolation, and heaven to hell? ↑Then let him weep on.↓ True philosophy hath a clearer sight, and remarks amid the vast disproportions of human condition a great equalization of happiness; an intimate intermingling of pleasure with every gradation, down to the very lowest of all. Pleasant and joyous are the connexions of our sympathy and affection — is proved by the very tear which marks their dissolution; and even that pang of separation and loss is relieved by its own indulgence. Are we nothing else but downcast downtrodden worms twisting ourselves in pain? What is literature, science, poetry, taste? [n] Are these only sources and stings of torment? [39]

[30₁] Innumerable [n] springs of pleasure open upon the inquirer as he proceeds, even in paths where they are least likely to be found. There is a feast spread for the understanding in the Registers of the past, and even in the bloody and difficult roads of human crime or elemental ravage the imagination travels with a grateful sense of power & pride. What heart warms not to the stern triumph of martyrdom or ⟨to⟩ is not alive to a pleasing awe, as it detects the pace of undoubted Retribution stealing after the Agents of secret violence or open outrage? The same scene which if acted under our eye, would appal or disgust us to the last degree, is made by a fine provision to minister to our delight. Thus also we are pleased with the picture of a tiger devouring his prey, though the original would be frightful.[n]

[28₂] Moreover consider with attention whatever appears instinctive in our texture; for the bias of any instinct must determine [29][40] our belief of the design of the Creator. And if there be any one feeling which is universal and untaught, it is *Hope*,[n] that darling

[39] After "torment?" Emerson inserted a large caret. At the end of the paragraph on p. [30] which follows he wrote: "Insert this paragraph near the bottom of 28 page."
[40] "BENEVOLENCE" is centered beneath "to any power, even" at the bottom of the page.

propensity to gild the future in unauthorized and exaggerated colours, Hope, which is faithful to its maker, and never impeaches his benevolence; Hope which is God's voice and prophecy — of a better state beyond the grave. ↑"Hope travels on, nor quits us when we die."↓[41] A very signal indication of kind design in the framing of the mind is that defect of vision which it has, when it looks either behind or before that it *sees only agreeable objects,* and oblivion veils all that are loathsome. We are proverbially blind in our anticipations of life to all that is dark; we dwell with covetous delight, in like manner, on our own pictures of the past, and are amazed at our ⟨own⟩ stupidity which under valued it.

Happiness lies at our own door. Misery is further away. Until I know by bitter personal experience that the world is the accursed seat of all misfortunes, and as long as I find it a garden of delights — I am bound to adore the Beneficent Author of my life. The young, the healthy, & the prosperous, — we will make haste to thank God for his goodness, before the evil days come and the years draw nigh when thou shalt say I have no pleasure in them. No representations of foreign misery can liquidate your debt to Heaven. You must join the choral hymn to which the Universe resounds in the ear of Faith, and I think, of Philosophy.

There are many things which being contrary to the nature of things are impossible to any power, even to omnipotence. [30₂][42] Thus we commonly say that the Deity himself cannot annihilate space and duration. If we knew more of the Nature of things we could add more to the list of impossible things. With regard to morals, we are ignorant of the bounds of power, but an enlarged understanding might perhaps inform us, that a portion of unhappiness[,] a rankling of discontent with the present moment, inducing a perpetual anxiety to aggrandize their lot, is a necessary element of intelligent creation, and can never be forgone.[43]

There remains to be considered an important objection, if it were well founded, to which Divine Benevolence is liable.

---

[41] Pope, *Essay on Man,* II, 274.

[42] "BENEVOLENCE" is centered beneath "founded, to which" at the bottom of the page.

[43] Here follows the passage printed on p. 60 above.

[31]⁴⁴ Our feeble judgements are apt to make a war among the Divine perfections, and ↑to↓ oppose the *Justice* to the *Benevolence* of God. As if it was impossible for a Being who permits and forces Justice to work out its inevitable results, — ever to pardon sin, though the penitence of the sinner ⟨was⟩ ↑may have been↓ wet with tears of blood. But the infinite Justice which ⟨gives to⟩ administers laws to the moral universe, is no partial, finite, or ignorant principle; is no poor semblance of human judicature, bewildered and misled by false evidence[,] corrupted or disobeyed in its uncertain decisions. That tribunal weighs every particle of influence, of temptation, of education, ⟨de⟩ examines motives instead of actions, sees the undisguised sources of the event, the end and beginning of action. Upon these complicate circumstances, beyond the reach of human sagacity, are grounded its unerring decrees. Of course, under its inflexible law, Reformation atones for crime, and imperfect virtue, by the goodness of its intentions, wins its way to heaven. Causes in Heaven's chancery, are neither betrayed by negligence, nor won by a bribe.

A blind Justice, which, with a single regard to every act, dispensed its promiscuous rewards of blessing & vengeance would chain down the Arm of Omnipotence to a limited and unworthy operation. It would fare ill with that part of created intelligence which is liable to fault, if its cause was condemned before its existence were out.

[32]⁴⁵ You go nigh to abolish human virtue if you pronounce its first fall the cause and inheritor of perdition. And you abridge the Freedom of a Being whose freedom is at the foundation of things. It is not worth while to conciliate the favour or deprecate the wrath of any being who can never indulge his inclination to protect and gratify you, when once you have violated the least of his laws. And Reason speaks plainly to the heart th⟨e⟩at the God of its fervent worship is no such fettered lord.

As we thus discover that his Benevolence is necessary to his Justice, when surveyed on a broad scale, so a corresponding view informs us, that Justice is necessary to the true & perfect exercise of Benevolence. For, if a boundless absorbing Mercy swallowed up the

⁴⁴ "BENEVOLENCE" is centered beneath "condemned before its" at the bottom of the page.
⁴⁵ "BENEVOLENCE" is centered beneath "Continued p. 34" at the bottom of the page.

recollection of guilt, and delighted itself in the indiscriminate accumulation of happiness upon every head, unmindful of the daring transgression that forfeited a title to pardon, — it is manifest, that, heaven
would be filled with spirits little prepared for its enjoyments; and
the just and the holy would be associated with demons. This would
subtract from the delight of Paradise, and an enforcement of the
law of Justice would be demanded to restore that sublime order which
is heaven's first law.

1 Dec., 1822.

Continued p. 34

[33][46] Arthur wandered in the wood of Cornwall as the day
dawned and, by the better vision of his eye, he discerned, as he
passed among the trees, the dauncing fayries in companies, that had
not yet departed before the face of the sun. By and By he fell into a
path which was very sweet & refreshing by reason of the honeysuckles
that grew thereabouts; and very many throstles and singing birds,
saluted him from the branches that grew over the way. And when two
young kids of spotless white, frisked before him with many gambols,
Arthur said unto himself — "Would God, my crown were in the
Dead Sea, that I might live alway in this wood." After this, the path,
by many turnings, wound deeper into the wood, but Arthur, enticed
by the frolic & beauty of the kids, followed them as they raced along
this embowered lane. By fits, also he heard music, which was not the
music of birds, but was marvellously soft and tuneable; and [n] the
path terminated in a large cavity of a rock, into which the kids leaped.
Then the king, when he had curiously considered that entrance, espied
certain characters deeply cut in the stone, and emblazoned with gold.
There was a picture ↑of the cup↓ of the Sangreal thereon, and under-
neath was written *Let the bold enter.* So Arthur went into the cave;
and presently the mouth of it closed together behind him, with a loud
crash. Without terror the royal knight held on his way keeping his
eye fixed upon the cheerful light before him which resembled a ball
of fire resting on the ground. As he advanced the rock around him
gradually enlarged into a magnificent arch and upon his path were

---

[46] "ARTHUR" is centered beneath "champions of the Round" at the bottom
of the page.

scattered many glistening gems. And this was the porch of the Palace
of the Lady of the Lake. And long and sorrowfully did the champions
of the Round Table bewail the absence of their King.

[34]⁴⁷   Sabbath Evg., Dec. 8th, 1822.
     Certain questions of Natural Theology deeply affect our views
of its very foundations. Wherein consists the Benevolence of ↑a↓ God
who persists in creating minds which his Omniscience foreshows him
will be finally and exquisitely miserable? This is one of those dark
questions which many pious Divines tremble to approach, and which
they prefer to hide from the profane eye of controversy under the
name of a *Mystery*. This I deem a false and unauthorized delicacy,
because it certainly does impeach the divine Wisdom or goodness to
suppose that he would set our minds loose upon the moral world,
without an understanding of the exhibitions of his character which
he has made; and ↑that he would↓ open to our view terrific doubts,
which, our ray of reason was insufficient to satisfy. At the first, therefore, we have cause to believe, that, upon a fair and comprehensive
examination of the glimpses of God's economy, some explanation will
occur to us of the difficulties that instituted the inquiry.
Dec. 9. This question would stagger the believer if it related to but
one created being. If God had never made but one inferior mind, &
that individual had failed in his hour of trial; if the anguish of remorse, and the miseries of eternity began to darken around his head;
this tremendous punishment would no [35]⁴⁸ doubt lead that being
to tax the benevolence of his omniscient ⟨a⟩Author. And no reason of
ours could justify the fate by which he suffered. God has vouchsafed
to us another view of his Providence, which, properly considered, will
go far to solve our doubts, and reconcile Reason to the merciful
equity of his Government[.]
     I shall state this view briefly. God has created an Universe.
↑Upon this single fact rests our defence.↓ Instead of a solitary mind
depending directly & only upon ⟨Himself⟩ ↑Deity↓, there is a great
community of minds whom their Maker has formed to depend much

    ⁴⁷ "BENEVOLENCE" is centered beneath "tremendous punishment" at the bot-
tom of the page.
    ⁴⁸ "BENEVOLENCE" is centered beneath "hundred generations" at the bottom
of the page.

and constantly upon each other, for example, for information, for cooperation; linked & leagued together by eternal & indissoluble bonds; and though resting all ultimately upon Him, yet are they separated at an infinite distance from *his* character and perfections, and closely allied by the equality of their littleness to their fellow-beings.

We learn so little of ourselves in our span of earthly existence, that we are Altogether unable to discover the nature and limits of this common connection of finite minds. But a careful eye reads on the history of man traits of an influence and union of mind to mind which cannot be mistaken. It remarks features of character which are propagated from sire to son for a thousand years in continual repetition. It remarks how the great congregation of mankind is divided into groups that severally take up their abodes in different parts of the earth and through an hundred generations continue the same. [36][49] That these differ all from each other in radical distinctions of feeling & life; while each group retains within itself the same distinctions from age to age. In short it discovers that there is an important effect of connection which is called *Education*. Upon a long review of any great ↑pro↓portion of the facts and events that the passage of men's lives ha⟨ve⟩s developed, it also discerns undoubted marks of a system, sometimes shaken & shattered by un⟨d⟩toward accidents but holding on its way till it ends in some definite results affecting the condition of the world.

From this external survey the Mind retires with a conviction that no Chance or Fortune sits as the blind lord of the changes that take place[n] but that an Order is appointed, a System is proceeding. It can percieve a harmonious whole, combined & overruled by a sublime Necessity, which embraces in its mighty circle the freedom of the individuals, and without subtracting from any, directs all to their appropriate ends. It percieves a purpose to pain, and sees how the instruction and perfection of myriads is brought about by the spectacle of guilt & its punishment. That great & primeval Necessity may make impossible an Universe without evil, and perhaps founds happiness *everywhere*, as *here*, upon the contrast of suffering. This

---

[49] "BENEVOLENCE" is centered beneath "contrast of suffering." at the bottom of the page.

question [37] lies at the sources of things, and we are only indulged with an intimation that may make out the just goodness of the Deity.

(This connection may be[n] deeper and more intimate than we are apt to imagine, and[n] the circumstances observed just now, seem to indicate that it is. That connection, which subsists *here* in *character*, will subsist in *condition* hereafter. And some plan will be developed, in which, the good of *Evil*, will be made plain, on the general scale, that cannot be explained upon the particular. It was with a vague idea of this kind, that I started, and fear I have involved myself in a bold speculation. My results can be only detrimental to myself as they shall never be exhibited to bewilder others, ↑if↓ I find they terminate in darkness. —)

Propositum thesis.

Choose ye this day whom ye will serve. As for me, and my house we will serve the Lord.[n] A race of intelligent beings is set down in a Universe filled with objects of attraction. A golden idol is set up on every side. Innumerable crowds flock unto Mammon; others unto the Shrine of Pleasure; others to Self; others to Fame; and a few gratefully adore the God who made them. They shall all have their reward.

The Being who created can destroy. I concieve that if we can find a refuge in nothing else, we can find one in the belief of this fact. Annihilation is a prerogative of God, and as long as its exercise is secured to himself, you cannot arraign his mercy in creating beings who would be frail, and who would fall. ⟨F⟩Virtue which [38][50] passed the ordeal of time, which has endured the hard martyrdom of the privations of sense, which has triumphed over all temptation, —by the firm hope of a reward hereafter—believes that God is pledged to renew and to perfect its existence when it quits its house of clay; and every rational mind admits, without question, the justice of the plea. Eternity therefore is perfectly safe to the intelligent beings who have fulfilled the conditions that the Deity has prescribed to his children. But he may deny the gift of eternity to those whose

[50] "BENEVOLENCE" is centered beneath "formidable objections" at the bottom of the page.

guilt has forfeited the promises, and in stern mercy may annihilate the mind when he stops the warm current of human life. They who have proved themselves unworthy to exist, may be blotted at once from the Divine Universe of which they are unworthy, and their places on the book of life be supplied by new creations. This opinion I believe has been broached before, and published by no very respectable oracle to the Christian world; but to my mind it presents no absurd or unnatural view of Providence and seems to open a fair means of obviating the formidable objections which meet the young theologian.

[39][51]

    Continued from W. No 4[52]   Saturday Evening, Dec. 15.

    The observation of every day, and our earliest acquaintance with the distinctions of character set us upon the inquiry after the nature of Greatness. What is the idol that God hath set up for the mind's worship? How is it that he appoints one man to be the model & master of a thousand? I looked diligently to understand the foundation of the individual's claim upon my praise & imitation. I saw the demigod whom the partial multitude consented to admire. The sun illumined his visage; but so it illumined the vassal crowd of idolaters. He walked in dignity and joy, — but the same earth and heaven that opened light & beauty upon him, the same senses that fed his pleasure, the same nerves that sustained his form in the image of God, the same *mind*, to see the invisible world, and the same hope of eternity — gratified, supported, & inspired all the world alike. He was made full with bread, and his heart was rejoiced with wine; he was wedded to earth's joy, and stung by human sorrow, and bereaved by the tyrant, death, as other men are. In society he was governed by the same forms, constrained by the same necessities, excited by the same causes; in solitude he was merry and melancholy, he wept & prayed like the other creatures of God. Heaven seemed to hoard no joy, & Evil no pain for the rest of mankind which befel not him, equally with all.

    [51] "GREATNESS" is centered beneath "which befel not" at the bottom of the page.
    [52] See *JMN*, I, pp. 100–102.

[40][53]   Tuesday Evg.

Whence then his distinction, and what was the purpose of God, in creating this aristocracy among men? Take generally those minds which the multitude acknowledge great & I believe that all which can be found that is common to them will rather be a certain capacity to adapt themselves & the exertions of their intellects to the desires & wants of all,— than any ⟨thing else.⟩ separate or characteristic property. I am here taking greatness in its loosest acceptation & applying it, of course, to *many* members of society. Certain it is, that, an accustomed observer very readily distinguishes the individuals of his species whom it has been his lot to see, into two classes, separated by a pretty definite line of demarcation — Men of talents, & Men of none; and in general I think it will be admitted, that, the line is drawn *at their birth,* though not percieved by men, till the approach of years of discretion; and that universally they *remain*[54] upon that side on which they were born. Education makes useful men of the dull, & more useful men of the gifted; but it neither gives the first the keys & command of character & society nor does its absence take them from the second; Nature establishes her yoke over the kingdom of men in defiance of their petty opposition of books, laws, institutions.[n] Every man who enumerates the catalogue of his acquaintance is privately con[41][55]scious, however reluctant to confess the superiority, of a certain number of minds which do outrun & command his own[,] in whose company, despite the laws ↑of↓ good breeding & the fences of affectation his own spirit bows like the brothers' sheaves to Joseph's sheaf. He remembers the soothsayer's faithful account of Antony's guardian Genius which ⟨alone⟩ ↑among other men↓ was high & unmatchable, but quailed before Caesar's. He remembers also other some of his companions, over whom his own spirit exercises the same mastery. And let no man complain of the inequality of such an ordination or call Fortune partial in the distribution of her blessings. Because moral goodness & moral grandeur

---

[53] "GREATNESS" is centered beneath "his acquaintance" at the bottom of the page.

[54] A circle, line, and caret carry "universally" from after "*remain*" to its present position.

[55] "GREATNESS" is centered beneath "of the internal" at the bottom of the page.

which are our chief concern in this world plainly do not at all depend upon the richer or poorer endowment of the intellect. Besides
there remains an answer which forever stops the mouth of the queru-
lous, and refers the inquiry to another decision — There is another
World. As this is but the infancy of existence we can form at best
but very vague & indeterminate ideas concerning the laws & nature of
the following scene. It may be that in Heaven the scale of greatness
which prevailed on earth will be reversed and that Genius may be
the reward of Piety. At all events creatures that are altogether ignorant of the internal administration of the next world [42][56] speak with
presumption & ignorance, when they arraign the eternal Equity
which appoints & measures their doom. They might be convinced
of their folly by entertaining the supposition, for a brief space, that,
the same gift of mind was apportioned to every man alike. If you
take the same *quantum* of intellectual power that is in the world
today, & divide it anew ↑by an Agrarian law↓[57] into equal shares
for every son & daughter of Adam; radically equalizing all; adding
to the ideot, & subtracting from the sage; you[n] would shortly have
a world too weak to be ashamed of themselves, but a spectacle of
ridicule or commiseration to whatever higher angel contemplated,
from above, a great community without literature, institutions, science, enthusiasm; — ⟨which⟩ ↑for these↓ things are produced only
by emulation, & the sense of superiority, feelings[n] which this mental
Reformation has abolished. In the tremendous Monotony that would
prevail, no transcendant genius would soar above his kind, to bring
down from higher spheres than theirs, fruits of surpassing excellence.
In our state of affairs, we clearly see how the economy of mind is
conducted, — not by the *many*, but by the few. A very few, the
Bacons & Newtons, ascend to sources of knowledge which are locked
to the rest, & [43][58] bring back stores which are to be the gospel of
science to the ages that come after; which are to be high points to
which the patient labour of many generations will hardly attain.
Without these models and landmarks to guide the young aspirations
of ambition the loose & ill directed ⟨minds⟩ efforts of inferior minds

[56] "GREATNESS" is centered beneath "which are" at the bottom of the page.
[57] This careted insertion is written in pencil but is apparently in Emerson's hand.
[58] "GREATNESS" is centered beneath "the ability of" at the bottom of the page.

would fail of good effect and would end in nothing. And a levelling democracy of intellect without leaders and without stings of ambition would produce a pigmy republic of ⟨flat⟩ insipid triflers. Away with the scheme; it is the vanity of vanities.

One or two remarks I wish to add with regard to the carriage & culture of Greatness where Heaven has actually entrusted the jewel. Because we are improvable beings, and improvable to a vast and infinite extent, he is a wretch who having recieved the gift diminishes its splendid effect by letting it lie neglected.

With regard to this, *many men's fellest foes are those of their own household.* For, many, whom God marked with his own signet, who had all the germs within them of great public influence, and who, if their lot ↑of early life↓ had been cast in solitude, might have nourished up their latent powers to the ripeness of strength and the ability of giving a tone & character [44]⁵⁹ to a whole state, — have failed here. They have been seduced to look on the easy & pleasant side of life, ⟨have n⟩ and instead of resolutely departing from the luxurious indolence of the social fireside, ⟨and⟩ have wasted their days & nights, in the endless, flat, unprofitable idleness of common conversation; have stolen from God & man the span of time, that should have plotted & executed schemes of hope & salvation for the world, to lavish it upon idols of clay.

Tuesday Evg. (*4 pp. & a half at a sitting.) ⟨‖ ... ‖⟩

Dec. 20.

Beside the stupendous greatness which men rather believe than behold, and which is imparted from heaven only once in a thousand years, there is a lesser distinction, which is the one to which I have been alluding in these remarks, and which is the star that heaven gives, to cheer with its radiance each ordinary day of common life. I have observed that it is difficult to ascertain distinctly wherein it consists. It often soars no higher than merely to feel its preeminence, and contents itself with the bare consciousness of standing on the better side of the line. It enjoys the majesty of beholding as from a height the various prospects of the intellectual world and reaps a refined amusement from the displays of character that come under

---

⁵⁹ "GREATNESS" is centered beneath "character that" at the bottom of the page.

its ob[45]⁶⁰servation. Vulgar minds quail, ⟨from⟩ ↑by↓ selfishness or weakness, and noble ones, under the same circumstances, calmly resolve, & sternly perform. Individuals pursue everyday the same trodden track in their ordinary avocations and are fretted in their petty interests by customary obstacles and never once suspect, through their lives long, that they ⟨can⟩ ↑might↓ rise above these wearing & contemptible contentions. Other individuals see the sources of these pains, & leave them behind, and disdaining to run always the same disgusting round invent varieties of thought, sacrifices to duty, and objects of enthusiasm. And thus, to differ⟨n⟩ent minds, the same world is a hell, and a heaven. This is the exhibition of character and conduct which makes the theme whereon many of those ↑high-born↓ spirits use to dwell. They please themselves with the idea that they have stronger wings and a broader range, in the universe, than the multitude have. Happy, if they exercised this glorious liberty in making nearer acquaintance with the Principle of being, and the supreme stages of moral excellence. That they do not, & that the paths to heaven contain no greater proportion of wise than of unwise men, is a thing extraordinary to the eye of the mind. It is this which makes the world so complex, so unaccountable, & so diversified a picture, leaving ample room for the speculations of philosophy [46]⁶¹ and also giving birth to the vagaries of doubt. Heaven's Revelations have illuminated a portion of the dark, and at least have lit the road to happiness, but still hath left, upon every side, a wilderness where his errors & ignorance grope; in whose shadows, no powers, no light, which God hath vouchsafed to man, will be sufficient to guide him. If we seek a reason for this jealous⟨y⟩ care, with which Heaven debars us from the light, it may satisfy inquiry to remember, that, the world is a school for the education of the mind; that doubt exercises the faculties ⟨that⟩ ↑which↓ would lie dormant & passive under perfect light. But, because of the stern principles of Justice & Retribution, which prevail in the Universe, a deeper sight than ours might discern a dreadful compensation taking place. The race ↑of existence↓ is not to the swift, nor the battle of moral competitions to the strong; and,

⁶⁰ "GREATNESS" is centered beneath "the speculations" at the bottom of the page.

⁶¹ "GREATNESS" is centered beneath "of their existence." at the bottom of the page.

perchance, in the palaces of ⟨the⟩ heaven, not the *great*, but the *good* are enthroned; & those fallen spirits, who took pride to themselves here, in the lavish goodness of God, may find *that* fatal *Greatness* the curse of their existence.   Dec. 20.

[47] Dec. 21.

    There is everything in America's favour, to one who puts faith in those proverbial prophecies of the Westward progress of the Car of Empire. Though there may be no more barbarians left to overrun Europe & extinguish forever the memory of its greatness yet its rotten states like Spain may come to their decline by the festering & inveteracy of the faults of government. Aloof from the contagion during the long progress of their decline America hath ample interval to lay deep & solid foundations for the greatness of the New World. And along the shores of the South Continent, to which the dregs & corruption of European society had ⟨tra⟩been unfortunately transplanted, the fierceness of the present conflict for independence, will, no doubt, act, as a powerful remedy to the disease, by stirring up the slumbering spirits of those indolent zones to a consciousness of their power & destiny. Here then, new Romes are growing, & the Genius of man is brooding over the wide boundaries of infant empires, where yet is to be drunk the intoxicating draughts of honour & renown; here ⟨is⟩ ↑are↓ to be played over again the bloody games of human ambition, bigotry, & revenge and the stupendous Drama of the passions to be repeated. Other Cleopatras shall seduce, Alexanders fight, and Caesars die. The pillars of social [48] strength which we occupy ourselves in founding thus firmly to endure to future ages as the monuments of the wisdom of this, are to be shaken on their foundations with convulsions proportioned to their adamantine strength. The time is come, the hour is struck; already the actors in this immense & tremendous scene have begun to assemble. The doors of life in our mountain-land are opened, and the vast swarm of population is crowding in, bearing in their hands the burden of Sorrow & Sin, of glory & science, which are to be mingled in their future fates. In the events & interests of these empires, the old tales of history & the fortunes of departed nations shall be thoroughly forgotten & the name of Rome or Britain fall seldom on the ear.

In that event, when the glory of Plato ↑of Greece↓, of Cicero ↑of R[ome].↓, & of Shakspeare ↑of E[ngland].↓ shall have died, who are they that are to write their names where all time shall read them, & their words be the oracle of millions? Let those who would pluck the lot of Immortality from Fate's Urn, look well to the future prospects of America.

Friday Evg., Dec. 21, 1822.

> Whilst the fat fool prates nonsense to the pack
> Filled with the folly echo blab[s] it back.[62]

[62] Part of the date was written over the couplet, which is in pencil.

Wide World 9

1 8 2 2 – 1 8 2 3

The first of four journals which were later bound together, Wide World 9 continues the regular sequence of Wide Worlds. The journal was originally entitled "Wideworld No 9," but at some later time the letter designation I (the ninth letter in the alphabet) was added and then altered to the Roman numeral IX by adding X. The dated entries continue without interruption from Wide World 8, beginning on December 21, 1822, and ending on March 13, 1823.

The manuscript is composed of thirteen folded sheets of unlined paper hand-stitched into a single gathering and later attached by white thread to Wide World numbers 10, 11, and 12. All are enclosed within a blue paper cover labeled "Nos. IX, X, XI, XII" (see *JMN*, I, p. 404, note 1). The twenty-six leaves vary in size from 16 to 19.2 cm in width and from 16.5 to 21 cm in length. The pages are numbered from 1 through 51. Attached to the unnumbered verso of the final leaf are two scraps of paper containing notes, one measuring 10.7 x 17 cm and the other 6.5 x 13 cm.

[1][1]   Timeo Danaos et dona ferentes.[2]   IX

Wideworld.   No 9 —

"Pass not unblest the Genius of the place."
                    [Byron, *Childe Harold's Pilgrimage*, IV, lxviii]

---

[1] "Wideworld" is enclosed in an ornamented oval. The Latin motto is inside the oval, following the upper curve, and the English quotation is below the lower curve. Because the lefthand margin of the page has been pasted to the blue cover enclosing this and Wide Worlds 10, 11, and 12 in one gathering, four of the words, as the vertical bars show, are partly obscured.

[2] "I fear the Greeks, even when bringing gifts." Virgil, *Aeneid*, II, 49.

Saturday Evg., Dec. 21, 1822.

DEDICATION.

This night, the worm & the reptile are ||a||t work, in ten thousand sepulchral grottoes, upon the pitiful relics of human clay. Ever since the ||G||olden Age, & the hour when the royal Saturn descended from his throne, and laid himself down in the tomb, ever since men first left their flocks & herds and the labours of the living for the rest of the dead, — this desolate & disgusting corruption has proceeded. Meantime the living generations have signalized their successive ||oc||cupation of the globe, by waking within it the fierce ||vo||ices of Discord, Agony, & Revenge, by staining with blood its laughing fields, by cursing with malevolent passions its human abodes, and helping on, with ready officiousness, the carnage of Nature. The past — in all its grand characters of horror & evil — lies open before us. The whole of it amounts to what? The bones of its [2][3] children ↑which↓ lie about & beneath us, and the monument of its bad example, its terrific wrongs, and its Gothic ignorance, as the inscriptions tell, written on the mausoleum by the genius of its redeeming minds. Amid this hideous picture, the eye traces a few golden lines, writ specially by heaven; but the darkness sits grosser around.

God forbid that the mind should bow down before this huge chaos to worship; or, that, the world's dark barbarism, or darker vice, should be the best idol that the intellect can set up.

There is another prospect before. We have gathered what we could that was precious from the past; we are preparing to add the results of present science & civilization to these, and thus shall form a legacy to the future, which men shall think it worth living to attain. Not yet is the night departed; not yet shall Passion & our evil Destinies resign their victims; for a few more centuries, men shall still play the same wild bacchanalia of war & avarice, but all beyond is Hope. The collateral progress of Christianity & Philosophy may work out blissful results in the remotes||t|| corners of Libya and the frozen zone, and realize, in [3] some adequate manner, the splendid dream which the bards of all ages have portrayed, as the consummation of

[3] "DEDICATION" is centered beneath "and the frozen" at the bottom of the page.

Time. To the men of that age, the idolatrous fancy may look; She will never degrade her hopes by fixing them there. But if this also be an illusion, and Time hoards no halcyon scene as a retribution for his sorrows — mine eye passeth over his bound, for a glimpse of thy shoreless abyss — Eternity! There are beings and events involving felicity *there*, — if such there be in the Universe. To the Genius of the Future, I dedicate my page.

> "Incipe. Vivendi recte qui prorogat horam,
> Rusticus expectat dum defluat amnis; at ille
> Labitur et labetur in omne volubilis aevum" [4]

It is not the freak of a youthful or Utopian imagination to anticipate more ⟨of⟩ ↑from↓ the future than the past has produced. A benevolent disposition which finds the darkness disappearing continually before the light of goodness and truth, may be easily damped by the vague charge of enthusiasm. Casual & general /recurrences/ appeals/ to the melancholy uniformity of human history may plausibly support the declamations of those false prophets who denounce tribulation & wrath to all the years of man as they rise in the long succession of futurity. But a cautious & profound philosopher would be loth to believe the denunciation. For his survey of mankind suggests the opinion that there is no experience in its annals, from which a fair judgement could be formed, with regard to its future history — because there is no age in its whole history bearing any tolerable likeness, in its character, to the present. Besides if the misanthrope take refuge in *analogy* — it will fail him. [4][5] For, though we bewail the imperfection of ⟨the⟩ sublunary things yet all things in the ⟨anim⟩ mineral, vegetable, and animal kingdom have a *perfection*, which, though not attained in the hundred instances, — *is* attained in the thousand; is attained much oftener than not. Man in many trials has

---

[4] "Begin! He who puts off the hour of right living is like the bumpkin waiting for the river to run out: yet on it glides, and on it will glide, rolling its flood forever." Horace, *Epistles*, I, ii, 41–43. Emerson was fond of these lines, especially of the last one, — see *JMN*, I, 90, and pp. 101, 106 and 250 below. It may be no coincidence that Montaigne quotes the lines (see *The Essays*, ed. W. C. Hazlitt, 2 vols. in 1, New York, 1892, I, 157) and so does Cowley, in "The Dangers of Procrastination," *Essays, in Prose and Verse* (London, 1819), p. 121, a volume which Emerson quotes below, p. 88 (see also p. 94, n. 42).

[5] "⟨DEDICATION⟩" is centered beneath "to the developement" at the bottom of the page.

failed; Assyria, Egypt, Greece, & Rome, have successively made the
experiment; have attempted to carry human nature by the Sciences,
the Arts, & the Refinements accumulated through ages of civilized
life — to some near approach of his Perfection, and have only succeeded in making his sensuality more daintily luxurious, his crimes
more ingeniously abominable. But now a preparation is made for
another experiment which begins with infinite advantages. I need not
name the daily blessings which are diffused over the present generation & distinguish them above antiquity. I notice only that they possess
Christianity, and a civilization more deeply ingrafted in the mind
(by reason of the extraordinary aids it derives from inventions &
discoveries) than ever it has before been. It is the nature of these
advantages to multiply themselves. Providence ordains that every
improvement extend an influence of infinite extent over the face of
society. For centuries back the progress of human affairs has appeared
to indicate some better era; & finally when all events were prepared
God has opened a new theatre for this ultimate trial. This country
is daily rising to a higher comparative importance & attracting the
eyes of all the rest of the world to the developement of its embryo
greatness.

[5][6]   Christmas, Dec. 25. ——
    If, (as saith Voltaire) ⟨the⟩ all that is related of Alfred the
Great be true, I know not the man that ever lived, more worthy of
the gratitude of posterity. I hope the reservation means nothing.
There is not one incredible assertion made either of his abilities, his
character, or his actions. Besides it was not an age, nor were Saxon
monks the men, to invent and adorn another Cyropaedia. Sharon
Turner[,] an ambitious flashing writer, & elsewhere a loon, hath
done well by Alfred.[7] His praise rests not upon monkish eulogy or
vague tradition, but upon *facts*. Crit‖ics‖ may quarrel upon the reputed foundation of Oxford; it is not at all necessary to his fame. In
the first place he had the smartest man of his age for his enemy, with

---

    [6] "ALFRED" is centered beneath "invasions of the sea-kings," at the bottom of
the page.
    [7] Turner's *The History of the Anglo-Saxons. . .*, 4 vols. (London, 1802–
1805), was withdrawn from the Boston Library Society November 30–December 12,
1822. The account of Alfred occupied most of Book IV, chs. IV–XI, and all six
chapters of Book V. Voltaire's tribute is quoted in French from *Essai sur les Moeurs*.

whom he repeatedly, constantly, & vigorously fought until he finally drove him utterly from the kingdom. *Hastings,* in despair, retired to France, & obtained some little settlement from the king, where he obscurely died. The fact, that after his entire loss of every acre of England & every man of his armies he should be able to reproduce *ab initio* his cause & kingdom, equals the Return of Bonaparte. The skilful policy of domesticating the conquered Danes and thus lulling the opposition of those myriads which swarmed in Northumbria, and at the same time creating upon his shores a formidable bulwark to the future invasions of the sea-kings, by giving their [6][8] brothers a stake in the commonwealth to defend; — this policy was not unworthy of the profound art of Augustus Caesar. The admirable military genius discovered in his position between the two divisions of Hastings' Northmen so as to menace at the same time both armies & to separate both from the East Anglians, (too ready to join the aggressions of their countrymen,) the ⟨st⟩ vigilance of his patrolling bands & the strict adherence to ⟨the plan⟩ ↑measures↓ of *defence* alone, — indicate his masterly generalship. An instance is likewise recorded of military skill which discovers an active invention. When Hastings went up with his ships the River Lea, Alfred ⟨th⟩ dug three new channels below, & thus drew off so much water as to leave the ships aground. He built a castle on either bank to protect his works & the Northmen were obliged to abandon their ships[n] and escape as they best might from their strongholds in Essex. His enthusiastic attachment to learning (the more laudable as it was solitary,) his care of courts & ministers of justice, his zealous & useful piety, all these combined in so extraordinary a manner with his warlike talents, are the foundation of his surpassing fame, of his tit⟨t⟩le to the surname of Great. I am anxious to understand fully the merits & honesty of the records in which he is transmitted to us. Asser, his friend & instructer, is the chief source. Turner says nothing about his authenticity.

[7][9] There is a book which Alfred translates containing one of the most singular funeral ceremonies I ever met with. The book is the narration of the voyage of Wulfstan towards the east of the

---

[8] "ALFRED" is centered beneath "Turner says nothing" at the bottom of the page.

[9] "ALFRED" is centered beneath "dear." This is" at the bottom of the page.

Baltic.[10] The custom among those of "the Eastland" is that when a
man dieth his body is preserved one, two, or even six months according to the wealth of the deceased, unburnt. For the E[a]stmen have
a mode of producing cold so as to prevent the body from becoming
foul. All the time that the body lieth within, the wealth of the deceased ⟨lies⟩ furnishes the revelry of his kinsmen without. "Then
the same day that they chuse to bear them to the pile his property
that remains after this drink & play is divided into five or six parts,
sometimes more as the proportion of his wealth admits. They lay
these along a mile apart; the greatest portion *from* the town, then
another, then a third till it be all laid at one mile asunder; and the
least part shall be nearest to the town where the dead man lieth.
Then shall be collected all the men that have the swiftest horses in
the land for the way of 5 miles or 6, from the property. Then run
they all together to the property. Then cometh the man that hath the
swiftest horse to the first portion & to the greatest & so on, one after
another, till it be all taken away; he taketh the least who is nearest
the town & runs to it: then each rides away with his prize and may
have it all. And because of this the swift horse is inconceivably dear."
This is Turner's translation from Alfred. —

[8][11]   Dec. 26th, 1822.
     I have heard this evening & shall elsewhere record Prof.
Everett's lecture upon Eleusinian mysteries, Dodona, & St Sophia's
temple.[12] The modes of response in the Dodonean Groves were full
of poetical beauty; by bells, by fountains, by the wind in the oaks, &
by doves; to interpret these signs was the peculiar faculty & prerogative of the priests. For two thousand years the celebrity of the Mysteries continued, originating in a natural & simple harvest home &
proceeding to august ceremonies in which sound moral truths were
no doubt always inculcated & the best views though imperfect which

[10] The voyage of Wulfstan, as Turner makes clear, is Alfred's own work, inserted
into his translation of Orosius' *Adversos Paganos Historiarum Libri VII*.
   [11] "LECTURE" is centered beneath "of the Protestant." " at the bottom of the
page.
   [12] According to P. R. Frothingham, Emerson is referring to one of "a course of
lectures in Boston on Antiquities." See *Edward Everett, Orator and Statesman* (Boston,
1925), p. 66.

antiquity entertained of God & his providence. Just in proportion as Christianity advanced, the Eleusinian Mysteries declined in splendour & importance, until they were finally suppressed by Theodosius in 404 A.D. Though the Lecture contained nothing original, & no very remarkable views, yet it was an account of antiquities bearing everywhere that "fine Roman hand" & presented in the inimitable style of *our Cicero*. "Bigotry & Philosophy are the opposite poles of the judgement & the scepticism of Hume, & Gibbon is as different as the superstition of the Catholic from the freedom of the Protestant." Pr. E.[13]

[9][14]   Sunday, Jan. 5, 1823.

                                                     Wednesday, 8th.

In the grave, the passions rest peacefully; the riot of pleasure, love, & revenge is silent; and that banquet which life offered to youth & health, is most foully disordered. The distinctions of society are levelled in that stern republic, and the badges of those distinctions are cast away.

The soldier's helmet rusts beside him and there is no fear of his shield or his sword. The priest hath found these abodes but his chalice & his crucifix will not fright away the worm. Vassals & lords, gownsmen, peasants, matrons, & nuns have mixed their dust in this common urn, of which your boasted mausoleums & tombs are but the little marble compartments. The life that you led & the contemplations of the spirit while it stirred amid the upper elements, — though this life & thought were stainless & perfect as the Angels, can afford you no partial exemption from this tax of death which the universe levies on its children. Your hand was never red with blood, was never closed to the necessities of the poor, never toiled at the work of avarice & crime; you lived upon earth without soiling your fame; — it is well; — there is a Moral End & Retribution alike with the Natural and the soul will mount by its native instincts to that Paradise which her sacrifices & self-denials have won. But the body too hath its instincts & its term; nor can the strength wherewith its lineaments and sinews are knit, nor the disobedient will of the

[13] Undoubtedly Professor Everett.
[14] "GRAVE" is centered beneath "claim." at the bottom of the page.

possessor nor the defiance of spiritual pride save it from the lord of death. The tenement which was leased for the habitation of the mind, when the lease is out must return to its lord, and subt⟨el⟩lety and wit would vainly efface a letter of his claim.   What is your life? [10] A vapour and a cloud. I see upon it a fair painting of many hues. I see within it the forms of men, & the motions of manifold phantoms; the freshness of beauty & the glory of the sun is upon it — but it is still a vapour, and already vanisheth away.

Saturday Ev.g., January 11th.

My bosom's lord sits lightly on his throne; I cannot distinctly discern the cause; tomorrow he will sit heavily there; and after a few days more, he shall cease to be. The connexions which he nursed with earthly society shall be broken off, and the memory of his individual influence shall be obliterated from human hearts. It may chance that he will resume his thought elsewhere; that while the place from whence he passed forgets him, he shall nourish the fires of a pure ambition in some freer sanctuary than this world holds. It is possible that the infinity of another world ↑may↓ so crowd his conception, as to divest him of that cumberous sense of *self* that weighs him down, — until he lose his individual existence in his efforts for the Universe.

I am the tenant of a transitory Universe. Its pleasures & pains, its sights & sounds, its peace and /disturbance/revolutions/ are nothing & vanity [n] to me. They may be of stupendous magnitude and of infinite variety, but they are short, & shall shortly die. It is curious to see how like shadows those events have come and gone. I was a child, and I exhausted all my little powers of mind & body upon the sports of childhood[;] the baubles & pleasures of the moment filled my faculties and seemed of momentous importance. ⟨Youth followed upon childhood⟩ ↑The years of infancy fled↓ and those [11][15] toys dwindled away to make room for the splendid hopes and enthusiastic resolutions of youth. The sky was not so bright and alas! not so changeable as its promises. It revelled in the sight of beauty, and the sound of music, in the motion of the limbs, in the intercourse of friends, and in all the joys of a pleasant & gorgeous

[15] "TIME" is centered beneath "more value" at the bottom of the page.

world. But the crimson flush went from its cheek, and the joyous light from its eye; its bones hardened into manhood and its years departed beyond the flood. Reason watched them as they departed and was bitterly mortified to find how insignificant they became in the view. ⟨t⟩Those changes and events which had engaged the mind by their gigantic greatness sunk now to pigmy dimensions and so dim were their images upon the memory that it was hard to believe they were not ↑altogether↓ a dream[.]

After a few more turnings of the globe in its orbit, manhood, age & life itself will have passed, and as I advance, that which I have left behind will continually grow less & less. As I reach & pass successively the several epochs of existence the things of former pursuit will degenerate in my esteem. All, all will be unremembered as if they had never been. The mind writes daily, in its recollections of the past, but one Epitaph upon Time — "Vanity of Vanities, all is Vanity!" [16] God forbid that this be the /true/faithful/ history of the Universe! Are the years and ages that are gone, nothing but a ridiculous bubble to move ⟨their⟩ our scorn today? That *Time*, which the soul deemed so precious and bewailed the pernicious liberality which was lavish of its least portions, is Time and its treasured events of no more value than the vapour of smoke, or [12][17] the chime of a bell? Have all the scenes and acts, & the multitude[n] of beings that moved therein, astonishing the mind by their prodigious variety — sunk to this? There is one distinction amid these fading phenomena — one decided distinction which is real & eternal and which will survive nature — I mean the distinction of Right and Wrong. Your opinions upon all other topics and your feelings with regard to this world, in childhood, youth, & age, perpetually change. Your perceptions of right & wrong never change. You can dismiss the world from your mind, and almost abolish in your imagination the dominion of sense; but you can never bury in your breast the sense of offended Justice. You can never make a lie appear innocent as truth or lay quietly asleep the fierce demon who curses unrepented transgression. The mind may lose its acquaintance with other minds, and may

---

[16] Eccl. 1 :2.

[17] "MORAL SENSE" is centered beneath "many passing shadows" at the bottom of the page.

abandon, without a sigh, this glorious universe, as a tent of the night to dwell in; but it can not part with its moral principle, by which it becomes akin ⟨with⟩ to the extraordinary intelligences that are to accompany its everlasting journey to the throne of God. If there be any thing real under heaven or in heaven, the perception of right & wrong relates to that reality. Dogmatists & philosophers may easily convince me that my mind is but the abode of many passing shadows ⟨and⟩ by the belief of [13][18] whose existence about me I am mocked. I shall not very sturdily combat this ancient scepticism because, to my mind & to every mind it has often seemed problematical whether ↑or not↓ it was ⟨not⟩ cheated by an unsubstantial edifice of thought. But it is in the constitution of the mind to rely with firmer confidence upon the *moral principle,* and I reject at once the idea of a delusion in this. This is woven vitally into the thinking substance itself so that it cannot be diminished or destroyed without dissipating forever that spirit which it inhabited. Upon the foundation of my *moral sense,* I ground my faith in the immortality of the soul, in the existence & activity of good beings, and ↑in the promise↓ of rewards accommodated hereafter to the vicious or virtuous dispositions which were cultivated here. The great citizenship of the universe, which all souls partake, has *this* for its common bond & charter which none may violate, without taking upon themselves the peril of losing its infinite privileges. Upon the bounded field of this earth, nations upon nations of men have expired in succession & borne to other and unseen countries the minds that dwelled here, for a space; and[n] all ↑the individuals of↓ this host have consented together[n] in one respect alone, namely the acknowledgement of this inward tribunal of thought & action. They obeyed or disobeyed its law, they suffered or rejoiced, as they might; but not one ever escaped from this high, unyielding,[19] universal thraldom which the ⟨a⟩Author of Mind has created upon the mind. In all ages & districts of the earth, these minds fell from their native celestial purity by offending against the law but in all instances they were likewise conscious that they did offend, & derived a punishment from that very consciousness.

[18] "MORAL SENSE" is centered beneath "from that very" at the bottom of the page.
[19] The word is partly blotted.

[14]²⁰   January 19th, 1823.——
⟨It is related of Cybele⟩
The ideas of Deity and religious worship readily find admission
to the mind, and are readily abused. The clown on a dunghill can
exalt his capacity to these truths and is delighted and flattered by
this ⟨proof⟩ ↑consciousness↓ of a new and transcendant /feeling/
power/. God is infinitely above the whole creation, and he that aspires to worship Him, feels that his mounting spirit leaves the rest
of the Universe beneath his feet. Enthusiasm is therefore apt to
generate in uncultivated minds a rash and ignorant contempt for
the slow modes of education and the cautious arts of reasoning by
which enlightened men arrive at wisdom — because they have themselves acquired this surpassing conception without the irksome toil
of the intermediate steps. The boor becomes philosopher at once and
⟨dauntlessly⟩ ↑boldly↓ issues the dogmas of a religious creed from the
⟨rank abundance⟩ⁿ ↑exuberance↓ of a coarse imagination. The tumults
of a troubled mind are mistaken for the inspiration of an apostle, and
the strength of excited feelings is substituted for the dispassionate
& tardy induction, the comparison of scripture & reason, which /regu-
lates/sanctions/ the devotion of moderate & liberal men.

This has been everywhere found to be the history of religious
error; not merely in the fanaticism of sects, but in the mistakes &
superstitions of individuals. Every man's heaven is different; and
is coloured by the character [15]²¹ and tone of feeling most natural
to his mind. And, in like manner, his conceptions of the Divine
Being will vary with the narrowness or justness of his modes of
thinking. A mind which is remarkable for the truth and grandeur of
its views in physical or metaphysical science will seldom be found
the dupe of an unrelenting bigotry in its religious faith. We do not
so easily put off and on the leading features of character as to think
↑in the same hour↓ greatly & wisely of the next life, & foolishly of
this. Whatever topic ⟨starts⟩ is under review, our trains of thought
pursue their accustomed route, whether ⟨habit has taught them to end
in⟩ ↑they ⁿ have ⟨habitual⟩ ↑⟨ultimate⟩↓ regard to↓ the good of self,

²⁰ In the top margin, opposite the date is some practice penmanship. "Enthusiasm" is centered beneath "coloured by" at the bottom of the page.
²¹ "PRAYER" and "☞" are centered in the bottom margin of the half-filled
page.

or the good of the universe. Intellectual habits are not the /rapid/ sudden/ productions of ↑an↓ accident ⟨or a moment⟩, but are formed slowly, and confirmed from day to day by the influence of events, until they acquire a↑n immutable↓ strength that may outlast the ⟨limits⟩ ↑period↓ of this ↑mortal↓ life. We think of God, therefore, as we think of man. Our views of human nature are liable to mistake, so are our views of the divine.

[16₁]²² I have made these remarks with a particular view to the subject of Prayer, because I think that the misapprehensions to which this subject is liable commonly arise from a too great extension of the analogies which we draw between human & divine things. The origin of Prayer is no doubt to be traced in our comparison of finite beings with the infinite Being. To obtain bread, we prayed our neighbour to impart from his store. But to obtain more than bread, to obtain our health or the life of a friend, to change the course of events, is beyond our neighbour's power. Man remembered in his hour of need that there was a Power above him, and uttered an ejaculation of his distress and his hopes dictated by precisely the same emotions which moved him to address his earthly friend. Thus far the analogy is unexceptionable, but if pursued farther it fails. A judge has decreed the death of a criminal; the father & friends of the unfortunate man come ⟨to⟩ ↑before↓ the tribunal to pray for his life, and plead with such importunity and eloquence that the judge consents to set aside the sentence. The character of the culprit is not amended, but the free course of justice is stopped ↑and society wronged↓ by the earnestness of the supplication. [17₁] [In the ancient Persian religion, it is forbidden to petition for blessings to themselves individually; the prayer must extend to the whole Persian nation.] See M. XIX p. 19 ²³ [16₂] In like manner, men came to their maker to ask the favour of a partial event, a particular blessing that will prove prejudicial to the whole; and reasoning erroneously from human experience they concluded that there was a certain force in prayer that would extend some controul ²⁴

---

²² "Prayer" is centered beneath "prayer that would" at the bottom of the page.
²³ The sentence and the reference appear on p. [17] with the notation "Insert on opposite page" and a penciled circle, line, and arrow to show the intended location.
²⁴ Continued on p. [18].

[172] This subject is closely connected with that of Particular Providence & has all its difficulties in common with it. The opposition of a General to a Particular Providence is often implied in prayer. Antiquity viewed the gods as the Particular, & Fate as the General Providence, and reconciled them by making Fate absolute in the administration of the Universe. Our perplexity springs from the union of both in the hands of One God.

[18] even over the Mind of Deity. Pity and irresolution in the human judge triumphed over his knowledge and his virtue and the worshipper flattered himself with the hope that even God might ↑be induced to↓ hesitate by the ↑offering of↓ hecatombs and clamorous petitions. The ⁿ idolatry of every nation has had a tendency towards this belief that the arm of Omnipotence could be chained down by sacrifice and entreaty, which the Hindoo mythology has pursued to extravagant lengths. Prayer & penance by their intrinsic virtue will raise the worshipper above the power of gods & men until it ⟨dethrones the Supreme Being⟩ ↑hurls the Highest from his throne↓ to make room for the devout Usurper. Such a creed shocks the mind; but a secret bias to this belief is by no means uncommon in Christian countries. We are prone to think that the prayers of righteous men avail with God to check or change the ⟨tide⟩ ↑course↓ of events, which implies, ↑either↓ that those events were ill-ordered before, or that they will take a wrong direction now; but both these hypothe⟨t⟩ses are inconsistent with our trust in the superintendence of Providence over human affairs. It is not ↑to be↓ supposed for a moment, that, ⟨⟨if God be wise & omnipotent⟩⟩ the petitions of so humble and ignorant beings as men, who know but few causes and can penetrate but a few effects should alter the ordinations of a wise & omnipotent God. Is the importunity & blind passion of men to ascend & enter into the councils of heaven; and cannot Providence be intrusted with the government of the Universe? A good man prays God to alter [19] the circumstances of his lot. But prior to this prayer, God owed it to Himself & to the Universe to place that individual in certain circumstances adapted to his virtues or his wants. Because that good man ignorantly desired a change pernicious to his true interests, will

²⁵ The matter on this page, including the bracketed passage transferred to p. [16], is written in a somewhat different ink and may have been added at a later time.

the Most High reverse his decree & punish the petitioner with com-
pliance? When God has ordained a change of events, & the aspect
of the world suggesting the benefits of such a change to the mind,
induces man to pray for it, in this case, the event coincides with the
prayer, and is interpreted as an especial interposition. With this solitary exception, men's prayers and the succession of events have no
direct connexion at all ⟨up⟩ with each other. When a dread of impending vengeance had ⟨ame⟩ cleansed the corruptions of Nineveh,
that dread was taken away because its end was accomplished. But the
prayers of the people, independent of their reformation, could never
have averted their fall. God knew that they would repent & therefore knew that he should not destroy the city. This view should be
kept in mind to prevent a misconstruction of the expressions used in
sacred story. An argument of this nature should be fortified by instances.

Human curiosity is forever engaged in seeking out ways &
means of making a connection between the mind & the world of
matter without or the world of mind that has subsisted here or an
uniting bridge which shall join to future ages our own memory &
deeds. This laudable ⟨en⟩ [20₁][26] curiosity should not neglect the
formation of a bond which proposes to unite it not to men, to matter,
or to beasts, but to the Unseen Spirit of the Universe. Our native
delight in the intercourse of other beings urges us to cultivate with
assiduity the friendship of great minds. But there is a Mind to whom
all their greatness is vanity & nothing; who did himself create and
communicate all the intellect that exists; & there is a mode of intercourse provided by which we can approach this excellent majesty.
That Mind is God; and that Mode is Prayer.

[21] X[27]   And, if by prayer
            Incessant I could hope to change the will
            Of Him who all things can, I would not cease
            To weary Him with my assiduous cries;
            But prayer against his absolute decree

    [26] "HISTORY" is centered beneath "or that" at the bottom of the page.
    [27] This "X" mark appears here and on several following recto sheets which
appear to have been left blank to permit the insertion of additional commentary or
illustration. The quotation from Milton is placed where Emerson apparently intended it to go, with the comments on prayer.

No more avails than breath against the wind,
Blown stifling back on him that breathes it forth.
                    Paradise Lost   B. XI. [ll. 307–313]

[20₂] In reading History it is hard to keep the eye ⟨c⟩ steadily fixed upon any distinct moral view of the species, to which we may readily refer all the facts recorded of individuals. When we lay aside the book, & think of man, our habitual theories regard him as a being in a state of probation, & we elevate the whole human race to an exalted equality of condition & destiny. Resume the page, and you are convinced at once, that whatever opinions you are yourself pleased to entertain concerning them, — it never entered the minds of the majority of mankind in past ages that any such equality prevailed or that they sustained any very [22₁]²⁸ sublime rank in the scale of Creation. They have themselves shewn a melancholy apathy (that is madness in the eye of a philanthropist.) to every supposed nobleness of moral or intellectual design; they, that is the majority, have uniformly preferred the body to the mind, have ⟨indulged⟩ ↑permitted↓ the free and excessive enjoyment of their sensual appetites and chained down in torpid dreams the noble appetites of the soul. Instead of eating, to live, men have lived to eat, to drink, & to be merry; and when ordinary means failed to bring about these grand purposes, then the extraordinary means of lies, murder, & robbery have been resorted to. No doubt good men are also found in the dramatic variety of the tale, to recal[l] the mind to the theory from which it has wandered, but a good man in the world is aptly represented by a stag in the chase as the ⟨hapless⟩ ↑one↓ mark & victim at whose cost the enjoyment of all the rest is procured. [23] "If 20,000 naked Americans were not able to resist the assaults of but 20 well armed Spaniards, I see little possibility for one honest man to defend himself against 20,000 knaves who are all furnished with the defensive arms of worldly prudence & the offensive too of craft & malice." Cowley Essays p. 104[.] Dangers of company[.]²⁹ [22₂] There is nothing in fable so dark & dreadful but had its first

²⁸ "Depravity" and "History" are centered beneath "new wine of their imaginations" at the bottom of the page.
²⁹ The quotation is the first sentence of Cowley's "The Dangers of an Honest Man in Much Company." It appears on p. [23] opposite the sentence on p. [22] after which it is here inserted. See Cowley's *Essays*, 1819, p. 104.

model in the houses & palaces of men. Iniquity, malice, & rage find many homes with the lords of the creation & Devils were not *invented* for our poetry, but were copied from ⟨our⟩originals among ourselves.

It seems to be a mockery to send us to this howling wilderness to pluck roses & fruits. The rose *is* blooming there & the wild flowers hanging luxuriantly, but they cast their perfume in the tiger's den. Fanciful men heated by the new wine of their imaginations have attempt[24]ed to woo the indignant Reason into a better love of this darkened world. Epicurean pencils have painted it as perfectly accommodated to our powers of enjoyment, as fraught with every luxury, grace, & good which we desire to gain, as the palace of beauty & love, the ↑vast↓ mart of thought, friendship, society & distinction, the home of Virtue & the End of Hope. So it is pictured, & so we believe in childhood; but our first mature glance at the actual state of society falls upon so much real deformity & such low moral and intellectual turpitude that the fair fabric of the imagination is speedily undermined. We find it difficult or impossible to reconcile the phenomena which we observe with any plausible hypotheses that heaven or earth have told us of their design; but humanity always resembles itself —, and we readily recognize the imposture that attempts to describe better beings than men. For, this more brilliant & seductive faith concerning man & the earth, is deduced from false & partial representations of human nature and makes only momentary converts, when it is aided by the gay exhilaration which nature within and without awakens in youth, or by the few hours or moments that happen in a man's life, when the heart is swelled & imagination is feasted at seasons of ⟨festivity⟩ ↑revel↓, magnificence & public joy. Whereas the times when the contrary conviction is forced upon the soul, outnumber these moments a thousand fold. They sadden our thoughts in the [26][30] streets, & at home; by night, & by day. It is a melancholy spirit, whose acquaintance, if we could, we would most gladly drop. It is the nightmare which rides our thoughts and will not be shaken off. It makes many hearts sick &[31] weary of the world

---

[30] An unnumbered recto page between pp. [24] and [26] is blank except for an "X" in the upper left corner.

[31] The phrase "sick &" is circled.

and eager for an introduction into a better. That there is another world, a more splendid scene of life & thought is the consoling inference which they draw from this.ⁿ ⟨a⟩And this belief lends a majesty & joy to the funeral rites that attend his departure; the hearse & the pall become pleasant spectacles to his eye, and the way smooth from whose bourne no traveller returns.

From these views, which it is apt to suggest, it happens that history leaves a melancholy impression upon the mind, where it leaves any deep interest at all. Experience may not in every instance verify this observation, because the activity of ⟨the⟩ mind which the reading of history excites, the mere succession of imposing images ⟨is apt to awaken an intellectual⟩ ↑produces a↓ pleasure which counterbalances the disagreeable effect of the facts themselves. The history of an intelligent accountable race like the human, ought to abound with splendid & honourable anecdotes of virtue, with the records of cultivated & profitable mind, with blessed events produced by the irresistible weight of united & wise communities, with the rapid improvement of each generation [32]

[27][33] X   The history of America since the Revolution is meagre because ⟨no no⟩ it has been all that time under better government, better circumstances of religious, moral, political, commercial prosperity than any nation ever was before. History will continually grow less interesting as the world grows better. Professor Playfair of Edinburgh, the greatest or one of the greatest men of his time died without a biography for there was no incident in the life of a great & good man ↑worth recording↓. Nelson & Buonaparte[,] men of abilities without principle[,] found four or five biographers apiece.

The true epochs of history should be those successive triumphs which age after age the communities of men have achieved[,] such as the Reformation, the Revival of letters, the progressive Abolition of the Slave-trade.

[32] Continued on p. [28].
[33] The material on the page, written in pencil, was apparently added at another time in extension of the discussion of history. Two male heads, probably caricatures, are sketched in pencil at the bottom of the page.

[28] upon the improvement of the last, & the conversion of men to a race of demigods. Humanity mourns at the contrast to this, which her annals exhibit. Socrates, ⟨Alfred,⟩ Antoninus, Alfred, Washington, at intervals of a thousand years, assert the honours of the species which have been deeply degraded, & good men scattered thinly among mighty generations lament in solitude that their light is lost to the world. He that can most easily "feel his way up & down in Time," finds most reason to bewail man's depravity; and an unsatisfied & melancholy wonder becomes familiar to him. Those multitudes whom iron Necessity has forbidden to drink ⟨of⟩ at the fountain of the Muses & to explore the books of knowledge while they earn their bread by daily labour, have less time or room to be astonished; ↑satisfied with the present↓ they are not accustomed to look with anxiety beyond it, & demand the causes & designs of the motley scene ↑wherein they stand↓. They ask not Why do men build these houses of brick & stone along the ground which presently they are to leave without a hope of return? Why do they plant vineyards, & invent luxuries & crowd their lives with the engrossing pursuits that have their end here? I see that when they ↑have↓ amassed a little wealth & have fed the body & laughed & wept — then are they stuck with a loathsome evil which gnaws into the vessels of life, and they /are taken away from the face of the sun /[have] no part in things done/ & their names are no more counted among men. Will[n] the things which they have done in their life serve them in the unknown places to which they are gone? [n] The skill of the hand which [30][34] was acquired in a mechanical craft; the de⟨s⟩xterous & lucrative trades which they plied, through thirty, forty, or fifty years; the bargains which they made; the merchandise which they collected from every shore of the globe; the plots of their long sighted caution & worldly wisdom; will[n] these only fruits of their existence here, help forward their present greatness? Is there no latent connection between the two worlds which unites all their zeal in this life to some objects in the next?   Feb. 1, 1823.

Whoever considers what kind of a spirit it is which prompts

---

[34] An unnumbered recto page between pp. [28] and [30] is blank. "Domestic Manners" is centered beneath "subjects swelled to an" at the bottom of p. [30].

men to write, will remark the improbability ⟨of⟩ that a knowledge of the domestic manners of an ancient people should be transmitted to a remote age, except by /the most accidental fate/ any but the most fortuitous event/. Literature grew out of the necessity of written monuments, and in its first expansion into an elegant art while yet its mechanical advantages were rude & poor it was devoted only to those great features on the face of the world which ↑first↓ forced themselves ⟨first⟩ on the mind of the writer, — to the history of laws, of colonies, of wars, and of religion. (For his illustrations, the ↑writer↓ appealed to nature and upon the early discovery of the delight given by ⟨these⟩ appeals, was formed a new department of the Art which was called poetry.) The magnitude & variety of these subjects swelled to an indefinite extent, [32][35] as the mind became more habituated to them. It was an elevation of the soul to think & speak of these and it never entered the penman's thoughts to describe the tent or house which he inhabited & the habits of life familiar to his race. Other men ⟨lived⟩ ↑fed↓ & clothed themselves as he did and would find little to admire in the most accurate account of these wellknown matters. Not until many generations had lived & scattered themselves, and changed their customs by a⟨n⟩ ↑slow↓ accommodation to the climes & events into which they had come, was the distinction of manners a topic of attention. The most rapid progress of civilization in a community is so gradual that it is unmarked. Marble palaces do not rise immediately upon the ruins of mud hovels; nor till after the successive improvement of lime, of wood, & of brick houses. Much less can the unpractised eye discern the progress of the finer improvements in society which regard the intercourse of men ↑& women,↓ the government of the passions, the refinement of taste, & the ⟨style⟩ ↑tone↓ of conversation. When the knowledge of barbarous nations comes to the ears of a polite people, the historian gains an opportunity of describing the domestic institutions of his country by drawing a parallel; but even then the hints which we glean are very imperfect, because ⟨after the great & obvious points of distinction⟩ the historian contents himself with ⟨making⟩ manifesting the obvious points of distinction without indicating the nicer shades

[35] An unnumbered recto page between pp. [30] and [32] is blank. "Domestic Manners" is centered beneath "at last it is undertaken," at the bottom of p. [32].

of his picture. It is indeed a difficult task when at last it is undertaken, because

[33]³⁶ Falstaff saith — "It is certain that either wise bearing or
ignorant carriage is caught as men take diseases one of another."
[Shakespeare, 2 *Henry IV*, V, i, 83–85]

[34₁]³⁷ the observer is at a loss where to begin or how to discriminate
amid the forms in which he has always lived those which are common to all nations from those which are artificial & peculiar. Moreover he stands in peril of the charge of impertinence in offering to
his age the elaborate enumeration of the common usages of life.

All our researches into antiquity look to this ultimate end — of
ascertaining the private life of our fellow beings who have occupied
the different parts of the globe before us. But these domestic manners
are fleeting & leave no trace where they are not themselves transmitted. If we had a⟨n⟩ series of faithful portraits of private life in
Egypt, Assyria, Greece, & Rome we might relinquish without a sigh
their national annals. The great passions which move a whole nation,
[35] and are made up, it should be remembered, of the passion &
action of the individuals³⁸ [34₂] ⟨of⟩& the common sense of mankind are alike everywhere, and these determine the foreign relations & the political counsels of men. But private life hath more delicate varieties, which differ in unlike circumstances; and the barbarian
in his tent by the Rhine,ⁿ ↑the Tartar burrowing in the ground↓ the
Spartan in ↑the humble↓ house of the Republic, the Roman in the
luxurious palace of the Emperors, the Chinese in his floating house,
& the Englishman in his comfortable tenement ⟨spend⟩ ↑fill up↓ the
hours of the day with ↑very↓ different thoughts & different actions:
and he who enables us to form just estimates & comparisons of all,
unfolds an instructive page which we can never [36]³⁹ hope to see.

----

³⁶ The page is numbered in pencil and is blank except for the single quotation,
which appears opposite the sentence, "Other men . . . matters." on p. [32].

³⁷ "Domestic Manners" is centered beneath "instructive page which" at the bottom of the page.

³⁸ The inserted clause "and are . . . individuals" is written in pencil on the
opposite recto page, otherwise blank, with a directing line to indicate its insertion
here.

³⁹ "Domestic Manners" is centered beneath Emerson's note at the bottom of the
page.

Exactly to appreciate the weight of influence which these several situations cast upon the love of action & the love of pleasure (Gibbon's two ultimate principles) ⟨in the human breast⟩ would be to ⟨learn⟩ ↑get↓ ⁿ well that most useful of all lessons — the knowledge of human nature. Our vague & pompous outlines of history serve but to define in geographical & chronological limits the faint vestiges we possess of former nations. But of what mighty moment is it that we know the precise scene of a Virtue or a Vice? Give us the bare narrative of the *moral* beings engaged, the *moral* feelings concerned & the result — and you⟨r⟩ have answered all our purpose[,] all the ultimate design which leads the mind to ⟨the⟩ explore the past. (That is of a speculative mind — apart from all purposes of government and policy *). For the history of nations is but the history of private Virtues & Vices collected in a more splendid field, a wider sky. It would be to little purpose you would show the curious philosopher a mighty forest extending at a distan⟨t⟩ce its thousand majestic trees; ⁿ a ⟨leaf⟩ single branch, a stem, a leaf in his hand is of more value to him for all the purposes of science. Even the Eternal Geometer, in the fancy of Leibnitz deduces the past & present condition of the Universe from the examination of the single atom.⁴⁰

[38]⁴¹ The gods & wild beasts are both, to a proverb, fond of solitude; thought makes the difference between the solitude of the god & that of the lion.⁴² This community & equality of pursuits, ↑among all beings↓ but with different design & effect may be remarked throughout the Universe. Good men & great knaves cultivate with similar assiduity the same faculties; but *these* do it for Heaven; and *those,* for Earth, or, perchance, for Hell. Thus the ⟨sta⟩ⁿ ↑golden↓ corn ripening to the harvest, & the foul ratsbane suck up the same juice from the earth; but the one to feed & the other to destroy man.

 * For the purposes of another world, rather than for this.

⁴⁰ Emerson's source is Stewart's *Dissertation* (see *Collected Works,* ed. Sir William Hamilton, 11 vols., London, 1854, I, 264, n. 1).
⁴¹ An unnumbered recto page between pp. [36] and [38] is blank. On p. [38] the word "Equality" is written vertically in the left margin, from "the same" below to "*these* do" above.
⁴² Cf. Cowley, "Cogitation is the thing which distinguishes the Solitude of a God from a wild Beast" (*Essays,* 1819, p. 31).

In the entry of the saloon there has been considerable bustle; but an individual now stood there to throw off his blue cloak whose figure arrested at once the whole attention of two or three guests who chanced to be looking towards the door. A whisper instantly circulated to inform the party of the presence of a most distinguished & welcome guest. Every one rose at his entrance and the stranger advanced with an air of dignified majesty towards the centre of the hall. Franklin ⟨wel⟩ saluted him with evident respect & introduced him to the company as the first American President. There was no brilliant sparkle in his eye which attracted notice, nor rapid change of expression in his countenance; his countenance was composed and a graceful dignity marked every motion so that he was rather the Jupiter than the Apollo of the group. This however was manifest, that from the time of his entrance, during all [39] that long conference, the first place in that society was invariably, & of right, as it seemed, conceded to him. A most melodious voice which rolled richly on the ear and was that of Cicero, addressed the last mentioned person. "I esteem myself happy to stand in the company of one to whom ⟨fortune⟩ ↑heaven↓ seems to have united me by a ↑certain↓ similarity of fortune & the common glory of saving a state. But the fates have given you an advantage, O most illustrious man, above my lot, in granting you an honourable decline & death amid the regrets of your country, while I fell by the vengeance of the flagitious Antony." Gibbon put up his lip at this speech; and Franklin, who sat with his hands upon his knees between Washington & Gibbon, &c &c[.]

Tush, he said, thoughts & imaginations! I tell thee, man, that I who have got my bread & fame by informing the world, can write in twenty lines, all the *thoughts* that ever I had; while the imaginations, would fill a thousand fair pages.

[40] March 6, 1823.

My brother Edward asks me Whether I have a right to make use of animals? I answer "Yes," and shall attempt to give my reasons. A poor native of ⟨Greenland⟩ ↑Lapland↓ found himself in mid winter destitute of food, of clothing and light, and without even a bow to ⟨procure⟩ ↑defend↓ himself from the beasts. In this perplexity he met with a reindeer which he killed & conveyed to his hut. He now found himself supplied with oil to light his lamp, with a warm covering for his body & with wholesome & strengthening food, and with bowstrings withal, whereby he could again procure a similar supply. Does any mind question the innocence of this starving wretch in thus giving life & comfort to a desolate family in that polar corner of the world? — Now there is a ↑whole↓ *nation* of men precisely in this condition, all reduced to the alternative of killing the beasts, or perishing themselves. Let ↑the↓ tender hearted advocate of the brute creation go there, & choose whether he will make the beasts *his* food, or be himself, *theirs*.

Just such a picture may be made of the Arabian & his camel; and of the Northern Islanders & their Whales; in[n] all these instances, the positive law of Necessity asserts our right. But the use of the sheep for clothing, the ox, the horse, & the ass, for ⟨f⟩beasts of burden ⟨are⟩ ↑is↓ parallel to these, and their necessity though less ⟨forcibly⟩ seen is equally strong. "Increase & Multiply" said the Creator to Man; and caused all the brute creation to pass before him & recieve their names [41] in token of subjection. The use of these enables man to *increase & multiply* a thousand fold more rapidly, than would be practicable if he abstained from their use. Their universal application to our purposes & especially that remarkable adaptation that is observed in many instances of the Animal to the wants of the country in which he is found constitute the grand Argument on this side. (Besides Camel, Whale &c, that were mentioned, I believe the Mule, surest footed animal which walks, is found in the mountains to transverse whose precipices man wants his steady step.)

But it will be said they have rights

[42][43]   March 10th.

The mixture of the body & soul is the great wonder in the world, and our familiarity with this, puts us at ease with all that is unaccountable in our condition. Providence, no doubt, scrupulously observes the proportions of this mixture, and requires for the soundness of both, a fixed equilibrium. The gross appetites of the body are

[43] "TEMPERANCE" is written vertically in the left margin from "Even the body," below to "through which," above.

sometimes indulged, until the mind by long disuse lo⟨o⟩ses the
command of her noble faculties, and one after another[,] star after
star they are gradually extinguished. Those passages & conduits of
thought, of divine construction, through which, God intended, that
the streams of intellect should flow in various directions; — because
they have never been used have fallen to ruin, and are choked up;
Mind, from being the free↑born↓ citizen of the Universe & the inheritor of glory has become the caterer & the pander of sense. Even
the body, from being the upright lord of the lower creation, and
the temperate owner of a thousand pleasures, has abused his liberties, until he is the slave of those pleasures, & the imitator & peer
of the beasts. This is one mode of destroying the balance that Nature
fixed in our compound frame. We will see if it ⟨is⟩be in equal danger
on the other side, from the undue preponderance of the spirit.

Ascetic mortification and an unintermitting livelong [44][44] martyrdom of all the sensual appetites although far more innocent than
the contrary extreme is nevertheless unwise because it fails of its intended effect. Hermits who believed that by this merciless crucifixion
of the lusts of the body they should succeed in giving to the winds
the rags & tatters of a corrupt nature, and elevate & purge the soul
in exact proportion to the sufferings of the flesh have been disappointed in their hopes; at least if they have succeeded in decieving
themselves, they have ↑grievously↓ disappointed the world. ↑The
age ceased but a few centuries since when↓ the [n] cells upon the mountains of Palestine, the dreary caverns of Lybyan desart ⟨have⟩ echoed
⟨to the remorseless lash⟩ day & night for hundreds of years to the
remorseless lash & ↑half↓ suppressed groan of those mad tormentors
of themselves. In their own age, Fame told far and wide the story
of their self devotion and men came out ↑in processions↓ from the
cities & the fields to find these Christian Stoics & ⟨see⟩ ascertain the
success of that bold experiment which they had made upon their
nature. They looked to see their earthly parts faded, and the spirit
waxed brighter & brighter, and breaking out from the clayey tenement, in effulgent manifestations of celestial love. They looked to
find in those who had forsworn the seductions of the world & come

[44] An unnumbered recto page between pp. [42] and [44] is blank. "HERMIT"
is written beneath "benevolence," at the bottom of p. [44].

out ↑with disdain↓ from the active contamination[,] the Sodom &
Gomorrah ⁿ of human society for the avowed purpose of conversing
with God & Christ & his saints, — some ray of fervid & burning benevolence, some extraordinary [46]⁴⁵ ↑force↓ of mind to speak or of hand
to work, *good*; or in their dwelling, some footstep of their etherial
visitants. ∧ But these golden dreams of a rapid amelioration of the
world to issue from the prayers & penances that stormed heaven from
these solitudes, vanished away. The solitary man was as other men
are. His sufferings had soured his temper, or inflamed his pride;
theⁿ current of thought had been checked & frozen. His powers &
dispositions were diverted from useful ends & were barren & selfish.
Instead of the blessed plant which they thought had sprung for the
healing of the nations, was a dry & withered branch; ⟨that⟩it was
sundered from its root, producing neither blossoms, nor leaves, nor
fruits, ⟨to be cast into⟩ ↑'twas fit only for↓ the fire.

March 12th.   These then, however they may so appear, are
not instances of a victory gained by the mind over the body; because
the zeal which dictated this extraordinary effort was found to be mistaken & did not confer that distinction which had been attributed to
it. True, it may be said ⟨to be⟩ ↑we are↓ incompetent to decide upon
the other priv⟨e⟩ileges to which those famous austerities laid claim;
namely: a large reversion of favour and dignities in heaven as the
reward of an exemplary ⁿ obedience to the command that man should
deny his fleshly lusts. But there was an elder [47]⁴⁶ Scripture, a
prior command; Love thy neighbour; amid your righteous war
against your passions forget not that you are a man; ↑that you are↓
one individual of ↑a great↓ and immortal company, who, with you,
are labouring on to the attainment of objects which demand all ↑&
more than all↓ their ⟨c⟩faculties to appreciate & reach; that thousands
of these are fainting or falling by the way and will task your utmost
benevolence to lend them needful aid. And when a man has duly
considered all the great accumulation of inconveniences, mortifica-
tions, & obstacles which embarass the ways of this world & retard

---

⁴⁵ The recto page numbered [45] is blank. Emerson originally wrote "martyrdom of all the ⟨human⟩ ↑sensual↓ appetites" at the top of p. [46], and seeing that he
had skipped a page, canceled it and rewrote it at the top of p. [44].

⁴⁶ "SOCIAL" is written at an angle beneath "into the" at the bottom of the
page.

or divert men's ↑moral↓ progress in it, I think ⟨t⟩he⟨s⟩ will be led to undervalue the precious qualities of that man's virtue who like the Priest & the Levite of the parable goes on the other side & extricates himself as he can from the importunity of want or the cries of the dying — even though he thinks it meet to purchase his own freedom at the expense of abstinence & stripes.[n] The Earth which supports him upon her bosom, the common mother of us all, has a right to ask at his hands some return for her bounties and what immunity ↑it is↓ entitles him ⟨far removed⟩ to nurse his own unprofitable existence, without putting his shoulder to the wheel or bearing his part of the burden of life; without giving help to the weary or pouring one drop of balm into the wound⟨s⟩ed heart.

[48][47] But to return. There is force, no doubt, in the mind to carry away & subdue the body, and to vanquish, by great motives, all natural fears, or positive suffering. And here the mind seems to compensate itself for that quenching & absorption of the spirit into the flesh which was noticed before. The scholar is amazed in the annals of the Saracens at the absolute sway exerted upon the conduct of rude & ignorant hunters & shepherds by their religious opinions. Their subtle prophet, a master in the science of ⟨the⟩ human nature, inculcated that he who died in battle, entered instantly upon the enjoyment of voluptuous delight; & that God would forever punish him who turned his back in the fight. Upon this fierce incitement they fought, as the Christians relate, more like madmen than soldiers & threw themselves without hesitation upon the extremest dangers of fire & sword. History is rich in similar examples, and every man's memory will furnish him with some season of excitement when peril ⟨or⟩& death lost their wonted consideration in his eyes. There are likewise moments when the first charm & novelty of a theory or the stirring power of an engrossing conception diminishes the magnitude of all other things; and in opposition to the whole mass of a life's recollections, we doubt of the reality of the [49][48] world, and do not believe that we shall live for the future as we have lived heretofore. But these thoughts, vast & glorious as

[47] "SARACENS" is centered beneath "recollections, we doubt" at the bottom of the page.
[48] The page number is in pencil. "GREATNESS" is centered beneath "destinies of" at the bottom of the page.

the rainbow are equally fleeting & the clouds of life & the storms return.

I am persuaded that God enforces the law which was hinted at above, to make the perfection of man's nature consist in a fixed equilibrium of the body & the mind. Those masters of the moral world, who have preserved an undisputed lordship over good minds for ages after they themselves have died, have not gained that rare fortune by any extraordinary manners of life, or any unseemly defiance of the Elements, or of death. Temperate unassuming men, they have conformed to the fashions of the times in which they fell, without effort or contempt. God, in their minds, removed the ancient landmarks of thought, or ↑else↓ gave them strength to overleap the boundary, so that ↑they↓ took in a mightier vision of the state of man than their fellows had done. In all this they did not see *differently* from them, but sa⟨y⟩w *beyond,* the /common/vulgar/ limit. Accordingly it was no part of their pride to be at discord with men upon ⟨the⟩ common matters of everyday's observation. Upon trifles of time & sense they ↑all↓ thought alike. Deeper thoughts & remote consequences, far beyond the ken of vulgar judgements and yet intimately con⟨cerned⟩↑nected↓ with the progress & destinies of society were the points they fixed [50][49] their eyes upon; and upon the distinctness with which they were able to detect these, they chiefly valued themselves. It is a delightful relief in the afflicting history of the world, it is a crystal fountain ↑gushing↓ in the wilderness — to remember the men who exercised this peaceful & sublime dominion over human hearts,[n] not cemented by ↑the↓ blood nor shaken by ↑the↓ curses of enemies. Bound like other men to the complicated machine of society, & their fortunes perhaps inseparably linked[n] to the greatness of another house — these minds quietly founded a kingdom of their own which should long outlast the ruins of that transient dynasty in which it grew. The despots under whom they were born have been buried in the earth & forgotten under the sun, while these, in our reverted view, walk alone, with giant port, a⟨m⟩bove the pigmy throng of their contemporaries. Men of God they were, — children of a clearer ⟨light⟩ ↑day↓ walking upon earth keeping in their hands the Urns of immortality out of which there

[9] The page number is in pencil.

streamed a light which reached to far distant generations that they might follow in the↑i↓r track. The Pagan also blest them,

> Pauci quos aequus amavit
> Juppiter, aut ardens virtus ad sidera tollit.[50]

March 13th. And what a motley patchwork of feelings may be found in ↑the↓ crew of their admirers behind them. How many brows are knit, how many hearts [51][51] yearn, of those who resolve to follow, or are content to ⟨venerate⟩ worship them. Upon what meat did these Caesars feed, that they have grown so great? Did God or Man, time, or place, or chance sow the immortal seed? And how many seats at the Table of the Gods are yet vacant? And the store-houses of Genius & Goodness from which each child of the Universe may pluck out his share — are they yet exhausted or locked up? And shall those hearts which have throbbed to the secret urgency of the spirit, (perchance it was the same spirit that urges all existence) shall they faint in the outset? Onward, onward, the Sun is already high over your head! Or ⟨da⟩fearest thou because the day is waxed late that time shall lack? I tell thee, the race is for Eternity. The windows of heaven are opened, and they whose faces are as the day[,] Seraphim & Cherubim beckon to the children of Man & bid him "Be bold!"

> 'Incipe! Vivendi recte qui prorogat horam,
> Rusticus expectat dum defluat amnis; at ille,
> Labitur et labetur in omne volubilis aevum.' [52]

[52][53] "The World is not thy friend, nor the world's law."
> [Shakespeare, *Romeo and Juliet*, V, i, 72]

'Advantage feeds him fat, while men delay.'
> [Shakespeare, *1 Henry IV*, III, ii, 180]

> 'The soul's dark mansion battered & decayed
> Lets in new light through chinks that time has made.'
> [Waller, "Of the Last Verses in the Book," ll. 13–14]

[50] "Some few, whom kindly Jupiter has loved, or shining worth uplifted to heaven. . . ." Virgil, *Aeneid*, VI, 129–130, inaccurately quoted.
[51] The page number is in pencil.
[52] See p. 76 above.
[53] Two scraps of paper are tipped onto this page over the quotations. They are designated below as inserts by the addition of subscript letters to the page number.

'Talk, is a tinkling cymbal, without love.' [54]

> Nature's tears are reason's Merriment
> [Shakespeare, *Romeo and Juliet*, IV, v, 83]

'If there be any curse which ⟨is heard in heaven⟩ ↑brings damnation↓, it is not the curse of the pope but the curse of the poor.'   Shenstone [55]

'Flattery is a foolish suicide; she destroys herself with her own hands.' Gibbon

> Convey a libel with a frown,
> And wink a reputation down.
> [Swift, "Journal of a Modern Lady," ll. 192–193]

[52ₐ]

> The Greek who won the Muses to the Porch
> Said that the world was God, in this same form
> Existing from eternity himself.
> "Thy God is round," the merry scoffer said,
> "And since the Arabian desart is one part
> "Why ⟨can⟩ ↑cures↓ he not his sandy palsied side?" [56]

> Glory is fond of heaven; Passion rests here
> Polluting all the earth; Her se⟨p⟩rpent trail
> Winds through low huts & golden palaces
> To mar alike the sultan & his slave.
> God save me from this dragon, whose foul clutch,
> If I once 'scape, Glory's proud wing will stoop,
> And lift me joyful to her own abode.[57]

Rea‖ . . . ‖ truly,

[52ᵦ] The Chronicles of Norway say that in the year 982, Eric the Red, a Norwegian youth of noble family sailed from Iceland with

---

[54] Cf. Bacon, "Of Friendship": "For a crowd is not company; and faces are but a gallery of pictures; and talk but a tinkling cymbal, where there is no love."

[55] "Of Men and Manners," inaccurately quoted. See *Essays on Men and Manners*, (London, 1868), p. 238.

[56] The verses are written on the recto of the first scrap of paper pasted to p. [52].

[57] The verses are written on the verso of the scrap of paper used for the preceding verses.

102

25 ships, in quest of adventure & discovery. His fleet took a south-westerly course & came to a pleasant land full of lofty timber & of fresh & verdant vallies. Pleased with the beautiful coast, which he called Greenland, Eric resolved to settle there. After building their houses, they wasted the short summer in the pursuit of the game which was very abundant. But a summer of unusual mildness was followed by the stern winter of those high latitudes. Their harbour was frozen & the ill fated colonists beheld with despair a vast barrier of ice accumulating on the coast to shut them out forever, from all communication with the rest of the world. They are supposed to have perished miserably with cold & famine. The court of Denmark sent out several ships to ⟨exp⟩ search after the lost Colony, in vain. The sailors believe the ghosts of the settlers guard the coast & make all access dangerous.[58]

[58] The account of Eric the Red is written on one side of the second scrap of paper attached to p. [52].

Wide World 10

1823

Originally entitled "Wideworld No 10," this journal was later given the letter designation K. The second in the sequence of journals bound together, the journal continues with only a brief interruption from Wide World 9, the dated entries beginning on March 18 and ending on June 11, 1823.

The manuscript is composed of twelve folded sheets of unlined paper hand-stitched into a single gathering and then sewed together by white thread with Wide World numbers 9, 11, and 12. The manuscript is in ink except for one passage on the page numbered 36. The leaves measure 17 x 21.3 cm.

[1] "Vinegar is the Son of Wine."

K

Wideworld [1]   No 10

"Optimus ille animi vindex laedentis pectus,
  Vincula qui rupit, dedoluitque semel." [2]

Boston, March 18, 1823.

DEDICATION

When God had made the beasts, & prepared to set over them an intelligent lord, He considered what external faculty he should add to his frame, to be the seal of his superiority. Then ⟨h⟩He gave him an articulate voice. He gave him an organ exquisitely endowed, which was independent of his grosser parts, — but the minister of his mind & the interpreter of its thoughts. It was designed moreover

[1] The title "Wideworld" is enclosed in an ornamented oval or scroll.
[2] "He best wins freedom for himself who has burst the bonds that hurt his soul, and once for all o'ercome the smart." Ovid, *The Remedies of Love*, ll. 293–294. Emerson's source was doubtless Bacon's "Of Nature in Men," which has "animi" for the customary "sui." Emerson's "laedentis" is an error for "laedentia."

as a Sceptre of irresistible command, by whose force, the great & wise should still the tumult of the vulgar million, & direct their blind energies to a right operation. The will of Heaven was done, & the morning & evening gales wafted to the Highest, the harmonious accents of Man. But the generations of men lived & died, while yet their expanding [2] powers were constrained by the iron necessities of infant civilization, & they had never, with, perchance, a few solitary exceptions, ascertained the richness of this divine gift. Suddenly, in a corner of Europe, the ripe seeds of Greatness burst into life, & covered the hills & valleys of Greece with the golden harvest. The new capacities & desires which burned in the human breast, demanded a correspondent perfection in *speech*, — to body them forth. Then a voice was heard in the assemblies of men, which sounded like the language of the gods; it rolled like music on the ear, and filled the mind with undefinable longings; it was peremptory as the word of Kings; or mournful as a widow's wailing or enkindling as the martial clarion. That voice men called Eloquence, and he that had it, unlocked their hearts, or turned their actions whithersoever he would. Like sea waves to the shore, like mountain sheep to their shepherd, so men crowded around this commander of their hearts to drink in his accents, & to mould their passions to his will. The contagion of new desires & improvements went abroad, — and tribe after tribe of barbarians uplifted the banner of Refinement. This spirit stirring art was propagated also and although its light sunk often in the socket, it was never put out. Time rolled, & successive ages rapidly developed the mixed & mighty drama of human society, and among the instruments [3][3] employed therein, this splendid art was often & actively used. And who that has witnessed its strength, and opened every chamber of his soul to the matchless enchanter, does not venerate it as the noblest agent that God works with, in human hearts? ⟨This⟩[n] My Muse, it is the idol of thy homage and deserves the dedication of thine outpourings.

After two moons I shall have fulfilled twenty years. Amid the fleeting generations of the human race and in the abyss of years I lift my solitary voice unheeded & unknown & complain unto in-

---

[3] "TIME" is centered beneath "heaven over his" at the bottom of the page.

exorable Time. 'Stop, Destroyer, Overwhelmer, stop one brief moment this uncontrollable career. Ravisher of the creation, suffer me
a little space, that I may pluck some spoils, as I pass onward, to be
the fruits & monuments of the scenes, through which I have travelled.'
—Fool! you implore the deaf torrent to ⟨stop⟩ ↑relax the speed of
its cataract,↓ [at ille]

Labitur et labetur in omne volubilis aevum.⁴ How many thousands before, have cast up ↑to Time↓ the same look of fear & sorrow
when they have contemplated the terrible flight of Time. But this
infinite Extinguisher or ⟨c⟩Changer of being, continues his supreme
agency without exception or interval. Among the undistinguished
myriads ↑thus↓ hurried on & off the stage of mortal life, a few, parted
by long periods asunder, have made themselves a longer memory
in this world, (& perchance in worlds beyond,) by pouring out all
their strength in the service of their fellow men. They rightly judged
that if a benevolent God keeps watch in heaven over his family in
earth, the sight [4]⁵ would be grateful to ⟨h⟩Him, of patient study
& intense toil accomplished by magnanimous Minds in behalf of
human nature & for the avowed design of its improvement. Men
grope, they said, in a night of doubts & falsehoods, for the light of
Truth is quenched, or burns dimly in the midst; ⟨and they set themselves to⟩ ↑come let us↓ restore the flame, and ⟨add⟩ feed it with fuel,
until it sh⟨ould⟩all grow up again in a beacon ⟨blaze⟩ ↑light↓ blazing
broadly & gloriously to illuminate the world. Then our sons & our
sons' sons shall walk in the brilliant light and shall pray God to
bless us long after we have gone down to the chambers of death.
That glorious company of martyrs who took up the cross of virtuous
denial & gave their days & nights to study, meditation, & prayer,
were indeed 'Blessed' of Heaven & Earth. God, in the watches of
the starry night, fed their imaginations with secret influences of
divinity, and swelled their conceptions with ⟨celestial hope & radiance.⟩ ↑showers of healing water from the fountain of paradise.↓
They could not contain their joy of these sweet & silent promptings,
this interview as they deemed it, between God & man, and they

⁴ See p. 76 above.
⁵ "Greatness" and "Milton" are centered respectively beneath "grew daily upon"
and "me" at the bottom of the page. "New Year's" is written vertically in the right
margin from "their joy" below to "the watches" above.

mounted to a constant elevation of thought which left far below them, the cankering & ignoble pursuits of life. They have left inscribed in their writings frequent & bold appeals to the grandeur of the spirit which lodged in their breasts, confident that what was writ would justify the truth of their claims. The sublimest bard of all — he who sung "Man's disobedience & the fruit of that forbidden tree which brought death into the world & all our woe"[6] felt himself continually ⟨called upon & urged⟩ ↑summoned & inspired↓ by a Spirit within him, and which afterward he says grew daily upon me — to do God's work in the [5] world by ↑sending forth↓ strains which "aftertimes would not willingly let die. Not a work to be finished in the heat of youth or the vapours of wine; nor yet by invocation of Dame Memory & her siren daughters, but by devout prayer to that Eternal Spirit who giveth knowledge,"[7] ↑thereby↓ he hoped to release in some great measure the hearts of posterity from th⟨e⟩at ⟨bondage⟩ ↑harlotry↓ of voluptuousness, whereinto he percieved with grief his own age had fallen. A kindred genius born for the exaltation of mankind, who preceded the poet and who fell (alas for humanity!) into a snare & ruin for his integrity did yet contribute a mighty impulse to the cause of wisdom & truth. And he also was nowise unconscious of the magnitude of the effort & the power which supported him. —

It ⟨has been confidently⟩ ↑is often↓ alleged with a great mass of instances to support the assertion, that the spirit of philosophy & a liberal mind is at discord with the principles of religion, so far at least as to imply tha⟨n⟩t hoary error that religion is a prejudice which statesmen cherish in the vulgar as a wholesome terror. Those whom Genius or Education have rescued from the common ⟨bondage⟩ ↑ignorance↓[8] have openly discarded the humble creeds of men and vaunted their liberty. They have mounted, it is pretended, to some loftier prospect of man's dependance or independence upon God & have discovered that human beings foolishly trouble themselves by their shallow & slavish fear of some great Power in the Universe who

---

[6] Milton, *Paradise Lost*, I, 1–3.

[7] "Not a work . . . knowledge," is a paraphrase of a passage in Milton, *Reason of Church Government urged against Prelaty*. See *The Works of John Milton*, 18 vols. (New York, 1931–1938), III, Pt. I, 240–241.

[8] The word "ignorance" is circled, perhaps for further revision.

(cons) notices & remembers their actions. For these clearer-sighted intellects have darted their glance into the secrets of the other world & have satisfied [6]⁹ themselves, either that there is no Divinity at all, beyond the vain names & fantastic superstitions of men, or else, if there *be*, — a sphered & potent Dweller in the Abyss, he is incurious and indifferent to the petty changes of the world. In this confidence therefore, these bold speculators cast off the fetters of opinion & those apprehensions which so cleave to our poor nature & are willing to survey at ease the gorgeous spectacle of the Universe, the fabric of society, & the closet of the Mind; and to make themselves proud of this birthright of thoughts — this rare /workmanship/chance/ which fell upon them they know not how; and even to vaunt of their incomprehensible immortality, if perchance they shall outlast the changes of death. This perilous recklessness, I find with regret in many of the intellectual Guides of these latter times engendered in some, no doubt, by the too faithful copying of the others from whom they had themselves recieved the first impulse, and arising in the↑m↓ ⟨former⟩ from feelings of superiority & spiritual pride. Hume, Gibbon, Robertson, Franklin, certain Scotch geniuses of the present day, & the profligate Byron have expressed more or less explicitly their dissent from the popular faith. Composing in themselves a brilliant constellation of minds variously & richly endowed they have taken out its welcome influence from the cause of good will to men & set it in the opposite scale. Like the star ↑seen↓ in the Apocalypse they have cast a malign light upon the earth, turning the sweet waters to bitter &c[.]

That there may be a transient pleasure in such freethinking I will not deny, nor that pride of opinion has its gratifications. I will not dispute that to a man inclined so to consider it, [7]¹⁰ the majesty of nature is a puppet show of rarest entertainment abounding with devices which will repay the toil of his curiosity. I will not deny that this disciple of Democritus may find the human soul & human society rich sources of merriment; but I shall say that laughter in the mouth

⁹ "Freethinking" is centered beneath "dispute that to a" at the bottom of the page.
¹⁰ "MILTON" is centered beneath "Nothing of ⟨prose⟩" at the bottom of the page. Pencil sketches of two men in profile, one wearing a plumed helmet, the other with long flowing hair, appear toward the center of this page.

of a maniac is, in my judgement, as becoming. Standing, as man stands, with the thunders of evil fate suspended over him, bound on every side by the cords of temptation; and uncertainty ↑sweeping↓, like a ↑dark↓ cloud, ⟨sweeping darkly⟩ ↑⟨like⟩↓ before his path, — is it for him, ⟨whose⟩ ↑if his↓ understanding is strong enough to appreciate this condition — to acknowledge his melancholy lot by unseasonable mirth? A sober firmness on his brow, & purity ⟨at⟩in his heart, is the best armour he can /wear/gird on/. I believe nothing is more un-grounded than the assertion, that, scepticism is, in any manner, the natural fruit of a superior understanding. The legitimate fruits of a master spirit are a dearer love to virtue, and an ardent & thrilling desire to burst the bonds of the flesh & begin a perfecter existence. In those moments which every wise man counts the best of his life — who hath not been smitten, with a burning curiosity, to rend asun-der the veil of mortality, & gaze, with pious violence, upon the un-utterable glories beyond? — The names which I mentioned as apos-tate, weigh nothing against the greater names of Bacon, Milton, New-ton, & the like, whose hearts cleaved to the divine revelations as the pledge of their resurrection to eternity. Nor can I concieve of any man of sense reading the chapter of Milton to which I have referred (Reason of Church Government urged against Prelaty ↑Book 2, c. 1↓) [11] without his heart's warming to the touch of noble sentiments; & his faith in God & ↑in↓ the eternity of virtue & of truth, being stead-fastly confirmed. Nothing of ⟨prose⟩ ↑human composition↓ is so akin to inspiration.

[8][12]   Sunday Evg., March 23d, 1823.
    A man is made great by a concentration of motive. Bacon might have lived & died a courtier, disgraced & forgotten, but for a fixed resolution at eighteen years old — to reform Science. Milton should have slumbered but for that inspiration to write ⟨p⟩an epic; Luther, but for his obstinate hatred of Papacy; Newton, but for his per-severance, thro' all obstacles, to identify the fall of his apple ↑&↓ ⟨&⟩of the moon; (Shakespeare is an outlaw ⟨to⟩from all systems and would be great in despite of all.) So of inferior men; Peter the Hermit

----

[11] See p. 107 above.
[12] "IMPROVEMENTS" is centered beneath "with the most" at the bottom of the page.

sent men to die in Crusades; Modern Mr Lancaster, a stupid man, fills the world with his schools; only from a concentrated attention to one design. Human power is here of indefinite extent; no one can prescribe the bound beyond which human exertions cannot go with effect. But *times* must be observed, and ↑in great things↓ a man always acts with more effect when the evil is far gone, than when it is nascent. Thus if Luther had preached one or two centuries earlier it might have been vain. For it is with nations as with individuals. A man altogether in the wrong may more easily be convinced than one half right; for when ⟨convinced of his error⟩ ↑the error is pointed out he is obliged to↓ give⟨s⟩[n] up the whole, at once; whereas, the other, is so much the more tenacious of his opinion as he percieves it to be partly right. And a nation may be more violently roused to ↑a↓ reform when the mischief is great & indisputable than when it is concealed & may be denied. In like manner a man with the arts of civilization would be recieved by a nation of savages with admiration & gratitude, while a small positive improvement arising among them would obtain very slowly. — Compare also the fate of Socrates, Galileo, Roger Bacon, who made vast discoveries, with that of Hermit Peter, or the silly Schoolmen lauded to the skies — which may perchance force me to reverse the last sentence about savages. —

¶ A child may be made to believe the greatest absurdities & to act upon his belief; he casts them all off as he grows up & those with the most contempt which are [9][13] most palpable. A tribe of savages is a moral child, and will tolerate, from the same imperfection of faculties, the grossest errors without a suspicion. They may often arrive at a considerable ⟨advan⟩ growth of Civilization without being prepared to recieve an useful innovation upon them. The doctrine you would teach them, though true, is far above their years; and though they may give it their assent, they cannot give it that practical & enthusiastic approbation which is necessary to exterminate the error which you combat,[n] an approbation that will be the warmer, the longer it is delayed. Such a society of half civilized barbarians was Europe in the Middle Ages; old enough to see & denounce some errors, and, at last, to spread the Reformation; but not old enough

[13] "IMPROVEMENTS" is centered beneath "Thus in the savage" at the bottom of the page.

to appreciate or believe Galileo — or in earlier times to learn from
Friar Bacon even his useful arts of life. It ⟨often⟩ ↑commonly↓ happens, moreover that the educated portion [of] society, (although
poorly educated) is far in advance of the other & major portion.
Socrates therefore who brought down from heaven most unusual
communications, was taunted as a blasphemer, & condemned to death.
But Athens nevertheless furnished him with competent disciples who
treasured up & transmitted to another age thoughts & precepts
which will never be forgotten. This therefore should be stated as
the exception to the remark of the last page — and remark & exception will stand thus —. ⟨That a nation recieves an improvement with
greatest effect when it is far gone in error, except where the improvement is of a refined nature,⟩ ↑viz.↓ that, that improvement which
takes great effect must be in the farthest extreme from the recieved
custom, excepting in cases where the improvement is of a refined &
metaphysical nature. Thus in the savage islands of the Pacific, where
[10]¹⁴ armour of the natives is rude & simple, little improvements
of the bow & ⟨a⟩the arrow which were made in one island, spre⟨d⟩ad
no further than its shores. But when the European brought them
muskets, the whole Archipelago were eager to exchange their weapons
at once. The same Europeans brought them a sublime religion; infinitely more superior to their own than were firearms to their
↑pointed↓ reeds; but the islanders were wedded to a most gross &
stupid idolatry & they found that Christianity was too refined & advanced for their infant understandings.

It should be observed here that it is a well known fact that arts
have generally been carried to their perfection very soon after the
first attempts & have seldom afterwards surpassed this first success —
e.g. Napoleon's imperial press never published any better specimen
of typography than was exhibited within the first century of the Art
of Printing. (40 or 80 years after the discovery.)

¶ I have rambled far away from my original thought, still there
is a loose unity which binds these reflections together and which leads
me back to the dubious theme — myself. One youth among the multitudes of mankind, one grain of sand on the seashore, unknown in

¹⁴ "IMPROVEMENT" and "FORTUNE" are centered respectively beneath
"which he mistakes" and "for the" at the bottom of the page.

the midst of my contemporaries, I am hastening to put on the manly robe. From childhood the names of the great have ever resounded in my ear. And it is impossible that I should be indifferent to the rank which I must take in the innumerable assembly of men, or that I should shut my eyes upon the huge interval[n] which separates me from the minds which I am wont to venerate. Every young man is prone[n] to be misled by the suggestions of his own ill founded ambition which he mistakes for the promptings of a [11] secret Genius, and thence dreams of a⟨s⟩n ↑unrivalled↓ greatness. More intercourse with the world and closer acquaintance with his own faults wipes out from his fancy every trace of this majestic dream. Time, who is the rough master of the feast, comes to this concieted & highly-placed guest, and saith, 'Friend come down to this lower seat, for thy neighbour is worthier than thou.'[15] Nevertheless it is not Time nor Fate nor the World that is half so much his foe as the demon Indolence within him. A man's enemies are those of his ↑own↓ household. Men sometimes carelessly & sometimes ⟨wilfully⟩ ↑profanely↓ cast off the blame of their insignificance in society, upon God their maker, or upon Circumstance, the god (as they term him) of this world. ⟨But⟩ It is a skilful masquerade which they have vamped up to tickle the sense & to lull them to repose. They thus contrive to lay quietly an oppressive burden upon the Atlantean shoulders of fate. But if ⟨they⟩ a man shall diligently consider what it is which most forcibly impedes the natural greatness of his mind, he will assuredly find that slothful sensual indulgence is the real unbroken barrier, and that when he has overleaped this, God has set no bounds to his progress. The maxim is true to an indefinite extent — "Faber quisque fortunae suae."[16] We boast of our free agency. What is this but to say God has put into our hands the elements of our character, the iron & the brass, the silver & the gold, to choose & to fashion them as we will. But we are afraid of the toil, we bury them in a napkin instead of moulding ↑them↓ into rich & enduring vessels.

[15] Cf. Luke 14:10.
[16] "Every man is the architect of his own fortune." (Ed.) The quotation appears often in Bacon, notably in *De Augmentis Scientiarum*, *The Advancement of Learning*, and "Of Fortune." See *The Works of Francis Bacon*, ed. James Spedding et al., 15 vols. (Boston, 1860–1864), III, 89, VI, 360, and XII, 215–216. Emerson's source is probably "Of Fortune" (see p. 364 below).

This view is by far the most animating to exertion. It speaks [12] life & courage to the soul. Mistrust no more your ability, the rivalry of others, or the final event. Make speed to plan, to execute, to fulfil; forfeit[n] not one moment more in the dalliance of sloth; for the work is vast, the time is short, and Opportunity is a headlong thing which tarries for no man's necessities. Habits of labour are paths to Heaven. — It commands no outward austerities. Do not put ashes on your head, nor sackcloth on your loins nor a belt of iron for your girdle. — But Mortify *the mind,* put ↑on↓ humility & temperance, for ashes, and bind about the soul as with iron. The soul is a fertile soil which will grow rank & to waste if left to itself. If you wish therefore to see it bud out abundantly & bring an harvest ↑richer↓ an hundred and a thousandfold, ↑bind it,↓ bind it with the restraint of Cultivation. (March 26) It is overgrown with tares & poisons. Suffer no longer this noisome barrenness. Harrow it up with thoughts. Fill it with the joys & ↑wholesome↓ apprehensions of a reasonable being, instead of the indifference of a brute. There are a million loiterers in the moral ways, laughing as they stop to pick flowers of sin or pleasure in the fields; — but their gaiety hangs ill upon a haggard countenance, and they are covered with rags. — Far before them ⟨are⟩ ↑I see↓ a chosen /few/company/, clad in shining garments, and pressing eagerly forward with honourable industry. ↑*Make Haste.*↓ Cast off your burden of apologies & compliances which retard your steps, and flee after them lest they reach their ⟨l⟩Lord ↑& enter in↓ before you and the door be shut.——[17]

These are the clamours with which conscience pursues & upbraids me — happy if they were undeserved — happiest could they accomplish their end! But the inscrutable future, comes down in darkness and finds us in the thrall of [13] the same old enemies, with all our hopes & ⟨good⟩ ↑fullblown↓ intentions ↑thick↓ on our heads. — For your life, then, for your life! crawl on a few steps farther in the next twelvemonth!

[17] The final dash has been extended into an open-mouthed snake's head with sharp fangs.

March 28.

A Shout to the Shepherds.

Freshly, gaily, the rivulet flows
Beside its emerald bank
Each silver bubble in beauty goes
Adown the stream & briefly glows
Till it reach the broad flags & the alders dank.
  Shepherds, who love the lay
Of untaught bards in oaken shades
Brighteyed Apollos of the forest glades
  Hither, hither, turn your way.
Come to the grassy border of the brook
Here where the ragged hawthorn dips
His prickly buds of perfume in the wave
And thence again ⟨the⟩ a costly fragrance sips
Drinking with each balmy floweret's lips
Pure from the Naiad's welling urn
While overhead the embowering elms
Bow their broad branches & keep out the day.
  Hither, hither, turn your way.
   Good bye.

April.

[April 8, 1823] Powerful & concentrated motive, it was remarked above, is necessary to a man, who would be great. And young men ⟨may⟩ whose hearts burn with the desire⟨s⟩ of distinction may complain perhaps that the paths in which a man may be usefully illustrious, are always taken up and that they have fallen in too late an age to be benefactors of mankind. Truly I wish it were so. I wish that human grandeur had gone so high — if the thing were possible — that it had exhausted all the stores [14][18] from which the mighty pile was supplied — and that there remained no ignorance to teach, no errors to correct, no sin to purge. ↑But alas!↓ The wildest dreams of

---

[18] Beneath "obvious causes . . . square miles" are two faint pen and ink sketches of men's heads, one in profile and one full face.

poetry have uttered no such thing. There *is* a huge & disproportionate abundance of *evil* on earth. Indeed the good that is here, is but
a little island of light, amidst the unbounded ocean. What mind
therefore (that is stirred by ardent feelings) looks over the great
desart of human life without fervently resolving to embark in the
cause of God & man? And without finding ⟨a⟩puissant motives calling
out the strength of every root & fibre ↑of his soul↓? But he finds the
field too spacious and the motive not ↑enough↓ concentrated. Contract it. —— Leave out of sight all those vast barbarous countries, and
continents, (I may say) of Asia & Africa & the Northern & Southern
regions of the globe; and leave out also the civilized Europe and
the field will be still large enough. Let the young American withdraw
his eyes from all but his own country, and try if he can find employment there,[n] considerable enough to task the vigorous intellect he
brings. I am of opinion that the most extraordinary powers that ever
were given to a human being would lose themselves in this vast
sphere. Separated from the contamination which infects all other civilized lands this country has always boasted a great comparative purity.
At the same time, from obvious causes, it has leaped at once from infancy to manhood; has covered & is covering millions of square miles
with a hardy & enterprizing population. The free institutions which
prevail here & here alone have attracted to this country the [15] eyes
of the world. In this age the despots of Europe are engaged in the
common cause of tightening the bonds of monarchy ⟨and⟩ about the
thriving liberties & laws of men and the unprivileged orders, the bulk
of human society gasping for breath beneath their chains, and dart-
ing impatient glances towards the free constitution of other countries. To America, therefore, monarchs look with apprehension &
the people with hope. But the vast rapidity with which the desarts
& forests of the interior of this country are peopled have led patriots
to fear lest the nation grow *too fast* for its virtue & its peace. ↑In↓
the [n] raw multitudes who lead the front of emigration ↑men of respectability in mind & morals↓ are rarely found — it is well known. The
pioneers are commonly the offscouring of civilized society who have
been led to embark in these enterprizes by the consciousness of ruined
fortunes or ruined character or perchance a desire for that greater
license which belongs to a new & unsettled community. These men

& their descendants ⟨of⟩ compose ⟨a⟩the western frontier population of the United States and ↑are↓ rapidly expanding themselves. At this day, the axe is laid to the root of the forest; the[n] Indian is driven from his hut & the bison from the plains; — in[n] the bosom of mountains where white men never trod, already the voice of nations begins to be heard — haply heard in ominous & evil accents. Good men desire, & the great Cause of human nature demands that this abundant & overflowing richness wherewith God has blessed this country be not misapplied & made a curse of; [16] that this new storehouse of nations shall never pour out upon the world an accursed tribe of barbarous robbers. Now the danger is very great that the Machine of ⟨g⟩Government acting upon this territory at so great distance will wax feeble or meet with resistance and that the Oracles of Moral law and Intellectual wisdom in the midst of an ignorant & licentious people will speak faintly & indistinctly. Human foresight can set no bounds to the ill consequences of such a calamity if it is not reasonably averted. And, on the contrary, if the senates that shall meet hereafter in those wilds shall be made to speak a voice of wisdom & virtue, the reformation of the world would be to be expected from America. How to effect the check proposed is an object of momentous importance. And in view of an object of such magnitude, I know not who he is, that, can complain ↑that↓ motive is lacking in this latter age, whereby men should become great. — April 8 — 1823 ——. [They represented their Supreme God as one whose cheek, (& they trembled not to express it) blanched with fear, who fled away & hid himself in a beastly form while a Giant held his Heavens.] [19]

The balancing and adjustment of human pleasures, privileges, & graces so that no man's share ↑shall↓ outrun⟨s⟩ all competition, nor ⟨is⟩be diminished to an extreme poverty, — is so obvious in the world, as to be a daily topic of conversation. And the system of compensations takes place as much in the *difference of good,* as in the apportioning of evil & good. Thus knowledge is a good; but it must be acquired in different ways and ⟨he tha⟩ there is no ↑single↓ way

[19] A faint pen and ink sketch of a man's head is beneath this bracketed sentence. An ornate scrolled line (here printed as a short rule) separates the date and bracketed sentence from the following paragraph.

which combines the advantages of all the others. The advantages which one man enjoys by access to unusual sources of im[17]^{20}prove-ment, do, by some necessity, deprive him of admittance to other sources ⟨as⟩ ↑equally↓ rare & rich. Is he opulent & commands the privileges of libraries & schools? he wants th⟨e⟩at vigour & eagerness to use them, which *Necessity* gives. Is he a traveller & borne by the winds to every foreign clime & does he transact affairs am⟨ong⟩idst the famous ruins of ⟨all the⟩ ↑each↓ continent⟨s⟩? then his taste has been uncultivated & he views them all with indifference. Has he wit & industry sufficient to grasp all knowledge? poverty shuts up with iron bars every avenue to him. Men are alike only in infancy; afterwards every man takes a path which leads out from the common centre, and every step separates ⟨th⟩ him further from all the rest. (The rest is somewhat more systematic but is elsewhere.)

↑The following is a gross mass, which is to be the skeleton of a sound & logical Discourse, whenever I have leisure & power to work upon it↓[.] ^{21}

I seek to prove the immense pressure of moral obligation, upon every man, both from Scripture & reason. I ask indulgence to re-marks upon an old & familiar topic, but for that not ^{n} to be despised. Turn not away because it is old unless you have also found that it is ^{n} false or of no use. It is no objection to your friend that he is an old friend — he is the more tried, & the more trustworthy. You do not reject bread because you have tasted it a thousand times; so much the more you confide in its wholesome sweetness. So it becomes you to give unwearied attention to this imposing theme of your moral obligations to God unless you have already tried their efficacy & found yourself harmed by them.

———Permit me to observe then that the very reason why they are not considered as supremely binding upon our attention is the same reason why they are not considered binding upon our conduct

---

^{20} "(Moral obligation)" is centered beneath "why they are not considered" at the bottom of the page.

^{21} The sentence appears to have been squeezed between the two paragraphs at another time. It is enclosed between two crossed double-slashes.

[18]²² viz. our ignorance of their character & claims. That ignorance is sometimes sin is undeniable. The partial judge who refuses to hear a part of the evidence lest he be compelled to contravene his inclinations by his decision, is sinful. And the man who is afraid to examine his relations to God & man lest the result should condemn himself, is sinful. We are bound therefore by the first & plainest dictates of conscience to study with care that moral constitution under which we stand to find out the boundary lines where innocence ends & guilt beg⟨an⟩ins; not to give all our life & thought to accidents & trifles which meet us by the way & let that alone go by unheeded upon which character and eternity depend. — Take heed therefore and although it should rend every fibre of the heart (too intimately allied to its iniquity) though it cost you pangs of reproach or perchance the sharpness of ridicule from without — to expose the true character of the relations in which you have stood & compare it with the relations you ought to sustain to beings, below & above; — take heed that you make this scrutiny without delay. Grope no more in the fogs & shadows which your own inconsistent affections have cast around you. Make haste to let in the broad daylight, to scatter the clou⟨l⟩ds & let the sun of Righteousness shine in.

To this end, — I shall try to compare the apparent condition of men with their real condition; the conduct which their apparent condition seems to sanction with the conduct which their real condition demands.

Men always act from some motive and though it be their own duty to see that their motive is good, yet when they act unworthily they act from some puissant impulse. Pass by the actions then ⟨which flowed from this motive⟩ & purge the fountain ⟨w⟩from whence they flowed. What is the cause then that after so many generations of examples the majority of mankind do still act with a [19] reference to this world & not to another? Seers & moralists have never been wanting. It is not that they have never been told that the eye of faith discerned a better & greater scene beyond. Watchmen have always stood upon the intellectual towers and warned those be⟨low⟩neath, faithfully, of the distant & the near enemy. But like infatuated

²² "MORAL OBLIGATION" is centered beneath "the majority of mankind do" at the bottom of the page.

victims of destiny they have shut their ears to the philosopher's
lesson & the Watchman's cry. What is the cause of this fatal disregard to God's first law — Love thyself — ? What is the secret
sorcery that has bewitched men's souls? I will tell you. It is because
men are blindly[,] madly attached to the present moment, and will
hazard the infinite future rather than forego the gross and inconsiderable joys which are soliciting their appetites today. It has been
pretended of old, (and they disbelieved it who started the pretence)
that this rankling — in the breasts of the multitude — of a sense of
duty was the result of superstitious & superficial views; that by much
thinking they had themselves ⟨had⟩ arrived at the correct conclusion,
that since man, in his best circumstances, is, on every side, encountered
by trouble it is wisdom to drown the sense of this manifold evil in
the surfeit & intoxication of pleasure,[n] & to bury, as they best can,
this gloomy memory of a God ↑& this uncomfortable sympathy with↓
⟨&⟩[n] Men in the rapid succession & impetuous mirth of a livelong
jubilee. It was[n] not by thinking much, it was by thinking little, that
they attained this shallow conclusion. But though it is not now commonly repeated, for men mistrust it too much to state it too distinctly to their own understandings — yet it is daily implied in the
actions of men. Need therefore is, that it be weighed & shewn wanting,
as it most certainly will appear.

The great illusion by which men suffer themselves to be mocked
is the idea of their independence. So far as any sense of dependence
stares them in the face — social[,] physical dependence as that of a
child on its parent, of an injured man on his deliverer, [20][23] of a
poor man on his benefactor — so far they are willing to acknowledge
an obligation and act as that obligation requires. They easily percieve
also, without much reasoning[,] an obligation which their own interest imposes to behave in society with decency & honesty; — but,
beyond this, they are apt & anxious to believe their human condition an independent one. They were not suddenly placed in this
goodly frame of nature and organized society; then they might have
been led to ask the curious questions of Whence? & Why? But they
have grown slowly up in it, making personal interests and in a man-

[23] "MORAL OBLIGATION" is centered beneath "Nature without anxiety," at
the bottom of the page.

ner acquiring rights & claims herein as they grew; learning to view mankind *as a society*, acting freely for itself & to distinct & finite ends — not as the machinery of another Being concealing secret agenc⟨y⟩ies of another World. When they have arri↑v↓ed at years of discretion, they are got to be so absorbed in affairs, that the questions, which, it should seem, would force themselves upon the mind, ⟨rare⟩ seldom occur, or are most foolishly answered. To what purpose is this gorgeous firmament displayed, in such rich & inimitable colours, with such glorious variety? What is this curtain of darkness which is hung abroad, unaltered in its regularity, unrivalled in its grandeur[?] I stand in a Paradise. And the pleasant winds of heaven fan me as they move, and scatter health & odours through all their outgoings. Custom has made familiar to me the marvels of the world; nevertheless [n] its mighty magnificence will sometimes break upon the sense in overpowering sensations and fill the mind with unspeakable ⟨sentiment⟩ conception⟨t⟩s of the Cause and Design and with awful shame for its own ingratitude. But men are much more apt to let their thoughts rest in the works, to behold Nature without anxiety, to see Nature's [21] [24] God; it [n] is Custom, the tyraness of fools, that suffers them to gaze vacantly upon this fair & noble miracle[,] this sublime & exquisite world without exacting an unbounded homage to the Author of it all. — But ⟨C⟩perchance Custom is right, and I owe no homage; stand forth now and shew, if thou canst, some grounds for this superlative clai⟨i⟩m upon my affections & life. For, if you say well, then I am checked in that liberty which I have exercised and (in the full view of my whole hopes) I shall be free to do right, but I shall no longer be free to do wrong. For he that is bid to go one way, and a sword is pointed to his breast, is not free to go another. Explain to me then my obligations, for ↑else↓ I cannot consent to resign that free & entire license to go right or to go wrong with which I hitherto believed I walked in the world's ways.

Infra, quote 6, 7, 8, Ver. xxxv. Job [25]

[24] "Continued" is centered beneath "repugnance to God, of" at the bottom of the page and separated from that phrase by a long line. The line may be either a dividing line or an underlining of "repugnance to God," for emphasis. The page is evidently a continuation of the discussion of "Moral obligation," like pages [23], [24], and [25].
[25] A circle, line, and arrow connect this citation with the passage beginning

First, then, you are not your own, but belong to another by
the right of Creation. This claim is the most simple, perfect, and
absolute of all claims. Nothing is akin to it in the universe; we[n]
cannot reason about it from analogy; but when we think of it, it is
the most reasonable & satisfactory of all claims. God animates a clod
with life in a corner of his dominions: By his own power he first
orders it to be, — to hold a passive existence as a clod, out of nothing;
then, he breathes into it life — and thus from an imparting of Om-
nific Virtue, a thing is, which was not; having come from himself,
it is a part of himself; it takes the tone of existence from him alone;
can[n] aught be said to be so absolutely inevitably[,] unchangeably
God's? And for this new creature to manifest a repugnance to God,
of whom it is, is ↑incoherent[,] outrageous↓ like the rebel[22][26]lion
of my hands against my head, of my feet against my hands. Relations
are reciprocal, and the intimate unconditional sovereignty which God
holds over this being implies the most unreserved submission to his
will on the part of the creature. A denial of such implicit allegiance,
we see, we feel, outrages nature. In extreme cases, we feel that the
same law prevails. If we concieve the Divine Being inflicting pain
upon these creatures, — we[n] cannot satisfy ourselves that even persecution authorises their rebellion against his Will. For, he has as
close & near an interest in what he makes from himself as that which
he makes has for itself; and for him to pain such a creature is to
pain himself. I said above we cannot reason here from analogy, for,
men are not creators. Not even the paternal relation (which approaches the nearest to that of creation) can bear the comparison.
Because, if a father abuses his child, forgets the ties of nature, ↑&↓
encroaches upon his human rights or seeks his life — the son is not
left without resource — he can renounce those mutual claims which
his sire has refused to respect, and divesting himself of all other support can sustain himself on the simple grounds of natural rights, —

"God animates a clod. . ." below. The verses from Job read: "If thou sinnest, what
doest thou against him? or if thy transgressions be multiplied, what doest thou unto
him? If thou be righteous, what givest thou him? or what receiveth he of thine hand?
Thy wickedness may hurt a man as thou art; and thy righteousness may profit the
son of man."

[26] "Moral Obligation" is centered beneath "induced to renounce" at the bottom
of the page.

merely as a man, a citizen of the universe. [But it is important to observe how unwillingly virtue allows this ultimate resort and requires the son to honour even a brutal father. A ⟨great⟩ cogent argument which Nature offers upon this topic] That is[,] upon ⟨rights⟩ ↑relations↓ yet more native than the filial character. But the case is radically different with the creature of God & ↑with↓ ⟨the⟩ ↑a↓ son of Man. For the former has no ultimate & primal rights to throw himself back upon when he is induced to renounce his submission to God; [23][27] for God is his Maker and made those very rights which he possesses. There is no other being in the abysses of existence who might erect a hostile standard against the Throne of the Deity that afflicts him, about which the disaffected might rally and /resist/ hope/. There is no other separate ultimate resource, for, God is within him, God about him, he is a part of God himself. Nothing therefore can destroy, nothing can abridge the claim of obedience which ⟨God⟩ a Creator advances upon his creatures. Hence, the first ground of moral obligation consists in this, that, the Being who ordained it, is the Source, the Support, & the Principle of our existence and it were a kind of denying our nature to reject, that which is agreeable to him. ——

Thus far, therefore, we have considered our relation to God, as *barely existing creatures*, and shewn the impossibility of our escaping from those relations, — without any reference to the forms & circumstances of our condition. Mere animal life, in the basest & most loathsome forms, is dependent upon the Supreme Being by this law and under obligation to him. Now we add to this simple existence, a capacity ⟨of⟩ ↑&↓ means ⟨and⟩ of enjoyment, and of course accumulate the obligation by every new favour. Instead of being worms crawling in the clod, God has wrought man in a perfect mould, quickened him with exquisite senses and lastly inspired him with intelligence. To make these gifts of value, he has accomodated to them a mighty world rich with innumerable objects of beauty & grandeur; and no solitary dwelling — but crowded with beings like himself. And so constituted are they all, that from their intercourse and connection, springs the sweetest solace ⟨to their hearts.⟩ and com-

[27] "Continued" is centered beneath "complacency. Such" at the bottom of the page.

placency. Such an abode is it, that it would seem [24]²⁸ to be framed
by a mind in love with beauty and constituted with a view to that
sole end. Live as long as man may, its fairness & freshness never grows
old upon him. The bloom of summer fields; the colours of the rainbow & the cloud; the song of birds; mountain & valley ↑throughout
the changing seasons ↓; ⁿ & the heaving interminabl⟨y⟩e ocean are beautiful & grand to the last moment of life & to the last fragment of
ruined intellect. This is the pavilion God built in the beginning for
the residence of man. This is the Lord's doing & it is marvellous in
our eyes. [XII Job 7, 8, 9, 10, v.] Under every condition that we
can concieve, blessings & favours on one part, create obligations of
gratitude upon the other. And this rich inheritance of native blessings wherewith God has crowned man, lays the latter under a correspondent debt — which ⁿ must form the second ground of moral
obligation[.]

But what is the thinking organ which recieves all these enjoyments? Its endowments naturally demand a distinct consideration; for, although its agency is implied in the mere fact that we
enjoy this external nature, (as being the receptacle wherein all these
living pictures are painted) yet are its attributes so unlike those of
the world it converses with, and of such a solitary and unmixed excellence, that, as a piece of rare workmanship only, it deserves study.
God who is in our view one great congregation of all moral powers
& virtues — Who is himself the pure abstract of the moral system
has lit a ray in us of his own intelligence, has given us capacities to
see the moral distinctions he has established. Powers to understand
the Scheme upon which the Deity acts & to which he [25]²⁹ exists,
are, methinks, no small gift to a mind, nor in reality less valuable
because the Benefactor has vouchsafed them to many. ↑Nor in His
eyes is the gift small.↓ Ignorance alone can believe that the common-
ness of a blessing reduces its value. But, with these powers in his mind,
this key of the Universe in his right hand, — man, instead of opening
the sources of good, unlocks the sources of evil. A perverse infatuation which has confounded the wisdom of sages dwells upon man —

---

²⁸ "Continued" is centered beneath "the Deity" at the bottom of the page.
²⁹ "Continued." is centered beneath "the practi⟨s⟩ce of vice" at the bottom of the
page.

of which no account can be given; turning[n] aside from the road⟨s⟩
of eternity & virtue along which the light of God is burning forever,
and in which direction alone, knowledge, ↑the real glory↓ and the
final grandeur of his being reside, he forgoes it all, he barters it all,
for a base & sordid price; he strays into a slippery road of sensual
indolence & pleasure,[n] and forgets that the crooked path leads down-
wards to death. Too late he opens his eyes to its accursed accursed
seductions, and seeks in vain to let go his hold on existence and bids
the cycles of eternity which roll wearily over his head to forget him
that he may die. Memory torments him with ⟨the idea⟩ ↑those notions
to which we have just referred,↓ that his election was free of vice &
of virtue; that his mind was furnished ↑with↓ instruments & modes
of action with just views of God's moral government,[n] that motives
of such deep interest, & powerful character knocked loudly for admittance at his heart's doors. And this clearness of moral vision to determine between good & evil must be regarded as the third source of
moral obligation. Next a man's experience in the world daily adds new
ties to his moral obligations. I refer to the different emotions he is
conscious of in the practi⟨s⟩ce of vice & in the practice of virtue,[n] [26]
by which he is certified that the former is agreeable to the order of
nature and to the deeper & mightier feelings of his soul and that the
latter, however varnished by pleasure and palliated by the pleadings
of passion is deformed in its nature, pernicious in its consequences, —
and as such condemned by the high tribunal within. The sentiment of
moral approbation is moreover so unreserved, so pure & so satisfactory a feeling that it speaks to the heart in all times with a weight
& authority which belong to nothing else, and which convinces us
of its affinity & origin in real systems of right & wrong in a real
Heaven and a true God. No man in his closet enjoys the memory
of a bad action; no man colours with shame, at the sweet memory
of a good one; in[n] the battle of life when desire endeavours to make
vice amiable, when the encouragement of parasites & wrong-doers
befriends it, when opportunity seduces, and a clamorous crowd of
sinister motives ⟨rise up⟩ ↑take up arms↓ in its cause — there still ⟨is⟩
↑remains↓ enough of spiritual strength & truth; to keep down the
unquiet & peremptory protest Man cannot wholly deny his noble
nature.[n] Happy, if he give heed to the ↑unpolite but↓ wholesome

monitor and curb his mutinous passions to its law. Let your little
narrowminded bigotries of sin give place to just views of life, — not
considering it longer as an appointed day of business & lucre — nor
yet as a wild holiday of the senses which purposes to remove every
scruple & impediment to their license nor lastly as a season of soft
repose to be dreamed away in sloth — but rather as a porch & avenue
to other scenes of Being which must be traversed with circumspection
and activity if we would arrive safely at its termination in a better
country. "When a few years are come, I shall go the way whence I
shall not return." [30]

[27][31] Experience binds with the greatest tenacity because it
is so infallible a test. And I rejoice in making an appeal to it, confiding in its favourable response. What then is the character in society
which your secret ambition /has marked/ aspires after/ for your own
and who are the patterns according to which you would mould your
own condition? I am safe in asserting they are irreproachable, highminded, and virtuous men who enjoy your unreserved respect; — and
not little low lived sordid minds without any merit but diligence or
craft in the accumulation of wealth. Perchance you are under a momentary delusion, and cannot at once reconcile your ↑present↓ opinions
to this judgement. I do not ask your rash and youthful sentiment,
for I know well many snares beset and pervert it; but I appeal to
the ⟨fixed⟩ ↑solid↓ & deliberate judgement of manhood, confirmed by
the evidence of many years; — to that fair & venerated image of
moral worth which often haunts your breast, and finally folds its
wings & settles there; — I appeal to your hearts, and let them answer,
if Virtue be a deformed and loathsome thing rendering its votaries
unfit for trust and companionship or if it is not rather by the native
b⟨y⟩uoyancy & strength of virtue that individuals are forced up to
the high places of society. Immoral and unprincipled men win their
way up also to the rank & honours of the world but do they also obtain the same veneration and unshaken trust from you that the good

[30] Job 16:22. A single diagonal line running from "Let" through "shall not"
is probably a use mark.
[31] "MORAL OBLIGATION" is centered beneath "of conduct essentially" at
the bottom of the page and separated from that phrase by a long dividing line. A
small pen and ink sketch of a man's head in profile is centered in the lower third
of the page.

obtain? The secret of their unhappiness also, ever leaks out, and suppresses the wish to possess their place. A reasonable creature who sees a certain course of conduct essentially contributing to his [28]³² welfare is constrained by obvious obligation to pursue that course, and avoid an opposite one.

The next ground & the chief & last is God's Revelation to men. Before, we enjoyed his blessings without being distinctly told whence & wherefore they came. Sufficiently inclined to do homage for the physical & moral riches to which the gift of life made them heirs, they were left to grope in darkness after the Source of all; to spell out, in uncertainty, the deep enigma of His name, his will, & his designs, and no mind doubted, that, were the cloud & darkness scattered in which he clothed himself, and the bright form & perfections of the Lord of the Universe revealed to the Universe, men would welcome with ↑thankful↓ heartfelt & unmeasured hallelujahs this vision of the most high. That men would bow down, that all beings would bow down in the dust, ⟨would⟩ with eager & prostrate adoration; that one accord of gratitu⟨t⟩↑d↓e & obedience sho↑u↓ld be seen & felt when mankind were summoned from the turmoil of insignificant affairs, the bickerings of interest to behold the true image of an Omnipotent Eternal & Benevolent Mind, whom the ardent imaginations of a few ⟨minds⟩ ↑of the greatest & best of men↓ had vainly attempted to pourtray. This was the hope which men would have entertained in the prospect of such a revelation. And further, it was natural to think, that, such ⟨be⟩ gift & gospel of God would form an era in the history of the world; that it would impart a new tone to human character which would never cease to be felt, that Utopian & poetical schemes of human perfectibility of which enthusiasts had dreamed long ago but which wise men had long abandoned would now begin to be realized, and that Nature which is perfect in her ways would now be in[29]habited by beings perfect in theirs. All this appears no extravagant hope to be entertained of a revelation of the Divine being by men without such a revelation. (To be inserted before— It seemed natural & unquestionable that when God should tell men how he wished them to live and offered them an unbounded blessing

---

³² "MORAL OBLIGATION" is centered beneath "her ways would" at the bottom of the page.

& menaced them with a tremendous curse, there would be but one course to pursue, — the strong minded & the weak, the feeblest & the frailest would be so bound down to rectitude by this last moral obligation as to find it impossible to go astray.) But alas for the disappointment of these hopes! Signs & miracles & a heavenly host (procla) attended the promulgation of the Divine Character & designs in man. The most remarkable personage who ever appeared on earth brought the errand from the skies[,] a being who whether his character partook most of human or divine — came not unannounced nor departed unknown. ↑Voices in the temple↓ hundreds ⁿ of years before, — his advent, his character, his claims, & his fate were distinctly & repeatedly declared. His life fulfilled its promise. The unbeliever will admit that in the lowest condition of life he made himself venerable. The purest philosophy inculcates a spirit such as his, for the high unattainable aim of its efforts. The final catastrophe of his life was altogether worthy of him and has forced all ages to look back with awe and gratitude to the ignominious death of a reputed criminal ↑crucified↓ upon a tree — with ⁿ an insolent rabble offering the most cruel indignities around, & common malefactors beside him. Jesus Christ the Saviour of the World passed his life in publishing the character of God & his intentions respecting man and in this way chiefly has increased the weight of our moral obligation. Before, we pleaded ignorance as an apology [30][33] transgression; we can plead it no more; the ⁿ way is strait & narrow; we cannot swerve from it unwittingly.

I have now enumerated the chief grounds of moral obligation. We wish to propose the question if they could have been augmented or if they are not already as powerful & numerous as justice demands. I am [of the] opinion that we cannot augment the amount of this influence, without ⁿ subtracting from our free agency, and this is a ↑sacred↓ province upon which no claims unsupported may infringe. We are prone also in our unchastised thoughts of God's Omnipotence to think he does little or nothing in merely supplying our minds with a few vague motives when the force of the Universe is at his disposal. But ask your own better reason how else he can work upon

[33] "MORAL OBLIGATION" is centered beneath "could never persuade" at the bottom of the page.

you. It is not to curb your headlong passion and to check its mischief; it is not to vanquish your bodily strength that the Deity acts. The puny strength & rage of mortal Nature containing in itself the uneradicable seeds of decay, can never be formidable to Him; — one [n] moment, and it will crumble in dust at his feet. It is your moral will, he desires to bias, free as it is — free as his own /right hand/ omnipotence/ —; to induce it to approve the good & to hate evil. And this is an end to be compassed by none but moral means. Physical enginery & the thunder of his power can avail nothing here. Light & heat[,] fire & sword act upon bodies but have no nature or organ to move the soul. Matter contains endless forms of torture for the living body — shrinking from the acute pain of every extreme; but when the senses are shut, & the soul is separate, matter is an independent, incommunicable substance that can neither affect it nor be affected by it. And you are perfectly convinced that all the matter in the Universe could not be made to come in contact with one of your thoughts; could never persuade you, for instance, [31] that you did not exist, while you felt conscious that you did. Motives then are the engines by which God must act to gain your Will. Motives — which you derided as vague & unsubstantial things; and, which, however they may now strike us in the mire of our Clayey tabernacle, will by & by in a nobler scene command our admiration as the instruments & angels by which the whole spiritual universe lives & moves when this perishable * *material universe* shall have passed away. (* This organ of our trial or education)

It is plain common sense, it is in the alphabet of moral wisdom, that you are not fit for heaven, are not a prepared denizen of a place of perfect purity, whilst your mind is not perfectly pure. Consequently ↑even↓ if it should be according to your unreasonable desire, and God should interpose his visible omnipotence to confirm you in the right & drive you from the wrong; if you should be persuaded that instant torture would take hold on avarice, fraud, and idolatry; that fire would fall from heaven to consume the liar & blasphemer; that the earth would swallow the ⟨hom⟩↑patr↓icide; [n] in this case, though you would cease to do wrong, you would not be virtuous; fear of danger being the agent & not love of goodness, you would not be a fit inhabitant of heaven. Until your will is subdued by the discipline &

contemplation of Virtue to its love, Paradise can do without you.

Thus from the nature of the thing, Deity was reduced to one mode of influencing his creatures in their thoughts upon the good & evil of eternity. That mode he has abundantly used. All motives that were efficient he has crowded upon their notice. No violence which they may do themselves can release the⟨m⟩ir understandings from their ↑tenacious↓ hold. He has unveiled the world of Spirits to your view and intimated to you that this was to endure & the world of matter to fade that you might learn to bind [32][34] your fate to the eternal pillars of the first and risk nothing on the shortlived frailty of the last. He has spoken also in thunder to your fears & warned you of wrath to come. There is nothing in the history of human suffering, nothing in all the compass of man's inflamed & melancholy imagination which bears comparison with the tremendous menace which the violated law, utters. If infinite benevolence be exhausted in the joys of Paradise, an equal omnipotence is taxed in the punishment of crime. The sacred bards by whom God hath revealed his will to man have told this errand in dark & thrilling eloquence. No voice on earth, no accents of man ever called such awful images out of the abyss as they have invoked to strike transgression with salutary dread. Thus they have connected the commission of crime with the most revolting anguish and allured I might almost say seduced us to virtue by the pleasant security which attends it. Pass away then from the fatal way which is broad & whose gate is wide. Turn ye[,] turn ye[,] for why will ye die?[n] It will not be the fault of God nor of his prophets & priests. They have done all they could,[n] first to accumulate the load of obligation & then to shew it. ——

(I have finished the treatise begun upon the 17th page; and it is not worth much, in its present form. The operations of the Refining furnace and of the file upon it may by and by give it value.)
         Sunday Ev.g,   May

We very properly attach a degree of veneration to ⟨object⟩ things durable, as if nature had assigned to them a date proportioned to their value; and man [33][35] never feels his insignificance so forcibly

[34] "MORAL OBLIGATION" is centered beneath "proportioned to their value;" at the bottom of the page.
[35] "GOLDEN MEAN" is centered beneath "prize of existence" at the bottom

as when he compares himself to her everlasting hills, which, unchanged themselves, have beheld all changes ⟨from⟩ through the hundred generations of his race. Now the eternity of physical nature is but a metaphor of speech; an occasional comparison between the longevity of nature and man's momentary life. For in fact the whole period of the material universe may be but a span of time considered in relation to the existence of mind. (In the infinity of God, the whole system is but a spec[k] of decaying matter, whose very brightness indicates that it is consuming away.) But there is no waste no period to the Moral Universe. An antiquity that is without beginning and a futurity that is without end is its history. A principle of life & truth in itself which it is impossible to concieve of, as liable to death or suspension, or as less than infinite in the extent of its rule, binding God & man in its irreversible decree, — is coexistent with Deity. As moral beings, created into these relations of good & evil, you must partake of their nature; these relations you can never lose; this immortal duration then gives[n] them a claim paramount to all other claims. Quit then your tenacious hold upon the gay world without to make closer acquaintance with the world within. Extinguish the Sun. Annihilate[n] this solid fabric of earth. Forget the forms of li⟨v⟩fe & beauty which adorned it. What is any worth? What are all worth that they should detain the soul a moment from studying the secrets of that universal & immortal kingdom which alone will survive[n] this fair & perishable World?

It is now a very old fact that in the vulgar & equable course of human affairs, extremes of character are to be deprecated. If a man would succeed in life, he must not be too bold, nor too cautious; too close nor too kindhearted, ↑too much studied nor too ignorant↓ — nor even as the Spanish adage says — too good,[n] because a man's character must not, in all respects, run counter to his condition, but must chime in easily with it; and the equal & average mixture of elements in the constitution of the world would certainly not harmonize with an excess of any single quality in the moral disposition. To get the prize

of the page. A circle, line, and arrow direct the phrase to the paragraph beginning "It is now" above.

of existence we must comply with the terms on [34][36] which alone
it can be found. That it is well to avoid or relieve pain is plain enough,
& one might thence conclude that a light & joyous spirit which refused to be weighed down by untoward events was best fitted to en-
gage in the world. Time corrects this error. We see the need of arms
of better proof & finer temper to contend with such dangerous & inveterate foes. Human life is beset with a crowd of sorrows who never
forsake the path till it terminates in the grave; and a light heart
however graceful & becoming it may be to youth, is unable to stand
in the battle long & either falls a victim to the unnatural effort or
loses its sensibility to misfortune, & degenerates into a frivolous &
ridiculous old age. For, suffering is real & abundant & he that would
always laugh — contradicts the sympathies & bias of his nature. Suffering is the law of our condition; the great & troubled element which
girdles our world, wherein our little joys & comforts are but green
islands that are bounded by it on every side; and however we may
escape from it, for a moment into pleasant retreats yet the roar of its
waters is ever in our ears, and its barren main is ever in our eye. This
gives the human mind its melancholy cast, and forces its deepest
emotions to borrow that character, and men look with pity, as on a
zany or maniac, upon him whose hour of heartless mirth is always
present. — Our constitution would be equally defective if we could
never doff the cowl and crown ourselves with the rose & vineleaves;
if this dark shadow which eclipses & embitters our days could never
give place to gleams of light. We should ⟨in that case⟩ sink pre-
maturely with sorrow in the grave because the sinews of youthful
strength are too weakly strung for this fatal load. The true character
which God & nature indicate, and to which ↑tissues↓ God has tempered
our clay is ⟨a⟩ one of a mingled & compound texture whose prevailing
feature is a firm & temperate sobriety, lightened ever and anon by
gay & cheerful feelings — [n] dictated by a reliance upon ourselves, and
a yet firmer reliance upon Providence; by a sense of the tremendous
perils that encompass frail humanity, and a willing gratitude [35][37]
for the riches & felicity of our nature. This well compounded char-

[36] "GOLDEN MEAN" is centered beneath "frail humanity, and a" at the
bottom of the page.
[37] "MEAN" is centered beneath "better than" at the bottom of the page.

acter, this careful mean between many extremes is the golden rule for ↑all↓ our powers intellectual & moral. It is moreover the proud distinction of our human nature whereby man is privileged to stand in the lower world akin to the beings of the upper—in himself forming a golden link in the system of things to unite unlike orders. — In the brute creation, each animal is distinguished by some peculiar animal power—some one habit of life—in which he is excellent beyond all others and as long as he lives, he enjoys & improves it, without any effort to ripen other powers that may lie dormant.—— The skilful beaver is never tempted to climb the precipice & build on the mountain, and the surefooted goat never descends to dwell by the river side. Who ⟨has seen⟩ ↑ever saw↓ the ⟨sagacious⟩ elephant abandon his summer clime and endeavour to inure his frame to a polar cold, or cater for his appetite by changing his food? Who has known the bee to forsake the thrifty trade she learned of nature, and gather corn like her neighbour the ant? Where is the lion of the desart? Will he not leave his bloody prey and come to browse pleasantly on the fragrant herb? These wait all on God; they have few & single powers which they cannot alter ⟨&⟩or restrain; they can do no violence to their sensual nature, for they have no other. But Man is made their lord, and can accommodate his mind to any condition[,] his body to any clime. He can improve all his faculties and give up the reins to none. He is not so strong as they, he is not so fleet, he is not so patient of fatigue; but by tempering & harmonizing his powers each to all, he is better than the brute.   This is an idea that agrees with what we observe in nature. There is no single object so beautiful & glorious as ↑is↓ the ⟨o⟩union of many; no colour so fair as the harmony of many dies, (in the evening cloud); no stars so magnificent as the firmament of stars. One rational being is a good thing but a society of rational beings is much better. God, indeed, is *alone*, better than the Universe beside, but God [36] is the maximum of that very character we recommend to imperfect man; for he is neither all Power, nor all Justice, nor all Benevolence but the perfect proportion of all these moral elements.—— May 25.

Empire, partakes of the nature of all machines and must occasionally be wound up. Perpetual motion has never been discovered, and a perfect government must not be expected. It will answer its end more or less perfectly, and endure for a longer or shorter time in proportion to the skill of its construction. Moreover different exigencies demand different machines. The peasant wants nothing more than an hour glass to measure his day, but the astronomer must be furnished with a ↑more↓ delicate time piece; so the savage is content with the rudest mode of government, whilst Europe demands a complicate & nicely balanced policy. ——

No propitious God thundered on the left to ratify the vile, Heaven hung out no fiery cross amid the clouds to encourage the heart of the conqueror. No voice was heard but the roaring of the inhospitable main[.]

[38] With regard to the manner in which we percieve our moral obligations — we cannot if we would abstain; they surround us palpable as the air we breathe. It is no effort, it is an intuition which teaches them to us. And it is long afterward, when by learned abstraction we have learned to doubt, that in our occasional wantonness to get rid of them, we attempt to evade their force by arguments against their rigors. The pure uncorrupt mind, in retirement or in society needs no elaborate exposition of their divine source & eternal strength; (for where the noxious reptile ⟨doubts⟩ errors have not crept in, the fences of criticism are not wanted) and to such this essay is not addressed. It is directed to those, on whose minds a philosophic scepticism has had its full force,[n] — ↑and is designed↓ not to discourage but to provoke the ⟨most⟩ strictest scrutiny into this divine science. For if it will not bear this, it is not a fit code to sway the destiny of beings that ↑are↓ intellectual & immortal. It is designed not to give a full history of moral science, but to indicate some of its chief points of strength that the mind may form an adequate notion of its outline.

[37][39] [The numberless connections which ally each individual to the world seem to him by a natural delusion to be so many props giving permanency to his existence. He forgets, man in madness for-

[38] The paragraph is written in pencil in Emerson's hand.
[39] "The numberless . . . shall be" is written in the left margin from the bottom to the top of the page.

gets, notwithstanding the overwhelming mass of experience in favour of the fact that these ⟨are⟩ties are all severed at once. The parade of innumerable connections, & the habits of perfect solitude sink undistinguished[.]

> How loved how honoured once avails thee not
> To whom related or by whom begot
> A heap of dust alone remains of thee
> 'Tis all thou art & all the proud shall be]
> > [Pope, "Elegy to the Memory of an
> > Unfortunate Lady," ll. 71–74]

[Mas.] [40] "When will the plague depart? Will all my sons
            Snuff death from the wild wind, and go away
            To the dim land of spirits o'er the hills?

Seer   The bisons fed in safety in this valley
            Until thy sire set up his wigwam here
            Now they are gone to see the setting sun
            Thy people dwelt in safety in this land
            But they must flee to see the setting sun.
            Come let them now dig down the tree of peace
            Cut reeds from rivers for their poisoned shafts
            Pluck up keen flintstones for their tomahawk[s]
            And ⟨fi⟩ battle with the thunder gods of heaven,
            Hear the bald eagle scream amid the clouds
            His voice betokens blood; his eye glares bright
            O'er the great Waters to the misty isles.
            Out of the clouds Big Warriors shall come
            In swift canoes that fly on shining wings
            I see them leap like giants on thy shore
            With thunder in their hands and thy Great Spirit
            Is frighted at their Gods and leaves his skies.
            I tell thee chieftain that the coward Gods
            Fear the white tribe that ride across the deep,
            And hide their ↑shamed↓ heads ⟨behind the clouds for
                shame.⟩

[40] "Cawba." is written in pencil in the left margin opposite the first line of the poem, but it is probably not Emerson's addition. Other penciled corrections and additions in the following passage, which do not appear to be by Emerson, have in general been ignored (but see the Textual Notes).

Ah! Red Men are few;ⁿ Red men are feeble ⁿ
They are few & feeble and the eagle tribes
Must crumble ↑fast↓ away & fall in pieces

Mas.   You sing the deathsong of my tribe. Ay me
Now by my father's soul, Old Cawba say
Why are the tall warriors weak? and why does God
⟨Whom you see sitting on the mountain's top⟩
⟨Why does God⟩ ⟨s⟩Suffer the wolves to ⟨dr⟩ lap
     his children's blood?
Does the great spirit betray, or does he fear?

[38] Seer. ——ⁿ Eagle! He loves his ⟨sons⟩ children; feeds them when
They famish, saves them in the winter's storm
⟨a⟩And sends the pleasant summer full of joy
Fattening the forest families — for them. —
Then see thou blame Him not; for ⟨h⟩He is good.

Mas   Sometimes he darts his thunder at my sons
Can he not kill my enem⟨y⟩ies?

Seer   There are gods
Besides thy god, as other tribes have chiefs
Besides thy own. Eagle, thy God is weak
Waxing & waning like yon horned moon
The white man's god eternal as the sun.

Mas.   Out on your god! I'll be my people's god
Since the great spirit is afraid to fight;
They shall not lack an arm strong as his arm
And when the white canoes come o'er the sea
↑Oh may↓ ⟨T⟩their God ⟨and⟩ ↑with↓ me ⟨shall⟩ wrestle ⁿ for life
⟨O⟩Then I will fall upon them like the night
And sing my war song in their ears, and kill
⟨Until the Ocean foams with crimson waves.⟩
And stain the waterside with crimson foam
And if my warriors ⟨die⟩fall and if the foe
Prevail — then I will die, as the Eagle Chief
Should die — in fight, last of a noble tribe
And white men's dying groans ⟨shall⟩ lull ⟨me to death⟩
    ↑my last sleep↓.

(Add this to the "Moral Obligation")

Great force is given to morals if you consider the object & integrity they contribute to human life. They are strong; if they were weak, and but a faint hint or indeed no suggestion at all of this law were imparted to the mind — Life, instead[n] of being a noble & harmonious order would immediately become a wild & terrible dream. Men would ask one of another the cause & meaning of this unexplained enigma. To what purpose stand we here? Shall a tremendous event shut up this troubled scene? These tem[39]pestuous passions of ours — come let us gratify them though we slay each other, & ourselves also, to avoid some darker calamity that uncertain existence may be storing for us. A Chaos more frightful than that of nature — the Chaos of thought would make life an insupportable Curse. The intelligent universe would be deprived of the salutary restraint that supports & prolongs its awful beauty. Rend away the darkness, & restore to man the knowledge of this principle, and you have lit the sun over the world & solved the riddle of life. Now man lives for a purpose. Hitherto was no object upon which to concentrate his various powers. Now happiness is his being's end & aim. One course leads to it & the prize is secure. The distant & dark intimation of such an end, which in case of total previous privation, we should have hailed with rapture & have pursued with unconquerable diligence is made to us a rich & majestic[n] revelation and can the zeal with which we conform to its edicts ever become intemperate. Never in the eye of God; never in the eye of Seraphim & ⟨c⟩Cherubim; but often ill-timed & intemperate it would seem in the eye of men. So unerring perhaps & so judicious is human sagacity that it is ever loth to enter zealously into this subject; afraid it would seem of jeopardizing some whit the stately dignity of human nature by falling into a momentary enthusiasm in this inquiry. Out of this world, all the active intelligences that move in the heavens are absorbed in these views, are incessantly pursuing on the fiery wing of Contemplation the wonders of God's Providence into the Abyss of his works. Mind, which is the end & aim of all the Divine Operations, feeds with unsated appetite upon moral & material Nature, that is, upon the order of things which He has appointed. It is perpetually [40] growing wiser & mightier by digesting this immortal food,[n] and even in our feeble conceptions of the heavenly hosts we seek to fill up the painful chasm that divides God from his humble creatures upon earth by a magnificent series of godlike intellects. Worlds like ours were the cradles of their infancy. Their minds like ours learned the rudiments of thought from the material creation. Their ripened & godlike understandings revere the law & study the foundation principles of Morals. But man, in his nook of earth, knits his brow at the name of his Maker, & gravely apprehends that the discussion of his laws may lead to fanaticism. ↑It seems to me↓ ardour ⁿ & enthusiasm are the appropriate feelings which belong to things of Eternity and make the *habits* of Angels; but Man waxes cold & slow at the word; & fears to commit himself upon these topics in the presence of his fellow worms. But this waywardness, in the end, grows to presumption & there is a time when ⟨the⟩ slighted opportunity ceases to return. He that is deaf to the suit of Virtue must make up his mind to pay the debt to Vengeance. This law, this violated law of morality, which you refused to study, is still the statute of the Eternal Universe, and your fate hangs upon its decree. The stern compensation which it enacts, may mete out ⟨a⟩ ↑some↓ tremendous retribution of wrath upon the head of Crime that violated, of Apathy & Frivolity that spurned it.

June 1, 1823.

"Praise is the salt that seasons right for man
And whets the appetite for moral good."
[Young, *Night Thoughts*, "Night VII," ll. 420–421]

Dat veniam corvis, ↑vexat↓ censura columbas.⁴¹

[41]⁴² Men so universally draw their characters after the pattern of their times that great regard is due to any who spurning the character & humour of an ignoble age, act upon principles not apprehended by the vulgar. Upon this ground we claim veneration for the forefathers of N. England, who were an association of men that for once in the history of the world forgot to found their plans

⁴¹ "Our censor absolves the crow and passes judgment on the pigeon." Juvenal, *Satires*, II, 63.
⁴² "TRADE" is centered beneath "and faint;" at the bottom of the page, and the insertion is crowded in just above it.

↑exclusively↓ upon the interests of *trade*, and preferred to *trade*, the finer interests of Religion & literature. Trade was always in the world, and indeed, to judge hastily, ⟨of the world⟩ we might well deem trade to have been the purpose for which the world was created. It is the Cause, the support & the object of all government. Without it, men would roam the wilderness alone; and never meet in the kind conventions of social life; Who is he that causes this busy stir[,] this mighty & laborious accommodation of the world to men's Wants; ⟨and⟩ Who is he that plants Care like a canker at men's hearts, and furrows their brows with thrifty Calculations; that makes Money for his instrument, and therewith sets men's passions in ferment & their faculties in action, unites them together in the clamorous streets or arrays them against each other in War? It is Trade — Trade — which is the mover of the nations and the pillar whereon the fortunes of life hang. ↑All else is subordinate.↓ Tear down, if you will, the temples of Religion, the Museums of Art, the Laboratories of Science, ⟨and⟩ the libraries of Learning — and the regret excited among mankind would be cold, alas! and faint; a ⁿ few would be found, a few enthusiasts in secret places to mourn over their ruins — but destroy the temples [42][43] of Trade, your stores, your wharves & your floating castles on the deep; ⟨and⟩ restore to the Earth, the silver & the gold which was dug out ⟨for⟩ ↑thence to serve↓ *his* purposes; — and you shall hear an outcry from the ends of the Earth. Society would stand still & men return howling to forests & caves which would now be the grave, as it was once the cradle of the human race. This partial & inordinate success by which this institution of men ⟨h⟩ wears the crown over all others is necessary; for the prosperity of trade is built ⟨a⟩upon desires & necessities which nourish no distinction among men; which, all — ↑the high & humble, the weak & strong↓ can feel, — and which must first be answered, before the imprisonment of the mind can be broken & the noble & delicate thoughts can issue out, from which Art & Literature spring. The most enthusiastic philosopher requires to be fed & clothed before he begin his analysis of nature[,] and scandal has called poetry, taste, imagination, the ⟨ph⟩ overflowing phantasms of a highfed animal. True, Archimedes forgot for a moment in the Sicilian Capital the rigid laws of decorum when he

[43] "TRADE" is centered beneath "*traffic*, which he" at the bottom of the page.

found the theory of the tides, & fiery poets have lived who defied the vile necessities of the flesh & wrote obstinately on, until they starved; but these are ↑instances↓ rare & extraordinary and are only quoted ↑in evidence,↓ as *miracles* by which the reality of these ⟨things⟩ ↑lower revelations↓ was to be attested; and [n] ↑in despite of them all↓ the Scholar is quickly taught the unwelcome ⟨truth⟩ ↑conviction↓, that, his studies are the later luxuries, which the world can easily forego; whilst it cannot spare its meat & its drink & the interests of *traffic*, which he holds in contempt.

[43] [44] The justice and propriety of this early preference to trade we are not so blind as to doubt; we only lament the poverty of our nature which makes us heirs to such inconveniences. But we complain that here we find new instances of the imperfection of our mind — which by that universal misapprehension of the means for the end — after the wants are gratified, which trade proposed to gratify, continues to pursue with unslaked appetite these concerns which have ceased to be necessary — to the exclusion of those nobler pursuits which bring honour & greatness upon our race. This mistake is a sore evil under the sun and under some broad form or other offends us every day. The Merchant said in his heart, I will amass treasure & then buy me these pleasures of Refinement & Science; when [n] I am free from the fear of want, I will call the Muses from Helicon & sacrifice at their altars. And he unfurled his canvass on the sea and sent men on his errands of gain to all corners of the earth. And his purpose seemed good in the eye of the Genii of the air & the Mermaids of the deep. His white sails were swelled with favourable winds and the Mermaids sung pleasantly to his Mariners to cheer them on their way. ⟨The o⟩Ores of gold & silver, Mines of diamond & shores of pearl, spice groves of the East & plantations of the West were ransacked to heap the amount of his wealth; but when his will was done & the progress of years added new accumulations to his wealth, — in the abundance of his schemes he [44] forgot his youthful promises for the application of his wealth, he forgot to invoke the Muses & call the Arts and Philosophy to adorn his dwelling. Alas he was fast yoked into the thraldom of Care, — painfully gathering riches for another to enjoy — and niggardly denying himself the

[44] "TRADE" is centered beneath "in the abundance" at the bottom of the page.

best fruits of his toil. This history of the individual is the history of the nation. Thousands wished well to the scanty Godlike band who kindled & bore the torch of improvement thro' the darkness of the world; — and were well nigh persuaded to abandon their own sordid pursuits & ally themselves to their cause. Nations ripened into civilization & crowded with an enlarging population the narrow confines God gave them to possess, but it was Trade who sent out the superfluous numbers in colonies to people distant territories. Phoenicia, Greece, & Rome, vaunting the liberality of their policy had no loftier motive than the extension of their taxes & their trade. ——

A reading selected from *29 & 30* chapters of Job, admits of great eloquence — Note the pauses after "now" which occur thrice
____ [45]

[45] [46] The obligation of all the virtues is nearly the same as their foundation is one; viz, their conformity, however unexplained or little understood, to the laws of an intuitive sense. It is mere affectation [—] though sometimes supported by subt⟨e⟩lety & sometimes by effrontery [—] it is a vain affectation & known to be such to the Pretender himself, to deny the force of this law. All objects in the universe, far as the eye can reach & thought can comprehend them, fulfil some purpose, and are parts of some plan; and [n] whatsoever things the infancy of knowledge once regarded as exceptions to this prevailing order, the advancement of knowledge has brought in to fill a chasm in the regular series of things & beings. Mind, which in human nature creeps ⟨i⟩on its ⟨progress⟩ ↑long journey to the source of things↓ with a snail's pace, (compared with the intellects he is fond of imagining,) by the excellent necessity of its nature, *expands*, as it proceeds; and, in this late age, when it looks no longer with the timid glance of a child, but with the experienced eye of Centuries

[45] In chapter 29 Job reviews the glories of his former years; in chapter 30 he laments their loss. The "pauses" occur in the following verses: 30:1, "But now they that are younger than I have me in derision . . ."; 30:9, "And now am I their song, yea, I am their byword"; 30:16, "And now my soul is poured out upon me. . . ."

[46] "MORALS" is centered beneath "the question" at the bottom of the page. Near the lower right corner " 'The X H" is written over the text downward from "the object" above to "where the" below.

into the bosom of nature, it is able to unite things severed by long
intervals, to compare mean beginnings with remote & mighty results,
& thus to restore order to a Chaos of mighty things, where, in time
past the grandeur of the object outwent the capacity of the Observer;
so that ↑even↓ the slow & halting march of human science continually
discovers the divine adjustment of circumstances to fulfil purposes.
This is the amount of all our insight into nature, the discovery of
the purpose; and wherever we are at fault in our search our whole
views ⟨are⟩ become loose & unsettled; the fact where the study fails
is regarded as monstrous. Now, in all the varieties of this investigation the question recurs to the investigator — What [46] is the purpose of Man? Or is all nature, from suns & stars, to the root & the
clod — instinct & dignified with design, & Man alone, the thinking
inhabitant & the peerless lord of all — an insulated & casual creation?
In this vast theatre of being, in the tremendous uncertainty that shuts
up the future around the ⟨action⟩ present activity of Nature's immense
family of worlds & beings; what,[n] & where, I pray you, is his security
from its possible convulsions? Is his lot cast upon the waters of chance?
Is he ⟨independen⟩ unallied to Nature & independent of God? Then
when Change & Destruction, those terrible agents in the Universe,
obey their lord, & take hold on life & matter & dissipate the parent
elements, when[n] Thought is gathered ↑through all its infinite chan-
nels↓ to its Divine Fountain, & Goodness to its reward, & Matter is
dissolved — ↑then↓ can his will bridle the ministers of the Universe,
& stop the⟨ir⟩ almighty operation? But the man who denies a moral
design to his existence, thus sets himself adrift upon wild & unknown
seas. — Man's early impulse & abiding feelings distinctly indicate an
obedience to certain laws of moral action as the design of his present
being; leading him up to a qualification & fitness for better existence.
Obedience to each command of this law is Virtue & disobedience Vice.
— *Else* — to what purpose have these useless thousands & millions
of men lived, &c[.]

There is an important view striking the very foundation of
moral accountability which I shall attempt to present. I cannot blame
for I do not feel a contradiction to Divine Justice in the alarming
result of God's experiment on earth. Men have thought, that if a
fair & equal election of good & ill & their respective rewards be

offered to Man, it cannot be that so huge a majority of wrong doers should burden the Earth. Sin they say is too strong, it hath too many pleasures & too [47] many apologies, — for our integrity. If purity be necessary to my salvation↑,↓ — God should not have made it so difficult to be pure.[n] I answer, if Temptation were tenfold stronger than it is, I see not, with what face, this poor palliation of guilt could be advanced. For, all the most clamorous invitations that Vice ever offered, ⟨when⟩ ↑the moment↓ they are brought into close comparison with the Recompense offered to Virtue do so shrink into mute & secret insignificance that they lose every shadow of effect. Nothing ⟨that⟩ ever occurred to man's fiery imagination bearing any proportion as a picture of delight to the promises granted to Obedience. Being then so infinite in their excellency & out of all comparison with meaner things, it follows that the moment they are considered they must be embraced. It is hard then to find any counterbalance which should present an⟨y⟩ obstacle in the way of innocence, any opposite induce-ment of weight enough, to create an election, — & thereby Virtue. God gave man Senses which he might pervert, passions that he might indulge to excess — these acting, not to balance the just influence of Eternal Happiness but to lead him astray from making the Com-parison. At the same time ↑he is↓ not kept aloof ↑from↓ opportunity & knowledge[n] for comparing these principles. The Revelation is full[,] the knowledge is obtruded upon his notice from without, & by the importunate whisper of Conscience within; and[n] if he persists in barring out from his thoughts the light & beauty of Heaven, I know not how he can deem himsel‖f‖ hardly dealt by.

[48] June 11. ——   Epilogue.

When Memory rakes up her treasures, her ingots of thought, I fear she will seldom recur to the Muse's tenth son; and[n] yet it should have been able to gather & condense something from the wealth of fancy which Nature supplies in the beautiful summer. I have played the Enthusiast with my book in the greenwood, the huntsman with my gun; have sat upon rocks, & mused o'er flood & fell, have indulged the richest indolence of a Poet & am therefore a creditor to Nature for some brilliant & unusual inspiration. But the Goddess is slow of payment — or has forgotten an old bantling. If she was partial once,[n]

she is morose now; for Familiarity, (if awful Nature will permit
me to use so bold a word,) breeds disgust; & Vinegar is the son of
Wine; [47] peradventure [n] I may yet be admitted to the contemplation
of her inner magnificence, & her favour may find me, no shrine indeed, but some snug niche, in the temple of Time. 'Tut,' says Fortune — 'and if you fail, — it shall never be from lack of vanity.'
[R. W. E.]

Labour is the son of Resolution & the father of ⟨g⟩Greatness,
of Health & Wealth. The family is a very thriving one, though it is
infested not uncommonly by an execrable vermin called ⟨c⟩Care.

> Go if your ancient but ignoble blood
> Has crept thro' scoundrels ever since the flood
> Go & pretend your family is young
> Nor own your fathers have been fools so long
> What can ennoble sots or ⟨fools⟩ ↑slaves↓ or cowards
>   [Pope, *Essay on Man*, ll. 211–215]

[47] See p. 104 above.

Wide World II

1823

The third in the sequence of journals bound together, this journal was originally entitled "Wideworld No 11" and was later given the letter designation L. The dated entries begin on June 13, 1823, immediately following the last entry of Wide World 10, but are interrupted during August when Emerson made the summer excursion recorded in the journal "Walk to the Connecticut." On his return early in September, Emerson continued to make entries in this journal, though somewhat sporadically, from September 6 until December 13, 1823.

Wide World 11 is composed of eleven folded sheets of unlined paper, measuring approximately 16.8 x either 20 or 20.8 cm. The twenty-two leaves have been sewed separately into three gatherings of six, eleven, and five leaves each, hand-stitched together, and subsequently sewed by white thread with Wide World numbers 9, 10, and 12. The pencil pagination (probably not by Emerson) runs sequentially from 1 through 40. The final two leaves are unnumbered except for the last page, erroneously numbered 42. The pages numbered 13, 36, 39, and 42 carry writing which appears upside down in relation to the other matter on the page. In addition, the final two leaves carry a sequence of back to front writing that ends on the page numbered 40, which page is designated by subscript numbers as a repeated page.

[1][1]   1823.   Wideworld   No 11   L
June 13.

The writings of men, & the pictures they have drawn of the world are not for the most part histories of facts but of feelings. We are tangled round in such a web of associations that scarce any thing affects ⟨us independently of all else, in one solitary manner⟩ ↑*the whole world in one manner*↓ but awakens ↑a thousand↓ trains of ideas

---

[1] Four pen sketches of male heads, possibly intended as caricatures, appear in the left margin, from "⟨us independently" down to "monsters" below. A large profile of a man's head in ink appears in the text, from "*world in one*" down to "door is one" below.

in a thousand different persons connected in each with the peculiar
circumstances of his Education. The ordinary views under which
society is regarded by many minds, would appear altogether extravagant to others and the same scenes & one wor⟨d⟩ld are multiplied into unnumbered varieties in their modes of affecting men. For
this reason, broad caricatures have been gravely drawn of human
nature & long & obstinately supported as truth. The history of philosophy is in great part a list of such systems. ⟨The world is represented
as⟩ ↑Here is a man who calls the world↓ a den of monsters in ⟨ma⟩
divers shapes agreeing only in malignity & next door is one who paints
it in rich & gaudy hues[,] whose pencil of light has hardly a shade to
darken any corner of this Paradise where Virtue & Happiness abide
in every form. And Man is an Angel of light walking in the Universe [2] with the dignity of an immortal being. Because of the essential
inseparable individuality of every mind, the universe is new & distinct to it as much as if there were no fellow to share in the destinies
& enjoyments of the growing being. Important as [2] our sympathies
are to our happiness & close & tender as they are to our hearts still
they are so remote as not to hurt our /personal integrity/individual-
ity/ or abridge in the least our responsibility. The ways of good &
ill are open & unobstructed. No man can interfere with our Walk
therein and no apology can be pleaded for the perversity of our
choice. Though the moral way be clear & uniform, the intellectual
path is devious & grotesque. ——Phantoms of sight that have no real
existence, distorted pictures of life, & changeful spectacles that flutter
in the horizon of hope give wild & various aspe↑c↓t to the journey
↑on↓ which he is travelling. Truth requires that the fabulous accounts
of man be sifted carefully and that we neither believe the world to
be peopled with unthinking varlets of blood & dust, nor yet with
tribes of majestic demigods. If, in this dreamy world, we would
keep the path of Common sense, we must carefully pick our way between many extremes — and we shall everywhere find that Nature
mixes ⟨up⟩ the Angel & the brute in the moulding of Man. We shall
mark every where the certain traces of Nature's hand in her equal &
pervading Compensations, taking an unit from the rich and adding

[2] "Universe" is encircled by a line that also encloses "every" in the preceding
sentence.

an unit to the poor, strictly economical in all her immense liberality, dealing out the qualities of human character in the same just measure that gives fleetness to one animal, might to another, & cunning to a third without suffering any one to monopolize all her favour. This mixture & community of nature's gifts ⟨man⟩ is remarkable throughout the Universe & especially in man. The proud lord of the lower creation finds for himself no partial exception [3]³ from Nature's law. He is never permitted to indulge the imagination that there is no higher power present than himself or that mighty Nature relaxes ⟨in favour to him⟩ ↑for his sake↓ one iota of the Statutes of the universe. —— (Dead ere it reached its original idea. One more of my extensive family of still born trains.) Aceldama Aceldam

Shell   — Upon the aversion of Men of taste to
hell   Evangelical Religion.⁴ — Steam
ell

In the world, we are perpetually reminded of natural connections & adaptations of parts to parts, & systems to systems. In material, & in human nature, this design is alike evident. It is ⟨res⟩ sufficiently extraordinary that a pause[,] a chasm in this order should appear in man's greatest relation, viz. his intercourse with Deity. In our daily observation of men we ⟨find⟩ ↑see↓ every mind seek & find its appropriate food. Little minds ⟨grasp little things⟩ are content to grasp trifles. The hard mysteries & difficult conclusions of science, the sublime secrets of the mind — they abandon with indifference. Ardent & profound genius pursues these, and finds the easy & grateful exercise of its powers, in the toilsome search. And men fall so readily into their several habits of intellectual nourishment, that if we find an abstruse problem, an elevating moral sentiment, a conundrum or a straw, [4] we can generally indicate with sufficient precision our neighbour, to which each will be welcome. Thus it is in general, & these sympathies are not commonly contradicted. The madman &

³ Five pen and ink sketches of male heads are scattered in the lower half of the page.
⁴ The little essay on pp. [4]–[6], including the title, is crossed through by a single wavy line on each page, probably to indicate use.

ideot stand on equal ground; philosopher shakes hands with philosopher; but yoke Newton & a clown in unequal society & you find the⟨ir⟩ intercourse insufferably tedious to both. Heaven opens its broad arch to one & fills with mighty visions his mighty mind. The other drivels, perchance, upon ↑rags &↓ vermin. Having made this observation in innumerable instances we hope that such a harmony finds place in all; that Mind matches mind, Weakness hath pleasure in weakness, Greatness meets greatness. If the observer should find a mind which by the exercise of transcendant powers & the possession of unrivalled advantages had acquired a manner of thinking vastly superior to any other & to all other minds and should ⟨hav⟩ see this superiority proved by numerous undoubted instances of profound contrivance & grandeur of design, he would anticipate the joy with which all ambitious & generous spirits would welcome his approach & seek to ally themselves to him. It is with surprise therefore & sorrow that he finds that men of lofty genius turn with aversion from the idea of GOD. Instead of that uncontrollable delight with which we thought the soul would attempt to link itself mind to mind in unequal companionship with the Spirit which encompasses the universe — it ⟨tur⟩ recoils or [5] limits itself to a cold confession of his existence & attributes. So unwelcome & unnatural facts demand a careful explanation. A pardonable indignation has led many minds astray, and has permitted them to account for the ingratitude of man by assigning him a perverse nature which reflects upon the Justice & Wisdom of his ⟨nature.⟩ Maker.

The moral relations by which God has encompassed man in order to enable him by a free election of opposite principles to work out his own salvation, to deserve a reward, lie at the foundation of all our feelings. According to the manner in which these relations have been sustained, whether wrongly or rightly, so is the tenor & spirit of all our thoughts. Cherish them or violate them — we can never divest ourselves of them[,] we can never become independent of their influence. They are too inseparably interwoven[5] into our minds, — too much a part of us — to be readily torn away. Very early in life we become acquainted with these strange & sacred elements for which life is given. They admit of no middle course or neutral ground

[5] "P." is written opposite "interwoven" in the left margin.

& therefore we very soon begin to resist or obey their stern & pure laws. Of course all our feelings towards God[,] the author of those laws[,] are immediately affected by our choice. Human virtue is frail. Youth surrenders its integrity to temptation and by the law of our nature which I have named cannot keep its feelings pure when actions, which are their source have become impure. Then comes in, besides, the stinging [6]⁶ slighted & insulted kindness. We know among men how the sense of old & injured love envenoms present hatred; & our hearts are obliged to carry something of this feeling to our thoughts of God when they swell with remorse for the violation of his law. ——

Upon Men's Apathy to their Eternal interests.

Man sows the wind today to reap the whirlwind tomorrow. Youth is a mistake; Manhood is the bitter disappointment of a discovery; Age with its tardy crutch retraces the wrong steps but ↑belated in the Night of Death↓ is interrupted by the grave which yawns in its path. This is the history of the species; & ⟨the history of⟩ all the individuals var⟨g⟩y little from each other. Ambition, Avarice, Fame, Love, Patriotism, whatever be the ruling passion — its fortunes are nearly the same. It is nourished in the beginning by extravagant hopes & poisoned at last by their failure. The respective lots of life of different men though variously coloured are wrought of one substance & cast in one mould. To keep society from one uniform monotony, producing an absolute stagnation of character[,] we magnify the differences which exist and affect to draw a wide interval between Alexander & Diogenes[,] between Cicero & Cataline. In the pageant of life, Time & Necessity are the stern masters of ceremonies who admit no distinctions among the vast train of aspirants. In the relentless [7]⁷ conformity which is exacted to their iron law, all minor inequalities ⟨are obliterated⟩ ↑disappear↓. And though the appetite of

⁶ "APATHY" is centered beneath "train of aspirants." at the bottom of the page. "Random" is scrawled across the page upward from "failure" below to "yawns" above, and below it is apparently a careless attempt at the same word.
⁷ "APATHY" is centered beneath "progress of" at the bottom of the page. A pen and ink sketch of a man and eight pen and ink profiles are scattered across the page. "Sand" is scrawled crosswise on the page and repeated three times in smaller letters. "Vade in Pace" (Go in Peace) and "Pax" (Peace) also appear near the bottom of the page.

youth for marvels & beauty is fain to draw deep & strong lines of
contrast between one & another character we early learn to distrust
them & to acquiesce in the unflattering & hopeless picture which Experience exhibits. We dreamed of great results from peculiar features
of Character. We thought that the overflowing benevolence of our
youth was pregnant with kind consequences to the world; that the
agreeable qualities in the boy of courage, activity, intelligence, & good
temper would prove in the man Virtues of extensive & remarkable
practical effect. The momentary ardour of childhood found that manhood & age were too cold to sympathise with ↑it↓, & too hastily in-
ferred that its own merit was solitary & unrivalled & would by and
by blaze up, & make an era in Society. Alas. As it grew older it also
grew colder & when it reached the period of manhood & of age it
found that the ⟨course of nature⟩ ↑waters of time, as they rolled↓ⁿ
had extinguished the fire that once glowed & there was no partial
exemption ⁿ for itself. The course of years rolls an unwelcome wisdom with them which forcibly teaches the vanity of human expectations. We learn in season to cure our hopes on this side death, that
the magnified differences of mind & nature are really very small, &
that the progress of years melts these varieties [8][8] down into an
uniform mass. And hence we gather an important inference[,] that
intellectual nature does not take the first rank in the scale of excellence but that it is subservient to one still higher. We begin
to discover that our understandings have an ultimate aim beyond
their own perfection — viz to be employed about moral excellence.
Two Elements there are to which the Universe exists, Mind &
Morals. Strangely & essentially connected as they ↑are↓ our most
curious speculations are employed in discriminating them. Morals we
cannot concieve existent without mind: though perhaps it is not impossible to concieve mind without morals. In their adjusted combination we feel that they ↑form↓ object[s] for whose pursuit we are introduced into being. All in whom is once kindled the unquenchable
spark of life look forward to a change of being & a subsequent allotment of condition for the great Duration they are just beginning to
partake. That allotment comes sooner to some than to others but
comes to all. The change that precedes it we call Death. That the

[8] "APATHY" is centered beneath "makes a parade" at the bottom of the page.

allotment of condition depends upon the character stamped upon our existence previous to the change, is the only fact regarding this awful Universe of which we can speak with certainty. Man makes a parade of his knowledge [9][9] of the little corner in space which he is permitted to inhabit,[n] or rather of its appearance in his imagination; — but what the living Universe ⟨is⟩[,] the moral existing System of things really is, we do not know. We have a vague notion of an inconcievable infinity [10] extending around us in life & thought necessarily existing & existing forever — something in which by and by we shall be called to take a part. We give to this magnificent mystery, and[n] to our own connexion with it, An Author, who is God; — & this is the limit of our view. This glimpse which we catch of our nature & fates is full of solemn majesty; but there is another part of the picture, which, when we have duly pondered this, is likely ⟨f⟩to surprise & disappoint us. That stage of the existence to which our actual knowledge is confined is the first period or the passage of the young candidates for Eternity from the birth of /their/his/ being to the Change which is to introduce /them/him/ to the world of spirits. I behold the millions of my fellow beings who are on this perilous way, who are in the present expectation of the prodigious revolution which ⟨it⟩ is to come upon their lot. I see them standing on the brink of this unknown & infinite existence but their brows want that care[,] that awful anxiety which is so becoming to their condition & which I expected to see. On that tremendous brink they sported with indifference; amusing themselves at their ease, each one with his toy. I say that phi[10]losophy is surprised & disappointed to see this stage of life. When we had a right to expect in the youthful probationer a⟨n⟩ wakeful and active mind keeping watch in the Universe if, by any means, he might pry into the secrets of Eternity. He Continued (A) [11]

Does the consent to an injury lessen the crime? In what does the crime consist? ↑I↓ If it consists in the ⟨evil⟩ ↑mischief↓ brought upon the victim ↑& on the world↓, that mischief is not the less because

---

[9] "APATHY" is centered beneath "with his" at the bottom of the page.

[10] Tiny x's under "inconcievable infinity" may indicate emphasis, like underlining.

[11] See below p. 155. "A" is encircled. "Coquetry" is written upside down beneath it.

the victim recieved it freely. Those who build up all morality upon a general Expediency, will find a verdict against the Wrongdoer; because the interests of society as peremptorily required that he should abstain from the action as if the Victim had also forbidden it. Take the familiar instance of Adultery. The injury done to the world by one known instance of this crime far exceeds it appears to me the mischief of a Rape. The crime ⟨un⟩consented to has a less atrocious but not less pernicious form. And in the immediate personal effect upon the victim is altogether as bad. It may be said that the ⁿ wretched woman who consents to be an adulteress is already depraved to the last degree & is not made worse by the indulgence of her passions. Depraved she is to a very great, [11₁] but not to the last degree. The shocking familiarity with vice which she here learns, is a fatal stroke to whatever remains, there might be, of moral life; there is no hope beyond. And the Accomplice of her Crime has therefore done her an immense & irreparable injury.

Besides what is *Consent?* It is not a *request* — it is ↑only↓ an abetting of the injurer's intentions on the part of the victim's passions. It would not have been given, the crime would not have been committed but ⟨i⟩on the application of the offender. Knowing this, it was his imperious duty to have fled far away and (setting aside his own criminality) have saved those pernicious effects to the world & the unfortunate individual. ¹²And it is vain to ⟨say if⟩ urge as a palliation of the offender's guilt, that if he had not been a sharer in the crime, the crime would nevertheless have been perpetrated by some other. Let me ask if the ↑man↓ would be innocent who should murder a convict on his way to the gallows? —— Besides, it should [12₁] have been observed above, that, this species of Consent is unlike any other; — and when well considered is nothing but an ignorant & foolish sacrifice of what would not have been, at any rate, forfeited, if the individual had distinctly understood the exact condition in which she (or he) stood.

[11₂] II   But those who did not build upon Expediency and who claim to human agency an intuitive moral sense will make another

---

¹² The passage from "And" to "stood." begins near the bottom of the page and is headed "Insert". It is placed here in accordance with Emerson's directions — an asterisk after "individual." and one before "And".

⟨case⟩answer to the question ⟨oft⟩ concerning the nature of ⟨the⟩ Crime. Crime consists not in the effect upon others nearly or remotely ⟨but in the motive⟩ nor in the mere doing of the deed, but in the determination to that effect existing in the mind.

[12₂][13] Though the ruffian's hand be arrested as he is planting his dagger in your heart, he is a murderer still & if he die that moment dies with the same responsibility as if his hand were red with your blood. The Crime consists in that breaking over the ⟨command⟩ ↑law of conscience↓ which was necessary to that determination he has formed. Now can the consent of the offended party annul this law which the ⟨criminal⟩ ↑offender↓ violates? Does it not amount to this? the thing which he doth — man says — 'thou shalt do,' — & God says — 'thou shalt not do.'   To be Continued [14]

Sept. 6.[15] —— A young man who is gathering up his bundle of experience counts many matters of old observation to be his own discoveries. Many of these are notices of manners & the peculiarities of ordinary social intercourse, which as they are ⟨seldom⟩ evanescent & seldom recorded, it is obvious must be left to the acuteness & industry of each young person to ⟨gather up⟩ collect for himself. Each one [13] enjoys the satisfaction of making these discoveries anew. The subjects to which they relate are the noblest in nature — his fellow men; & the period in which they are made, adds enthusiasm to the interest with which they are regarded. The meeting of man with man and the new impulse given to two minds by their communion, and the ↑rapid↓ accomodation of their unlike tones ⟨of two minds⟩ ↑of thought↓ to each other, are, to his mind, new & curious phenomena. He remarks how fast the adjustment is made of rival intellectual claims; how easily each mind ascertains the inferior or superior nature of its neighbour to its own & how quietly this ⟨&⟩ dear preeminence is conceded with a submission that makes no appeal. He notices the harmony of some minds & the discordance of others. Two individuals

[13] Four pen and ink profiles of male heads and two full face sketches are scattered on this page.

[14] The continuation appears not to have been written.

[15] During a part of the period between this and the preceding entry, from Aug. 22 to Sept. 4, Emerson took a walking trip to the Connecticut River. The journal of this trip is printed below, pp. 177–186.

will sometimes meet, who both stand on cordial terms with the rest
of the world, but find themselves constrained to assume towards each
other a sour caustic tone[.]

[16] It is easier a thousandfold to love justice, sincerity, humility,
& grandeur of soul, than to be just, sincere, humble, & magnanimous.
It is easier to love, than to forbear loving them. By the beneficent
necessity of our nature we are ↑thus↓ constrained. And then we swell
with pride at this fancied rhapsody of virtue. It is a fine remark
which I once heard from a popular preacher of the present day,ⁿ that
⟨we⟩men always judge themselves by their best moods; judging ⁿ
then that we are highly virtuous from our momentary disposition to
be pleased by virtue, we decieve ourselves.

[14]   Canterbury Sept., 1823.
    I have often found cause to complain that my thoughts have
an ebb & flow. Whether any laws fix them & what the⟨y⟩ ↑laws↓ are
I cannot ascertain. I have quoted a thousand times the memory of
Milton & tried to bind my thinking season to one part of the year
or to one sort of weather; to the sweet influence of the Pleiades, or
to the summer reign of Lyra. The worst is, that the ebb is certain,
long & frequent, while the flow comes transiently & seldom. Once
when *vanity* ⁿ was full fed, it sufficed to keep me at work & to produce
some creditable scraps; but alas! it has long been dying of a galloping
starvation & the Muse, I fear me, will die too. The dreams of my
childhood are all fading away & giving place to some very sober &
very disgusting views of a quiet mediocrity of talents & condition —
nor does it appear to me that any application of which I am capable,
any efforts, any sacrifices could at this moment restore any reasonableness to the familiar expectations of my earlier youth. But who is he
that repines? Let him read the song about the linter-goose.[17]
    Melons & plums & peaches, eating & drinking & the bugle, all
the day long. These are the glorious occupations which engross a

[16] The following paragraph is written upside down at the bottom of the page.
[17] There is almost no textual justification for this reading, which seems to be
"linber-goose", but "linber" has been found in no dictionary, and in *J*, I, 285, it
is printed "linter." This is a form of the American colloquial word "lean-to," and in
Massachusetts it meant also "a cattle-feeding trough." Whatever Emerson's intention,
the song has not been located.

proud & thinking being, running his race of preparation [15] for the eternal world. Man is a foolish slave who is busy in forging his own fetters. Sometimes he lifts up his eyes for a moment, admires freedom, & then hammers the rivets of his chain. Who does not believe life to be an illusion when he sees the daily, yearly, livelong inconsistency that men indulge, in thinking so well & doing so ill. Young men, who from time to time, take pleasure in ascertaining their own rights & claims on the universe, who measure with laudable eagerness what portion of good, life is heir to[,] [18] of the esteem of mankind th⟨a⟩ey ⟨have a⟩ ↑may↓ fairly expect to reward their future powers & virtues — though they resolve fervently & ponder much on the goodness of their ⟨att⟩intentions [n] though for ⟨a time⟩ sometime their hearts are wrapt & their faces glow with magnanimous hopes & fancied selfdevotion to the cause of God & Man — yet these — when by & bye, the flush has gone from the countenance, & the ordinary temptations of indolence, of sensual gratification, return upon them — are accustomed to forget the noble promises they ↑just now↓ plighted to heaven & their own souls, & the lavish good dispositions of their excited hours. They forget for a long & weary interval that ⟨not⟩ to eat, ↑&↓ to drink, ⟨is⟩& to lie down in sleep is not the life of man but the life of swine; — that meats & ⟨drinks⟩ wines & dress ⟨do⟩ are not the real ends of existence, but *thought, affection, & virtue,* [n] [16][19] that God is not honoured nor man served by misspent or vacant time. To sit day after day[,] nay month after month amid the sufferings & cries ↑of↓ ⟨the⟩ barren ignorance & rank depravity — to hear on every side the frightful burden of human lamentation, curses, & fears rising on the winds to heaven, to read by our warm & ⟨pea⟩ idle firesides the miserable report of all evil that is done under the sun; & this without a solitary effort of charity[,] without stirring hand or foot to rescue & save ⟨is a mean & accursed resignation⟩ because we are given up to a mean sloth which is accursed of God & good men — is the sort of approbation which we deem fittest to secure ↑our future↓ happiness. We ⟨are content to⟩ bury in an undefined procrastination, all our obligations. We should be shocked at any formal resignation in words of our hopes of activity in life, while our abominable list-

---

[18] The phrase "of good, life is heir to" is circled, possibly for revision.
[19] "APATHY" is centered beneath "man had" at the bottom of the page.

lessness amounts to the same. You call the squandered hour — a
reverie. — It is, say you[,] a casual relaxation which nature requires
but the real objects of existence will grow dim[n] & dimmer in your
sight, until your eyes are shut fast, & you will sleep out life in this
⟨disastr⟩ desperate reverie — the purposes for which you live un-
sought[,] unfound.

Continued from A [20]

We borrowed a dye from our own fresh emotions to colour the
thoughts we supposed them to entertain. We shuddered when we
looked at the majestic lines in which the fate of man had been drawn
[17][21] and easily supposed that they also would be alive to our
alarm. When an eternal life was risked, and infinite happiness to be
/lost or won/bought or sold/ — we were not able to be calm. We
thought we should catch some outward sign of this burdensome responsibility in the children of men; [n] that the⟨ir⟩ brow would labour
with doubt; that their joy would burst out into jubilee, when the
⟨p⟩hope of heaven grew into confidence. & when it fainted into despair,
we listened for its desolate & miserable cry. ⟨When m⟩Man contemplated his lot — & remembered that he was no hermit in the spacious
universe — that though his cold & indifferent gratitude might be unlike all that existed beside — yet he was not alone — but the uncounted
myriads of ⟨g⟩God's sons & servants were above & around him thro'
a thousand ↑great↓ worlds; — he was encompassed by a glorious Company & he put his finger on his lips and almost listened to hear their
voices. It would seem like mockery & burlesque, if we strictly compared these natural expectations with what is fact. If[n] we should
enter the doors of each house & make ⟨ours⟩ faithful acquaintance
with the actions of every day. And[n] ascertain how many of an individual's thoughts & actions spring from his earnest regard to his great
moral obligations. How[n] many times he sordidly sacrifices to Mammon, & how many to the universe of moral beings. What[n] he does
with a view to lay up money, & what, having heaven in his eye.

[18][22] The causes of this indifference, this hare-brained contempt

[20] See p. 150 above.
[21] "APATHY" is centered beneath "heaven in" at the bottom of the page.
[22] "APATHY" is centered beneath "Providence unlocks" at the bottom of the
page.

of a danger, to which all other jeopardies which men fear & shun, are safety itself, are easily seen but do not diminish the wonder. Men think they will hazard what has been hazarded before & is risked by the living generation; since so, neither the sin nor the penalty can be fatal beyond example. Crimes that they would not dare do in Solitude, when none but Heaven would be privy to the trespass, — in society they hardily commit; they lose themselves in a crowd & grow bold. ⟨Is⟩Hath heaven ⟨spiteful⟩ ↑a grudge↓? saith the offender to himself, or will the thunder strike me, when my neighbour is worse, & hath provoked it so long? Hungers the worm for me? is the bed of penal fire spread for me? and not for him whose corrupt example led me astray? Well, let the worst come to the worst I shall be no outcast from God's rejoicing creation nor shall I alone be the prey of malig-nant fiends; I shall but share with unnumbered thousands of my fellow men, sufferings which the weakest can support. Thus they alleviate the terrors that grow out of compunction & remorse. They find a treacherous consolation in this sad misapplication of the social principle. The pang will be less intolerable which throbs in a thousand breasts. Wherever God shall open the scene of their suffering, they shall go down that dark & tremendous way, in company and when Providence unlocks the doors of vengeance [19][23] & commissions unknown ministers & weapons of suffering, they dream of braving the fiercest[n] anguish omnipotent wrath can frame, because a mighty host gasp under it together.

When[n] this mockery of a consolation is broadly stated, one wonders how it could ever suggest itself, even to desperate atrocity. It denies with presumptuous scepticism the Omnipotence of Divine Justice, by confining its exercise to a manner & place, which the scep-tic's fancy allotted. Where is the foundation of this last hope. ⟨I⟩Can-not almighty power find room in the depths of space to separate the victims of vice? Is not the Universe spacious enough to find prisons for souls in its dreary Corners? Cannot God shut you out in pitiless solitude from all the sympathies & society of beings like yourself? Can he not make that society more odious than the most frightful loneliness?[n] Can he not curse you with an indignation so dire & ↑so↓ deep with such ⟨dark⟩ ↑concentrated↓ remediless /everlasting/inex-

---

[23] "APATHY" is centered beneath "explains no" at the bottom of the page.

orable/ woe as to wipe out the notice of all things from the brain, to make solitude & society indifferent in the bitter extremity of suffering? Alas, for the glory of this world[,] alas for the pleasures of sin! and woe to their miserable consolation. It is a fearful thing to fall into the hands of the living God. —

Another cause & the chief is, that, men are habitually & fatally unthinking. Conscience unread, untaught, prompts us to do good, & refuse evil. It is the human instinct, & is ⟨spread⟩ bestowed as universally as reason. It tells us not to do wrong, but does not tell us why. It shews the ultimate fact of the distinction between vice & virtue, but explains no consequences.

[20]24 The cause & end of this distinction we gain from Reason ↑& experience↓. We ⟨d⟩see how hateful vice makes human nature, how it alters it from a beautiful harmony of excellent qualities to ↑vile &↓ incongruous wretchedness. And the more we study ⟨our communications⟩ the nature of man, the more intensely 25 laboriously we think out our relations to God & our fellows, the better we get the lesson ↑we↓ were sent to this school below to learn. We learn ⟨a⟩more accurately the number & nature of our duties, we see more clearly, the connexion & symmetry of all the parts of the moral world. We see that goodness is better than greatness; we learn that goodness & beauty are one. I know there are deplorable instances to the contrary but I believe that, *in general*, the tendency of habits of thought & reflexion is decidedly propitious to morals. God never gave so glorious a gift as a strong understanding with a bias towards ruin. By the strong necessity of its nature, it aspires. The wisest being, is not *one*, & the best being *another* ⟨G⟩god. They are one. He n is supremely good *because* he is supremely wise. A man of transcendant genius is sometimes profligate, because his ill habits got a rooted & incurable encouragement in an ill-starred infancy before his intellectual powers were developed, to discriminate & reject the wrong. Active imitation, in a forward child, led him in [21]26 the way of wrong example, & he walked downward so far that the light which broke in,

24 "APATHY" is centered beneath "in a forward" at the bottom of the page.
25 The word "intensely" is circled, possibly for revision.
26 "APATHY" is centered beneath "who have not" at the bottom of the page. Nearby, Emerson penciled the profile of a man around some random ink marks, using them for eyes.

served only to shew the inextricable labyrinth in whose mazes he was lost. It is impossible for me to believe that God lighted up the beautiful ray of Genius, to be quenched in a premature & ominous night or to mix its celestial illumination with the lurid fires of malignant & infernal passions. God's works are fruits of his character; copies, (as ancient philosophy expressed it) of his mind and wishes. ⟨W⟩One could not venerate him if he were only good. Who could bow down before a God who had infinite instincts of[n] benevolence, & no thought; in whom the Eye of Knowledge was shut; who was kind & good because he knew no better; who was infinitely gentle as brutes are gentle? The[n] poor Egyptian plebeian layman might do so, who worshipped a divine Ox for his gracious tameness, but an enlightened Man, ↑with the spirit of a man,↓ would bid them bring the stake & fire & make him Martyr, ere he surrendered his mind & body to such a prostration. Man reveres the Providence of God, as the benign & natural *result* of his omniscience; and expects in the imperfect image of God an imperfect copy of the same eternal order. He, therefore, that thinks soberly in season, before his habits have been by evil influence corrupted, will probably embrace goodness, from conviction of its incomparable advantage. For there are few men who have not felt how shallow & superficial [22][27] is the vulgar view of moral existence which ↑mis↓cal⟨l⟩s sin, pleasure, & self-government a martyrdom. It is an old truth & not an old cant, that, the prosperous revels of libertines, whose joyous appearance sometimes disheartens the wavering & short sighted, are counterbalanced by an ample measure of burdensome vacant hours, of insipid idleness or scorpion remorse. Pleasure in ceasing to be new, loses its ↑brightest↓ attraction, & has hardly grace enough left to cover its stings withal. There is not a voluptuary on earth who does not eagerly hope that he may sometime break the thraldom which he has not strength to throw off. (B)

Fine marble form! Would it might wake to life.[28]

[27] "APATHY" is centered beneath "thraldom which" in the last line of the first paragraph.
[28] The line is written in a heavier hand and seems to have been added later, perhaps in regret at failure to achieve the vitality Emerson wanted in his writing.

Oct. 5. Milord W.[29] from Andover let me into his mystery about Edwards on the Will & told me withal that the object of the piece was to prove that President E. has not advanced human knowledge one step, for, his *definition* includes the very proposition which the book is designed to establish. W. saith, moreover, that perchance the President has done something albeit his definitions be imprudent & entangled. And perchance, the fault of apparently proving an identical proposition lies in the nature of the subject which, though so intricate before as to have ever been debateable ground, is made so plain by the able & skilful statements of Edwards, that we ⟨wonder⟩ [23][30] are made to see the truth, & wonder that it ever was disputed. Waldo E. will please consult upon this topic, on one side Edwards, Priestl[e]y, & Belsham; [31] on the other, Clarke, & Stewart (?) Dr Reid is to be read by me, quo citius, eo melius; [32] & Ed. Rev. of La Place's Calculation of Chances; [33] also ⟨is⟩ ↑are↓ to be stated anew the two propositions unanswerable concerning Necessity. One of them has occurred in Wideworld — No 8[.] [34]

Continued from (B) There is a nightmare upon men's thoughts which constrain them into a hideous inactivity while they are pierced with a sense of the necessity of action. Men indulge a restless expectation, which soothes their remorse, that, next day, some kind change

[29] William Withington, a college classmate, and later an Episcopalian minister (*J*, I, 286, n. 2). In a letter to John Boynton Hill, March 12, 1822, Emerson calls him "Lord Withington" (*L*, I, 107).

[30] "APATHY" is centered beneath "& which" at the bottom of the page.

[31] Emerson is referring to Thomas Belsham (1750–1829), whose *Elements of the Philosophy of the Human Mind* . . . (London, 1801) stated and answered objections to the freedom of the will and asserted the fallacy of the doctrine of necessity (ch. IX, sections V–VIII). Stewart quotes Belsham's " 'the *fallacious* feeling of *remorse* is superseded by the doctrine of necessity' " (*Dissertation, Collected Works*, 1854, I, 312, n. 1).

[32] "The sooner, the better" (Ed.). There is no evidence in the reading lists that Emerson read Thomas Reid (1710–1796) at this time, but Emerson may have read about Reid's attack on the ideal theory of Hume and Berkeley in his *Inquiry into the Human Mind* in Stewart's *Dissertation* (see *Collected Works*, 1854, I, 456–466).

[33] Laplace's *Essai Philosophique sur les Probabilités* (Paris, 1814), was reviewed in *The Edinburgh Review*, XXIII (Sept. 1814), 320–340.

[34] Presumably Emerson is referring to his statement that "No event therefore in mind or matter starts up into an independent existence, but all have an immediate dependence upon what went before. This is the foundation of the doctrine of human necessity." See p. 53 above.

of fortune will turn up, that will effectually reform these habits of apathy that are growing inveterate. They are scared by a casual glimpse of th⟨e⟩ose infinite perils they go to encounter, & it may be pour out a fervent resolution of amendment or give way to a half wish that one of those avenging Ministers whose way among their fellow men ⟨is⟩ ↑they have seen↓ marked [n] by Death & Pain & Ruin may deal his bolts even within the circle of ⟨his⟩their own sympathies; in confidence that the thunder may appal the heart which a whisper could not move. All this passes in their minds, but they will not forsake for a day or an hour the dull unsatisfactory world to which their customs & feelings cling & which passes before them daily [24][35] in an uniform & joyless reverie. They will wait in expectation of this admonishing judgement — but they will not awake & reform.[n] It is ↑a↓ curious fact & the abstrusest mystery that darkens our existence, how men should hold such a transcendant gift as Thought in their hands[,] such a key to infinite pleasures[,] & ⟨manifest⟩ ↑shew↓ such painful reluctance to use it. In youth they often appreciate its un-speakable worth & the imagination sometimes revels in the pictures of its wealth. They are impatient to begin the journey of greatness[,] to enter upon the expanding scene glowing & towering in magnifi-cence afar before their eyes. But ere the days of youth have gone over their heads ↑an ungrateful & unaccountable↓ Indolence comes in like a lethargy to shut ⟨up⟩ his eyes ⟨from⟩ ↑upon↓ the glorious prospect or rather to stop his pursuit without removing its brilliant object. The sick men of this malady have the choice viands of the world set before them & while they feel the need of being fed, lack the appetite to eat. There are a few ⟨|| ... ||⟩ whom the restless ambition of duty awakens out of this sleep & who disdain like the Nazarite to wear these Philistine fetters, who having once drunk the draught of im-mortal thought thirst again for this water of life & cannot be satisfied.

[25] Sunday, Oct.   I heard Dr Channing deliver a dis-course upon Revelation as standing in comparison with Nature. I have heard no sermon approaching in excellence to this, since the Dudleian Lecture.[36] The language was a transparent medium, con-

---

[35] "APATHY" is centered beneath "for this water" at the bottom of the page.
[36] "The Evidences of Revealed Religion," delivered by William Ellery Channing

veying with the utmost distinctness, the pictures in his mind, to the minds of the hearers. He considered God's word to be the only expounder of his works, & that Nature had always been found insufficient to teach men the great doctrines which Revelation inculcated. Astronomy had in one or two ways an unhappy tendency. An universe of matter in which Deity would display his power & greatness must be of infinite extent & complicate relations and of course too vast to be measured by the eye & understanding of man. Hence errors. Astron. reveals to us infinite number of worlds like our own accommodated for the residence of such beings as we of gross matter. But to kindle our piety & urge our faith, we do not want such a world as this but a purer, a world of morals & of spirits. La Place has written in the mountain album [n] of Switzerland his avowal of Atheism. Newton had a better master than Suns & Stars. — He learned of heaven ere he philosophized. & after travelling through mazes of the universe he returned to bow his laurelled head at the feet of Jesus of Nazareth. Dr C. regarded Revelation as much a part of the order of things as any other event. It would have been wise to have made an abstract of the Discourse immediately.

> O keep the current of thy spirits even;
> If it be ruffled by too full a flood, —
> 'Tis turbid; or, if drained, goes dry. The mind,
> In either case, obeys the animal pulse,[n]
> And weeps the loss of unreturning time,

[26] Mr Hume's Essay upon Necessary Connexion proves that Events are conjoined, and not connected; that, we have no knowledge but from Experience.[37] We have no Experience of a Creator & there-[fore] know of none. The constant appeal is to our feelings from the glozed lies of the deciever but one would feel safer & prouder to

---

at Harvard, March 14, 1821. The "discourse upon Revelation" was preached in Boston at the Federal Street Church Sunday, October 12 (see *L*, I, 138).

[37] "One event follows another; but we never observe any tie between them. They seem *conjoined*, but never *connected*. And as we can have no idea of any thing, which never appeared to our outward sense or inward sentiment, the necessary conclusion *seems* to be, that we have no idea of connexion or power at all, and that these words are absolutely without any meaning, when employed either in philosophical reasonings, or common life." "Of the Idea of Necessary Connexion," *Philosophical Essays*, 1817, II, 72.

see the victorious answer to these calumnies upon our nature set down in impregnable propositions.

> Pride carves rich emblems on its seals
> And slights the throng that dogs its heels
> Fair vanity hath bells on cap & shoes
> And eyes his moving shadow as he goes.

We put up with time & chance because it costs too great an effort to subdue them to our wills, and minds that feel an embryo greatness stirring within them let it die for want of nourishment. Plans that only want maturity, ideas that only need expansion to lead the thinker on to a far nobler being than now he dreams of; good resolutions whose dawning was like the birth of Gods in their benevolent promise,[n] sudden throbs of charity & impulses to goodness that spake most auspicious omens to humanity[38] are suffered to languish & blight in hopeless barrenness. And is it supposed, is it to be suggested that this [is] a vague & groundless alarm? I would to God it were! [27] I would to God that none of the good purposes of his children upon earth failed of their accomplishment;[n] that every humane design; every heart bleeding for the sorrows of men; every liberal feeling which would pardon their faults or relieve their woes — might go on to the fine ultimate issues which it contemplated. The melancholy truth is that there are ten thousand abortive to one successful accomplishment. Who does not know, who has not felt that ⟨a⟩unnumbered good purposes spring up in the clean & strong soil of the youthful breast, until Sloth gives a relaxing fatness to the ground, which kills the growth. I call every man to witness whatever be his lot, be he the minion of fortune or the child of sorrow, ⟨C⟩Pagan or Christian, bond or free, that ↑if he be sinful↓ his hands have not ⟨ever⟩ ↑always↓ ministered to his designs[,] that virtue is not a name unknown to his ears or overlooked in his thoughts. No there is an impulse to do good continually urging us, an ⟨illuminated⟩ eternal illumination upon virtuous deeds that attracts the beholder. His heart applauds; it is ↑this↓ hands that fail. It strikes my mind as a beautiful

[38] The phrase "to humanity" is circled, possibly to indicate intended revision. The two words are omitted in *J*, I, 292.

& adorable truth that the good spirit who made all things is daily
working in this lower sphere by presenting to ten thousand thousand
minds images & occasions of goodness,[n] striving as he can, without
infringing [28] their freedom to bind them to the right interest, in-
viting them with benignant importunity to thought & duty, & imparting a bias which if obeyed will make the heart burn with gratitude. The more we magnify this benevolence the more depraved &
besotted is man's negligence or frowardness. He averts his sullen
eye from all the riches to which his nature made him heir[.] ——

It will not be a very wide digression from the somewhat desultory
train of thoughts which I have strung together, if I here consider a
notorious fact which is strange as it is common. I mean the coldness
& poverty of our views of *heaven* &, what is the result of this, the
meagreness & hollow declamation of all uninspired descriptions of
the same.

It is not a characteristic of our joys that the hope of them should
be languid, & the consequent desires of them, cold. Nature has not
iced our passions & affections in their prospect of gratification. In the
perfectly confident hope of future indulgence, the labourer toils.
The hope of the lover is not apathy. Political & literary ambition are
not apathy. Hope is so strong that on it is founded the uninterrupted
sedulous labour of many years. Imagine it removed from the human
breast & see [29] how Society will sink, how the strong bands of
order & improvement will be relaxed, & what a deathlike stillness
would ⟨take the place of⟩ ↑come over↓ the restless energies that now
/move/shake/ the world. The scholar will extinguish his midnight
lamp, the[n] merchant will furl his white sails & bid them seek the
deep no more. The anxious patriot who stood out for his country to
the last, & ⟨plotted⟩ ↑devised↓ in ⟨a⟩ ↑the last↓ beleaguered citadel,
profound schemes ⟨for its⟩ ↑of↓ deliverance & aggrandizement, will
sheath his sword & blot his fame. Remove hope, & the world becomes
a blank & rotteness. Human breasts lose their indestructible impulse
to improve that now triumphs over time & disappointment & altered
fortunes: the human eye loses its fire; the voice its eloquent tones of
joy & animation; the hand its cunning, & the heart its feeling. Kill
this bright lord of the bosom's throne & man's imagination will leave
↑going forward with him &↓ decking the future with gay colours, &

will go out instead into the melancholy past, into the forlorn history of old time, to walk among comfortless graves, into the infamous scenes of human guilt, into fields whose grass is /crimsoned/discoloured/ with blood. Distempered fancy will give a ghastly life to darkness & curdle the blood with the apparition of a thousand fell spectres. If the past were presented to our hearts in all its dark reality relieved by no ↑contrasted↓ Hope for the future, men would ⟨instinctively⟩ rebel in spirit against the [30] ⟨Spirit⟩ Providence which placed them here & had darkened their lot with such deep & damning shades. Why does omnipotence, they would murmur, ↑send↓ the poor slaves of its power into this wide prisonhouse to run the selfsame round of madness & sorrow that the long train of generations have run already; to bear the same burden of curses & infirmities: to be disfigured by the same angry passions; [n] to be crushed by the same unrelenting course of events; to be thrown & abandoned without friend or strength upon the same tremendous theatre amidst the play of human passions, a ⟨prey⟩ lamb before the lions[,] a prey to the fighting Kings & Nimrods of the earth, to be eaten up by their rage, or tortured by their Caprice? — Indeed the most benevolent philanthropist when in sober thought he reverts his eye to the solemn annals of departed Time must sometimes shudder at the suspicion that if the delusions of Hope were dispelled Futurity might be modelled on this pattern. He sees how a wretch's extravagant ambition in one hour strowed in ashes cities that had struggled up into civilization & magnificence by the tardy & toilsome efforts of many hundred years; how nations are swallowed in one day; how vice mounts the throne & virtue retires to dungeons: how mind falls before barbarism[;] how God is forgotten whilst men pass thro' fire to Baal.

[31] If Hope ⟨is⟩ ↑be↓ the beautifier that out of such darkness creates such light; it must needs have potent energy. Now why does it limit its action to earth? If it brightens all the years of life as they rise in dim futurity, why cannot its rays reach over the abyss & illuminate the country beyond? Why [n] does Youth bound with rapture in the prospect of the emancipation & strength of manhood; and ⟨why does not⟩ ↑why↓ [does] the ↑youth of the↓ Soul ↑not↓ rejoice in the hope of *her* deliverance ⟨of her⟩ from this mortal coil, & the shackles of a fleshly appetite? Is there anything intrinsically disagreeable in

those circumstances which divines describe as taking place at death in the man who has done well & worthily here? Can it be a distressing summons, which calls us to strip off what we call vile incumbrances? to get rid of the clods that shut in the soul & bar it from better society; that substitute the dim & obscure language of sensations, for the acquaintance with real beings; that subject it to the pollution of gross passions; to the poor temptations of Sense, & the uncomfortable agitations of little affairs? Or is it that we are to part with life, that is, with the trivial succession of wants, inconveniences, & [32] petty actions that occur every day; with the wretched & unceasing care of the body? for it is these drawbacks upon life & not life itself we are to lose. It can hardly be, that men are so loath to lose things of which they complain so strenuously & so often.ⁿ And yet it must be *here,* that the fear rankles; there ⟨is⟩ ↑must↓ need↑s↓ be some deprivation of body ⟨that⟩ the dread of which freezes in their spring the affections that should flow towards heaven. For I cannot bring myself to imagine that they are afraid of hurt from the other parts of that glorified state. The other parts are a nearer connexion with Deity; an unlimited [39] & increasing capacity of knowledge; pure & fervent affections; & ⟨a⟩the rich gratification of all our desires. A wise man who does not confine his attention to the words in which these promises are enumerated but recalls incessantly these thoughts, as things having a *real existence,* to his mind, will soon learn to give them a preference so decided as to go nigh to banish all other thoughts. All men, indeed, who could be induced to give these hopes their ⟨pro⟩ just weight (which is infinite,) would find the tone of all their associations rapidly changed. The difficulty is to rouse them from resting in the terms to an intense attention to the things[,] & this, though marvellous easy in its distant appearance [33] is the hardest labour appointed ⁿ to the human mind. Men's lives have been devoted sedulously to this attempt. Writing & preaching & example have been exhausted in the cause. The most mighty[,] the almost supernatural impulses of the intellect have been applied to it. The blood of martyrdom has been spilled in its behalf. And all this— to make men pass over words to things. But the invincible repugnance which the mind has shewn ⟨th⟩ is that ↑one↓ element which

---

[39] Beneath "unlimited" Emerson made a small cross mark.

neutralizes the good qualities & quenches the heaven directed ⁿ ardour of all the rest. There is a⟨n⟩ Vis inertiae of mind as well as of matter, an inherent almost uneradicable indolence in human nature which pauses at the threshold & is immoveably passive, where it is of the last importance that it should go on, & where delay is tremendous peril. The dull ear hears that Eternity is a solemn name & that vast meaning is wrapped up in it; & it is feared that the developement will cost much thought ↑& action↓, possibly much pain, & is therefore most unfriendly to that darling repose which is to be soothed at every hazard. So the dream is indulged[,] these obscure notions of heaven are repeated with plausible terms of respect, (as an apology to the world & to the inward monitor,) & the barrier which separates their ⟨mani[?]⟩ awful import from the understanding & the heart is never overleaped.

[34]⁴⁰ If I am asked ⁿ why the hope of heaven is thus broken — while the hopes of the lover, the scholar, the merchant & the states-man are active enough,ⁿ I answer that their objects are tangible & require no very farsighted sagacity to bring them home to the feel-ings. The mind of man is wrought upon by the eye & the ear, the taste & the touch when it is insensible to the cold representations of the understanding. Such is our constitution, that the affectionate eye of a friend, ⟨t⟩ which speaks of actions ⟨f⟩& feelings which we can w↑h↓olly understand, has more charms to our own, than the most magnificent spectacle of nature. And commonly the coarse applause of an unthinking worthless mob, because ⟨the circumstances do not surpass the measure of our narrow understandings⟩ ↑it is thoroughly intelligible↓ will vastly outweigh the unheard approbation of the uni-verse of good ⟨beings⟩ ↑spirits↓ — though the individual's faith in their existence & sympathies may be ⟨old &⟩ undoubting. And these earthly comforts that are the fixtures of civilized society, a family hearth, a spacious house, rich table, equipage & dress, fix the imagina-tion & regulate the conduct of life. Meantime a cultivated ⟨und⟩ mind in the very moment when it is arranging whole years of ⟨pr⟩ action with an immediate reference to these, sees & knows how insignificant

⁴⁰ The head of a man in left profile is sketched in the text, from "home to the feelings." to "spectacle of nature." below.

& valueless they are ⟨in⟩ when measured upon a true scale. In reference to a whole existence, these dainty conveniences of the flesh sink
to atoms, while the moral laws & truths which they banished from
[35] the mind, swell into ↑their↓ real stupendous magnitude.

It may also be queried, (if these truths do not easily become
practical owing to their abstruseness or remoteness from sense,) how
they differ from those lofty studies that absorb the intensest attention of the mightiest minds, while they [are] very far from being
very practical; such as some parts of pure mathematics, or ↑some of↓
Leibnitz', & Boscovich's researches.⁴¹ I answer there is also a very important difference ⟨in⟩between the nature of these researches & of
religious meditation. As the great end of abstruse study is not the
knowledge it procures but the cultivation of the intellect which necessarily results from these habits, God has connected ⟨with⟩ acute pleasure with the consciousness of progress and also an increasing curiosity.
So that if the mind can once conquer its indolence & begin to study,
it is almost impossible to stop for it gathers new impetus at every
step. So it is with the kingdom of nature, it is otherwise with the
kingdom of heaven. The truths of this Revelation are so simple &
intelligible that he who runs may read, that the meanest & the wisest
are made equal here. They give no triumph of the judgment or the
wit to please the pride of the scholar. All understandings, it may be,
were not made to comprehend Newton's Principia; but all were made
expressly to recieve the belief of a God, & ⟨of human[?]⟩ the distinction of right & wrong [36] & of human accountability. As the former
were only partial & incidental purposes, & the latter the immediate
indispensable object ⟨of⟩ ↑in↓ the creation of mind, it was of course
right, that profane knowledge should be the result of curious research, while the latter was to be the spontaneous fruit of the mind.
Hence the difference between ⟨these⟩ Religious & Scientific thought,
that the one is to be *felt*, & the other to [be] elaborated.

One more circumstance is important

⁴¹ Ruggiero Giuseppe Boscovich (1711–1787), Jesuit mathematician, astronomer,
and physicist, was the first Italian to support Newton's theories, and an early proponent
of the molecular theory of matter (1758). Emerson may well have read of him in
Stewart's second *Dissertation*, where he is linked with Leibnitz (see *Collected Works*,
1854, I, 423).

[Dec. 13, 1823] [42] Edinburgh Rev has a fine ⟨account⟩ ↑eulogy↓ of Newton & Dr Black &c in the first article of the 3d Vol.[n 43] No. XXXVI contains a review of Mrs. Grant on Highlanders, and, in it, good thoughts upon the progress of *manners*. 'A gentleman's character is a compound of obligingness & self esteem.' [44] The same volume reviews Alison & gives an excellent condensed view of his theory.[45] The charm of all these discussions is only a fine luxury, producing scarce any good, unless that of substituting a pure pleasure for impure. Occasionally this reading helps one's conversation; but seldom. The reason & whole mind is not forwarded ↑by it↓, as by *history*. The good in life that seems to be most *real*, is not found in reading, but in those successive triumphs a man achieves over habits of moral or intellectual indolence, or over an ungenerous spirit and mean propensities.—— Dec. 13, 1823.

[37] Love is a holy passion, & is the instrument of our connection with Deity, and when we drop the body, this, perhaps, will constitute the motive & impulse to all the acquisitions of an immortal education. As we are instinctively ashamed of selfishness, we venerate *love,* the noble & generous nature of which seeks ⟨the go⟩ another's good. It warms the mind into a ferment, which is prolific ⟨of⟩ in benevolent deeds. Then, embryo powers of which we were not hitherto conscious are nursed into the manhood of mind. A powerful motive is to the character what a skilful hypothesis is to the progress of Science; it affords facility & room for the arrangement of the growing principles of our nature. What lay in Chaos & barren, before, is now adjusted in a beautiful & useful order, which exposes to the light numberless connexions & relations & fine issues of thought not easily

[42] The following paragraph is written upside down on the lower half of the page.

[43] A review of Joseph Black, *Lectures on the Elements of Chemistry* . . . , 2 vols. (London, 1803).

[44] *Essays on the Superstitions of the Highlanders of Scotland* . . . , 2 vols. (London, 1811), by Anne Grant. Emerson's quotation seems to be a précis of thoughts from different passages, especially on pp. 485 and 487 of the review (XVIII, Aug. 1811).

[45] Archibald Alison, *Essays on the Nature and Principles of Taste,* 2 vols. (Edinburgh, 1811), reviewed in May 1811, pp. 1–46. A Dublin, 1790, edition was withdrawn from the Boston Library Society July 12–Aug. 2, 1823.

percieved until such a system is ⟨p⟩laid. A motive thus powerful &
of such benignant fruits is *love*. It is strong & active enough to vanquish in many a proud instance even the gross selfishness of the human
nature. It bears many forms, but is *love*. It is the attachment to truth,
to a sentiment, to our country, to a fellow being or to God, that has
↑won &↓ worn the crown of martyrdom & that has stirred up in men's
minds all the good which the earth has seen. Indeed pure love is too
pure a principle for human bosoms; and were it not mixed with the
animal desires of our nature, would not meet that unqualified & universal honour it now finds among men. It is not unwarrantable mo-
roseness to add that the depravity of the heart hugs to itself the
animal love [38] and rejects the intellectual, sucks out the poison
& leaves the aliment. What does the sensualist know of love?— of
such love as exists between God & man and man & God; of such love,
as the pure mind concieves for moral grandeur, for the contemplation
of which it was made? Love has an empire in the world, but Fear
has an empire also. And I wish on the comparison this palsied leprous
principle be not found to have the larger sway. The conventions, as
they are called, of civilized life, the artificial order & conversation of
society are propped on this miserable reed. Now & then, there are
minds of such indomitable independence as to overleap the wretched
restraints of fashion, & who let the Universe hear the true tones of
their Voice; unpracticed to ⟨a⟩ ↑the↓ "tune of the time," unembar-
rassed by fear; who venture to speak out, & to treat their fellow
creature as their peer, & the Deity as God. Such men embrace, in
their apprehension, a larger portion of existence than their weaker
brethren in the shackles of prudence. By casting a glance on the
future they discriminate between trifles & magnificent things & learn
to weigh the world in a true scale & to undervalue what is called
greatness below. I would not be understood to cast imputation on
good-breeding. In the human throng it is certainly a convenient,[n]
perhaps a necessary thing; and its absence could not be borne. But in
the higher connexions of which I speak — it is to be treated [39]
merely as a convenient thing, and when it pretends to higher claims
it is to be treated with contempt. Shall the fear which an expanding
mind entertains of the eye or tongue of each insignificant man &
woman in its way interfere with its progress to↑wards↓ the ripe⟨ness⟩

↑excellence↓ of its ⟨faculties⟩ ↑being↓? ⁿ There are times ⟨wh⟩ in the history of every thinking mind, when it is the recipient of uncommon & awful thought, when somewhat larger draughts of the Spiritual Universe are let in upon the Soul; and it breathes eloquent ejaculations to God, and would cease to be the plaything of petty events & would become a portion of that world in which it has sojourned. But that mind returns into the company of unsympathising minds, and the humble routine of their *small* talk is little akin to the revelations opening upon his soul; and ⁿ must what is called Good Manners freeze the tongue that should drop heaven's wisdom to ⟨silence⟩ ↑dumbness↓; and must the eye struck with the glory of Paradise be levelled to the earth?

Dec., 1823.

[46] When merry England had her virgin queen
And Glory's temple in the isle was seen

⟨A⟨n⟩ virgin queen⟨!⟩ wore England's lion crown⟩
⟨And trod with lordly grace bold Faction down⟩
⟨Yoked War's ⁿ red lions to the imperial car⟩
⟨And shewed to ⟨go⟩ distant lands her Redcross
        ⟨banner⟩ ↑flag↓ afar⟩
⟨Across the globe wheree'er her navies sailed⟩
On Avon's banks a child of earth was born
⟨In meads⟩ where fairies wind their midnight horns
The tiny dancers leaped in frolic wild
And o'er the cradle blessed the sleeping child

[40₁] There is danger of a *poetical* religion from the tend-enc⟨y⟩↑ies↓ ↑of the age↓. There is a celebrated passage in the prose works of the great Christian bard, which is precious to the admirers of Milton. I refer to the II ⟨Chap.⟩ ↑Book↓ of Reason of Ch[urch]. Government, &c. There is probably no young man who could read that eloquent chapter, without feeling his heart warm to the love of virtue & greatness & without making fervent resolutions that his age should be made better, because he had lived. Yet these resolutions,

[46] All the verse that follows is written upside down on the lower half of the page.

unless diligently nourished by prayer & expanded into action by intense study will be presently lost in the host of worldly cares. But
they leave one fruit, that may be poisonous; they leave a self complacency arising from having thought so nobly for a moment, which
leads the self deciever to believe himself better than other men.

[44]⁴⁷   Plato's Dialogue   De Virtute

Menon   Tell me, Socrates, if Virtue is ⟨not⟩ something to be
           taught, or is not rather to be practised, or is neither to be
           practised nor taught but falls to men by nature or in some
           other manner.
Soc.   Formerly, Menon, the Thessalians were esteemed by the
           Greeks for their wealth & their skill in horsemanship. Now,
           they are so, ⟨f⟩methinks, for their wisdom,ⁿ & chiefly for the
           wisdom of your friend Aristippus of Larissi. Gorgias is my
           authority. He being brought to the government as well
           from [the] Thessalian‖s‖ as Alevadi (of which Aristippus
           was one) made all the great men his friends,ⁿ and taught
           you this manner of answering ⟨boldly⟩ in bold & sweeping
           terms as if with thorough knowledge — whenever a question
           is put. x x But, here, methinks an opposite manner prevails, a
           kind of lowliness of knowledge, as if Wisdom had departed
           from us to you. So that if you should ask that question here
           no man but would laugh & reply — 'Methinks, sir, ⟨I⟩you
           mistake me for some wise man that I should know how virtue
           grew. But so far am I from knowing whether or not virtue
           can be taught, that I am altogether ignorant what Virtue is.'
           I also, my friend, share this ignorance of my countrymen, and
           confess myself absolutely in the dark with regard to the na-
           ture of Virtue. How then shall I know the *qualities* of a sub-
           stance I do not know; or how shall any one unacquainted

⁴⁷ The page is misnumbered [42]. In the bottom margin are sketches of two male
heads. "Vol 29 Edin. Rev." appears right side up at the bottom of the page. The
dialogue is written from back to front, ending on p. [40₂], and appears upside down
in relation to the preceding matter in the journal. That part of it which appears on
p. [40₂] was written down before the other material on that page ([40₁]).

with Menon, know if he be handsome, rich, and generous, or
the reverse? Does this appear possible?

Men. No; but[n] is it true, Socrates, you do not know what virtue is?
and shall I tell this at home?

Soc. Not only so, my friend, but also, that, I think I never met
with one who did know⟨?⟩.

Men. What, did you not converse with Gorgias, when he was here?

Soc. Yes, I did.

Men. And did not he appear to know?

Soc. I do not now remember; and am not at present able to say
how it then appeared to me. Perhaps he knew, & you may
remember what he said. Recall to mind the manner of his
discourse. Or, it may be you would prefer to give those opinions of yourself, if you assented to his doctrines.

Men. I did.

[43] *Soc.* We may dispense with him, then, since he is not here;
but, prithee, Menon, do *you* tell me what Virtue is, ⟨(↑al↓)⟩
though, (in case you & Gorgias be right) the lie be proved on
me in having said that I never saw one who knew the nature
of Virtue.

Men. It is not difficult to tell, Socrates; and, first, if you will, it is
better to name the Virtue of a Man. A Man's Virtue consists
in an ability to administer affairs of state; in being profitable
to his friends & dangerous to his enemies, and in providing
against personal dangers. — Or a woman's virtue in the well
ordering of her house, and in obedience to her husband.
There is a Virtue of a boy as of a Man & a Woman; of an old
man, of a Child, & of a Slave. And there are many other virtues, that there can be no fault in discovering its nature. For
in particular actions & ages, & to every case is its appropriate
Virtue. In like manner I judge of Vice.

Soc. Methinks, Menon, I am singularly fortunate, who asking the
meaning of one Virtue, am favoured with a catalogue of all,
but in like manner   if, when I had inquired what
was the nature of a bee, ⟨&⟩ you had ⟨t⟩answered that there
were many & various bees, — what should you say if I demanded whether, it was, because they were bees, that they

were many & different from each other; or that they did not
vary in this, but only in beauty, size, or something else. Tell
me, what would be your answer.

Men.   Indeed I should say they did not differ, one from the other,
in being bees.

Soc.   And if I should ask you what were the circumstances wherein
they did not differ, but were alike,—should you have any
answer?

[42]   *Men.* Certainly.

Soc   Well, so also the virtues, which are many & various, have
yet some quality whereby they are virtues, & to which *he*
should refer, who undertakes to answer what Virtue is. You
understand me?

Men.   Not quite as clearly as I could wish.

Soc.   Does this difference, then, which makes the virtue of a man
different from the virtue of a woman, &c, only prevail in
Virtue? or is it the same with health, & strength, & size,—
that the health of a man is different from the health of a
woman;—or is health the same quality whether in man,
woman, or any other animal?

Men.   The health of man or woman appears to me to be the same
thing.

Soc.   So of strength & size, do they differ in different individuals?

Men.   No.

Soc.   But Virtue in as much as it is virtue, varies in a man, a woman, a child?

Men.   Indeed, Socrates, this seems to me, to be unlike the others.

Soc.   Did you not say that the Virtue of a Man was to govern the
state & a Woman's to govern her house?

Men.   Yes.

Soc.   But can any one govern well either a house or a state or any
thing else who does not govern with justice & moderation?

Men.   ⟨Yes.⟩ No.[48]

Soc.   Man & woman then have both need of ⟨the⟩ justice & temperance in order to be virtuous?

---

[48] "Yes." is canceled in pencil and followed by a penciled dash. "No" is in ink,
written over "No." in pencil.

Men.   Certainly.

Soc   And were ever an old man or a boy virtuous who were petu-
         lant & unjust?

Men.   Never.

Soc   And, *if* temperate & just?

Men.   They were virtuous.

Soc.   All men then are good in the same way; for by obtaining the
         same things they become go⟨d⟩od. They would not be good
         in the same way if their virtue were not the same?

Men.   ⟨Yes⟩ No[.]

Soc.   Since then the Virtue of all men is the same, tell me now
         what Gorgias would say this Virtue is, & you with him.

Men.   Well then to command men, if you want one out of all the
         Virtues[.]

Soc   Yes. And I would inquire if this be equally the virtue of a
         boy, & of a *slave*, that he also be able to command his master?
         And is he a slave who commands?

Men.   No — he certainly is not.

Soc   Probably not. But consider this. You say — "to command."
         Shall we not say '*with justice*'?

[41]   *Men.* You are right; for, justice, Socrates, is virtue.

Soc   Virtue, or *one* Virtue?

Men   I don't understand you.

Soc.   On some other subject, I might say, for instance, of round-
         ness, that it is *one* figure, & not that it is simply *figure*. So
         also, that not justice alone is virtue, but that there are others.
         And as if I should tell you to name the other *figures* so tell
         me now what are those other virtues. —

Men.   Fortitude is a virtue, and Wisdom & Temperance & mag-
         nanimity & many more.

Soc.   The same thing has happened to me now which fell before;
         — asking one I hear many; but not in the same manner. But
         we have not been able to find that one quality which is com-
         mon to all these.

Men.   No, Socrates, I am not able to find *one virtue*, the same in all
         these, as was the case, in *health* &c.

Soc.   Right; but I will endeavour, if I can to direct our inquiry.

You see that this holds good in all. If any man ask you as I did — 'What is figure?' and you reply roundness and he ask again if roundness be *figure* or *one* figure? would you not say *one* figure?

Men.   Yes.

Soc   And would so speak because there are other figures?

Men   Yes[.]

S.   And if he ask '*what* other?,' you would still answer?

M.   Certainly[.]

Soc   And in colours likewise[,] that White is not alone Colour for there be many colours besides. If therefore the inquirer should pursue the subject as I did & should say — We always come to many things, — which pleaseth me not. But since you call all by one name, & there is none of all, which is not fig-ure. And this when they vary from each other; while that which you call figure contains a straight line and a circle, nor would you say a circle to be more a figure than a line?

Men.   *No*[.]

Soc.   Try to tell me of what this '*figure*' is the name. If you were thus pressed respecting figure or colour, you might say, 'Sir, I neither understand your meaning, nor can explain your doubt.' Perhaps he would say, 'I want to know what is the same in all these figures.' Should you not be able to answer? Now Menon, apply this order — to your answers respecting Virtue.

Men.   I cannot. Do you, Socrates, speak in my stead. x x x x
        x x x

Soc.   Now give me as you intended a general definition of Vir-tue[.]

Men   I think Virtue consists (to use the language of a poet) in the power to do & to take pleasure in whatever is beautiful. And virtue desires & produces what is beautiful.

Soc.   Say you that he who desires what is beautiful, desires what is good?

Men   Yes.

[40₂]   *Soc.* And there are some who seek what is good; others, bad?

Men   Yes.

Soc	Now do you think that the last mistake bad for good; or that knowing certain things to be bad, they still desire them? [n]
Men	I believe both cases happen.
Soc	What[,] that a man knowingly desires what is bad?
Men.	Yes.
Soc	Desires what? that they happen to him?
Men	Happen? Yes, for how else?
Soc	Does he suppose that bad things, can profit him whom they befal?
Men	There are men who suppose that bad things profit.
Soc	Do you suppose they understand the nature of bad things, who suppose them to profit? [n]
Men	
Soc	Is it not plain that they who do not know what is bad, do not desire it, but that what they imagine to be good, is bad? So that those who do not understand the nature of these thin⟨k⟩gs, but think them to be good do indeed desire what is good.
Men.	Yes[.]
Soc	Do they not percieve that it is by these very evils that those are injured on whom they fall? and do they not consider those men wretched in proportion as they [are] harmed by these?
Men	Yes.
Soc	
Men.	Is there any man who desires to be wretched?
Soc	No man therefore[.]

Walk to the Connecticut

1 8 2 3

This brief journal is a record of Emerson's walking excursion between August 22 and September 4, 1823. Chronologically, it precedes the entry of September 6 on p. 152 above.

The manuscript is composed of fifteen folded sheets hand-stitched into three gatherings of five, eight, and three leaves respectively and the whole then enclosed within a single folded sheet of the same paper. The paper meansures 10.5 x 17 cm.

[front cover recto] Journal.
　　　Aug. 1822[3].

　　　　　　"Have lights when other men are blind
　　　　　　As pigs are said to see the wind."
　　　　　　　　　　[Butler, *Hudibras*, III, ii, ll. 1107–1108]

[front cover verso] White & Sargent's.	37 1/2	
——	3	
Warren's	40	
farmer's	6 1/4	
——	6 1/4	
——	2	
Hovey's	8⟨3⟩0	
Leicester	6	
Bemis	25	
Stevens	11	
Rice	1.33 Comb 10	
Cutler	17	
Babcock	0	X
Clapp & stage	1.00	
Bartlett	1.20	

Washing	.25
Visit to Holyoke	80
Toll & Tavern at Northam	15
Mine	17
Greenfield	71 Toll 3
Ginn's–Montague	15
Hunter's–Wendell	25
Hemenway	6
Haven's N. Salem	40
Wilbur's Barre	12
Wright's Hubbardston	⟨42⟩ 25
Smith's Princeton	42
Sterling	16
Bolton	37 1/2
Sudbury	6
Waltham	6 Turn over

[back cover recto] Stage fare from	
Princeton to Waltham	225
Brookline	⟨12⟩
Sum Total	12.75

[1]   ↑*Walk to the Connecticutt.*↓

Framingham, Aug. ↑22d,↓ 1823.
↑Friday Noon↓
Warren's Hotel —

After a delightful walk of 20 miles I reached this inn before Noon, and in the near recollection of my promenade through Roxbury, Newton, Needham, Natick, do recommend the same, particularly as far as the Lower Falls in Newton, to my friends who are fond of fine scenery.

[2] ↑To↓ ⟨At⟩ this stage of mine errantry no adventure has befallen me; no, not the meeting with a mouse. I both thought & talked a little with myself on the way, and gathered up & watered such sprigs of poetry as I feared had wilted in my memory. I thought how History has a twofold effect, viz intellectual pleasure & moral

178

pain. And in the midst of a beautiful country I thought how monotonous & uniform is Nature; but I found now as ever that maugre all the flights of the sacred Muse, the profane solicitudes of ⟨dinn⟩ the flesh, elevated the Tavern to a high rank among my pleasures.

[3]   Worcester Evening 8 o'clock
    I reached Worcester ½ an hour ago having walked 40 miles without difficulty. Every time I traverse a turnpike I find it harder to concieve how they are supported; I met but 3 or four travellers between Roxbury & W. The scenery, all the way was ⟨very⟩ fine, and the turnpike, a road of ⟨most⟩ inflexible principle, swerving neither to the right hand nor the left, stretched on before me, always in sight. A traveller who has nothing particular to think about is apt to make a very lively personification of his Road & s⟨t⟩o make the better companion of it. The Kraken, thought I, or the Sea-Worm, is *three English* miles long; but this *land-worm* of mine is some forty, & those of the hugest.

[4]   Saturday, Rice's Hotel, Brookfield.
    After passing through Leicester, Spencer & North Brookfield I am comfortably seated in South B. 60 miles from home. In Leicester, I met with Stephen Elliot in the Bar room of the inn, on his way, it appeared, to Stafford Springs. He guessed with me a few minutes concerning the design & use of a huge white building opposite the house & could not decide whether it were Courthouse or whether it were Church. But the stageman called, & he went on his way. The building I found to be an Academy containing ordinarily 80 students —boys & girls. "Not so many girls now," added the bar-keeper, "because there is no female instructer, & they like a woman to teach them the higher things."—Ye stars! thought I, if the Metropolis [5] get this notion, the Mogul[1] & I must lack bread. At Spencer I sympathized with a Coachman who complained, that, 'ride as far or as fast as he ⟨co⟩would, the milestones were all alike, & told the same number.' Mr Stevens of N. Brookf[ield]. is an innholder after my heart—corpulent & comfortable, honest to a cent, with high opinions

---

[1] His brother William, like Emerson a schoolteacher.

of the clergy. And yet he told me there was a mournful rise of schisms since he was a boy, — Unitarians & Universalists — which, he said, he believed were all one, and he never heard their names till lately. I asked him the cause of all this frightful heterodoxy? The old Serpent, he said, was at work decieving men. He could not but think people *behaved* about as well now as their fathers did; but ⟨Mr⟩ then Mr Bisby (the Universalist [6] minister of B.) is a cunning fox. & by & bye he & his hosts will show what & how bad they really are. My good landlord's philanthropic conclusion was, that there was a monitor within and if we minded that, no matter how we speculated.

Sunday Evg., Aug. 24.

I rested this Sabbath day on the banks of the Quebog. Mr Stone, a worthy Calvinist, who had been already recommended to my respect, by the hearty praises of my last-named landlord, preached all day, and reminded me forcibly of one of my idols, Dr N. of Portland.[2] My lord Bacon, my trusty counsellor all the week, has six or seven choice essays for holy time. The [7] aforesaid lord knew passing well what was in man, woman, & child, what was in books, & what in palaces. This possessor of transcendant intellect was a mean slave to courts and a conniver at bribery. And now perchance if mental distinctions give place to moral ones at the end of life — now this intellectual giant who has been the instructor of the world and must continue to be a teacher of mankind till the end of time — has been forced to relinquish his preeminence and in another world to crawl in the dust at the feet of those to whom his mounting spirit was once a sacred guide. One instant succeeding dissolution will perhaps satisfy us, that there is no inconsistency in this. Till then I should be loth to ascribe any thing less than celestial state to the Prince of philosophers.

[8] Belchertown, Clapp's Hotel
Monday Afternoon.

After noticing the name of M. Rice upon the Hatstore, upon the Blacksmith's shop, & upon the Inn of S. Brookfield, I made inquiries

[2] Reverend Ichabod Nichols, pastor of the First Church (Unitarian) of Portland, Me., 1809–1859.

of my landlord, and learned that this omni-trader was he himself, who, moreover, owned two lines of stages! This morning, Phoebus and I set out together upon our respective journies; and I believe we shall finish them together, since this village is ten miles from Amherst. The morning walk was delightful; and the Sun amused himself & me by making rainbows on the thick mist which darkened the country. After passing through W. Brookfield I breakfasted among some right worshipful waggoners at the pleasant town of Western,[n] [9] and then passed through a part of Palmer (I believe) & Ware to this place. I count that road pleasant & that air good, which forces me to smile from mere animal pleasure, albeit I may be a smiling man; so I am free to commend the road from Cutler's Tavern in Western, as far as Babcock's in *Ware*, ⟨(?)⟩ to any youthful traveller, who walks upon a cloudless August Morning. Let me not forget to record here, the benevolent landlady of Ware who offered me her liquors & crackers upon the precarious credit of my return, rather than exchange my bills.

Monday Evg.
Bartlett's, Amherst.

I sit here 90 miles from home, & 3 from the Institution, and have the pleasure [10] & eke the honour, to waft, on the winged steeds of a wish, my best regards to the lords & ladye who sit at home; to the majesty of Tartary,—chiefest of men calling the young satraps to order from the elbow chair & secretly meditating golden schemes in an iron age; then to the young lion of the tribe, (to change the metaphor) now resting & musing on his honourable *Oars; next to my loudvoiced & sparebuilt friend, loving duty better, ⟨th⟩oh abundantly better than pudding;[n] last to the medalled youth[,] the anxious Driver & Director of the whole establishment; Peace to his Bones.[3]

My worthy landlord wishes blessings to the Amherst Institution, which, saith he, [11] howbeit it may have had a muddy foundation, yet the Lord hath blessed.

* A word which I take to be an abbreviation.

[3] Emerson has been referring to his four brothers, William ("the majesty of Tartary"), Edward ("the young lion of the tribe"), Robert ("my loudvoiced & sparebuilt friend"), and Charles ("the medalled youth"). See *J*, I, 274, n. 1.

Thursday, August [4]

Tuesday Morning I engaged Mr Bartlett to ⟨me⟩bring me to Mrs Shepard's and I think the worthy man returned with some complacent recollections of the instructions & remarks he had dropped on the way for the stranger's edification. Our wagon ride was somewhat uneasy from below but its ups & downs were amply compensated by the richness & grandeur visible above & around. Hampshire County rides in wagons. In this pleasant land I found a house-full of friends[,] a noble house — very good friends. In the afternoon I went to the College. The infant college is an Infant Hercules. Never was so much striving, outstretching, & advancing in a literary cause as is exhibited here. [12] The students all feel a personal responsibility in the support & defence of their young Alma Mater against all antagonists, and as long as this battle abroad shall continue, the ⟨g⟩Government, unlike all other Governments, will not be compelled to fight with its students within. The opposition of [n] other towns & counties produces moreover a correspondent friendship & kindness from the people in Amherst, and there is a daily exhibition of affectionate feeling between the inhabitants & the scholars, which is the more pleasant as it is so uncommon. They attended the Declamation & Commencement with the interest which parents usually shew at the exhibitions of schools where their own children are engaged. I believe the affair was first moved, about [13] three years ago, by the Trustees of the Academy. When the corner stone of the South College was laid, the Institution did not own a dollar. ⟨The stones⟩ A cartload of stones was brought by a farmer in Pelham, to begin the foundation; and now they have two large brick edifices, a President's house, & considerable funds. Dr Moore has left them six or seven thousand dollars. A poor one-

---

[4] Exactly when the rest of the journal was written is impossible to determine. If Emerson wrote this heading on Thursday, Aug. 28, he must have ended the entry at the first sentence on p. [15], for the following paragraph tells of events of the next day. In the paragraph beginning on p. [16] he speaks of Mr. Strong's, "where I have been spending a couple of days. . . ." This would argue an entry on Saturday, Aug. 30, especially since it is written in different ink from what precedes it. The paragraph on pp. [20]–[22] beginning "In the afternoon" and also written in different ink from what precedes it includes events from Saturday afternoon through Sunday evening, Aug. 31. The last section, from the bottom of p. [22] to the end, may have been written on various days after Sunday or it may all have been entered on Thursday, Sept. 4, after Emerson returned home.

legged man died last week in Pelham, who was not known to have any property, & left them 4000 dollars to be appropriated to the building of a Chapel, over whose door is to be inscribed his name, Adams Johnson. Wm Phillips gave a thousand & Wm Eustis a hundred dollars and great expectations are entertained from some rich men, friends to the Seminary who will die without children.

[14] They have wisely systematized this spirit of opposition which they have found so lucrative, & the students are all divided into thriving opposition societies which gather libraries, laboratories, mineral cabinets, &c, with an indefatigable spirit, which nothing but rivalry could inspire. Upon this impulse, they write, speak, & study in a sort of fury, which, I think, promises a harvest of attainments. The Commencement was plainly that of a young college, but had strength and eloquence mixed with the apparent 'vestigia ruris.'[5] And the scholar who gained the prize for declamation the evening before, would have a first prize at any Cambridge competition. [15] The College is supposed to be worth net 85000 dollars.

After spending three days very pleasantly at Mrs Shepard's, among orators, botanists, mineralogists, & above all, Ministers, I set off on Friday Morning with Thos Greenough & another little cousin in a chaise to visit Mount Holyoke. How high the hill may be, I know not; for, different accounts make it 8, 12, & 16 hundred feet from the river. The prospect repays the ascent and although the day was hot & hazy so as to preclude a distant prospect, yet all the broad meadows in the immediate vicinity of the mountain through which the Connecticutt winds, make a beautiful picture seldom rivalled. After adding our names in the books to the long list of strangers whom curiosity has attracted to this hill we descended in safety without [16] encountering rattlesnake or viper that have given so bad fame to the place. We were informed that about 40 people ascend the mountain every fair day during the summer. After passing through Hadley meadows, I took leave of my companions at Northampton bridge, and crossed for the first time the far famed Yankee river.

From the Hotel in Northampton I visited Mr. Theodore Strong, where I have been spending a couple of days of great pleasure. His five beautiful daughters & son make one of the finest families I ever

[5] "traces of the country" (Ed.).

saw. In the afternoon, I went on horse back (oh Hercules!) with Allen Strong to Round Hill, the beautiful site of the Gymnasium, & to Shepherd's Factory about 4 miles from the [17] centre of the town. Saturday Morning we went in a chaise in pursuit of a lead mine said to lie about five miles off which we found after great & indefatigable search. We tied our horse & descended, by direction, into a somewhat steep glen ⟨wh⟩at the bottom of which we found the covered entrance of a little canal about 5 ft. wide. Into this artificial cavern we fired a gun to call out the miner from within. The report was long & loudly echoed & after a weary interval we discerned a boat with lamps lighted in its sides issuing from this dreary abode. We welcomed the Miner to the light of the Sun and leaving our hats without, & binding our heads we lay down in the boat and were immediately introduced to [18] a cave varying in height from 4 to 6 & 8 feet, hollowed in a pretty soft sandstone through which the water continually drops. When we lost the light of the entrance & saw only this gloomy passage by the light of lamps ⟨we⟩ it required no effort of imagination to believe we were leaving the world, & our smutty ferryman was a true Charon. After sailing a few hundred feet the vault grew higher & wider overhead & there was a considerable trickling of water on our left; this was the ventilator of the mine & reaches up to the surface of the earth. We continued to advance in this manner for 900 feet & then got out of the boat & walked on planks a little way to the end of this excavation. Here [19] we expected to find the lead vein↑,↓ & the operations of the subterranean man, but were sadly disappointed. He had been digging through this stone for 12 years↑,↓ & has not yet discovered any lead at all. Indications of lead at the surface led some Boston gentleman to set this man at work in the expectation that after cutting his dark canal for 1000 feet, he would reach the vein, & the canal would then draw off the water which prevented them from digging from above. As yet, he has found no lead but, as he gravely observed 'has reached some *excellent granite*.'[n] In this part of the work he has 40 dollars for every foot he advances and it occupies him ten days to earn this. [20] He has advanced 975 feet & spends his days, winter & summer, alone in this damp & silent tomb. He says the place is excellent for meditation, & that he sees no goblins. Many visiters come to his dark residence, & pay him a shilling apiece for the sight. A young man, he said, came the day before us, who after going in a little way was taken with terrors & said he felt faint, & returned. Said Miner is a brawny personage & discreet withal; has a wife, & lives near the hole. All his excavations are performed by successive blastings.

In the afternoon I set out on my way to Greenfield intending [21] to pass the Sabbath with George Ripley.[6] Mr Strong insisted on carrying me to Hatfield, & thence I passed chiefly on foot through Whately & Deerfield over sands & pinebarrens, & across Green River to ⟨H⟩Greenfield, and did not arrive there till after ten o'clock & found both taverns shut up. I should have staid in Deerfield if Mr S. had not ridiculed the idea of getting to Greenfield that night. In the morning I called at Mr Ripley's, & was sorely disappointed to learn that his son was at Cambridge. The family were exceedingly hospitable, and I listened with no great pleasure to a sermon from Rev. Mr Perkins of Amherst in the morng & in the afternoon rode over to the other parish with Mr R. to hear Rev Lincoln [22] Ripley.[7] After service Mr L. R ⟨ca⟩returned with us, and in the evening we heard another sermon from Mr Perkins which pleased me abundantly better than his matins. He is a loudvoiced scripture-read divine, & his compositions have the elements of a potent eloquence,[n] but he lacks taste. By the light of the Evening star, I walked with my reverend uncle, a man, who well sustains the character of an aged missionary. It is a new thing to him, he said, to *correspond* with his wife, and he attends the mail regularly every Monday morng. to send or recieve a letter.

After a dreamless night, & a most hospitable entertainment I parted from Greenfield & through an unusually [23] fine country, crossed the Connecticut (shrunk to a rivulet in this place somewhere in Montagu). My solitary way grew somewhat more dreary, as I drew nearer Wendell and the only relief to hot sandy roads & a barren monotonous region was one fine forest with many straight clean pinetrees upwards of a hundred feet high 'fit for the mast of some

[6] The son of the Greenfield merchant Jerome Ripley, George (1802–1880) entered Harvard when Emerson was a junior, graduated first in his class, and gave the English oration at the Commencement in 1823, at about the time Emerson was in Greenfield. Later, he helped found the Transcendental Club and Brook Farm.
[7] As the brother of Emerson's step-grandfather, Reverend Ezra Ripley of Concord, who had married Emerson's widowed grandmother, Lincoln Ripley was Emerson's step-great-uncle.

great Admiral.'[8] All that day was a thoughtless heavy pilgrimage and Fortune deemed that such a crowded week of pleasure demand⟨s⟩ed a reaction of pain. At night I was quartered in the meanest caravansera which has contained [24] my person since the tour began. Traveller! weary & jaded, who regardest the repose of th⟨y⟩ine earthly tenement; Traveller, hungry & athirst whose heart warms to the hope of animal gratification; Traveller of seven or seventy years beware, beware, I beseech you of Mr Haven's Inn in New Salem. Already he is laying a snare for your kindness or credulity in fencing in a mineral spring for your infirmities. Beware——

From Mr Haven's garret bed I sallied forth Tuesday morng towards Hubbardston, but my cramped limbs made little speed. After dining in Hubbardston [25] I walked seven miles farther to Princeton designing to ascend Wachusett with my tall cousin Thomas ↑Greenough↓ if I should find him there, & then set out for home in the next day's stage. But when morning came, & the stage was brought, and the mountain was a mile & a half away,— I learned again an old lesson, that, the beldam ⟨d⟩Disappointment sits at Hope's door. I jumped into the stage & rode away, Wachusett untrod. At Sterling I learned that Oliver Blood studies physic in Worcester; at[n] Bolton I saw Nat Wood on his way to Amherst N. H. to [26] study law, his pedagogical career being terminated[9]— O fortunate nimium! [10]

Close cooped in a stage coach with a score of happy dusty rustics the pilgrim continued his ride to Waltham, and alighting there, spent an agreeable evening at Rev. Mr Ripley's.[11] Home he came from thence the next morning, right glad to sit down once more in a quiet wellfed family — ↑at Canterbury.↓

[8] Milton, *Paradise Lost*, I, 293–294, inaccurately quoted.

[9] Both Oliver Blood and Nathaniel Wood had been Harvard classmates and Blood was a charter member of the nameless literary society to which Emerson belonged. A student of medicine under Dr. John Green of Worcester, he received the M.D. degree in 1826. Wood, a tutor at Harvard in 1823, later became a lawyer and a member of the Massachusetts legislature.

[10] "O too fortunate one" (Ed.) — doubtless adapted from Virgil's "O fortunatos nimium" (*Georgics*, II, 458) rather than echoed from "Lydia," 9. Emerson meant, of course, that Wood did not know how well off he was to have escaped from teaching.

[11] Reverend Samuel Ripley, Emerson's step-uncle, in whose school he had taught for two summers.

Wide World 12

1823–1824

The last in the sequence of journals bound together, this journal was originally entitled "Wideworld No 12" and was later given the letter designation M. The dated entries, following immediately from Wide World 11, begin on December 14, 1823. The last dated entry is January 25, 1824, but Emerson may have added in February the few subsequent entries, since Wide World XIII, started at least as early as February 17, 1824, continues the undated discussion of "Institutions" at the end of Wide World 12.

The manuscript is composed of ten folded sheets of unlined paper, hand-stitched into a single gathering and then sewed together by white thread with Wide World numbers 9, 10, and 11. The twenty leaves measure 16.5 x 21 cm.

[1]¹   Δος που στω
Wideworld, No 12   Canterbury, Dec. 14, 1823.
           M

The world changes its masters, but keeps its own identity, and entails upon each new family of the human race, that come to garnish it with names & memorials of themselves, — certain indelible features and unchanging properties. Proud of their birth to a new & brilliant life, each presumptuous generation boasts its dominion over nature; forgetful that these very springing powers within, which nurse this arrogance, are part of the ⟨gifts⟩ ↑fruits↓ of that Nature, whose secret but omnipotent influence, makes them all that they are. The world which they inhabit they call their servant, but it proves the real master. Moulded of its clay, breathing its atmosphere, ⟨living in⟩

¹ "SAMENESS" is centered beneath "now, as upon" at the bottom of the page. "Prynne Puritan B" is written vertically in the left margin, from "its livery," below to "very springing" above. "Δos που στω" is framed in a rectangle. Archimedes' familiar statement reads in full, "Δός που στῶ καὶ τὴν γῆν κινήσω" — "Give me a place to stand on and I will move the earth" (Ed.).

↑fed of↓ its elements, they must wear its livery, ↑the livery of corruption & change↓ & obey the laws which *all* its atoms obey. The relations (growing out of their condition here,) which subsist between
its children, fasten themselves with the same unfailing precision now,
as upon the first family [2]² that tilled the earth. Nor has the great
lapse of time that separates the infant Empires of Assyria and Egypt
from the expanding dynasties of the New World altered to any considerable degree the character of the human mind, or the conditions
& relations of the race. The lively fancy of some men has induced
them to ⟨believe⟩ ↑entertain↓ fanciful anticipations of the progress of
Mankind, & of radical revolutions in their manners, passions, & pursuits, ⟨of the⟩ already forming in the womb of ages. But the quiet
wisdom of history as she winds along her way through sixty centuries, speaks of no wonders, & of little glory. ⟨Nimrod, long of yore⟩
Noah awoke from his wine as the sensualist awakes today, but without the patriarch's excuse. Nimrod, long of yore, hunted man & beast
from the same furious impulses that drove Alexander & Caesar &
Buonaparte over Europe. No vices, that we ever heard of, have
grown old & died. ⟨They are a vampire brood & live upon those whom
they destroy.⟩ They outlast the pyramids, & laugh at Destruction.
The same topics which the eldest moralist urged, are repeated [3]³
by our preachers now, & received with the same repugnance, by the
first & last offender. Suffering & sickness are the same thing now as
of old. No one passion has become extinct. Joy has not altered its
nature, nor learned to last. Man has died as a leaf. Families & Nations
have mouldered; but all the traits of their nature have been faithfully transmitted without an irregularity.

There is a much vaunted progress in the world from the rudeness
of savage habits to the prosperous refinement of civilized nations. But
the change is very short from the barbarian to the polished gentleman; at least, what is cast aside is very insignificant compared with
what remains — of the dull unmoveable nature. The world, I said,
holds more dominion than it yields — both the Natural & Moral System. The Sun's everlasting light does not wax dim; it ⁿ kindles the
animal spirits of youth in the Morning of life with the same rich &

---

² "SAMENESS" is centered beneath "moralist urged," at the bottom of the page.
³ "SAMENESS" is centered beneath "the world, had" at the bottom of the page.

fervent glow it has always imparted. But this identity of things is
still more extensive. Go back into time, ↑until↓ when the waters of
the Flood had ↑just↓ subsided; he that had lived twenty years in the
world, had passed through many [4]⁴ moods of thinking; he had entertained ⟨v⟩unmeasured hopes, & seen them vanish; he had felt
himself ⟨sent⟩ to be an apostle of joy to mourners, & of regeneration
to old & corrupt forms of society; he had also felt himself to be in the
Universe an abject worm of no use or account. He had known hours,
on which the consenting stars seemed to shed all the best influences
of heaven; hours of delightful hope, & enthusiastic devotion; when
his spirit expanded to be worthy of the universe in which it dwelt,
& became akin, ↑as it seemed,↓ to Cherubim & Seraphim, in its capacities as in its sentiments. He triumphed in existence[,] he triumphed
in the love of truth & the desire of communicating it. The heroic spirit
of martyrdom, elevated his mind. But, alas! Night follows Day, &
other hours quenched the glory of these. Melancholy seasons came,
in which he felt with force

> "How weary, stale, flat, & unprofitable
> Are all the uses of this world."
> [*Hamlet*, I, ii, 133–134]

He wondered how he could be created ⟨as⟩for so ignoble a life.
His mind that should be so quick with thought was a barren blank.
His heart, which should be so full of warm affections reaching out
to all beings, languished in a dearth of all sympathies. Such a being
is man, then, now, & ever.

> Alas our young affections run to waste
> Or water but the desert
> [Byron, *Childe Harold's Pilgrimage*, IV, cxx]

> The chimney of the
> volcano

[5]⁵ [December 21] Who is he that shall controul me? Why
may not I act & speak & write & think with entire freedom? What am

---

⁴ "SAMENESS" is written at the bottom of the page.
⁵ "PRIDE" is written beneath "tribunal" and "TASTE" beneath "will submit."
at the bottom of the page. This page is reproduced as plate I.

I to the Universe, or, the Universe, what is it to me? Who hath forged the chains of Wrong & Right, of Opinion & Custom? And must I wear them? ⟨Has Society a sceptre and⟩ Is[n] ⟨it⟩ ↑Society↓ my ↑anointed↓ King? Or is there any ↑mightier↓ community or any man or more than man, whose slave I am? I am solitary in the vast society of beings; I consort with no species; I indulge no sympathies. I see the world, human, brute & inanimate nature; I am in the midst of them, but not *of* them; I hear the song of the storm, — the Winds & warring Elements sweep by me — but they mix not with my being. I see ⟨its⟩cities & nations & witness passions, — the roar of their laughter, — but I partake it not; — the yell of their grief, — it touches no chord in me; their fellowships & fashions, lusts & virtues, the words & deeds they call glory & shame, — I disclaim them all. I say to the Universe, Mighty one! thou art not my mother; Return to chaos, if thou wilt, I shall still exist. I live. If I owe my being, it is to a destiny greater than th⟨ese⟩ine.[n] Star by Star, world by world, system by system shall be crushed, — but I shall live. Dec. 21. —

↑'Animasque in vulnere ponunt.'[6]
Virgil↓ [*Georgics,* IV, 238]

It is an ancient question which Mr Alison has ⟨de⟩helped to settle whether there be an ultimate standard of Taste.[7] Is there in Nature any final Test by which all tastes may be tried, & to the authority of which tribunal all will submit?[n] In matters of [6][8] religious Faith the Bible is such an ultimate standard. All over Christendom its authority is acknowledged and all doctrines stand or fall according to their conformity or disagreement with this book. A do⟨ctrine⟩gma which appears very rational to one man seems very whimsical to another and men might therefore (if left to themselves) go very wide of truth & one another in their creeds but are all brought back by the existence of this salutary Touchstone, to some similarity of belief. Now ⟨a s⟩ we shall clear our ideas very much by keeping this analogy in view in finding what is the Standard of Taste. Such a Standard should be a code of general principles capable of being so applied to

[6] "lay down their lives in the wound."
[7] See above, p. 168.
[8] "TASTE" is centered beneath "without any" at the bottom of the page.

every possible production of Nature or Art as to determine at once
its beauty or deformity. The field of Taste is so ample that it is obvious, no rules could be laid down which should embrace all or any
adequate part of its works, and the Code must consist rather of
Negative laws ordaining what may not than what may be done. In
religious faith, what is not *repugnant* to any part of Holy writ, albeit
not anywhere specially enjoined, may be neither criminal nor false.
So there may be an infinite diversity of good works of art, all different, but none offending.

The supposition will be fairer, & the parallel preciser, if we
substitute for a Bible given by heaven, the mass of moral maxims
gradually accumulated, without any supernatural aid, [7][9] by the
force of reason & observation in Greece. If a body of men had been
chosen ⟨to⟩ in the time of ⟨Aristotle⟩ Alexander the great to condense
into a volume all the moral laws which had been expressed, and
acquiesced in by ↑all↓ the ⟨series of professed teachers ph⟩ sages who
had taught in Athens, a body of morality might have been framed
containing all the fundamental precepts essential to the good order
of society & the self government of the individual. When this system of natural law had recieved ↑as it would have done↓ the express
or tacit sanction of succeeding generations, it might be appealed to
with confidence as an ultimate standard of morality. Indeed, the single
instance of the establishment & universality of the ↑International↓
law ⟨of Nations⟩, the work of three or four respectable individuals —
is decisive.

(See Ed. Rev. of Stewart's Introduction to the Encyclopedia.)[10]

Now it is not I concieve extravagant to suppose that a bible of
Taste might be also compiled, ⟨from⟩ by selecting the unanimous conclusions of judicious men. That no such code has yet been contrived
cannot prove the impossibility of its execution when it is remembered
that the su⟨l⟩btilety of these principles makes them difficult to be
detected — unlike those of morals which lie at the surface. If this be
practicable, there is an ultimate standard; for as that is to be framed

[9] "TASTE" is centered beneath "been embodied." at the bottom of the page.
[10] *A General View of the Progress of Metaphysical, Ethical, and Political Science, since the Revival of Letters,* Part II. . . . (Supplement to the *Encyclopedia
Britannica,* Vol. V, Part I); *The Edinburgh Review,* XXXVI (Oct. 1821), 220–
267.

of the conclusions of individuals, the nearest approach to it must always be the ↑private↓ judgements of those law givers until they have been embodied.

["A painted cup Dr Johnson says proves beauty is not utility"] [10a]

[8] [11] ⟨T⟩ I see no reason why I should bow my head to man or cringe in my demeanour. When the soul is disembodied, he that has nothing else but a towering independence has one claim to respect; whilst genius & learning ⟨will⟩ ↑may↓ provoke our contempt for their supple knees. When I consider my poverty & ignorance, & the positive superiority of talents, virtues, & manners, which I must acknowledge in many men, I am prone to merge my dignity in a most uncomfortable sense of unworthiness. But when I reflect that I am an immortal being, born to a destiny immeasurably high, deriving my moral & intellectual attributes directly from Almighty God, & that my existence & condition as his child, must be forever independent of the controul or will of my fellow children, — I am elevated in my own eyes to a higher ground in life & a better self esteem. But, ↑alas!↓ few men hold with a strong grasp the sceptre of self-government & can summon into exercise, at will, whatever set of feeling suits their judgement best. One is apt, ↑when in society↓ to be tormented ⟨,⟩ with this ⟨repugnant⟩ ↑odious↓ abasement, ⟨when in Society,⟩ to wonder reluctantly with a foolish face of praise, & to consent, with bitter inward reproaches, to things & thoughts he cannot combat; and, in solitude, only, to be uplifted by this manly but useless independence. A vigorous resolution is not enough to conquer this abominable habit. A ⟨fervent⟩ ↑humble↓ Christian would not wallow in his humility. His reverence for the Creator precludes an extravagant deference to the Creature.

[9] [12] Selfish philosophy & selfishness are so odious that whatever wears an opposite aspect to them comes recommended to our cordial esteem. One is as much elevated by the contemplation of the benevolent affections, as pestered by selfishness. Language like Cicero's or Virgil's; — & ruins of ↑the homes of↓ magnanimous minds

[10a] *Boswell's Life of Johnson*, ed. George B. Hill; revised and enlarged edition by L. F. Powell, 6 vols. (Oxford, 1934), II, 166. The "quotation" is a paraphrase.

[11] "⟨Self esteem⟩" is centered beneath "extravagant deference" at the bottom of the page.

[12] "FRIENDSHIP" is centered beneath "universal citizenship, & is" at the bottom of the page.

have we say a *classic* air but the generous feelings have a more than classic hand & imbue all things they touch with a tenderness & beauty of association; which is of no slight or partial application but touches every heart in the great electric circle of human beings. A man therefore is always safe in writing the eulogy of the kind affections. He is secure of being kindled by his theme, & of meeting the sympathy of his reader. And if ⟨writing⟩ ↑the account↓ of these be ⟨de⟩agreeable, much more their exercise. No flower is so beautiful to the eye, no proportions so pleasing as to create that refined delight that springs from beholding the face of a friend. Friendship is ⟨the⟩ ↑an eternal↓ practical triumph over all forms of malignant philosophy. It is not the rare fruit of a heated soil, nor the offspring of one ↑peculiar↓ stock of manners or religion. It is not Roman nor Greek; not the son of Antiquity or of Civilization, but the spontaneous offspring of the human nature under every sky & age & /circumstance/government/.

I know not why it is, that, though Friendship ⟨boasts⟩ ↑has↓ this universal citizenship, & is no Aristocrat to [10][13] Fortune, or Family, or Genius; though all conspire to praise it & all generations enter deeply into the feelings which the fabled Nisus & Damon indulged towards Euryalus & Pythias; — that notwithstanding this unanimous sympathy of all tribes & tongues, so few men should ally themselves to others by this intimate & excellent connexion. Is it the unlike constitution of the minds that commonly meet, which prevents them from sympathising; or some bar in the state of society, which is only occasionally overleaped, — that makes so few get what all admire & covet? [n]

(Continued on Page 16) [14]

Romance grows out of ignorance, & so is the curse of its own age, & the ornament of those that follow. Romance is never present, always remote; not a direct but reflected ray. It is things cruel & abominable in act that become romantic in memory. Unprincipled bandits are Red Cross Knights, & Templars & Martyrs⟨e⟩ even, in the Song of this Century.* In individual history disagreeable occurrences are re-

* In Greece, such a person was a hero in the second generation, a giant in the third, & a god in the fourth.

[13] "ROMANCE" is centered beneath "giant in the third," in Emerson's footnote at the bottom of the page. [14] See p. 198 below.

membered long after with complacency. A Romantic Age, properly speaking, cannot exist. Eating & drinking, ⟨hunge⟩ cold & poverty, speedily reduce men to vulgar animals. Heaven & earth hold nothing fanciful. As mind advances, all becomes practical. Knowledge is a law-giver, as fancy is an abolisher of laws, — & introduces order & limit ↑even↓ into the character of Deity.

[11][15] Nevertheless Romance is mother of Knowledge — this ungrateful son that eats up his parent. It is only by searching for wonders that they found truth. Omne ignotum pro magnifico;[16] if the unknown was not magnified, nobody would explore. Europe would lack the regenerating impulse, & America lie waste, had it not been for El Dorado. The history of all science is alike — Men guess & to verify their guesses, they go & see, and are disappointed, but bring back truth. —— That fables should abound, seems not to indicate any especial activity of mind, for though Greece had many,[n] stupid Indostan has more. It may be that theirs[n] are the ⟨gro⟩ traditionary ingenuity of that supposed ancient parent people of Asia, that Bailly[17] wrote of. She that is not gay or gaudy, pitiful or capricious, * 'that liveth & conquereth forevermore,' that is 'the strength & the wisdom, the power & majesty of all ages' is *Truth*.

↑A nation like a tree does not thrive till it is engraffed with a foreign stock.↓[18]

The tendencies of literature in different ages observable. In France & England has sometimes run strongly towards drama, as in the rude Mysteries; in England ⟨a⟩in the last Century was historical — Hume, Gibbon, Robertson. In this day runs to Periodical writing, to newspaper, magazine, encyclopedia, & review. Causes & uses. Newspapers not known in Greece or Rome; (the first was published in

* I. Esdras IV, 38, 40.

[15] "Newspapers" is centered beneath "citizens; that he" at the bottom of the page.

[16] "The unknown is ever magnified." Tacitus, *Agricola*, xxx.

[17] Jean Sylvain Bailly (1736–1793), whose *Lettres sur L'Atlantide de Platon et sur l'ancienne histoire de l'Asie*, . . . (Londres, 1779), mentions an ancient people who instructed the Indians (p. 6).

[18] Possibly a quotation.

England, in Elizabeth's time) ⟨?⟩ 1538 ⟨ha⟩their help & harm pretty evenly balanced. Inasmuch as it is good the peasant in his humble cot should be acquainted with his government, the actions, interests, characters, of his rulers & distinguished fellow citizens; that he should have [12][19] a rational & exciting amusement; that he should not be liable to be misled by rumours, parents of national evils — in so much, a newspaper is good. ⟨Wh⟩ In a nation large as the United States, without prints, to what unruly extravagance false reports about men & events would grow before they could be corrected, is easily concieved. For a report cannot be *denied*; but a *printed* rumour can. But as vehicles of slander, & virulent party spirit they are fatally convenient. Dr Channing thought them eminently useful in enlarging the sphere of human sympathy; confederating us with distant Greece,[n] enabling a nation to unite in one feeling & hence in one effort. —— But Crusades without prints excited intenser sympathy. This example will go in favour of newspapers, for, as was said above, they were, for want of rapidly circulating information, ignorant, foolish, uncorrected, excitements. — Newspapers, are the proper literature of America, which affects to be so practical & unromantic a land.

The Indian Pantheon is of prodigious size; 330 million Gods have in it each their heaven, or rather each their parlour, in this immense "goddery." "In ⟨its⟩ quantity & absurdity their superstition has nothing to match it, that is or ever was in the world." (See two ⟨fine⟩ articles on Hindu Mathematics; & Mythology in the 29 Vol. of the Edin Review.)[20]   IND.

[13] The theory of Mr Alison assigning the beauty of the object

[19] "Newspapers" is enclosed in a rectangle beneath "Mythology" and there is an ornate "H[?]" beneath "Review.)" at the bottom of the page.
[20] Reviews of *Algebra, with Arithmetic and Mensuration, from the Sanskrit. . .* , transl. by Henry Thomas Colebrooke (London, 1817); and of three separate volumes, W. Ward, *Account of the Writings, Religion, and Manners of the Hindoos,* . . . (Serampore, 1811); W. Ward, *A View of the History, Literature and Religion of the Hindoos. . .* , 3rd ed., 2 vols. (London, 1817); and Abbé J. A. Dubois, *Description of the Character, Manners and Customs of the People of India. . .* [n.p., n.d.], *The Edinburgh Review,* XXIX (Nov. 1817), 141–164, and (Feb. 1818), 377–403. Emerson draws upon statements on pp. 383 and 388, but his "quotation" is a paraphrase.

to the mind of the beholder, is natural & plausible.[21] This want of
uniformity is useful. It prevents us all from falling in love with the
same face & as the associations are accidental enables them to hope
& to succeed to whose form & feature partial Nature has been niggard
of her ornaments. A homely verse of blessed truth in human history
saith

> "There lives no goose so gray, but soon or late
> She finds some honest gander for her mate." —
> [Pope, "The Wife of Bath, Her Prologue," ll. 98–99]

— Byron's fine verses are ⟨in⟩conformable to this theory.

> "Of its own beauty is the mind diseased
> And fevers into false Creation" &c
> [*Childe Harold's Pilgrimage*, IV, cxxii]

"x x Who loves, raves; 'tis youth's frenzy," &c.   [*Ibid.*, IV, cxxiii]

Dec.
Dec. 31. — ⟨I bear no badge, no tinsel star⟩
  1823. — ⟨Glistens upon my breast⟩
     I   ⟨Nor jewelled crown nor pictured Car⟩
       ⟨Robs me of rest.⟩

       ⟨I am not poor, but I am proud⟩
     II   ⟨Of one inalienable right⟩
       ⟨Above the envy of the crowd —⟩
       Thought's holy light.

       Better it is than gems or gold
       And oh it cannot die,
    III   But thought will glow when the Sun grows cold
       And mix with Deity.

[14] 1824. — A merry new year to the Wideworld

[21] See *Essays on the Nature and Principles of Taste* (New York, 1854), p. 20.
Emerson may have remembered the idea from reading Alison or the review cited on
p. 168 above.

The theory of the strong impulse is true I believe, nor does it matter at all what sort of being ⟨e⟩or event impart it. ⟨The⟩ Religion was always one of the strongest. Few bodies or parties have served the world so well as the Puritans. From their irreverent zeal came most of the improvements of the British Constitution. It was they who settled N. America. Bradford & Winthrop & Standish, Mathers & Jonathan Edwards, Otis, Hawley, Hancock, Adams, Franklin, & whatever else of vigorous sense, or practical genius, this country shews, are the issue of Puritan⟨s⟩ stock. The community of language with England, has doubtless deprived us of that original characteristic literary growth that has ever accompanied, I apprehend[,] the first bursting of a nation from the bud. Our ↑era of↓ exploits & civiliz⟨in⟩a-tion is ripe enow. And, had it not been dissipated by the unfortunate rage for periodical productions, our literature should have been born & grown ere now to a Greek or Roman stature. Franklin is such a fruit as might be expected from such a tree. Edwards, perhaps more so. [15] The Puritans had done their duty to literature when they bequeathed it the Paradise Lost & Comus; to Science, by   [,] to Legislation, by   — ; to all the great interests of humanity by planting the New World, with their thrifty stock. If there be such a thing as the propagation of moral & intellectual character for many generations, the prosperity of America might have been safely foretold. The energy of an abused people whose eyes the light of books & progress of knowledge had just opened has a better title to immortality than that vulgar physical energy which some nations are supposed to inherit from ⟨their⟩ ↑Gothic or↓ Scandinavian Sires. Fam-ily pride engrafted on a pedigree of a thousand nobles yields to the pride of intellectual power, — the pride of indomitable purpose. A few stern leaders of that stern sect nourished in their bosoms settled designs of reform & gave to the design such shape & impulse, that when they slept in the earth, the hope failed not. It was the nursling of an iron race. Their prayers, thoughts, & deeds were brothers to the sentiment. It grew & throve mightily in England. Its tremendous activity outwent doubtless the expectations of its early friends & the apprehensions of its enemies. The old courses into which national feeling runs, were broken up. Wise men were aghast at the fury of the convulsion, and abandoned in so wild a tempest, the helm which no human hand could providently hold. There is a sort of great ruffians that appear in such crises in human society to profit by a timely boldness & intrude themselves in [16]²² the hour of peril into places, that are in quiet times alike above their capacity & fortune. They are like those foolhardy robbers who run over the burning lava to turn into brothels of riotous debauch the recently deserted palaces which the Volcano menaces. They cannot retain their illgotten eminence when order is restored, & lords that are wise as well as strong usurp their thrones. Bear witness England & France in their Regicide Revolutions. Nameless & birthless scoundrels climbed up in the dark, & sat in the seat of the Stuarts & Bourbons. Cromwell & Napoleon plucked them down when the light returned & locked their own yoke round the necks of mankind[.]

Continued from p [10]

Jan. 5. He defrauds himself of half his life who can & does not ally himself to his companion by stricter bonds than mere acquaintance. ⟨It is⟩ Friendship is the sole romantic thing in life, that remains romantic. All childhood's poetry of hope & love, all youth's poetry of love fades after a brief bloom; but the delight of man's mind in man, the pleasing expectation & memory of his society as well as its present excitement, the ups & downs, the caprices of friendship do not fade, for aught I know ever. [17]²³ When one man has established with another that perfect understanding to which I give the name he may laugh or weep, trifle or pray, sing or reason in his presence; ↑may, in short,↓ act out his nature, give voice to all the whims of his most fantastic hour — without fear or misapprehension. Now it is very clear, that this cannot be done under the prescriptions of aching affectation, in the bowing crowd, or with an indifferent person. It is good for a man to feel that he is cared for,ⁿ that anxious eyes are cast upon the course of his fortunesⁿ as they are tossed on Time's water. He will not ↑himself↓ distrust the ⟨powers⟩ ↑faculties↓ that another does not distrust. He will work harder — mind & body.

²² "FRIENDSHIP" is centered beneath "aught I know" at the bottom of the page.
²³ "FRIENDSHIP" is centered beneath "will be barren & cold" at the bottom of the page.

He will love existence more, which with all men at certain times is
a dubious boon.

The besetting sin of men in society & out, is selfishness. Every
man who aspires to high things is more or less susp⟨icious⟩↑ected↓ of
being more exquisitely self loving. The best way to ↑avoid the crime
& to↓ parry this charge, is to be deeply interested in another's welfare.
It will keep your affections & ↑the current of your↓ thought unsoured
& pure. And it will keep your name unstained in the popular eye. For
all men regard friendship as attractive, fascinating, noble. It is supremely pleasant in this life, & when ⟨the⟩ soul & body separate methinks his lot is good ⟨whose fervent ⁿ affections shall then expand,⟩
↑who goes out to explore the abyss with a kindred spirit↓ & who does
not roam alone thro' worlds of strangers; methinks even the immensity of existence & of knowledge will be barren & cold to him.

[18] "A friend should bear a friend's infirmities." [24] This does
not chime perfectly with my fancies. Friends should not have infirmities; that is, discordant infirmities; Friendship will melt like snow if
there be anything likely to disgust, between parties. I may be the
friend of a passionate man perhaps but not of an illhumoured one &
bear his ill humour nor of a proser, & bear his long stories; nor of a
⟨vulgar⟩ plebeian, & tolerate his vulgarities. Hearts must be of a
mould to match. I have heard of instances indeed where ⟨the⟩ contrary inclinations have agreed well, the projections of one character
happening to adjust themselves, as it seemed to the cavities of the
other. But I believe this was a companionship & no nearer love. For
there must be no hollowness or artifice in the sympathy that would
be permanent. As there necessarily must be where one cannot relish
or concieve the pleasures of the other.

[25] It is curious how deceptive history when most authentic, is. Fifty,
twenty, or ten men, sometimes one man become in it the representatives [of] a nation & what is worse for truth do not speak for the
nation but only for themselves. In very unquiet times the number
augments, but is always comparatively insignificant, & in this case

[24] Shakespeare, *Julius Caesar*, IV, iii, 85.
[25] Random writing — "⟨There⟩" "How" "⟨rel⟩" and "F Co[?]" — appears at
the left of the beginning of the following entry.

compensates the better [19]²⁶ number by a worse character. We gravely write or read as the history of ⟨the French Revolution⟩ France the ⟨hi⟩ account of a miscreant mob who in ⟨the⟩ pursuit of pillage & rapine acted out their own horrible will for a series of months without any ⟨other⟩ settled design, and who no ⟨more⟩ ↑further↓ dreamd of revolution than as far as it would gratify their own appetite for bacchanalian disorder. A great deal, perhaps the greater proportion, was done at random & afterwards taken advantage of from time to time by the bolder sort of men of influence who found themselves thrown by circumstances into power. Their views also, were not premeditated; but open⟨d⟩ed as events opened wider & wilder changes. The only connexion in these events was mere succession. But when the fray is over, comes the sage annalist, with wise political saws, affecting to give order to the Chaos, & ascends for remote causes two or three reigns to the profligate splendour of an elder King. Whil⟨e⟩st nobody doubts that with as imbecile a monarch & ill-advised a ministry Lord George Gordon's mob or Jack Cade's mob or Mr Cobbett's mobs might effect as bloody wonders in free & enlightened London. That the famine & despotism of France made the difference between their Revolution & ours cannot be doubted. But nevertheless the history is much farce.

[20]²⁷ Jan. 10, 1824. — I apprehend every thinking man's experience attests the accordance to Nature of the Baconian maxim, of not building our theories except upon the slow & patient accumulation of ↑a↓ sufficiency of experiments. Youth says I will be famed — I will write. But wheresoever Youth turns his eyes for the subject of his vast meditation, he is met by the barrenness of facts, & forced to go labour in the chronicles for the ⟨fo⟩ⁿ substance he pants to adorn.

A community's rigid morality, has it any known effect on mind? A community's abominable immorality — has it known effects? The sight of beauty has curious effects, it bewilders the Mind into ⟨f⟩

²⁶ "FRENCH REVOLUTION" nearly fills the bottom margin.
²⁷ "TASTE" is centered beneath "representation," at the bottom of the page. Sketches of two male heads appear in the text, in the last three lines of the first paragraph.

reveries profligate of precious time. It produces a stronger impulse on one's common hopes. Ambition's tide rushes faster & with more determinate purpose. It dissatisfies the admirer with ↑the playing of↓ his own part this time & begets deceitful intentions for the time to come. If there be, as there does not seem to be, aught of sensuality in that[n] gratification, it is exquisitely refined & disguised. There is least of that ingredient in the sight of most perfect beauty. We shall help then to acquit Plato of extravagance, who contemplated divine beauty under its ⟨ne⟩ closest representation, human beauty.

[21][28] Men are not aware, & pedagogues least of all, how much truth is in that tritest of commonplaces 'that one may study human nature to advantage in a school.' When a man has been reading or hearing the history of politic men, of insinuating contrivance which neutralized hostility; of arts that brought the sturdiest prejudices to parley; of men whose ⟨wor⟩[n] eye & tongue got them that ascendancy over other men's minds which the sword cannot give — from Pericles thro' Aug Caesar & unnumbered Italians down to Charles II & to Aaron Burr even, he is often stung ⟨him⟩ with the desire of being himself a cunning workman in that art of arts — human nature. But when he looks around on his acquaintances in search of materials, the force of habit is so strong that he cannot strip himself of the old feelings that always arise at the sight of those well known persons nor come to consider them as mere subjects to work upon. He cannot, if he try[,] keep on, nay, can seldom put on the ↑iron↓ mask he would assume. Nature will speak out, in spite of his ⟨toil⟩ grimace, in the old vulgar frankness of a man to his fellow. All his projected artificial greatness, his systematic courtesy, which under [22][29] the guise of kindness pride devises to keep men at bay, his promised self control; his wisdom that should drop only aphorisms, all falls ↑quite↓ down[n] ⟨down⟩. Ambition will drop asleep & the naked mediocrity of the man is seen as it was wont,[n] & he says & does ordinary things in a very ordinary way & his influence which was to be so enormous is quite insignificant. Before these disappointments occurred, the experiment wore a very practicable air, & afterwards

---

[28] "CHARACTER" is centered beneath "systematic courtesy," at the bottom of the page.
[29] "CHARACTER" is centered beneath "the theatre of a school." at the bottom of the page.

he always attributes the failure not to any absurdity or impossibility in the ⟨plan⟩ scheme itself, but to the unconquerable opposition he had to encounter, in the strength of the habits he long before formed. This in many instances gives rise to the expression of a wish to go among strangers. The aspirant very naturally believes that he shall get rid of the associations by escaping from their objects. It may be he cheats himself. He does not know that the feelings he blushes for are his feelings towards the species & not towards individuals. But if there be any hope for the experiment & I sometimes think there is a great deal, it is in the theatre of a school. The arti[23][30]ficial character & deportment assumed, the unstooping dignity which in all ages mark out the pedagogue to the reverence or ridicule of mankind is eminently propitious to this attempt.

Aristocracy is a good sign. Aristocracy has been the hue & cry in every community where there has been anything good, any society worth associating with, since men met in cities. It must be every where. 'Twere the greatest calamity to ↑have it↓ abolish↑ed↓ ⟨it⟩. It went nearest to its death in the French Revolution, of all time. And if, tonight, an earthquake should sink every patrician house in the city, tomorrow there would be as distinct an aristocracy as now. The only change would be that the second sort would have become first but they would be as unmingling[,] as much separated from the lower class as ever the rich men of today were from them. No man would consent to live in society if he was obliged to admit every body to his house that chose to come. Robinson⟨'s⟩Crusoe's island would be better than a city if men were obliged to ⟨live⟩ ↑mix↓ together indiscriminately heads & points with all the world. ⟨D⟩ Envy is the tax which all distinction must pay.

[24][31] Profound knowledge is good but profound genius is better, because one[n] obtains with greater ease all the thoughts of all wise men, which the other obtains slowly by adding himself conclusion to conclusion. Yet in the end when both have arrived at the same amount of knowledge the latter is much the richest. ↑For since↓

[30] "ARISTOCRACY" is centered beneath "which all distinction" at the bottom of the page.

[31] " X V Z" is centered beneath "thought" at the bottom of the page.

⟨T⟩they have not only a certain sum of intelligence to get, but a great expedition to perform. No petty circumscribed offices to discharge whose narrow details daily return; ↑no↓ functions wherein mechanical adroitness avails more than acquaintance with principles — but immortal life in an unbounded universe. They are both to be shortly introduced into the immense storehouse of eternal truth. Their faculties are to be tasked to solve the secret enigmas of science by whose successive development the history of nature is to be explained. The universe to the eyes of ignorance is but a shining chaos. And when the veil of flesh is rent & the eyes of the spirit ⟨are⟩ open⟨ed⟩↑,↓ human perception will shrink from the splendour of the spiritual world. But there will be no comparison between the ⟨armour⟩ fitness of one & the other of the pilgrims who are to go on that heavenly road, from knowledge to knowledge. He who has sharpened his faculties by long & painful thought enters ⟨o⟩in a mighty sphere [25] but upon an accustomed task. Education has armed him in the panoply of thought. He moves gracefully like one at home in that etherial country. But his companion whose habits have not ↑been↓ similar though he recognizes some bright forms in the scenery is a stranger ⟨&⟩to the customs & the tongue of that glorious land & must walk among its wonders in stupid amazement long ere their order is /percieved/ seen/ ⁿ & must forever loiter at a distance from the other. Considered with relation to our whole existence, ↑that,↓ habits of thought are better than knowledge — was the original position of my rhetoric. Jan. 25, 1824.

Sympathy is the wine of life. A man has comfort in his friend when he is absent & when he is nigh. "The pause" of physical strength "reinforceth the onset;" & so is the society of two men dearer to them, for the interval of interruption. Friends fill that interval with pleasant thoughts which borrow their charms from the magic of this gentle sentiment. They treasure up the occurrences & thoughts, the times & chances, that were mixt in their cup of life to regale each other with the feast of memory. Words may be free, thought may be free and the heart laid bare to your friend but nevertheless the freedom even of friendship hath a limit & ↑let a man↓ beware how ⟨you⟩ ↑he↓ pass↑es↓ it. I do not know but a man may safely say to his

friend transient unweighed opinions, low scandal, base & vicious words
—things in short he would not trust a bird of the air with [26]³² so
that the form & manner only be guarded—so that they come as
momentary caprices & not the irrepressible utterance of rooted passions. It is noble to be governed by a lofty passion as the love of
man or the love of God & pardonable to be thus transported to an
excess of zeal. ⟨But i⟩It is a higher & godlike virtue to have the perfect mastery of all the passions, & to do from principle the great
deeds ⟨f⟩done by feeling, before. ⟨But⟩ ⟨And⟩ ↑But↓ to be the slave of a
base passion is to be most humbly degraded. He that loosely forgets
himself here & lets his friend be privy to the words & acts which base
desires extort ↑from him↓ has forfeited like a fool the love he prized.
↑The waters of↓ affection ⁿ will soon dry up ⟨&⟩or disgust will flow
↑in↓ their ⁿ ↑place↓. And what is worse, your friend, if he has ↑up-
rightly↓ disdained to become the accomplice of your vileness, possesses
a cruel advantage over you. Whatever tears, whatever bitter remorse
the memory of your degradation may cost you, you cannot efface
from his mind ⟨its⟩ ↑the↓ scornful recollection. He may expose to the
whisper & the scoff of society the ⟨g⟩secret guilt that lowers you in
the scale of moral beings. Give away to your friend the richest
treasure God [27] imparts to intelligent creatures—your own self-
respect; & then go & eat grass in the field until seventy times be
passed over you for the lord of Babylon was less a beast than thou.

It is false that familiarity of intercourse breeds disgust. Affection
has clean hands, & a pure heart. * " 'Love,' " said one of our old poets,
'esteems no office mean.' & with still more spirit, 'entire affection
scorneth nicer hands.' There is nothing interesting in the concerns of
men whom we love & honor that is beneath our attention." * ³³

It is no argument against new views or radical improvements in

* Burke's Econ. Reform.

³² "FRIENDSHIP" is written beneath "friend the richest" at the bottom of the
page.
³³ " 'Love . . . attention.' " is quoted almost verbatim but in different order
from "Speech on . . . A Plan . . . for the Economical Reformation of the Civil and
other Establishments." See *The Works of the Right Honorable Edmund Burke*, revised ed., 12 vols. (Boston, 1865–1867), II, 308. The old poet is Spenser, but only
" 'entire . . . hands,' " is his (cf. *The Faerie Queene*, I, viii, 40).

society that nothing like them is known to the ages past. Men's faces
have been lighted & their hands warmed & society enriched by *fire*
several thousand years before Any man dreamed what Combustion
meant. Socrates & the men of Greece[,] Cicero & the men of Rome
breathed the atmosphere without a suspicion of its elements, & were
wet with water without knowing its composition.

Men pay a price for admission to the civilization of society.
Some pay 20, 30, 40, or 50 hundred dollars a year to be permitted
to take [28][34] certain high & higher seats therein. My mother & I
might subsist on 200 but we are ↑willing↓ to ⟨p⟩buy with twelve or
thirteen times as much a more convenient & reputable place in the
world. Every man who values this bargain which he drives so zealously must give the whole weight of his support to the public, civil,
religious, literary institutions which make it worth his toil. Keep
the moral fountains pure. Open Schools. Guard the Sabbath, if you
be a member or lover of Civil Society, as you would not tremble at
the report of its earthquake convulsions, & be shocked at the noise of
its fall.

It is excellent advice both in writing & in action to avoid a too
great elevation at first. Let one's beginnings be temperate & unpre-
tending & the more elevated parts will rise from these with a just &
full effect. We were not made to breath oxygen or to talk poetry,[n]
or to be always wise. We are sorry habitants of an imperfect world.
And it will not do for *such* beings to take admiration by storm. One
who would take his friend captive by eloquent discourse must forego
the vulgar vanity of a great outset, which cannot last, but dwindles
down to flatness & disgust. He must lull the suspicion of art asleep
by the unambitious use of familiar commonplaces. He must [29][35]
be willing to say 'How do you do?' and "What's the news?" He must
not disdain to be interested in the weather or the time of day. And
when the talk has gradually got into those channels where he wished

[34] "BEGINNINGS" is centered beneath "commonplaces." at the bottom of the
page. A vertical line in the lower left margin seems intended to call attention to the
sentence, "We are sorry habitants of an imperfect world."
[35] "ACTION & THOUGHT" is centered beneath "old established mode." at
the bottom of the page.

to lead it, knowledge that is in place & fervour that is well-timed will have their reward.

———————

Forms are not unimportant in society. It is supremely necessary ↑that↓ you regulate men's conduct, whether you can affect their princip1(s)es or no. For the thoughts of the mass of men are ever in a crude, ⟨unorganized⟩ ungrown, unready state. But their actions regular & ready. They *must act*; but there is no compulsion to *think*. Therefore when the understanding is sluggish & indicates no course ↑of conduct↓, they are forced to obey Example,[n] & surrender the whole ordering of life to the judgements of other men. Thus a whole community ⟨acquiesce⟩ go to church; acquiesce in the existence of a certain law, or in the government of a certain ruler while, if their hearts were all read,[n] it might appear that these institutions had ↑but a few↓ strong favourers, & that, for the rest, each man leaned on his neighbor; nay, a critical inquiry should make it plain that the majority of opinions rebelled in secret against the custom complied with,[n] but that doubts were too shadowy & unformed ↑[to] venture↓ to challenge an old established mode.

[30] ⟨Indeed⟩ Men[n] in fact so openly borrow their common modes of thinking, i.e. those outside modes on which their actions depend (for when they act in a certain way they commonly go armed with some obvious reason whether they believe it or no) that it is surprising how small an amount of originality of mind is required to circulate all the thought in a community. The common conversation that has place in a city for a year does not embrace more intelligence than one vigorous thinker might originate; & one who carefully considers the flow & progress of opinion ⟨th⟩from man to man & rank to rank thro' Society, will soon discover that three or four masters present the people with all that moderate stock of conclusion↑s↓ upon politics, religion, commerce, & sentiment which goes current. The kingdom of thought is a proud aristocracy.

1790   England had three great names in her parliament[,] Burke, Fox, & Pitt. The two latter interest us by the engaging shew of youthful might. They seem to be beardless boys, abandoning their college with youthful impatience to mix with men; they come among

the grayhaired statesmen who are aghast at the storm which gathers
around, & fearlessly grasp & hurl the thunderbolts of power with
graceful [31][36] majesty. Fox took his seat in parliament at 19 years
of age. Pitt was prime minister of England at 24. Burke, who lacked
the aristocratical interest to back him, which Fox who descended
from Henry IV of Navarre, ⟨was⟩& Pitt who was son of Chatham,
could muster — was somewhat later. The two former were friends;
true hearted & noble friends, so matched as the world hath seldom
seen & so parted, as ⟨the⟩ we would hardly have had it otherwise.
They were two large & philosophical understandings both lit with
↑the↓ fire of eloquence. Fox, with tears in his eyes lamented in parliament that an uninterrupted friendship of twenty three years should
be invaded by the intemperance of a debate, & that his friend should
have applied such violent & angry epithets to his name. Burke said
he did not recollect any epithets. The reply of Fox was in the spirit
of a gentleman. "My honourable friend has forgotten the epithets,
they are out of his mind, and they are out of mine forever."
Burke's *principle* was dearer to him even than his friend, & he broke
with a stoic's heart, his ancient attachment. Burke said afterwards of
Fox 'he was a man made to be loved.' & Goldsmith said of B.

> "⟨Who,⟩ born for the universe narrowed his mind
> And to *party* gave up, what was meant for mankind."
> [Goldsmith, "Retaliation: A Poem," ll. 31–32]

It is not easy, for a common mind perhaps it is not possible to appreciate this magnanimous sacrifice (of his friendship.) No man perhaps
was ever fitter to enjoy fully this best & purest of pleasures. F. & B
agreed upon the American & their foresight triumphed over their
adversaries who laughed at the "vagrant congress, one Hancock, one
Adams & their crew," who spurned them when they "might have
been led," as Franklin told them, "by a thread" [32] until they
broke chains & scattered armaments like flaxen strings. In the dark
tempest of the French Revolution, *Pitt* was "the pilot that weathered
the storm." Fox, in Westminster Abbey lies 18 inches from Pitt &
close by Chatham. Pitt, Fox, Burke, — since one was in office, one

[36] "BURKE FOX PITT" is centered beneath "been led," as Franklin told them,"
at the bottom of the page.

in favour, & one in neither, perhaps it is just to say Pitt was a practical statesman; Fox, a theoretical statesman; & Burke, a philosophic statesman.

Franklin was political economist, a natural philosopher, a moral philosopher, & a statesman. Invents ⁿ & dismisses subtle theories (e.g. of the Earth) with extraordinary ease. Unconscious of any mental effort in detailing the profoundest solutions of phenomena & therefore makes no parade. He writes to a friend when aet. 80 "I feel as if I was intruding among posterity when I ought to be abed & asleep. I look upon death to be as necessary to the Constitution as Sleep. We shall rise refreshed in the morning." [37]

"Many," said he, "forgive injuries, but none ever forgave contempt." — See Edin. Rev. [38]

That age abounded in greatness[:] Carnot, Moreau, Bonaparte, &c, Johnson, Gibbon, &c, Washington, &c[.]

Institutions are ↑a sort of↓ homes. A man may wander long with profit, if he come home at last but a perpetual Vagrant is not honoured. ⟨Minds⟩ Men may alter & improve their laws so they fix them at last.

[33] "Humanity does not consist in a squeamish ear." Fox.

Men in this age do not produce new works but admire old ones; Are content to leave the fresh pastures awhile, & to chew the cud of thought in the shade.ⁿ

"A Great empire like a great cake is most easily diminished at the edges." Franklin. [39]

---

[37] The paragraph on Franklin is based on the review of *The Complete Works, in Philosophy, Politics, and Morals, of the Late Dr. Benjamin Franklin* . . . , 3 vols. (London, 1806), in *The Edinburgh Review*, VIII (July 1806), 327–344. The quotations, from pp. 343 and 344, are not completely accurate.

[38] From "Rules by Which a Great Empire May be Reduced to a Small One," paragraph VIII. It does not appear in the review cited in n. 37 above.

[39] From "Rules by Which a Great Empire May be Reduced to a Small One," paragraph I.

[34]⁴⁰ It is a problem never solved whether ⟨the⟩ institutions affect ⟨the⟩ ↑a↓ people or ⟨the⟩ ↑a↓ people modify their institutions. For example does bigot⟨ted⟩ry in Spain produce the Inquisition,ⁿ or the Inquisition make the bigotry? Does the English Constitution make men skilful & free & bold ⁿ or the character of the men give this or that particular shape to the bill of Rights? ⁿ Nor will it do to answer that the second alternative is true in point of fact, & therefore the question is at rest. For though history ↑credibly↓ ascribes to certain individuals this political work yet it was not a sudden & rapid ⁿ convention but the accumulation of   hundred years; & improvements were successively added, by those who had grown up under the salutary influence of its adult strength. Moreover the men who devised the coarse rudiments of the plan & who had been born & grown under a barbarous empire were altogether unlike their posterity in character ⁿ who grew up under the tree which they planted. But if the other be supposed true, & systems mould the moral character of men, repugnant consequences will follow & if you transfer the huge British Policy to ⟨Tombuctoo⟩ central Africa, the ⁴¹

[35] Does *Marriage* produce good-Order in Society or the desire & necessity of good order give rise to marriage. Yea or Nay?

Perhaps the question is reducible to this. Is man infinitely improvable, or only to such extent & in such direction[?]

[36] next generation will hear of Tombuctoo glory in arts & arms & Sierra Leone be umpire of Europe. But the Ethiopian cannot change his skin. It is plain an institution is but a paper fabric without ⟨the⟩ it find something of the manners it is to authorise. It is ⟨a⟩the means discovered able to ⟨perpetuate⟩ ↑transmit↓ the modes of feeling of one generation distinctly to the next. The progress of opinion is often fluctuating & capricious & unless the ground that has been gained be diligently /fenced in/guarded/ the next tide may /overwhelm/wash away/ it. An Institution is the embodying some result of sagacity or experience in a practical & permanent form.

⁴⁰ "INSTITUTION" is written beneath "Policy to ⟨Tombuctoo⟩" and "SABBATH" is centered beneath "central Africa," at the bottom of the page.

⁴¹ Continued on p. [36].

The chief institutions in the civilized world at this day are (5?) ↑combien?↓ To wit, the Institution of Marriage, of Property, of Government, of Public Education, of Religion & lastly what is a part of the fifth[,] of the Sabbath. In all polished nations inst[itutions]. subsist under these names, but ↑in↓ all marked with essential discrepancies. Thus the great feature of primogeniture ↑& entailed estates↓ alone cr[e]ates another aspect in the people among whom it obtains. But all in some form are indispensable to civilization, are all the [42]

[37] Yet Czar Peter civilized Russia by the rapid introduction of the Press — of new Government, of Educ[ation] &c. Alfred too? Mahomet[.]

[38][43] natural fruit of ripened Man; ⟨T⟩they aid his faculties to their fullest development ⟨& then⟩ recieve an i⟨m⟩nfallible return in his care to secure & ⟨perfect⟩ finish themselves. This ↑⟨successive⟩ progressive↓ mutual support which is afforded from ↑⟨progressive⟩↓ Social Man to his inst[itutions]. & from inst[itutions] to Man again, seem to me a curious specimen of moral economy.

The great ↑common↓ object[n] of /a community/laws/ ⟨are⟩ ↑is↓ to check evil rather than to promote good. Good men educate themselves to worth and enlightened men will themselves /feel/burn [with]/ the charm of Moral beauty. But ⟨the⟩ laws are designed to affect the characters of that large class of ⟨minds⟩ ↑men↓ to whose imperfect understandings expansive views & liberal relations of men were never revealed,[n] whose intellects being too unsettled to govern their conduct are under the servitude of custom or worse — of their appetites. Such too is the aspect of the institutions, accomodated to the necessity of things.

The French Revolution was a crusade against all of them & they were all more or less violated[.]

No body of men in their sober senses ever departed from the ancient community & broke down ⟨these⟩ either of these systems. Wild Anabaptists &c have done so; & Jack Cade[.]

---

[42] Continued on p. [38].

[43] "INSTITUTIONS" is centered beneath "&c have done so; &" at the bottom of the page.

[39]   Tomorrow & tomorrow & tomorrow
         Creeps in this petty pace from day to day
         To the last syllable of recorded time
         And all our Yesterdays
                    [Shakespeare, *Macbeth*, V, v, 19–22]

         sleep that knits up the raveled
                              [*Ibid.*, II, ii, 37]

"girded the imperial sword upon his side. he will not take up ⟨danger⟩ peace at a heavy interest of danger to ensue. These things were too fine to be fortunate & successful in all parts, for that great affairs are commonly too rough & stubborn to be wrought by the finer edges & points of wit.ⁿ The memory of Richard was so strong that it lay like lees in the bottom of men's hearts. & if the vessel was but stirred it would come up." Bacon's Henry VII q.v.[44]

         'Women's reigns always good — because then
         men are sure to govern.'

         "L'etat, c'est Moi" Louis XIV

         I hope to live till every peasant in France puts a fowl in his pot on
Sunday   Henri IV

It has been supposed a tendency of religious liberty &c to go into all other fanaticisms headlong. Theⁿ Puritans of 1620 had not a rash or visionary thought about them. No orders of nobility, ↑no enslaving of captives↓ no digging for gold, no community of goods, no agrarian laws.ⁿ They erred after as bigots & erred on virtue's side[.]

[40][45] Indeed the whole class of the severe & restrictive virtues are at a market almost too high for humanity. Ed. Burke. Econ. Ref. q.v.[46]

[44] Emerson might have read Bacon in any one of several editions (see "Early Reading List," 321). "These things . . . wit" has not been located. Except for the last two sentences the other quotations are only partly accurate. See *The History of . . . Henry the Seventh*, in *The Works*, 1860–1864, XI, 119, 122, and 134.

[45] "Moyle Mrs [twice]" is written ornately at the top of the page. "Ister Spirit" appears below "by his acquaintance" but seems to have no meaning in the context. To the right of the *Edinburgh Review* citations is "Armstrong Antony [thrice] Moyle [twice] Hou The curled Antony" in irregular columns. "Armstrong" may be an identification of "Such a man . . . the world" but the sentence has not been located. For "The curled Antony," see Shakespeare, *Antony and Cleopatra*, V, ii, 304.

[46] "Speech on . . . A Plan . . . for the Economical Reformation of the Civil and Other Establishments." See *Works*, 1865–1867, II, 268.

Μισω σοφιστην ουκ αυτω σοφος [47]

EURIP. [Fragment 905]

"Virtue, (for mere good nature is a fool)
Is sense & spirit with humanity." [John Armstrong, *The Art of
Preserving Health*, Book IV, "The Passions"]

Such a man will grow wise not malignant by his acquaintance
with the world.

Edin. Rev XLIII   Mad de Stael
Edin Rev LXXI   Stewart
          LXXIV   Partitions [48]

Burke's Reflections [49]
Maclaurin's Newton
Leibnitz's Letters
Smith's Wealth of Nations
Turgot . . Existence

[47] "I abominate the professed wise man [who] is not wise for himself" (Ed.).

[48] The references are to reviews of de Staël, *De L'Allemagne*, 3 vols. (London, 1813), XXII (Oct. 1813), 198–238 (see below p. 215); Stewart, *A General View of the Progress of Metaphysical, Ethical, and Political Science*. . . , Part II, XXXVI (Oct. 1821), 220–267; and three works on the partition of Poland, XXXVII (Nov. 1822), 462–527. Emerson mentions "Sir James Mackintosh's . . . noble article on Partitions" in a letter to John Boynton Hill, June 19 and July 2, 1823 (*L*, I, 134).

[49] The following list was written vertically upward in the lower half of the page starting from the bottom margin. Titles or probable titles are here given, alphabetically by author:

Thomas Brown, *Lectures on the Philosophy of the Human Mind; Inquiry into the Relation of Cause and Effect.*

Edmund Burke, *Reflections on the Revolution in France.*

Baron Gottfried Wilhelm von Leibnitz. No specific volume seems intended. Emerson may have been stimulated to seek out Leibnitz's letters by Stewart's four references to them in his *Dissertation* (see *Collected Works*, 1854, I, 267–269).

Colin Maclaurin, *An Account of Sir Isaac Newton's Philosophical Discoveries.*

Charles de Secondat, Baron de La Brède et de Montesquieu, *L'Esprit des Lois.* Volume 1 of *Oeuvres Complettes*, 6 vols. (Paris, 1816), containing part of *L'Esprit des Lois*, was withdrawn from the Boston Library Society April 10–May 8, 1824.

Daniel Neal, *The History of the Puritans.*

John Playfair, *Dissertation Second, Exhibiting a General View of the Progress of Mathematical and Physical Sciences.* . . . The volume in Emerson's library, which lacks publisher and date, is inscribed "R. W. Emerson from E. B. E. 182—." and contains Emerson's notes ("Early Reading List," 323).

Neal's Hist. of Puritans
Stewart's Philosophical ⟨lett⟩ Essays
Brown
De Staelî's↓ French Revolution
Playfair's Dissertations
Rousseau
Voltaire
Montesquieu Esprit des Loix

There is nothing which God has judged good for us that he has not given us the means to accomplish both in the natural & moral world. If we cry like children for the moon like children we must cry on. Burke Econ [50]

Jean Jacques Rousseau. Volumes 13 and 14 of *Oeuvres,* 18 vols. (Paris, 1817), containing *Les Confessions,* was withdrawn from the Boston Library Society Jan. 16– March 22, 1823.

Adam Smith, *An Inquiry into the Nature and Causes of the Wealth of Nations.* Volumes 1 and 5 of *The Works of Adam Smith,* 5 vols. (London, 1812), were withdrawn from the Boston Library Society June 26–Oct. 2, 1824. There is no record of the withdrawal of volumes 2–4, which contain *The Wealth of Nations.*

Staël, Madame de, *Considerations on the Principal Events of the French Revolution,* 2 vols. (New York, 1818), withdrawn from the Boston Library Society, though not until April 1–June 1, 1826. Volumes 1 and 2 of the French version (3 vols., Paris, 1818) were withdrawn Jan. 16–March 22, 1823.

Dugald Stewart, *Philosophical Essays.*

Anne Robert Jacques Turgot, "Sur Quelques Preuves de l'Existence de Dieu."

François Marie Arouet (Voltaire), *The History of Charles XII, King of Sweden* (New York, 1811), listed in "Catalogue of Books Read" (*JMN,* I, 399).

[50] "Speech on . . . A Plan . . . for the Economical Reformation of the Civil and Other Establishments." See *Works,* 1865–1867, II, 357. The quotation is written vertically downward in the lower right half of the page.

Wide World XIII

1824

"Wideworld No XIII" is the last of the journals to bear the Wide World title. Continuing without interruption from Wide World 12, the first entry is dated February, 1824, and the final entry August 11, 1824.

The manuscript is composed of twenty-three folded sheets of unlined paper hand-stitched together by white thread into a single gathering and enclosed in a heavier paper cover. The forty-six leaves measure 17.5 x 21.2 cm. Pagination runs sequentially from 1 through 90 except for leaves 22 and 23, where the page numbers are repeated. The repeated pagination for pages 42 and 43 is indicated in the text by subscript numbers 1 and 2.

[1][1]   U   "Bonus vir tempore tantum a Deo differt." [2] Seneca
                                                    [*Moral Essays*, I, i, 5]

Wideworld.   No XIII.

"Nor fetch my precepts from the Cynic's tub."
                                        [Cf. Milton, *Comus*, l. 708]

Canterbury, Feb. 1824.
(Continued from W. 13.) [3]

The appetite for innovation whether it falls among cautious & severe thinkers, or among light-headed revolutionists is always of signal advantage to mankind. The lesson⟨s⟩ taught is of vast importance though there be wo to them by whom the information comes. For this is an unsated appetite & must perpetually recur↑;↓⟨s⟩ experiment therefore must establish what is safe & wha‖t‖ is unsafe.

[1] "INSTITUTIONS" is written beneath "which are words" at the bottom of the page.
[2] "A good man differs from God in the element of time only."
[3] An error for Wide World 12. Emerson is continuing the discussion of institutions begun on pp. [32]–[38] (see pp. 208–210 above).

214

We must seek instructors therefore not only among the wise & fortunate legislators who settled N. England in 1620, but also among
the bloody demagogues of the French Convention. For before the
trial of their respective constitutions, the Scheme which completely
failed in France was infinitely the most alluring of the two to popular
imagination. — Liberty & equality which are words now [2] con-
signed to Bedlam politicians, have always been favourite topics of
poetical & philosophical rhetoric. Plato, & Sir Thomas More, & I
believe Bacon also, (never esteemed frivolous speculators,) indulged
themselves in delineating this ideal government. And grave legislators would hereafter adopt what grave theorists have approved except for the monitory example of France.

"La nature," says Pascal, "confond les pyrrhoniens et la raison
confond les dogmatistes." & Sir J. Mackintosh call↑s↓ the sentence
the sublimest of human composition.[4] It is fortunate & happy but a
sublimity not difficult to gain, as it did not occur to Pascal when he
first revolved the subject, but is the last generalization at which he
arrives. And it is easier to build up one subject into a cone with a
broad base of examples narrowing up into a formula expressing a general truth, than to detach subtle facts from subjects partially known.

"Montesquieu's Lettres Persanes sold like bread."
                                                    Vie.[5]
'Please to praise me,' is the ill disguised request of almost all
literary men. All men are cheered by applause & vexed by censure[.]

↑——— Nihil est quod credere de se
      Non possit.[6] Juv.↓ [*Satires*, IV, 70–71]

[3][7] but literary men alone cannot do without it. The reason is obvi-

[4] Emerson's source both for the Pascal quotation and Mackintosh's praise is the
latter's review of Madame de Staël, *De l'Allemagne*, *The Edinburgh Review*, XXII
(Oct. 1813), 238.
[5] A life of Montesquieu appears in volume 1 of *Oeuvres Complettes*, 1816, which
was withdrawn from the Boston Library Society, though not until April 10.
[6] "There is nothing which a man won't believe about himself" (Ed.). The
quotation, in the form Emerson uses, appears as the epigraph to *The Rambler*, No.
104, cited below.
[7] "PRAISE" is centered beneath "dispraise. Perhaps" at the bottom of the page.

ous, — other[n] men toil for gold & get gold for their toil but scholars cannot get gold & appetite in them craves another food. They are no more insatiable for their proper reward, than are the pursuers of Mammon for theirs. But why are the askers of praise ridiculous & not the askers of silver?   (Minor negatur)[8] Idle beggars of praise or ↑of↓ money alike are treated with contempt but one who laboriously seeks for ⟨wealth⟩ ⟨praise⟩ ↑reputation↓ as one who laboriously seeks wealth, in their proper fields & by just means will find both reputation & wealth. Both must be earned; neither will be given on bare demand. As for Fortune, she will coquette with both.

The vice of wealth & of fame is an outward pomp. But as cautious rich men are not forward to publish the amount of their property for fear of the tax gatherer, so men of merit must beware how they vaunt their wares lest detraction which is distinction's tax make them repent their vanity.

See No 104 Rambler.[9]

In education it seems to be safer to praise ⟨or⟩than[n] to censure abundantly. For myself I have ever been elated to an active mind by flattery & depressed by dispraise. Perhaps a Muse that [4] soared on a stronger wing would scorn to be so slightly disheartened. I like the lines

> "Praise is the salt that season⟨ed⟩s right in man
> And whets the appetite of moral good." Young
> [*Night Thoughts*, "Night VII," ll. 420–421]

It is noticeable how much a man is judged of by the praise he gives. It is best not to be too inflammable,[n] not to be lavish of your praise on light occasions for it will be remembered long after your fervent admiration has cooled into disgust. ↑Milton was very frugal of his praise↓[.] A man is not more known by the company he keeps. Dat veniam corvis, vexat censura columbas[10] — is ↑a↓ decisive index of perverted character.

---

[8] Emerson seems to have meant that "the lesser [craving] is denied" — i.e., that the scholar is denied praise.

[9] Though Johnson's essay is concerned with praise and flattery, it does not seem to be a source for Emerson's ideas. He may have thought of it as providing possible material for the development of his discussion.

[10] See above, p. 137.

↑'Somebody conquered somebody — the amount of Caesar's fame,' says Wollaston.↓[11]

> ↑—— uxorem, Posthume, ducis?
> Dic quâ Tisiphone, quibus exagitare colubris?↓[12]

Beauty is but skin-deep. In some instances that I have known men that in matrimony have sought neither beauty or ⟨wisdom⟩ wealth have not found wisdom but folly. Choice has been the fruit of weakness of mind or body; it were too appalling to affirm that this is always or generally the case.

Pliny's uncle had a slave read while he eat. In the progress of Watt & Perkin's philosophy the day may come when the scholar shall be provided with a Reading Steam Engine; [13] when he shall say Presto —& it shall discourse eloquent history — & Stop Sesame & it shall hush to let him think. He shall put in a pin, & hear poetry; & two pins, & hear a song. That age will discover Laputa.   Feb. 17.

[5][14] "Tout Commence," says Father Bossuet of the first ages. All has the air of beginning. — They form societies, devise arts, polish manners, & make laws.[15] This return to the Cradle is useful. Now when all things are tried & trite when ⟨the children of⟩ Shem, Ham, & Japhet have strayed from their paternal tent as far as the limits of the⟨ir⟩ globe will let them & on the mind of each is writ in in-

[11] "Somebody conquered somebody" is quoted directly, the rest is paraphrased from Thomas Brown, *Lectures on the Philosophy of the Human Mind*, 1822, III, 94. See p. 234 below.

[12] "Postumus, are you . . . taking to yourself a wife? Tell me what Tisiphone, what snakes are driving you mad?" Juvenal, *Satires*, VI, 28–29.

[13] Emerson apparently had in mind the fact that Jacob Perkins (1766–1849), versatile Yankee inventor, had developed a nail-making machine.

[14] "ASIA" is written beneath "the" and "ORIGIN" beneath "grandeur" at the bottom of the page.

[15] "Tout commence: il n'y a point d'histoire ancienne où il ne paraisse non-seulement dans ces premiers temps, mais longtemps après, des vestiges manifestes de la nouveauté du monde. On voit les lois s'établir, les moeurs se polir, et les empires se former: le genre humain sort peu à peu de l'ignorance; l'expérience l'instruit, et les arts sont inventés ou perfectionnés." "Second Époque," *Discours sur l'Histoire Universelle* (Paris, 1892), p. 7. Volume 1 of *Histoire Universelle*, 2 vols. (Paris, 1814), was withdrawn from the Boston Library Society from July 18 to Aug. 8, 1822, and volume 2 from Aug. 8 to 15.

dellible lines his character, now the Spirit of Humanity finds it curious & good to leave the arm-chair of its old age ⟨& the weary monotony of the present scene⟩ & go back to the scenes of Auld Lang Syne, to the old mansion house of Asia, the playground of its childhood, the ⟨c⟩ land of distant but cherished remembrance. That spot must needs be dear where the faculties first opened, where youth first triumphed in the elasticity of strength & spirits & where the ways of Civilization & thought (*then* ⟨*thought*⟩ ↑deemed↓ⁿ *infinite*) were first explored. It brings the mind palpable relief to withdraw it from the noisy & overgrown world to these peaceful primeval solitudes. For this reason, perhaps, there is a species of grandeur in Ist Epoque of Bossuet, though it relate a threadbare tale.[16] It may be, this emotion will be only occasionally felt for though the grandeur is real, it is ever [6][17] present, as the firmament is forever magnificent but is only felt to be so when our own ⟨emoti⟩ spirits are fresh (& buoyant.) Asia, Africa, Europe, old, leprous & wicked, have run round the goal of centuries till we * are tired and they are ready to drop. But now a strong man has entered the race & is outstripping them all. Strong Man! youth & glory are with thee. ⟨T⟩As thou wouldst prosper forget not the hope of mankind. Trample not upon thy competitors though unworthy. Europe is thy ⟨mo⟩father — ⟨support her Asia⟩ bear him on thy Atlantean shoulders. Asia, thy grandsire, regenerate him. Africa, their ancient abused ⟨slave⟩ ↑bondman↓. Give him his freedom.

Boethius was great & good — from 470 to 524 A. D.

In the beginning, which I spake of a few lines above, there was some good. Would it not have been well to have lived in Nineveh or to have been the mighty hunter or to have floated on the Deluge or have been dead before? Hope at least would have been a Contemporary. Now she has long been dead or doating — as good as dead. Moreover men's thoughts were their own then.

* '*We*' means beings better than we.

[16] "Première Époque," subtitled "Adam, ou la création," retells the Biblical story of man from the creation through the deluge.

[17] "AULD LANG SYNE" is written beneath "*'We'* means beings" in Emerson's footnote at the bottom of the page.

Noah was not dinned to death with Aristotle & Bacon & Greece & Rome. The patriarchs were never puzzled with libraries of names & dates, with First ages & dark ages; & Revivals & upper empires & lower empires; with the balance of power & the balance of trade; with fighting chronologies & dagger-drawing creeds. [Life is wasted in the necessary preparation of finding which is the true way, & we die just as we enter it.] An [7][18] antedeluvian had ⟨an⟩the advantage — an advantage that has been growing /rare/scarce/ as the world has grown older of forming his own opinion & indulging his own hope without danger of contradiction from Time that never had elapsed or observation that never had been made. ⟨The t⟩Unknown troubles perplex the lot of the scholar whose inexpressible unhappiness it is to be born at this day. He is born in a time of *war*. A thousand religions are ⟨at⟩ ↑in↓ arms. Systems of Education are contesting. Literature, Politics, Morals, & Physics, are each engaged in loud civil ⟨contention⟩ ↑broil↓. A chaos of doubts besets him from his outset. Shall he read or shall he think? Ask the wise. The wise have not determined. Shall he nourish his faculties in solitude or in active life? No man can answer. He turns to books — ⟨to⟩ the vast amount of recorded wisdom but it is useless from its amount. He cannot * read all; no, not in Methuselah's multiplied days; — but how to choose — hoc opus est.[19] Must he read History & neglect Morals; or learn what *ought* to be, in ignorance of what *has been*? Or must he slight both in the pursuit of (physical) science, or all, for practical knowledge & a profession? Must he, in a last alter[8][20]native abandon all the rest to be profoundly skilled in a single branch of art, or[n] understanding none smatter superficially in all?

A question of equal moment to each new Citizen of the world is this; shall I subdue my mind by discipline, or obey its native inclination? govern my imagination with rules or cherish its originality?[n] Shall I cultivate⟨ion⟩ Reason or Fancy[?] educate one power with concentrated diligence or reduce all to the same level?

* One had need read as Pliny elder to accomplish anything.

[18] "NOWADAYS" is centered beneath "profession? Must" at the bottom of the page.
[19] "This is the task" (Ed.).
[20] "EDUCATION" is centered beneath "appreciate what" at the bottom of the page.

These & similar questions (which I challenge all the wisdom now collected[21] in the world to set at rest & I[n] should be glad at heart to be answered) are a real & recurring calamity. I do not know that it ⟨would be⟩ ↑were↓ extravagant to say that half of the time of ⟨many⟩ most scholars is ⟨wasted⟩ dissipated in fruitless & vexatious attempts to solve one or another of them in succession. It is ⟨a trouble⟩ ↑an evil↓ oftener felt than stated. It is an evil that demands a remedy. It requires that what master minds have done for some of the ⟨S⟩sciences, should be done for Education. Teach no more arts but how those which are already, should be learned. Feb. 17.
How few appreciate what they praise!

[9][22] Good it is to read & to think; the gorgeous array of vivid images that pass thro' the mind is good (as in Gibbon's illuminated style). Better it is to remember what was read & to think aright. ↑But↓ the[n] flush goes from the face, & the ardor from the mind. Study is wearisome to the flesh & the book is shut & the mind's eye sleeps while the body's watches. But there are visions whose freshness never fades, which are beautiful to you⟨th⟩↑ng↓ & ⟨to age⟩ ↑old↓ alike which the heart embraces with rapture & the understanding commends. Material beauty perishes or palls. Intellectual beauty limits admiration to seasons & ages; hath its ebbs & flows of delight. Age does not relish the wit that feasted youth. Nor youth love the severe excellence which age esteems. But Moral beauty is lovely, imperishable, perfect. It is dear to the child & the patriarch to Heaven, Angel, Man. Intelligent being can contract no habit so vile, can ⟨carr⟩[n] pervert his feelings to no such dire depravity that moral excellence should ever lose its charm.↑The sight of↓ a[n] virtuous deed will strike a chord in the basest bosom & make a little light in the thickest ignorance. And none that can understand Milton's Comus can read it without warming to the holy emotions it panegyrizes. [10][23] I would freely give all I ever hoped to be, even when my airblown hopes were brilliant & glorious,— not as now, to ↑have↓ given down that sweet

[21] The phrase "now collected" is circled, perhaps for revision.
[22] "MORAL BEAUTY" is written beneath "the holy emotions" at the bottom of the page.
[23] "MORAL BEAUTY" is written beneath "getting . . . side" at the bottom of the page.

strain to posterity to do good in a golden way, — to bewitch young
hearts by eloquent verses to the love of goodness, to bias manhood
& edify ⟨age⟩ gray hairs. Would not a man die to do such an office
to mankind? The service that such books as this & the "Prelaty" &
Bunyan &c render, is not appreciable but is immense. These books
go up & down the world on the errand of charity & where sin &
sorrow have been[,] where malignity festers & ignorance thickens,
pour their balm of Gilead, & cleanse the foul humours & purify the
channels of life. They pluck away the thorn from Virtue's martyr
crown & plant the rose ↑Sharon↓ & amaranth instead. Of this I am
glad. I am glad to find at least *one* unfading essential beneficent
principle in human nature — *the approval of right*; ⟨a⟩& that it is
so strong & ineffaceable. Popular preachers have with judgement
selected this mode of attack. Availing themselves of this inborn par-
tiality to Good they have painted in Truth's glowing light the beauty
of rectitude ⁿ & have won the understanding by /getting on the right
side of/engaging/ the heart.

[11]²⁴ I am ignorant if, in saying this, I analyze Bancroft's eloquence. His sermon on Temperance was of powerful effect but it
seemed to reach the *practice*, through an appeal to this moral poetry.
Thus one fine sentiment in it that was calculated to produce much
fasting was the representation of the body as the corruptible &
perishable "channel, thro' which flow⟨ed⟩ for a season the streams
of immortal thought." ²⁵ Feb. ⟨16⟩ 20.

Canterbury. Feb. 22. — 1824. ——
The war between sentiment & reason is the perpetual wonder
that lasts the 'Nine days' of human life. When we calmly think &
precisely reason, our life — (ever enigmatical ↑enow↓) ⟨life⟩ has most

²⁴ "SENTIMENT" is written beneath "for a moment his relations" at the bottom of the page. In a penciled note in the margin Edward Emerson speculates that
the passage "I am ignorant . . . thought." " is the possible origin of the early poem
beginning, in his words,
      "Oh what are heroes prophets men
      But pipes thro' wh the breath of God doth blow &c".
The poem is "Pan," *W*, IX, 360.
²⁵ Bancroft preached some thirty-six times between September, 1822, and July,
1823, and then gave up preaching. How Emerson could have such an apparently
immediate recollection of this sermon is not clear.

of sense & design. There is an arrangement percieved in education, & a growth in mind. But when we *feel* strongly, when we *love* woman or man, when we hope, or fear, or hate or aspire with vehemence,[n] the strength of a sentiment is so engrossing & exclusive that it throws all memory & habit for the moment into a remote background; the delusion waxes so strong that it alone remains real & all else shows as strong delusion. An educated man when he is star gazing or vividly considering for a moment his relations [12] as an eternal being to the world ⟨is⟩ frequently undervalues as nugatory the time & diligence bestowed by him on science & art; forgetting that to this very cultivation he owes that elevation of thought which disgusts him with this world's unsatisfactoriness. At any rate however, it is a hard lot to toil for golden fruit, & the fruit when found is poison & ashes. The eye too is enraptured with the peerless & indescribable beauty of form & tint that glow at evening in the western clouds; but the glorious pageant rolls nearer & breaks into a foul & bellowing storm. Thus ever the Mind is enlightened by Misery. If Knowledge be power, it is also Pain.

A melancholy dream it is, this succession of rolling weeks each like the last in ⟨disat⟩ peevish dissatisfaction & in diminished hope.

> ⟨The Int⟩
> "By pain of heart now checked & now impelled,
> The Intellectual Power, thro' words & things,
> Went sounding on a dim & perilous way."
> [Wordsworth, *The Excursion*, III, 699–701]

A. D. ⟨904⟩ ↑1820↓ Michael II ascended the Greek throne from the prison in which he was about to be executed, & a smith not being nigh he wore the irons on his legs some hours after his accession.

[13]   Dr Franklin

If any apology be demanded for the seeming neglect in classical journals of ⟨so⟩ a name so much the ornament of America as Franklin's, there is but one answer. It is not because we do not appreciate the manifold merits of this distinguished person or ⟨are⟩ ↑would↓ ungratefully ⟨debtors⟩ cancel the debt we owe to his philosophy or political wisdom; but because his fame has a wider circulation than our page & his character has that sort of commanding excellence which is as undisputed as it is unrivalled, it was not worth while to beat the air in ⟨asserting⟩ ↑vindicating↓ the justice of his claims to the veneration of mankind. It is never too early or too late to hold up moral & intellectual worth to respect & imitation.ⁿ ⟨The life⟩ The reputation of living heroes is almost always clouded by envy, distrust, & ignorance & the tardy compensation which posterity can make must on no account be with⟨drawn⟩↑held↓. For, if the pitiful ingratitude which /embittered/shortened/ the lives of Socrates, Columbus, Galileo,ⁿ were not ↑in some measure↓ ⟨compensated⟩ retrieved in the eye of their distant admirers by the regret & honours of another generation, the appetite of fame which has in all ages wrought so much good would altogether cease in despair of gratifi[14]cation. Franklin's lot was ⟨more⟩ happier than these; yet certainly we need no apology for adorning a page with his name.

The purest fame man can acquire is that of the creator of the institutions of social life & the arts that support & embellish it. This is doing good without suspicion. But this praise is monopolized in each nation while it is yet in infancy by a few individuals who are either anterior to history or leave only a fabulous memorial of their divine exploits. And where the love of wonder is not checked by the art of writing we know that the benefactor becomes a hero in the second generation, a giant in the third, & a God in the fourth.[26] The discovery of America & its settlement by civilized nations permitted these last ages to see in some measure ↑repeated↓ that part of the growth of kingdoms which was shrouded in the darkness of savage ignorance. It permitted men also to see their benefactors & to ascertain the true elevation of their characters by a just comparison of them with their contemporaries.

> Good bye, proud world, I'm going home
>   Thou'rt not my friend & I'm not thine
> Long I've been tossed like the salt sea foam
> ↑All day↓ ⟨Long⟩mid ⟨thy⟩ weary crowds I roam

The nonsense of pedants is shamed by the practical wisdom of an unlettered observer.

[26] See p. 193 above.

[15]   ⟨And o my home o holy home⟩
          Good bye to Flattery↑'s↓ fawning face,
              To Grandeur with his wise grimace,
              To upstart Wealth's averted eye,
              To supple office low & high
              To frozen hearts & hasting feet
              To noisy Toil, to Court & Street.
              T⟨h⟩o those who go & those who come
              Good bye, proud world! I'm going home.

              I'm going to my own hearth stone
              Bosomed in yon green hills alone
              Sweet summer birds are warbling there
                              ↑forever mair↓

The theological notions of a Chinese are anomalous I trust in besotted perversity. The godhead that infests his thoughts is a certain cleverness & skill that implies no merit in the divinity but of which the yellow man may avail himself as he would of the swiftness of a horse or the fecundity of the earth. So he prays to his God for an event; if his prayer be answered he puts a copper or two on ⟨the⟩his ⁿ shrine; if not, he curses & kicks him; the ⁿ day, it may be, is not distant when the huge & sluggard wave of oriental population shall be stirred & purified by the conflict of counter currents, when the Resurrection of the East shall cast off the ⟨nightmare⟩ ↑incubus↓ that has so long ridden its torpid mind.

                                        v. p. 21

[16] ⟨All⟩ Metaphysicians are mortified to find how entirely the whole materials of understanding are derived from sense. No man is understood who speculates on mind or character until he borrows the /emphatic/specific/ imagery of Sense. A mourner will try in vain to explain the extent of his bereavement better than to say a *chasm* is opened in society. I fear the progress of Metaphys[ical]. philosophy may be found to consist in nothing else than the progressive introduction of apposite metaphors. Thus the Platonists congratulated themselves for ages upon their know⟨ledge⟩↑ing↓⟨of

the) ↑that↓ Mind was a dark chamber whereon ideas like shadows
were painted. Men derided this as infantile when they afterwards
learned that the Mind was a sheet of white paper whereon any &
all characters might be written. Almost ⟨any⟩ every thing in language
that is bound up in your memory is of this significant sort. Sleep,
the cessation of toil, the loss of volition, &c., what is that? but
'sleep that knits up the ravelled sleave of care,'[27] is felt. Life is
nothing, but the *lamp* of life that blazes, flutters, & goes out, the *hill*
of life which is climbed & tottered down, the *race* of life which is
run with a thousand Competitors & for a prize proposed, these are
distinctly understood. We love tellers of good tidings is faint but
'how beautiful upon the mountains are their feet'[28] is [17] excellent.
'The world is the scaffold of Divine Justice,'ⁿ said ↑Saurin↓[29] ⟨a
churchman.⟩ ⟨Saurin⟩

How do you do sir? Very well sir. You have a keen air among
your rocks & hills. Yes sir. I never saw a country which more delighted me. A man might travel many hundred miles & not find so
fine woodland as abound in this neighbourhood. But the good people
who live in them do not esteem them. It is people born in town who
are intoxicated with being in the country. It certainly is a good deal
like being drunk, the feelings of a cit in the hills. In Cambridge
there is some wild land called Sweet Auburn upwards of a mile from
the Colleges & yet the students will go in bands over a flat sandy
road & in summer evenings the woods are full of them. They are so
happy they do not know what to do. They will scatter far & wide
too among some insignificant whortleberry bushes, pricked with
thorns & stung by musquetoes for hours for the sake of picking a pint

[27] Shakespeare, *Macbeth*, II, ii, 37.

[28] From Isaiah, 52:7.

[29] Jacques Saurin (1677–1730), a celebrated French Protestant preacher, wrote
discourses on the Old and New Testaments and the state of Christianity in France and
several volumes of sermons. An English translation of his sermons appeared in London in six volumes in 1824, and two American printings had been published: *Eleven
Select Sermons* (Concord, N. H., 1806), and *Sermon on the Repentance of the Un-
chaste Woman* (Boston, 1823). In January, 1824, Mary Moody Emerson wrote
Emerson that "the earth . . . has been termed by divines since the reformation, the
scaffold of the divine justice" (letter in Houghton Library). For a different version
of the quotation, see p. 307 below.

of berries; occasionally chewing a bug of indescribable bad relish. You count it nothing more to go among green bushes than on the roads, but those who have been educated in dusty streets enjoy as much from sauntering ⟨t⟩here as you would in the Orange groves & Cinnamon gardens of the East Indies. They say there is a tune which [18] is forbidden to be played in the European Armies because it makes the Swiss desert ⟨because⟩ since it reminds them so forcibly of their hills at home.[29a] I have ⟨of⟩ heard many *Swiss tunes* played in college. Balancing between getting & not getting a hard lesson[,] a breath of fragrant air from the fields coming in at the window would serve as a Swiss tune & make me *desert* to the glens from which ⟨he⟩ it came. Nor is that vagabond inclination wholly gone yet. And many a sultry afternoon last summer I left my Latin & my English to go with my gun & see the rabbits & squirrels & robins in the woods. Good bye, Sir. Stop a moment. I have heard a clergyman of Maine say that in his Parish are the Penobscot Indians & that when any one of them in summer has been absent for some weeks a hunting he comes back among them a different person & altogether unlike any of the rest,[n] with an eagle's eye, a wild look, & commanding ⟨po⟩ carriage & gesture; but after a few weeks it wears off again into the indolent drone like apathy which all exhibit. Good day Sir.

↑I notice that Words are as much governed by Fashion as dress, both in written & spoken style. A negro said of another today 'That's a *curious genius.*'↓

Such a change as Hume remarks to have taken place in men's minds about the reign of James I may be found also perhaps in [19] a careful observation of the early & later books of this country. ⟨Mr⟩ The race who fought the revolution out were obviously not of the same temper & manners as the first comers to the wilderness. They had dropped so much of the puritanism of their sires, that they would hardly have ↑been↓ acknowledged by them as ⟨good men⟩ ↑sound members↓ of their rigorous society. This nation is now honourably distinguished above all others for greater moral purity. But the

[29a] Emerson doubtless found the story in Alison, *Essays on the Nature and Principles of Taste* (see the 1854 edition, pp. 37–38).

constant intercourse with Europe constantly lessen⟨e⟩s the distinction;
& liberality of religious & political sentiment gain ground rapidly.
The great men of our first age were Bradford, Standish, Cotton, Winthrop, Phipps, & Underwood,[30] of our second the Mathers, John
Elliot, Witherspoon, & Pres[iden]t Edwards, and of the third Otis,
Adams, Washington, Franklin. Smith of Virginia would not have
been admitted to the Plymouth doors unless perchance on account of
the slaughter of the three Saracens. Liberality of religion & of politics do not always go hand in hand. For the ↑same↓ puritans ↑who↓
framed the Eng[lish] Constitution, ⟨&⟩ persecuted the quakers &
hanged the witches. The adventurous spirit which distinguished the
settlers was begotten ↑by the↓[n] fanaticism of the Reformation — a
spirit which confides in its own strength for the accomplishment of
its ends & disdains to calculate the chance of failure. It is strange
↑gratifying↓ to see how faithfully the feelings of one generation may
be propagated to another amid the adverse action of all outward circumstances, poverty, riches, revolution. From the close of Elizabeth's
reign the intolerance & bigotry of the Puritans continued & multiplied
until [20] its outbreak in England in 1640 (?) & in the branch of
the stock in America in the eccles[iastical]. tyranny. After that effer-
vescence men ⟨b⟩ corrected the faults of inexperience & the following
generation here were more marked by *Good Sense.* Of [which]
⟨Frankli⟩ Gibbon s[ai]d 'twas as rare as genius[.]

This huge continent shrink to an islet.

All human pleasures have their dregs & even Friendship itself
hath the bitter lees. Who is he that thought he might clasp his friend
in embraces so tight, in daily intercourse so familiar that they two
should be one? They met in equal conversation. I saw their eyes
kindle with the common hope that they should climb life's hill together & totter down hand in hand. But the violent flame of youthful
affection rapidly wasted itself. They foolishly trusted to each other
the last secret of their bosoms, their weakness. Every man has his
failing, & these no more than others. But Men prudently cloak up

[30] There seems to be no Underwood of any prominence in Colonial history.
Emerson may have meant John Underhill (1597–1672), a captain of Massachusetts militia in the Pequot War, of which he wrote a classical account, and a leader
in the campaign to secure New Amsterdam for the British.

the sore side, & shun to disgust the eye of the multitude. These erred in fancying that friendship would pardon infirmities & that a just confidence demanded that the last door⟨s⟩ of the heart should be unclosed, and even its secret sensuality revealed. They fell in each other's respect; they slighted, disliked, & ridiculed each other & regret & fear remained at last of the consequen[21]ces of the implicit confidence of their violent love. Men must have great souls & impregnable integrity of ⟨view⟩ mind, to run no risks from the indiscreet ardor of their attachments. Heroes can be friends. Belisarius might love Narses; Aristides, Themistocles; Fox, Burke; & Jefferson, Adams, in their old age; true[n] the warmest ⟨fr⟩ connexions subsist in humbler life & groom loves groom, & fat citizen, fat citizen; with as faithful an affection, (tho' destitute of romance, because it grew moderately up in humble acquaintance) as ever united in its hoop of gold the finest minds. The history of these sympathies is very curious; one cannot conjure up this violent fondness for a long known & highly valued acquaintance, but it is a stranger, of whom Nothing is known, & nothing will come, whose eye, hair, or coat takes the fancy. So James I's propensity to favourites, who successively disgusted him. Misery to himself & seed grew out of his intemperate fondness for Robert Carre, & George Villiers. . . March 1.

If divine Providence shall always mix the fates of man, if good & evil must ever encamp ⟨together⟩ ↑side by side↓ then Europe must decline as Asia rises & Civilization will not be propagated but only *transferred*. Travellers[,] those missionaries of science & scholars of Observation[,] [22] have in the case of China rather added to the marvel than otherwise; a case unusual. The romance which they refuted only gave place to another of a less brilliant but more original & extravagant sort, and of whose incidents the worst feature is that they are true. ⟨To believe as many generations of⟩ ⟨o⟩Our forefathers ↑believed↓ that in the East was a great empire whose simple political institutions had a recorded antiquity ⟨trip⟩ at least triple the ⟨poetical⟩ ↑fabled↓ period of any other; that this nation augmented its territory with its age, incorporating all it took by the inherent virtues of its policy; that by reason of its perfect adaptation to human wants the paternal yoke of the government embraced the densest population in the world; that this population had for ages enjoyed all the great inventions that had recently been imparted to Europe as the Compass, the Press, & Gunpowder, that it was possessed of science unknown in Europe & that the peasants of this sunny land lived in greater luxury than the priveleged orders in the Western nations. This plausible tale is true in the particular but false on the whole. The Celestial Empire,—hang the [23] Celestial Empire! I hate Pekin. I will not drink of the waters of the Yellow Sea. Exorciso *tea*, celestissime, even *tea*.[31] One is apt to mix up an idea of the productions of a nation in our opinion of the producers, & Tea the insignificant sop of an herb, wholly a luxury in the West, the frivolous employment of millions in the making & tens of millions in the drinking is a fit representative of China. It is useful to know the (productions) state of man in circumstances widely dissimilar. It is a help to an inference concerning our progress. 'Tis like getting two angles to compute a third. But I hate China. 'Tis a tawdry vase. Out upon China. Words! Words.—

There are questions of education which were hinted at some pages above, which the progress of philosophy has never solved.[32] How to use the events of life; how to apply the changes in the material world to the instruction of the spirit; how to choose between incompatible advantages, between opposite utilities, are the hard problems. Is it not reasonable to suppose that a constant intimacy with the beings who are to accompany me in all the future, an exact observation of their modes of thought & action, & of the degree & manner of the influence [24][33] which one can exert upon another— should be the fittest education? Undoubtedly this is the best view of the case. But the imperfection of the human understanding has been found to forbid the direct practice of what seemed so easy. All education has indeed an ultimate regard to this design but it is found that before it can safely mix in this observant intercourse with its fellows, the mind must be trained to a solitary self examination. The faculties have their infancy & must be carefully nurtured by intervals

[31] Emerson's atrocious bilingual pun, essentially untranslatable, means "I exorcise *tea* [*te* = thee], most heavenly one, even *tea*. See p. 379 below.
[32] See p. 219 above.
[33] "EDUCATION" is centered beneath "noisy world" at the bottom of the page.

of rest & exercise to a healthful maturity. They are each liable to
peculiar infirmities & a maladministration on the part of their guard-
ians would be foll⟨ed⟩owed by fatal consequences. Great are the evils
that would spring from the premature association of the youthful
scholar with men such as the irrevocable dissipation of the concen-
trating powers; a total inability to form just judgments from the
things presented to the mind. It is not, moreover, yet decided whether
a man (of yet unbalanced soul) grows wise or malignant by his intercourse with the world.[34] Yet evils as great attend the womanish
immuring of ⟨a⟩youth ⟨in⟩ ⟨beyond the⟩ ↑out of↓ hearing of the hum
of the great & noisy world[.]

[25][35] All agree that wisdom must be got but whether by way
of knowledge or whether by observation of men & things is sturdily
contested. It seems that Mr Hobbes said "If I had read as much as
other men I should be as ignorant"; [36] & that Dr Franklin & old
Socrates, & Shakespeare & many men of note & influence in all societies, centres, in their own age, of delighted circles but forgotten
thereafter ∧—all these it seems form an amount of practical testimony in favour of *men* versus books which is not to be evaded or
answered. The worst is that we do not know the art of detecting
in opening mind the marks & elements of greatness & cannot therefore
determine what was in the seed & what was in the ⟨seed⟩ soil. Moreover all ⟨the good⟩ ↑desireable↓ qualities might be compatible & so
blamelessly pursued if it were not that every advantage verges (if
not mixes) upon a flagrant disadvantage. Thus Speculation fast re-
cedes into Fancy & idleness, Study into Pedantry & ⟨undervaluing of
thought⟩ servitude of the understanding. Solitary nurture into Pride
of opinion; ↑habits of↓ good[n] society into dependence upon others.
Nor can fallible man name an advantage ↑so↓ obvious or just[n] but it
may be plausibly balanced & contradicted by danger 'as apparent.'
This I steal from Bacon.[37]

[34] See p. 212 above.
[35] "EDUCATION" is written beneath "apparent.' This I steal" at the bottom of
the page.
[36] An inexact quotation of Hobbes' remark from Stewart, *Dissertation* (see
Works, 1854, I, 89).
[37] Emerson seems to have borrowed his ideas chiefly from *The Advancement of
Learning*.

[26][38] There is a broad average result which is so important in itself that it may be esteemed decisive,ⁿ — & to cast others in the shade. I mean the ⟨diff⟩ superiority of a civilized ⟨nation⟩ to a savage nation & of the educated to the uneducated part of a community. If ↑the inventions of↓ Gunpowder, the Steam engine & the Press were casual events as likely to be hit upon in New Zealand as in Germany; if Newtons, Bacons, & Lockes were as often bred in shops & stables as in colleges — it would indeed be deeply discouraging to the cause of Education. But the fact is that *all* genius has owed its development to literary establishments. If Benjamin Franklin were born N. Zealander he would have been a clever swimmer, boatman & weather prophet doubtless but he would certainly not have left an institution or a name. The advantage derived from a college cannot be accurately ⟨weighed⟩ ↑measured↓ but is assuredly not confined to those immured in its walls. Nay it will not be thought paradoxical to assert that the society without ⟨is⟩ may be often more benefitted by the literary resources of an university than the society within its gates. Interest, rivalry,[39]

[27][40] March

Shall I embroil my short life with a vain desire of perpetuating its memory when I am dead & gone in this dirty planet? I complain daily of my world, that it is false, disappointing, imperfect, & uncomfortable; & reason would that I should get thro' it as silently & hastily as I can & especially avoiding to tie any hopes or fears to it. I make it my best boast that I am the citizen of a far country far removed from the low influences of earth & sea, of time & change; that my highly destined nature spurns its present abode & aspires after a mode of existence & a fellowship of beings which shall eclipse & efface the gaudy glory of this. When my body shall be in the clods my triumphant soul, glad of any deliverance, will think no more of it or its habîi↓tation. Am I then to give my days & nights to a gnawing solicitude to get me a reputation, a fame, forsooth among these worm[-]eaten, worm[-]eating creatures of clay, these boys of the

---

[38] "COLLEGES" is centered at the bottom of the page.
[39] Emerson does not seem to have continued this discussion.
[40] "FAME" is written beneath "Howard," at the bottom of the page.

universe, these infants of immortality as they all must be while they live on earth? Virtue says Go beg the impartial goddess to enrol your name on her historic scroll. Why? Because if you toil & deserve to write your name there, you will effectually contribute by the same efforts to the good of yourself & your species. The attempt is very laudable, ↑even↓ if it fail of success. The "ambition of immortality is chimerical" to all but a few. But in many instances doubtless the silver trumpets of angels will answer to the flourishes of earthly fame. As in case of Newton, Socrates, Howard, & more —

[28]⁴¹   The blackbird's song is in my ear
           A summer sound I leap to hear
           Day breaks thro' yonder dusky cloud
           O'er well-known cliffs, those giants proud.
           And I am glad the day is come
           To greet me in my ancient home.

           Rejoice with me melodious bird
           Whose merry note my childhood heard
           For I've come back again to see
           The wild woods of mine infancy
           For, o my home, I thought no more
           No More! No more! for Mercy, no more!

History it seems is not, an account of the order of society in any time or land, but an account of the *exceptions* to such order. But travelling is a practical history which answers both these ends, & Talleyrand said that in a ⟨l⟩new country as N America to travel 1 or 2000 ⟨years⟩ ↑miles↓ is as good as to go, in *time*, one or 2000 years; for,ⁿ in so doing, you pass from the highest pitch of Civilization, to the verge or the midst of savage life. Much is made of *sympathy*, as an efficient principle in carrying refinement to that point where a brilliant literature begins. Competition does much also. And in this country the 5 metropolises ⁿ dissipate & cool the talent which should be concentrated & warmed. These and much more are Everett's notions on history.

⁴¹ "HISTORY" is written beneath "Everett's notions" at the bottom of the page.

[29]⁴² The imperfection of the human faculties renders it an advantage by no means inconsiderable to live in a late age of the world. Present events it is vulgarly said assume in our eyes a disproportionate importance nor does our experience of the continual error of our judgments seem to prevent the eternal recurrence of the same mistakes. It is surprising what a⟨n⟩ ↑different↓ effect is produced by the same scene at an interval of 50 years. We are forcibly struck with the justice of that analogy which calls Time, distance. Circumstances are grouped in a juster order, & shew their true relation to neighbouring events after the lapse of this period which no sagacity, placed nearer, could interpret. From its nature, moreover this is an advantage which is forever improving. The farther we depart from a cluster of considerable transactions the more we lose sight of their details & the wider is the generalization we can draw. All that is particular & lessening is gradually withdrawn until nothing remains but the point of relation to the history of the Universe.

As our views of the world vary, so our estimate of the length of life varies. But in this light no finite length of time, no number of generations can be accounted long.

[⟨29⟩30]⁴³ The mind can grapple with any portion of time without difficulty, & we roll up the story of 5 or 6 or 10 hundred years, having a distinct apprehension of the character of so long a period of time. We rapidly discover that all history occupies too brief a space ↑to↓ ⟨p⟩ qualify us to judge clearly concerning it. Who of us knows but that the same eras & events which we affect to separate by a vast ⟨int⟩ chasm from each other, the better judgment of posterity will unite again as essentially one? Remote generations may amuse themselves with the simplicity of this early age which magnified the hairbreadth boundary between itself & its fathers, & accounted itself old & wise. * ⁴⁴

[*] See Ed. Review of Stael Considerations ⟨i⟩on the French Revol

⁴² "HISTORY" is written beneath "generations can" at the bottom of the page.

⁴³ "FAME" is written beneath "have been" at the bottom of the page. Following "& wise." is a double diagonal slash.

⁴⁴ The asterisk is in the margin. It presumably refers to the unkeyed footnote. The review there mentioned is in Vol. XXX (Sept. 1818), 275–317; pages 278–279 deal with the ideas Emerson is discussing.

Themes instead of analyzing the nature of fame content themselves with the sweeping assertion that it is an universal passion & the source of all the good & evil in the world. Buonaparte for fame overran Europe & Alexander for fame overran Asia. Who told you that this was the only impulse? It might have been restlessness; it might be love of power; it might be impatience of being controuled. And why Universal? Go out into the street & count how many persons are stung with the ambition of being remembered? ⟨They⟩ Nine tenths are content to grow up & make fortunes & grow old without knowing or caring who ⟨knows⟩ ↑wots↓ & who wots not of them. It should have been inquired — what it is? & Dr Wollaston would reply Caesar's amounted to — "Somebody killed somebody." It should have been noticed also that [3⟨0⟩1]⁴⁵ fame is chiefly or wholly of two sorts; viz. military & literary fame. The former cannot be ⟨acqui⟩ preserved without the other, but it commonly occasions the second. And it is singular fact that the success of the sword & pen are contemporary,ⁿ or that the period of the best literary refinement of a nation is the period of its greatest military success. Architecture is in vain, for the pyramids add no fame, not the name even of their founders. Of Sculpture, Art, Civilization, let a story tell. A city of Greece sent Nemeas to Pindar to request him to write an ode to immortalize the name of their community. Pindar said he would but demanded as the price   .

Why, with that sum said Nemeas we can procure a statue in bronze which will last for ages. 'You shall choose,' said the poet. Nemeas at last agreed to the sum, and Pindar wrote the ode. Mark the event. Every palace, temple, & pillar are swept from the city but the ode of Pindar is still read & admired. What is the sense of Erostratus's fame who burned the Ephesian fane? The fame of the Conqueror is ambiguous; nay, it is very bad.

> One self approving hour whole years outweighs,
> Of stupid starers & of loud huzzas.
>   [Pope, *Essay on Man*, IV, 255–256]

But the possessor of a good fame, the Washington, the Socrates, the Howard may reflect with deep delight, that long after he has gone

---

⁴⁵ "FAME" is written beneath "excellence," at the bottom of the page.

down to the silent tomb, he prompts & encourages to the pursuit of the same excellence, many youthful & aspiring hearts.

[3⟨1⟩2]   ⟨*⟩From (A) 29th page.⁴⁶
It is not therefore ⟨our⟩ ↑the↓ fault of our sagacity, but of our age, that we cannot accurately seize the distinguishing feature of what we call ancient literature, nor can arrive at such a view of it as all scholars shall pronounce satisfactory. Very few men ever felt competent to decide upon the comparative excellence of any modern with an ancient literature. All men are by no means agreed that those literatures (of Greece & Rome,) are excellent to any marvellous extent. Indeed most men have ⟨ch⟩ on that subject changed their minds many times. — V. p. 35.

[↑said Pliny, of Rhodes↓ Centum Colossi alium nobilitaturi locum. ↑Galba↓ sacris fatigans diis nunc alterius imperii. Tacitus.]⁴⁷

I love the voice of the bird
And the tree where he builds his nest
And the grove where man's mirth & man's grief are
        unheard.
Ye are my home, ye ancient rocks,
Who lift amid cedar shades, your rugged crest,
The flowers, like Beauty's golden locks
Adorn ⟨thy⟩ ↑your↓ brow & droop upon your breast.

Mountain & cliff, & lake, I am your child
Ye were the cradle of mine infancy
The playground of my youth

⁴⁶ An error for p. [30], originally and mistakenly numbered [29]. Emerson continues his discussion of history, left off at the end of paragraph one (Emerson's "(A)"?) on p. [30]. He apparently canceled the asterisk because he saw that it would have referred to an asterisk on p. [30] which referred to a footnote.
⁴⁷ The "quotation" from Pliny is actually a paraphrase of "sunt alii centum numero in eadem urbe colossi minore hoc . . . nobilitaturi locum" — "there are a hundred other colossal statues in the same city, which though smaller than this one would have each of them brought fame to any place" (*Natural History*, Bk. XXXIV, 42). The "quotation" from Tacitus is an even more careless paraphrase of ". . . Galba . . . sacris intentus fatigabat alieni iam imperii deos" — "Galba . . . intent upon his sacrifices, . . . was importuning the gods of an empire which was already another's . . ." (*The Histories*, I, xxix).

He who frequents these scenes where Nature discloses her magnificence to silence & solitude, will have his mind occupied often by trains of thought of a peculiarly solemn tone which never interrupted the [3⟨2⟩3] profligacy of libertines, the ⟨busy schemes⟩ ↑money getting↓ of the miser,[n] or the glorygettings of the ambitious. In the depths of the forest where the noon comes like twilight; on the cliff; in the cavern; & by the lonely lake; where the sounds of Man's mirth & of Man's sorrow were never heard, where the squirrel inhabits & the voice of the bird echoes, is a shrine which few visit in vain, an oracle which returns no ambiguous response. The pilgrim who retires hither wonders how his heart, could ever cleave so mightily to the world whose deafening tumult he has left behind. What are temples & towered cities to him? He has come to a sweeter & more desireable creation. When his eye reaches upward by the sides of the piled rocks to the grassy summit, he feels that the magnificence of man is quelled & subdued here. The very leaf ⟨beneath⟩ ↑under↓ his foot[,] the little flowers that embroider his path, outdo the art, & outshine the glory of man. What are his ⟨coarse⟩ unskilful contrivances & coarse workmanship to the exquisite delicacy, the richness, & the perfection of Nature's handiwork? And his pigmy structures, (too spacious for the dwarf who inhabits them,) what are they to the everlasting hills? Things here assume their natural proportions before distorted by prejudice. What, in this solitude, are the libraries of learning? The scholar & the peasant are alike in the view which Nature takes of [34] them. The barriers of artificial distinction are broken down. Society's iron sceptre of ⟨forms &⟩ ceremony is dishonoured here. Here in the footsteps of the Invisible, in the bright ruins of the original creation, over which the Morning Stars sang together, and where, even now, they shed their sweetest light. Whatsoever beings watch over these inner chambers of Nature, they have not abandoned their charge[,] they have never grown weary of adorning their beautiful homes. The structures of human pride, the capitals of empires which were founded on the rock and baptized 'eternal' by the fond inhabitant who entrusted to these stone tabernacles his hope of fame, they have surrendered their tenants to narrower houses, & posterity has tired of the palace or lost the power. The Cormorant & the bittern scream in its vaulted chambers & the fox looks out at the window. Nature never tires of *her* house and each year ⟨the⟩ ↑its↓ glorious tapestry is newly hung. I stand beneath the same rocks, I touch the same greensward & my heart is exhilarated by the selfsame scenery by which the patriarchs of the infant world pitched their tents, or the herald angels folded their wings when they descended from heaven.

[35] From p. 32

Youth is not the fault nations soonest mend [48] and it may be very long before the World's experience can be anywise pronounced mature. What are we who sit in judgement upon our fathers as if upon a remote & foreign race? Their stripling progeny; inhabiting their hearths, covered with the dust of their prejudices, dressed in their robes and using their wealth. When hundreds of ages shall have rolled away & the scholar's eye shall combine the entire history of a thousand nations in one view it will be less immodest & more easy to pronounce on the merits of their respective literatures. It will correct our vain ⟨antiquity⟩ pretensions to read often Franklin's scrap called the Ephemeris.[49]

Myself.   Sunday, Apr. 18, 1824.

↑"Nil fuit unquam sic dispar sibi." [50] Hor.↓

[*Satires*, I, iii, 18]

I am beginning my professional studies. In a month I shall be *legally* a man. And I deliberately dedicate my time, my talents, & my hopes to the Church. Man is an animal that looks before & after; and I should be loth to reflect at a remote period that I took so solemn a step in my existence without some careful examination of my past & present life. Since I cannot alter I would not repent the

---

[48] Cf. *JMN*, I, 326:

Youth is the fault whatever curs pretend
The fault that boys & nations soonest mend.

See also p. 244 below.

[49] Volumes 1 and 3 of Franklin, *The Complete Works*, 3 vols. (London, 1806), were withdrawn from the Boston Library Society Feb. 21–May 22, 1824. "The Ephemera" (not "Ephemeris") is the last bagatelle in vol. 3, pp. 508–510.

[50] "Never was a creature so inconsistent." The Loeb text reads "impar," not "dispar."

resolution I have made & this page must be witness to the latest year of my life whether I have good grounds to warrant my determination.

[36] I cannot dissemble that my abilities are below my ambition. And I find that I judged by a false criterion when I measured my powers by my ability to understand & to criticise the intellectual character of another. For men graduate their respect not by the secret wealth but by ⟨its⟩the outward use; not by the power to understand, but by the power to act. I have or had a strong imagination & consequently a keen relish for the beauties of poetry. The exercise which the practice of composition gives to this faculty is the cause of my immoderate fondness for writing, which has swelled these pages to ⟨such⟩ a voluminous extent. My reasoning faculty is proportionately weak, nor can I ever hope to write a Butler's Analogy or an Essay of Hume. Nor is it strange that with this confession I should choose theology, which is from everlasting to everlasting 'debateable Ground.' For, the highest species of reasoning upon divine subjects is rather the fruit of a sort of moral imagination, than of the 'Reasoning Machines' such as Locke & Clarke & David Hume. Dr Channing's Dudleian Lecture [51] is the model of what [37] I mean, and the faculty which produced this is akin to the higher flights of the fancy. I may add that the preaching most in vogue ⟨with⟩ ↑at↓ the present day depends chiefly on imagination for its success, and asks those accomplishments which I believe are most within my grasp. I have set down little which can gratify my vanity, and I must further say that every comparison of myself with my mates that six or seven, perhaps sixteen or seventeen, years have made has convinced me that there exists a signal defect of character which neutralizes in great part the just influence my talents ought to have. Whether that defect be in the *address*, in the fault of good forms, which ⟨I⟩Queen Isabella said, were like perpetual letters commendatory, or deeper seated in an absence of common *sympathies*, or even in a levity of the understanding, I cannot tell. But its bitter fruits are a sore uneasiness in the company of most men & women, a frigid fear of offending & jealousy of disrespect, an inability to lead & an unwillingness to follow the current conversation, which contrive to make me

[51] See p. 160 above.

second with all those among whom chiefly I wish to be first.

[38] Hence my bearing in the world is the ⟨ex⟩ direct opposite of that good humoured independence & self esteem which should mark the gentleman. Be it here remembered that there is a decent pride which is conspicuous in the perfect model of a Christian man. I am unfortunate also, as was Rienzi, in a propensity to laugh or rather snicker. I am ill at ease therefore among men. I criticize with hardness; I lavishly ⟨praise⟩ ↑applaud;↓ I weakly argue; and I wonder with a foolish face of praise.[52]

Now the profession of Law demands a good deal of personal address, an impregnable confidence in one's own powers, upon all occasions expected & unexpected, & a logical mode of thinking & speaking — which I do not possess, & may not reasonably hope to obtain. Medicine also makes large demands on the practitioner for a seducing Mannerism. And I have no taste for the pestle & mortar, for Bell on the bones or Hunter or Celsus.[53]

[39] But in Divinity I hope to thrive. I inherit from my sire a formality of manner & speech, but I derive from him or his patriotic parent a passionate love for the strains of eloquence. I burn after the 'aliquid immensum infinitumque'[54] which Cicero desired. What we ardently love we learn to imitate. My understanding venerates & my heart loves that Cause which is dear to God & man — the laws of Morals, the Revelations which sanction, & the blood of martyrs & triumphant suffering of the saints which seal them. In my better hours, I am the believer (if not the dupe) of brilliant promises, and can respect myself as the possessor of those powers which command the reason & passions of the multitude. The office of a clergyman is

[52] "wonder . . . praise" is quoted from Pope, "Epistle to Dr. Arbuthnot," l.212. See p. 365 below.

[53] Charles Bell (1774–1842) and his brother John (1763–1820) were Scottish surgeons and authors of numerous works on anatomy. Emerson may have known about *The Anatomy and Physiology of the Human Body* . . . , by John Bell; *The Anatomy and Physiology of the Brain and Nerves* . . . , by Charles Bell, 3 vols. (New York, 1822). John Hunter (1728–1793) was another Scottish physician and author of medical treatises. For favorable impressions of Bell and Hunter, see *Lectures*, I, 40, n. 19, and 81. Aulus Cornelius Celsus (1st century A.D.) wrote eight works on medicine.

[54] "something great and immeasurable" (Ed.). Emerson may have found the phrase in Bacon. See Vivian Hopkins, "Emerson and Bacon," *American Literature*, XXIX (Jan. 1958), 413.

twofold; ⟨the⟩ public preaching & private influence. Entire success in the first is the lot of few, but this I am encouraged to expect. If however the individual himself lack that moral worth which is to secure the last, his studies upon the first are idly spent. The most prodigious genius, a seraph's eloquence will shamefully defea‖t‖ its own end, if it has not first won the heart of the defender to the cause he defends,[n] but the coolest reason cannot censure my choice [40] when I oblige myself *professionally* to a life which all wise men freely & advisedly adopt. I put no great restraint on myself & can therefore claim little merit in a manner of life which chimes with inclination & habit. But I would learn to love Virtue for her own sake, I would have my pen so guided as was Milton's when a deep & enthusiastic love of ⟨G⟩goodness & of God dictated the Comus to the bard, or that prose rhapsody in the 3rd Book of Prelaty. I would sacrifice inclination to the interest of mind & soul. I would remember that "Spare Fast oft with Gods doth diet," [55] that Justinian devoted but one out of twenty four ↑hours↓ to sleep & this week (for instance) I will remember to curtail my dinner & supper sensibly & rise ↑from table↓ each day with an appetite; & so see if * it be fact that I can understand more clearly.

I have mentioned a defect of character; perhaps it is not one, but many. Every wise man ↑⟨‖ … ‖⟩↓ aims ⟨t⟩at an entire conquest of himself. We applaud as possessed of extraordinary good sense, one who never makes the slightest mistake in speech or action; one in whom not only every important [41] step of life, but every passage of conversation, every duty of the day, even every movement of every muscle —— hands, feet, & tongue, are measured & dictated by deliberate reason. I am not assuredly that excellent creature. A score of words & deeds issue from me ⟨every⟩ da⟨y⟩ily, of which I am not the master. They are begotten of weakness & born of shame. I cannot assume the elevation I ought, — but lose the influence I should exert among those of meaner or younger understanding, for want of sufficient *bottom* in my nature, for want of that confidence of manner which springs from an erect ⟨shameless⟩ mind which is without fear & without reproach. In my frequent humiliation, even before women & children I am compelled to remember the poor boy who cried, "I told you,

[*] N.B. Till Tuesday Evg next

[55] Milton, *Il Penseroso*, l. 46.

Father, they would find me out."[n] Even those feelings which are counted noble & generous, take in me the taint of frailty. For my strong propensity to friendship, instead of working out its manly ends, degenerates to a fondness for particular casts of feature perchance not unlike the doting of old King James. Stateliness & silence hang very like ⟨the⟩ Mokannah's suspicious silver veil, only concealing what is best not shewn.[56] What is called a warm heart, I have not.

[42₁][57] The stern accuser Conscience cries that the Catalogue of Confessions is not yet full. I am a lover of indolence, & of the belly. And the good have a right to ask the Neophyte who wears this garment of scarlet sin, why he comes where all are apparelled in white? Dares he hope that some patches of pure & generous feeling, some bright fragments of lofty thought, it may be of divine poesy shall charm the eye away from all the particoloured shades of his Character? And when he is clothed in the vestments of the priest, & has inscribed on his forehead 'Holiness to the Lord', & wears on his breast the breastplate of the tribes, then can the Ethiopian change his skin & the unclean be pure? Or how shall I strenuously enforce on men the duties & habits to which I am a stranger? Physician, heal thyself. I need not go far for an answer to so natural a question. I am young in my everlasting existence. I already discern the deep dye of elementary errors, which threaten to colour its infinity of duration. And I judge that if I devote my nights & days *in form*, to the service of God & the War against Sin, — I shall soon be prepared to do the same *in substance*.

I cannot accurately estimate my chances of success, in my profession, & in life. [43₁] Were it just to judge the future from the past, they would be very low. In my case I think it is not. I have never expected success in my present employment. My scholars are carefully instructed, my money is faithfully earned, but the instructor is little wiser. & the duties were never congenial with my disposition. Thus far the dupe of hope I have trudged on with my bundle at my back, ⟨with⟩ ↑and↓ my eye fixed on the distant hill where my

---

[56] Hashim ibn-Hakim al-Mokanna (?–c. 780), an Arab who pretended that his veil hid a divine light about his face, appears as hero in one of the tales in Moore's *Lalla Rookh*.

[57] Emerson shortly repeats page numbers [42] and [43], as the subscript numbers indicate.

burden would fall. It may be I shall write *dupe* a long time to come
& the end of life shall intervene betwixt me & the release. My trust
is that my profession shall be my regeneration of mind, manners, inward & outward estate; or rather my starting point, for I have hoped
to put on eloquence as a robe, and by goodness and zeal and the
awfulness of virtue to press & prevail over the false judgments, the
rebel passions & corrupt habits of men. We blame the past[,] we
magnify & gild the future and are not wiser for the multitude of
days. Spin on, Ye of the adamantine spindle, spin on, ⟨t⟩my fragile
thread.

Sunday evg.

We are prepared to review the history of one of that distinguished body of men who achieved the Revolution that separated
⟨E⟩America from [42₂][58] ⟨a⟩⟨A⟩Europe. A Revolution of which we
⟨anti⟩ speak in the language of posterity when we say that it bears
the palm away from Greek & Roman achievement whether we contemplate the magnitude of the consequences, the eminence of the
actors, or the ⟨p⟩ universal pervading patriotism which made it the
cause of the victory of every American. There are three things chief
which the human mind studies; itself, God, & the Universe. I know
not how these high pursuits can be better combined than in that ⟨dep⟩
branch of art which is called History which from the events of communities & individuals ⟨of⟩ gathers the character & nature of man;
which likewise indicates those passages in human affairs where the
hand of Providence most visibly comes in, apart from what may be
deemed its most instructive office the noting of those curious invariable results of the sound or diseased state of society from the varied
proportion of the same elements. (There are several very striking
facts which must be here set down as luxury or high civilization like
ripe fruit being nearest to decay, ↑contemporaneous success of sword
& pen.↓ &c. &c.) ⟨All⟩ These[n] are what may be termed the general
Rules of History deduced from an ample induction & the soi-[43₂][59]

[58] "FRANKLIN HISTORY" is written beneath "an ample induction" at the
bottom of the page.
[59] The line between the poetic fragments below is ornamental, and followed
by a penciled line.

disant History that contains them not is a barren chronicle. (Qu. Are these not peculiar to mod[ern]. historians and wanting in the ancient masters?)

For the third study — i.e. the Universe, as far as it ⟨relates to other men⟩ regards the relations of fellow-beings, it is comprehended in the first office we ascribed to the historic Muse. In a vague sense, history may be said to comprise also all the store of Natural knowledge, since it records all the victories of human science over the inanimate Creation & the eras & degree of intellectual greatness.

W   Waldo

    The wheels of Fortune turn
    The Car of Conquest rolls
    The blazing rays of Glory burn   Angel
    O'er each bright land, where ardent souls
    Have loved the good of man & spurned ignoble goals.

    In Eastern Lands was Empire born
    And Asia gave him a royal crown

———————

    I'm going to my own hearthstone
    Bosomed in yon green hills alone
    A secret shrine in a pleasant land
    Whose groves the frolic fairies planned
    Their twilight shade each summer day
    Echoes the blackbird's roundelay
    And vulgar crowds have never trod
    A spot that is sacred to Mind & God.
                RW.E
[44]   O when I am safe in my sylvan home
    I tread on the pride of Greece & Rome
    And when I am stretched beneath the pines
    Where the evening star so holy shines
    I laugh at the lore & the pride of man
    At the sophist schools & the learned clan
    For what are they all in their high conceit
    When Man in the bush with God may meet.

243

I rake no coffined clay, ⟨I puff no pride⟩
   ↑nor publish wide↓
The resurrection of departed pride
Safe in their ancient crannies dark & deep
Let kings & conquerors saints & soldiers sleep.
Late in the world too late perchance for fame
Just late enough to reap abundant blame
I choose a novel theme, a bold abuse
Of critic charters, an unlaurelled muse.

Old mouldy ⟨lands &⟩ men & books & names & lands
Disgust my reason & defile my hands
I had as lief respect an ancient shoe
As love Old things *for age*, & hate the new.
I spurn the Past, my mind disdains its nod
Nor kneels in homage to so mean a god.
I laugh at those who while they   & gaze [60]
The bald antiquity of China praise.
Youth is (whatever Cynic tubs pretend)
The fault that boys & nations soonest mend.

The Cardinals in Italy have studied with faithful zeal the successive lessons con⟨tained⟩↑veyed↓[n] in Æsop's fable of the Frogs & their Kings.

[45] Intervals of mentality are faint & few & the intent of existence by no means clearly made out. Seemingly obedient to the intimations of nature society has yet arrived at an artificial, tame & pigmy result. It puzzles & mortifies the bounding spirit to be brought so soon to a goal. A choice of three professions, in either of which but a small portion of time is professedly devoted to the analysis of those high relations which unite us to God & those inexplicably curious cords that fasten us to matter. Men's creeds can never, at least in youth, set the heart entirely at ease. They strike the eye ever & anon as fine spun textures through which rebellious doubt is impatient, sometimes desperate, to plunge. There is a dreaminess about

[60] The word "gape" is written in pencil in the blank space, but it is almost certainly by Edward Emerson.

my mode of life (which may be a depravity,) which loosens the tenacity of what should be most tenacious — this my grasp on heaven & earth. I am the servant more than the master of my fates. They seem to lead me into ⟨a⟩many a slough where I do no better than despond. And as to the life I lead & the Works & the days, I should blush to recite the unprofitable account. But prophets & philosophers ⟨h⟩ assure me that I am immortal and sometimes my own imagination goes into a fever with its hopes & conceptions. Tell me, my soul, if this be true; if these indolent days & frivolous nights, these insignificant accomplishments, this handful of thought, this pittance of virtues are to form my trust & claim on an existence as imperishable as my Maker's. There is no such thing accorded [46] to the universal prayer of man, as satisfactory knowledge. Metaphysics teach me admirably well what I knew before; setting out in order particular after particular, bone after bone, the anatomy of the mind. My knowledge is thus arranged[,] not augmented. Morals, too, the proud science which departs at once from the lower ⟨con⟩ creation about which most of man's philosophy is conversant, & professes to deal with his sublimest connexions & separate destiny, morals are chiefly occupied in discriminating between what is general & what is partial, or in tying rules together by a thread which is called a system or a principle. But neither metaphysics nor ethics are more than outside sciences. They give ↑me↓ no insight into the nature & design of my being & the profoundest scholar in them both is as far from any clue ⟨at⟩to the Being & the work behind the scenes, as the Scythian or the Mohawk. For, Morals & Metaph[ysics]. Cudworth & Locke[n] may both be true, and every system of religion yet offered to man wholly false. To glowing hope moreover 'tis alarming to see the full & regular series of animals from mites & worms up to man; ⟨a⟩ yet he who has the same organization & a little more mind pretends to an insulated & extraordinary destiny to which his fellows of the stall & field are in no part admitted, nay are disdainfully excluded. x x x x But for myself [47] wo is me! these poor & barren thoughts are the best in my brain[.]

> —— 'the glow
> That in my spirit dwelt, is fluttering faint & low' ——
> [Byron, *Childe Harold's Pilgrimage*, IV, clxxxv]

I am ambitious not to live in a corner, or, which is tenfold perdition, to be contemptible in a corner. Meantime my prospect is no better; my soul is dark or is dead. I will hope. 'She is not dead, but sleepeth.' [Matt. 9:24]   May 2.——

> Sleep on, ye drowsy tribes whose ⟨reverend
>   age⟩ ↑old repose↓
> The roaring Oceans of the East enclose
> Old Asia, nurse of man & bower of gods
> The dragon Tyranny with crown & ball
> Chants to thy dreams his ancient lullaby

Letter to Plato — The voice of antiquity has proclaimed, most venerable Shade, that if the Father of the Gods should converse with men he would speak in the language of Plato. In cloisters & colleges, lovers of philosophy are found to this day who repeat this praise. But the revolution of ages has introduced other tongues into the world & the dialect of Attica is well nigh forgotten. Rome succeeded to the honours of Greece: Italy, France, & England to the power & refinement of Rome & the children of the proud republicans who disgraced Xerxes, defied Asia, & instructed all Europe, are now cooped up in a corner of their patrimony making a desperate stand for their lives against a barbarous nation whose bondmen they have been. In these circum[48]stances the pillars of the ⟨p⟩Porch have been broken & the groves of the Academy felled to the ground. Philosophy discourses in another language & though the messages of Deity are brought to men they come in terms as well as on topics to which you, illustrious Athenian, (?) were a stranger. In this old age of the world, I shall therefore speak to the Spirit of Plato in a new language but in one whereinto has long been transfused all the wealth of ancient thought, enriched & perchance outweighed by productions of modern genius. I may add that I live in a land ⟨of⟩ which you alone ⟨among⟩ ↑to↓ your contemporaries ⟨believed⟩ ↑⟨discover⟩↓ ↑prophesied↓ where is founded a political system more wise & successful than Utopia or the Atlantis.

You have now dwelled in the land of souls upward of twenty centuries & ↑in the meantime↓ mightier changes than those to which

246

I have already alluded have appeared on earth. I have no design to interrupt your serene repose with the weary annals of political convulsion. These were always alike & the fortunes of ages may be told from an infancy as brief as man's life. The desperate State of the Greek Republic concerns me not; it has long ceased [49] to touch yourself. I write of higher revolutions & vaster communities. I write of the moral & religious condition of man.

[61] As the world has grown older the theory of life has grown better, while a correspondent improvement in practice, has not been observed. Eighteen hundred years ago a Revelation came down from heaven which distinctly declared the leading principles of ethics, & that in so clear & popular a form that the very terms in which they were conveyed serve the most illiterate as well as the great & wise for a manual, a Rule of life. The book which contains this divine message has done more than any other to sap the authority, I might say, to sweep away the influence of Socrates & his disciple. Men still commend your wisdom for indeed Plato thou reasonest well but Christ & his apostles infinitely better not through thy fault but through their inspiration. Thus a religious revolution has taken place in the midst of civilized nations more radical & extensive than any other which ever came be it religious, scientific, or political. Men are now furnished with creeds, animated by all the motives a gospel offers & they look back with [50] [62] pity on the proud attainments of the *pagan* Plato & his emulous successors, & around upon the living pagan nations of the East & West. This Dispensation of the Supreme Being is expounded & enforced to all classes of men by a regular priesthood.

That priesthood find riddles in their vocation hard to solve[,] wonders not easy to digest. They examine with curious inquiry public annals & private anecdotes of your age to ascertain the just level to which human virtue had then arisen; to find how general were integrity, temperance, & charity; to find how much the gods were reverenced; & then to compare accurately the result with the known condition of modern Europe & America. For it is not believed pos-

---

[61] A faint line appears in the left margin from "As the world" to "for a manual" below.

[62] A faint line appears in the left margin from "-ine with curious" to "your gaudy" below.

sible by those living under the influence of such new & puissant principles as our Gospel hath erected that any high standard could have obtained of thought or action under the patronage of your gaudy & indecent idolatry. But now & then a scholar whose midnight lamp is regularly lit to unfold your spirit, appeals from the long mythology which the poets forged, to your own lofty speculations on the nature of the Gods & the obliga[51][63]tions to virtue — which Christianity hath rather outstripped than contradicted; when a scholar appeals from that to these for the true belief of good men your contemporaries, he is told that the mass of men regarded your pages as fine spun theories, unsanctioned, unpractical, untrue; that you Plato did not know if there were many gods or but One; that you inculcated the observance of the vulgar Superstitions of the day. If the law of the universe admitted of exception & it were allowed me to depart to your refulgent shores & commune with Plato this is the information I should seek at your hands. How could those parts of the social machine whose consistency & just action depend⟨s⟩ entirely upon the morality & religion sown & grown in the community, how could these be kept in safe & efficient arrangement⟨?⟩ under a system which besides being frivolous was the butt of vulgar ridicule? [n]

Is it necessary that men should have before them the strong excitement of religion⟨s⟩ & its thrilling motives? One who was accustomed to the constant pressure of their yoke would pronounce it indispensable. It was so specially made for man & blends so intimately with his nature & habits [52] that it is difficult for the believer to concieve of Unbelief. Nay the influence seems to spread a great deal wider & to affect ↑all↓ those who belong to a religious country though the predominance of these feelings be no part of their character. But 'tis very possible that this may be illusory and it seems to me if we ⟨estimate⟩ study /particulars/the particular actions making up the aggregate which we call character/ & abandon generalities, we shall find that there is a great selfdeception practised daily in society where ⟨a⟩ gospels are promulged & that the ⟨continual des⟩ ↑proneness↓ of men to judge of themselves by their best moments combining with that unqualified ⟨moral⟩ approbation which every moral being ⟨of no⟩

[63] A faint line appears in the left margin from "tions to virtue" to "Superstitions" below.

must needs yield to a system so pure, leads men to suspect that the deeds they do from a broad view of their interest, they do from religious motives & a powerful bias to Virtue.[64]

Sunday Evg., June   , 1824.

It is not so easy a task as is ordinarily thought to sketch in general terms the character & merits of a nation. It is not easy to be the seneschal of Time; to assign to any nation the precise niche of honour to which it has claim[n] & mete out to each series of generations the ↑just↓ measure of fame.

[53] ⟨Methinks⟩ It should seem that in the poor imperfection of our faculties it were a little arrogant to assume the ability of writing in a line the annals [of] an age, of embodying into a single picture with a rapid pencil ⟨th⟩all that infinite ⟨a⟩dissimilarity of events, the chaotic mass of fact⟨ions⟩s, actions, & men which spreading over a large tract of the globe & a long period make up the history of a people. We are prone to generalize so rapidly that we decieve ourselves & forget that the ⟨proud⟩ phrase or even epithet to which we have ↑proudly↓ reduced whole epochs pregnant with the fortunes of our race, are only the subterfuges under which we hide our ignorance & incapacity. For they leave out ⟨the⟩ ↑a↓ thousand particulars which we are unable to grasp at once but which are necessary to the induction of which we are ambitious. So when we say the Dutch are phlegmatic, the Greek ↑is↓ acute, the ⟨Spania⟩ Castilian proud, it is a bold sport of the imagination which moulds into one image ten myriads of men to whom the alleged phlegm or the acuteness or the pride was by no means an universal or a sole ⟨char⟩ or perhaps even a general or conspicuous feature. Before this image, which, by being a pleasing picture, *although no likeness*, occupies beforehand in [54] men's minds the place which the true object should take up, faith learns to kneel & Reason is dumb. In numberless cases, it hence follows, men express astonishment at what they are pleased to call radical & unaccountable revolutions of the mind in certain circumstances; but closer inquiry ascertains to be the proper & natural fruits of the preceding train of events. Out of what we call the Dark Ages came the light of Science to illumine the world not because there was

---

[64] Emerson continues the Letter to Plato on p. [55].

a sudden change but because, as we find, they had all along cherished & augmented the sparks that Rome had left burning on the altar. Etruria was ⟨civilized⟩ refined & learned before Rome usurped the power & the glory of Italy. The Grecian genius did not start into life with the victories of Salamis & Plataea but was born & disciplined before Homer sang.

X X X X X X X X

From our inability to grasp the whole truth it thus happens that we select ⟨on⟩ some one accidental feature & by dwelling exclusively on this our imaginations magnify it till we come actually to mistake the part for the whole. Perhaps no nation near or remote[,] contemporary or ancient was ever appreciated. The parts moreover of a nation's history are often so widely sundered & of such contrary complexion that they set sys[55]tem at defiance and are rather many nations than one. It is a vulgar obeisance to names & not philosophy which makes but one story of the Rome of Kings, the Rome of Consuls, the Rome of Emperors, the Rome of Ostrogoths, & the Rome of the Popes. It is joining together what God has put asunder. And this is true, though not so obviously, of all histories. The union which is effected under the name of England, of China, is ⟨an⟩ ↑forced &↓ artificial, contrived for obvious purposes of convenience but not founded in truth.

⟨The stream of liberty which the Holy Alliance are striving to *dam* [—] at ille
　　　Labitur et labetur in omne volubilis aevum.⟩[65]

Continued ↑from p. 52↓　　It is a favourite point, Plato, with our divines to argue from the ⟨ancient⟩ misery & vice anciently prevalent in the world, a certain necessity of the Revelation. Of this Revelation I am the ardent friend. Of the Being who sent it I am the child & I trust I am disposed from reason & affection with the whole force of my understanding, the warmth of my heart & the constant attention of all my life to practise the duties there enjoined & to help its diffusion throughout the globe. But I confess it has not for me the same exclusive & extraordinary claims it has for many. [56] I hold Reason to be a prior revelation & that they do not contradict⟨ion⟩ each other.

[65] "Yet on it glides, and on it will glide, rolling its flood forever." See pp. 76, 101, and 106 above.

I concieve that the Creator addresses ⟨th⟩ his messages to the minds
of his children and will not mock them by acting upon their moral
character by means & motives which are wild & unintelligible to them.
The assent which fear & superstition shall extort from them to words
or rites or reasons ↑which↓ they do not understand, since it makes a
ruin of the mind, can please none but a cruel & malicious divinity.
The belief of such a God & such sublime depravity is absurd. His
house is divided against itself. His house, his universe cannot stand.
The errand which the true God sends, which men have hoped to
recieve, which philosophers waited for in your Porches & Schools, —
must be worthy of him or it will be rejected as a mountebank's tales
& wonders. What we do not apprehend we first admire & then ridicule.
Therefore I scout all those parts of the book which are reckoned
mysteries.

But one of the greatest of these is ↑of↓ external rather than internal character by which the Revelation is made but a portion of
a certain [57][66] great scheme planned from eternity in heaven to
be slowly developed on earth. It is made essential to the economy of
Providence & necessary to the welfare of man. I need not inform you
in all its depraved details of the theology under whose chains Calvin
of Geneva bound Europe down; but this opinion, that the Revelation
had become necessary to the salvation of men thro' some Conjunction
of events in heaven, is one of its vagaries. This is one which from
whatever cause has lingered in men's minds after the rest of that
family of errors disappeared. And — sober & sensible theologians
speak of the ⟨p⟩ ages preceding the event as a long preparation for
it & of the whole history of man as only relative to it. The cases are
so few in which we can see connexion & order in events by reason of
the narrow field of our Vision that we are glad in our vanity if we
can solder with our imaginations into ⟨a⟩ system, things in fact unconnected, can turn the ravishment of devotion or poetry into prophecies by searching up & down in the great garner of History for an
event that will chime with a prediction[.] ——

Unmoved by the motives of virtuous ambition that press upon
you, unawakened by the thun[58]ders of the Church eternal, the
boundless hopes of thy youth forgotten, careless of the prayers of

---

[66] A faint line appears in the left margin from "that we are" to "chime with".

friendship & the admonitions of age, thy mother's tears & thy father's gray hairs dishonoured — there thou liest in thy damnable debauchery. Revel & rot in thy sensual sty, hug thyself & embrace thy sin, thou defiled one! while thy brother man, who was nursed in the same cradle, & the fellow of thy infant studies & sports —— embraces Glory in *his* arms, and clasps with clean hands an imperishable crown. God & good angels look out from the windows of heaven & open its everlasting doors to welcome him in, his Virtue & honour shine gloriously in that immortal company — while thou art too low for their loathing; thy life which thou callest pleasure is food for the scorn of the Universe ⟨o⟩O miserable fool of thine own contempt! ——

July 8.

To deny a Providence with Epicurus & a God with the Atheist, is a mournful speculation. It is depriving ↑Nature↓ of that kindly sympathy, that majestic society it held with us whilst we thought it instinct with divine life. It is casting man back into a cold & com[59][67]fortless solitude. You leave him alone in a Universe exposed to the convulsions of disorder & the wrecks of systems ⟨you leave him⟩ where man is an atom unable to avert his peril or provide for his escape, you leave him destitute of friends who *are* able to control the order of Nature. While he feels himself backed by Omnipotence he can approve the nobility of his origin, can do the deeds of a godlike nature — but if you put out the Eye of the Universe, if you kill that life to which all his hopes, his virtues, his affections essentially attach themselves — that being is ruined. He thought his virtue was known & acknowledged by an omniscient & benevolent Mind; Night & Morning he lifted his hands to bless him that he had admitted him to this glorious society of intelligent beings; his heart yearned after that blissful communion which he hoped to enjoy with the Divinity — and now he learns that there is no God,[n] that virtue & vice are sick men's dreams and his h↑e↓art sinks within him & hope dies. Why should he live longer in this infinite wilderness of suns & stars; he has no security, no interest, no love, in this dire dominion of Chance.

[67] "THE AGE" is centered beneath "daily remembered." at the bottom of the page.

That you can tell which is the superiour of two men ⟨in⟩ ↑by seeing them together↓ five minutes, is a well known maxim of Dr Johnson.[67a] It requires a twenty years' acquaintance with the world to feel the force of this, & then the statement will be daily remembered. The whole ac⌈60⌉[68]tion & result of Society seems to be a perpetual *Comparison.* Man is compared with man & *minus* or *plus* written on his forehead.[69] One is immediately carried one way & his companion another to be measured again with new mates. Each individual is anxious to have his standard merit fixed & known, jealous of his neighbours and eager to know the success of every other. Those that are highly ranked are elated, & soon tire of the elevation when ⟨ambition⟩ ⟨has no⟩[n] ↑there remains no↓ reward to ambition & grow impatient to go ⟨elsewhere⟩ ↑away↓ into new communities to find rivals worthy of themselves. Those to whom the decision is unfavourable repine in silence, or resent the decision by calumniating their superiours. Some are overtaken by a melancholy spirit which makes them unprofitable or sometimes worse. Others spit their venom at every good thing, or fall below a dependence on Opinion by becoming enemies of mankind & make themselves feared as a sort of atonement to ⟨themselves⟩ ↑their selflove↓ for not making themselves respected.

This perpetual adjustment of claims makes most of the interest which men feel in each other and as it is not finally settled on the very first occasion that brings two men together and as a title to distinction is by no means established by the superiority of a single faculty ⌈61⌉[70] but always is the joint result of all, there is much of importance & interest in the discussion. Its practical value will not be denied.

This principle being thus universal & active in Society, it cannot be thought strange if it be regarded in the education of the mind. Those branches of art & Science will naturally be most warmly explored which are most in use & note, which promise to give the most decided advantage over our peers.

This is one of those hermaphrodite principles ⟨of⟩ which it is alike plausible to blame & to praise, which we know not distinctly whether it be a blessing or a curse; which is a[n] ⟨essential⟩ ↑part↓ qual-

[67a] *Boswell's Life of Johnson,* 1934, II, 13 (a paraphrase).
[68] "THE AGE" is centered beneath "superiority" at the bottom of the page.
[69] Both *"minus"* and *"plus"* are underlined in pencil.
[70] "THE AGE" is centered beneath "the evils" at the bottom of the page.

ity of our ambiguous nature & may be admired as the ↑moral heart which is↓ [the] very seat of vitality or condemned as the fruit of inordinate selfishness. But its buds swell & its fruits ripen under the sunlight of refinement & in the progress of society men grow more sensitive to each other's opinion as that opinion is better worth.

Men have now nearly done with every visionary pursuit. The Madhouses are the only Schools where Alchemy and Astrology, Magic & ⟨d⟩Dialectics, once the study of the world are taught. Hope ↑it is true↓ is an eternal deciever. ↑The fraudulent↓ memory[n] conceals the evils of the past & these two [62] still make a fairyland in the youthful & the ancient breast; but all romance beside, is forever fled & the age claims & eminently deserves the name of *practical*.

φρονειν γα⟨r⟩ρ [n] οι ταχεις, ουκ ασφαλεις.[71]

In the succession of ages, the times must always assume & utter a decided tone some time, before its spirit can be embodied in a proportioned system of education which shall be faithful to public sentiment. It was perhaps a late generalization to speak of the spirit of an age but it escapes the imputation of paradox. For men are so close in their connexions & press so hard on each other that it is improbable a strong sentiment, or a marked character should anywhere arise without sending its strong contagion to an indefinite extent. Sympathy's "electric chain wherewith we are darkly bound"[72] is true to its office of transmitting common excitements of whatever sort. Man of every hue & race is sensitive to the lot of man & though the drops be severed a moment from the mass of waters they always rejoice to reunite in a perfect union.

Those who would distinguish their names by a permanent fame must not ↑affect to↓ overlook present success in the prospect of future reversion.

[63] For though the solace of neglected numbers which is offered to ⟨the ear of⟩ a youthful poet that posterity shall crown with a sure though tardy reward his unappreciated merit may sound plausibly in his ear, it must be a very strong or a very weak mind that will put faith in it,[n] strong enough to foresee that progress to which he

---

[71] "[For] swift councils are not sure." Sophocles, *Oedipus Tyrannus*, 617. Johnson used this as the epigraph to No. 111 of *The Rambler*.

[72] Byron, *Childe Harold's Pilgrimage*, IV, xxiii.

feels his work⟨s⟩ will correspond or weak enough to be the dupe of
unfounded hope. I know it is currently said that very many if not all
the capital productions of human genius have been crowned with
posthumous rather than contemporary fame. & the story of Milton
& Shakspeare as well as old Maeonides are the apposite examples.
But what is true of prophecies is true of this[,] that they are only
marked when they succeed & these three or four successful trials are
quoted out of innumerable failures. These men did not embark in
foreign or contrary channels to those in which the spirit of their times
moved but they launched farther down in the same stream & not at
too great a distance to be overtaken. Had they been more abstracted
from the world and sacrificed this commerce to an absorb[64]ing
delight in their own imaginations, the subsequent age would no
more have come up to that refinement of taste (which was wanted
to relish their works) than their own had done & the books would
thus be lost long before the day arrived to whose temper they were
suited. Without a very earnest faith in the commonly recieved maxims
of the universal uniformity of taste ⟨wh⟩ we are confident of that
writer's success who shall charm two generations, for in that space,
prescription grows so strong that he who has armed it on his side
may expect to vanquish for ages the opinions & it may be the reason
of men. Men we believe ⟨have well nigh got through⟩ ↑without giving
up↓ the admiration of Homer ⟨& few would⟩ are agreed that the Iliad
would prove a total failure today. Yet is there no danger that a ray
should part from the old bard's glory because he was so sensible or
so happy as to fall in precisely with the ⟨old⟩ Spirit of ⟨the⟩ his age.
                                                              U [?]
    Upon these remarks ⟨respecting the⟩ we build certain admoni-
tions to those men who are ambitious to occupy the same space in
American history which is already filled in Greek, Roman, [65]
French, & English Annals. Such ↑[as]↓ are greedy of fame[,]↓ as
think it not foolhardy to attempt the works of Bacon, of Shakspeare,
of Newton must devote themselves to the diligent study of the
Spirit of the age in which they live. And this must not be supposed
to be easily apprehended. It is no superficial glance that will penetrate
the secret disposition & partialities & antipathies of the great body of
civilized men and that mind is rarely gifted that can discriminate

between what is accidental & transient & what is permanent; between the ⟨prod⟩ works of individual & of popular taste; between the local effects wrought by an event, a custom, a character, a book & the consequences whose causes spread their deep & broad roots from the centre to the extremes of human society. It is never thought slight praise to say a man is a good judge of character. It is considered a ⟨d⟩ hard matter to determine from a man's daily action & speech which he is at no pains to conceal ⟨from the world,⟩ what particular merits distinguish him, & what trait is predominant in the mixed & complex texture of ⟨his⟩ ↑one↓ mind. And will it be thought easy when the field of observation is expanded from a single object to a painful infinity to cull ⟨from⟩ ↑out of↓ the great chaos of pursuits & characters the subtle particulars wherein they generally agree? Is not fluctuation the only abiding feature of all national character? This which gives zest to life, matter of lamentation to the aged, & of hope to the young — is [66] not this an insuperable obstacle in the way of all rational speculation? [n] We think we have seized the very principle which fixes the expression of our day & generation but while we contemplate it, it has ceased to be a feature of the times; it has given place to another as elusive & as brief. Nevertheless there are substantial principles which are out of this fluctuation. They are to be studied in the institutions, manners, letters, inventions, & history, of a people. They are to be studied in acts of senates & the conversation of private men. The camp, the temple, the parlour, the theatre, the inn are all ⟨the⟩ schools which this proficient must frequent. The temper of the Age will not suffer an observer to be immured in —— Hark! hark! the dogs bark! [73]

When this country is censured ⟨as⟩ for its foolhardy ambition to take a stand in its green ⟨infancy⟩ years among old & proud nations it is ⟨no objection &⟩ no reproach & no disqualification to be told ⟨b⟩But you have no literature. ⟨We⟩ ↑It is admitted we↓ have none. But we have what is better. We have a government and a national spirit that is better than poems or histories & these have a premature ripeness that is incompatible with the rapid production of the latter. We should take shame to ourselves as sluggish & Boeotian if it were righteously said that we had done nothing for ourselves ⟨in⟩

[73] Emerson added the apparently derisive comment later.

neither in learning nor arts nor government nor political economy.
But we see & feel that in the space of two generations this nation has
taken [67] such a start as already to outstrip the bold freedom of
modern ⟨anticipatio⟩ speculation which ordinarily (universally, but
for this case) is considerably in advance of practice. No man calls
Mr Hume an old fashioned & short sighted politician yet many pages
of his history have lost their credit already by the practical confuta-
tion of their principles. ↑'Tis no disgrace to tell Newton he is no poet
nor America even.↓

There are harder crosses to bear than Poverty or sickness or
death. Are you armed with the supreme stoicism ⟨that⟩ of a pure
heart & a lowly mind? Can you hear unconcerned Pride's /super-
cilious/deriding/ taunt, & Derision's[n] obstreperous laugh? Can you
lift a serene face against the whisper that poisons your name with
obloquy?[n] Can you ⟨face⟩ set unconquerable Virtue against the seductions of the flesh? Can you give the care of the tongue to charity
& caution? Can you resist the soft encroachments of sloth & force
your mind ↑&↓ your body to that activity which duty demands? These
are the real difficulties which are the harder to overcome as they are
the less feared. These are the duties which appal & press heavy upon
a serious mind. July 18, 1824. ——

Apocryphal

[6⟨7⟩8][74] It is wrong to say generally that the suicide is a hero
or that he is a coward. The Chin⟨a⟩ese[,] the most timid people in the
world, die as often in that as in another manner. The old Romans
& Greeks as Cato & Themistocles, who killed themselves, were brave
men, far braver than the mass of their countrymen who survived to
the sufferings which they avoided. The merit of the action must
obviously depend in all cases upon the particular condition of the
individual. It may be in one the effect of despair, in one of madness,
in one of fear, in one of magnanimity, in one of ardent curiosity to
know the wonders of the other world. 'If the smoke be troublesome,'
said the Stoic, 'I leave it; The door is open.'[75]

[74] "SUICIDE" is written beneath "grace and" and "MANNERS" is centered
beneath "match the" at the bottom of the page.
[75] The quotation is a paraphrase of Arrian, *Discourses of Epictetus*, I, xxv, 18,
but the real source may be Marcus Aurelius Antoninus. See *JMN*, I, 226, n.50.

Pericles, Caesar, Chesterfield, Henry IV of France.

It certainly is worth ⟨a man's⟩ ↑one's↓ while who considers what sway elegant manners bear in society & how wealth, genius, & moral worth[,] all extrinsic & intrinsic good in men[,] do in society feel their empire, [—] it becomes a clear command of reason to cultivate them. There are some men, wittily called Nature's Gentlemen who need no discipline but grow straight up into shape & grace and can match the proudest in dignified de⌈69⌉meanour & the gentlest in courtesy. Of these the line in the old song is a thousand times quoted "My face's my fortune, Sir, she said."[76] The eye of Beauty brightens at their approach. Age smooths its wrinkles & remembers ⟨the⟩ ↑its↓ daft days ⟨of its youth⟩. Patronage extends its gracious hand & proposes its ⟨own⟩ ↑plausible↓ plans. The vulgar admire at a distance & prognosticate greatness to come. I speak here ⟨only⟩ of ⟨the⟩ no transient success in tying a neck↑c↓loth aright & making a fashionable bow & speaking in the precise nick of time & the just length but of manners ↑of a sensible man↓ when they become the chief channel in which a man's sense runs; of those which ⟨make⟩ are the plain index of fine sense & fine feelings, which impress all & offend none. The specimens of this sort are to be searched ↑for↓ in the summits of society for these manners are invariably successful or among the young not yet advanced. They had better be observed in youth, for there is nothing in art or nature so charming as the brilliant manners of one of these candidates for eminence before adulation has got to be an old song with him while hope & love dazzle him. Their address is marked by an alacrity of manner arising from elasticity of spirits & of limbs that no eye can watch unmoved. The spectacle these afford is a perfect tonic in its physical effect like light or like wine. It imparts an [⟨69⟩ 70][77] impulse of cheerfulness not easily withstood to all within their influence; it effaces ⟨the om⟩ for a moment the omnipresent consciousness of sin, sickness, sorrow. It is an attractive subject & we will think of it more particularly.

When men are accurately compared it is found that 'tis in the ⟨distinctions⟩ success in life as in writing not so much matter *what*

---

[76] In its familiar and innocent nineteenth-century version the song begins, "Where are you going to, my pretty maid?"

[77] "MANNERS" is written beneath "one of Saturn" at the bottom of the page.

as *how* men do. Those who think says the judicious poet must govern those who toil.[77a] Very true. But 'tis only a part of those who think. Our common-places on character, our adages on life, every one's observation concur in the sentiment that those men whom their talents have raised to the ⟨ho⟩ places of honour ⟨a⟩or profit which ordinarily reward the thinkers are by no means superior to tenfold their own number in the people not so rewarded. Not superior ↑I mean↓ in intellect; able to take no juster, broader, or quicker views; but ↑they are↓ enriched with that fine taste or sense of propriety or whatsoever name it have which is at the bottom of manners. A judgement which keeps the golden mean between testy gruffness & obsequious pusil-lanimity[,] between Parisian frivolity & the oppressive gravity that reminds one of Saturn digesting his children. Besides [71][78] there must be more than a golden mean in this art of Arts. All men of fine manners are not alike. Nothing is more common than the comparison of unlike or even opposite excellences in ⟨the⟩ ↑men of elegant↓ ad-dress↑.↓ ⟨of accomplished gentlemen.⟩ And it is always agreeable to remark some decided expression of /agreeable/good/ or /admirable/ great/ qualities which shall distinguish them from ⟨imitations⟩ copies ↑& so↓ win them the praise of nature.[n]

> ↑Many men[,] said Montaigne[,] I have known of super-celestial opinions & subterranean manners.↓[78a]

In general, it may be remarked they are the safest passports to credit because their worth can never be questioned. Men are apt to distrust the grounds of your rep↑u↓ted learning or the solidity of your genius — or fling a doubt on the stability of your credit in trade or the sound-ness of your professions in life. ⟨They are say they, much less real than they seem.⟩ ↑And the Roman hint↓ Esse quam videri[79] ⟨they will hint was a Roman word.⟩ ↑may be thrown in your teeth.↓ But your manners are opened to their admiration and if they be dazzling they cannot, feeling their inimitableness, deny them a particle of

---

[77a] The poet is Goldsmith. See p. 363 below.

[78] "MANNERS" is written beneath "They are" at the bottom of the page.

[78a] Cf. "I have ever observed supercelestial opinions and subterranean manners to be of singular accord." "Of Experience," *The Essays*, 1892, II, 620.

[79] "To be, rather than to seem" — a well-known comment of Sallust upon Cato.

praise. I would not be misunderstood. I speak not of pretty but of majestic manners. And as sublimity of ⟨th⟩ conduct ⟨can⟩ must proceed from sublimity of motive so a magnanimous deportment will not be ⟨found⟩ a gem thrown before swine, an ornament worn by a fool. Nature gives no richer grace. They are never formed [7⟨1⟩2] by the dancing Master's fiddlebow. Monsieur Kickee can never give them.

Science is comfortless; she can describe what she has seen but she cannot shew those that are greedy of excellence how to get ↑this↓ Coat of Charms. But there is an atonement in the invariable compensations of the Universe, provided for this as for all inequalities of fortune. The charm of manners is mortal. The goods they have bought the possessor must be consumed while Day lasts, for they will not give a↑n↓ ⟨year's⟩ hour's date to his epitaph. The hand of Caesar & of Pericles has lost ⟨its⟩ ↑the↓ greedy welcome it gave and its vehement & graceful gesture[;] the foot no more measures with lofty stride the floor of the Capitol[;] no fascinating glance eyes you as you pass their graves[;] no smile of ↑condescending↓ ambition ⟨&⟩ illuminates their mouldering visages. This is one of the things over which ⟨the Angel⟩ power is given to the angel. Over what is well written though by obscure & uncouth hands he has not power. Over what is nobly *done* for the world or what is secretly done for the Cause of God [73] & man in solitudes & closets he has no power; these shall be recorded here or remembered hereafter. But the personal elegance & tasteful propriety of action that are here on earth of so high account & here have their reward are subordinate things[,] graceful lines traced in the sand that the next wave will obliterate forever.

> Thou art dead who wast my friend
>   Staff of my life friend of my soul
> And I am left vain sighs to send
> To wish my journey at an end
>   And hate the sluggish moments as they roll.
>
> Livest thou, o my friend?
> Art thou near me even now

Though thy dust to dust descend
And I who thought thy wreaths to blend
    See the worm embrace thy brow.

I thought that life would always leave
    In its dark hours a track of light
    For thy kind love would aye bereave
    Life of its poisoned pangs that grieve

The examiner of manners is struck commonly rather with the reasonableness & propriety of each gesture & expression in a gentleman than with any ↑nameless↓ charm. Sometimes the fitness of such demeanour may be felt when it would not be easy to describe it. But when he assays to copy

page 78

[74] Flattery is always tolerated even in the best society, as sugar mixes in the richest viands. Indeed one aspect of fine manners is only a secret flattery. For we are decieved by the elegant attentions paid us into the belief that a marked personal respect was shewn. There is a deeper art & more complete success sometimes ⟨e⟩ shewn in an affected reserve, which abashes you at first with the aspect of a thundercloud & then slowly smooths its scowl & thaws its ice, refines into elegance, & warms into sympathy & leaves you at last flattered by the complete victory you seem to have gained.

Reputation. It is no new saying but is worthy of all acceptation that those objects ⟨are⟩ most ardently pursued are not the most worth. In the hot chase of visionary good[,] solid advantage is passed by. It is accounted a laudable ambition to give your life to the acquisition of that credit which measures a man's standing in trade, or to that finished decorum & propriety of action which secures ⟨a m⟩ respectability & favour among the great, or to the practise of the profession of arms, the rules of tactics, & the etiquette of authorized murder,[n] or to the studies which shall provide literary distinction for the scholar. [75] And a man is applauded who shall not spare from these pursuits a moment of time that the scanty refection of the body does not exact. You desire to be remembered by such good ⟨fam⟩ repute as these will give. I can tell you ⟨of⟩ where you may be better remembered than in Courts or Camps, in the Marts of business or the halls of learning. Be remembered in the poor man's prayer.ⁿ Be ⟨remembered⟩ ↑heard of↓ in the fervent gratitude, which the widow & the fatherless utter to heaven. Be known in sick chambers & by dying beds. Let the benedictions of ⟨the⟩ admonished youth, of fostered poverty, of converted sin be your record. Its letters will not be effaced. They are copied into the Book of Life.

Be not deluded by the love or the fear of man & in that balance that men are disposed to make between personal esteem & public applause, forget not how much better it is to be loved than to be extolled. There is no comparison between that vague unprofitable eye-service which the exhibition of great powers procures you from the multitude, & the deep useful influence which daily goodness & uncompromising inexorable ⟨virtue⟩ rectitude will command in those who see & love you. It will save souls; it will train men to heaven; it will shed a pure influence which is illimitable.   There are some of the delusions of life which are known as such,ⁿ and some which are not. [76] There are some which depart with childhood, some which charm ⁿ ⟨bind⟩ us till manhood is ripe; some which cling on later nor leave us till we leave the world.

↑Literary reputation is one that is most & longest deceptive.↓ It is with these moral deceptions precisely as it is with those of the eye & the mind. The savage & the child, all who have had no opportunity of adding the experience of other men to their own or have had but limited opportunities themselves, are the dupes of a thousand crude superstiti⟨t⟩ons. In like manner the poor cannot bend their stubborn bigotry to believe the united voice of all ages & states of society when they call wealth disquieted & unblest. *They cannot believe but that it is rhetorick & that cushions & coaches ⟨are to⟩ ↑do↓ yield a softer repose than boards & streets. But those who have once under the aches & privations of penury ↑thus↓ coveted the luxury of

* Vide "Moral Sentiments." ⁸⁰

⁸⁰ Adam Smith, *The Theory of Moral Sentiments*, which is in volume 1 of Smith's *Works*, ed. Dugald Stewart, 5 vols. (London, 1812), withdrawn with volume 5 from the Boston Library Society June 26–Aug. 7, 1824.

the rich, & then have ⟨a⟩ themselves stood in the high places of fortune have sorrowfully owned that the man within the breast did not so suddenly change his language & aspect as the external state,ⁿ that the Worm of Care which dieth not had but changed his food without diminishing his appetite [77] or dulling his fangs. There are some conditions which are not so readily reached as that of opulence & these of course the unknowing multitude sigh after with whet⟨e⟩ted appetite. The interval is wider between ⟨a great ⁿ lite⟩ the great states-man's or great scholar's reputation & obscurity than between the rich & the poor. More people therefore are under this last delusion than under either of the others. I write not thus to dispraise or discourage literary efforts. I know them to be wholly commendable. I know there is danger of their being sought too little rather than too much but there is no need of urging what is urged every day an ardent applica-tion to them. But I write to set them upon their proper grounds, ⟨to put them u⟩ to raise up another science side by side with them, to put them in proper connexions with it, to recommend them as *means* & not as an *end*. &c. &c.   Sunday

                                                              July, 1824.

Mem.   Pope's proper merit & the now & then Centennial books.
Sunday.   July,   1824. I read today 5 verses in Prov III C.
Monday   A chapter in Lardner [81] & 8 verses in Prov.
Tuesday   Chap. in Lardner
Wednesday — *Sic nos non nobis* [82] E.B.E[merson]. at home

[78][83] th⟨i⟩ese fair proportions, he finds it requires an unbending attention & a power of face ↑too↓ that he may not be master of & which were incompatible with the ⟨matchless⟩ eas⟨e⟩y & modest ele-gance he admires in the original. It is for this reason that a book on Manners is of no use except to a small minority of its readers. When it has told how the masters of the world are to be vanquished, it

---

[81] Probably Nathaniel Lardner (1684–1768), in whom Emerson apparently read further when he withdrew volume 3 of his *Works*, 11 vols. (London, 1788), from the Harvard Divinity School Library in 1829.

[82] "Thus we [work] not for ourselves" — doubtless derived from Virgil's "Sic vos non vobis" — "thus you work not for yourselves."

[83] Continued from p. [73].

exacts so much resolution to meet its rules that very few observe them. Manners ⟨are⟩ is a fourth fine art & like Painting, Poetry, & Sculpture is founded on fiction. It is a mask worn by men of sense to ↑decieve the vulgar↓ [and] ape the conduct of very superior intelligence. Thus I know models who affect to drop carelessly the most subtle wit or profound thought. Every virtue is spoken of with respect, even those to which their private life bears little love. Every event is treated with its exact measure of interest[,] sickness & death, a balloon & a butterfly being discussed with the same cool philosophy.

In the practise of these wise Masters, I know different theories of manners prevail and ⟨all⟩ are as many as the systems of philoso-[phy] [79] for this is a species of second philosophy, & may be termed the philosophy of life. Thus the sect of the Stoics will have their mannerists who would command in good company ⟨by inflexible reception of good and ill⟩ m[any followers,][n] Democritus has many[,] even Heraclitus a few. Socrates has some disciples who use plain speech & practices as John L.[84] but the predominant sect are those who hold fast with the Epicureans,[n] independent & good humoured.

⟨Men may dispute about the features of Washington, each being positive and all being wrong; for they have seen different & incorrect pictures & have formed correct judgments on false premises.⟩

The multitude of books is the great good & evil of the present day & when our times ⟨are⟩of whose reputation we are so tender ⟨ar⟩come under the rude comparison of posterity to be grouped at will with Augustan or Middle Ages the extraordinary fecundity of our press may by dint of overdoing have damned us to oblivion or have nursed up a learning that will record us. These books naturally divide themselves into several classes[,] some of great use & some worse than vain. [80][85] ↑Apart from↓ the vast mess of transitory volumes which occasional politics or a thousand ephemeral magnalia elicit[,] books for the most part record the progress of science or

---

[84] Perhaps John L. Gardner, one of Emerson's classmates at Harvard. See p. 359, n. 15, below.

[85] " 'Twas a custom of philos. to describe a perfect man each in his age; now we'll try" is written vertically the length of the left margin.

exhibit only successive forms of taste in Poetry, letters & fiction ⟨not to mention⟩.[n] But there is another sort of ⟨w⟩book which appears now & then in the world once in two or three Centuries perhaps and which soon or late gets a foothold in popular esteem. I allude to those books which collect & embody the wisdom of their times & so mark the stages of human improvement. Such are the Proverbs of Solomon, the Essays of Montaigne, & eminently the Essays of Bacon. Such ⟨too⟩ also (though in my judgment in far less degree) is the proper merit of Mr. Pope's judicious poems[,] the Moral Essays & Essay on Man which without originality seize upon all the popular speculations floating among sensible men & give them ↑in a↓ compact & graceful form to the following age. I should like to add another volume to this valuable work. I am not so foolhardy as to write Sequel to Bacon on my title page, and there are some reasons that induce me to suppose that [81] the undertaking of this enterprise does not imply any censurable arrogance. Although it is perhaps a generalization which the mind but tardily makes to speak of the character of a *Nation* or *Age,* it is yet a manner of thinking which has a foundation in fact. There is frequently, perhaps invariably, a spirit & tone of thought according to which a multitude's habits of feeling may be guided without any one reaching all its results or viewing more than a few subjects in that light. (Thus in a *practical* day or day of small things, like the present, those who have heard the word & known its influence will be so wedded severally to their own prejudices that each man ⟨his⟩ will spare ↑out of the censure he bestows↓ his /own particular extravagance/ewe lamb/ from the censure he casts upon useless & fanciful plans. And no one man shall be found to have weighted & applied all the popular maxims.) It may be made clear that there may be the Wisdom of an age indepen[den]t of & above the Wisdom of any individual whose life is numbered in its years. And the diligence rather than the genius of one mind may compile the prudential maxims[,] domes[82]tic & public ⟨rules⟩ maxims[,] ↑current in the world↓ [n] and which may be made to surpass the single stores of any writer. . as the richest private funds are quickly exceeded by a public purse. Compound Interest V.

Read what Hume says in Wm Rufus' reign, touching the

Crusades. Read their history in Gibbon & Hallam.[86] See how the ↑two↓ ends of the scale of advancement meet, inasmuch as a work of that generosity is undertaken in the rudeness of Europe[,] and Abolition of Slavery, & Greek enthusiasm are reckoned as proofs of its refinement. Sympathy. Peter Hermit was sent on before with the ruff-scuff, whil⟨e⟩st the great lords engaged, followed with the disciplined & furnished troops. You go before with*out* bottle & bag & I'll follow after with little Jack Nag.[87] Rhetoric dwelling on modern distinctions might say that modern Europe does or that it does not the same wild deed, with like truth.

BRAWNY   Plague[88]

We have said above that the age was *practical*. It is common to *hear* this name affixed to it with high praise as if it were the best eulogium. ⟨We⟩ I think th⟨e⟩is is true but not exactly as the cognomen is vulgarly understood. I rather suppose this name will blow over in its turn while the spirit it was ⟨intende⟩ ⟨designed⟩ ↑to↓ [83][89] designate[n] shall long survive it. History tells us that the whole province of Biscay (?) was for some good deed to a great man, ennobled. ⟨Every p⟩ For a moment nobility ceased to be aristocracy for not a boor but was a lord. A similar enlargement of the republic of letters has been made in modern times. The ⟨freedom of her city⟩ gift of citizenship has been ↑as↓ lavishly bestowed in this country as the right of *voting*, instead of being, as ⟨formerly⟩ once, the pride of a few gowned oligarchs. It was a quick consequence that

Crusades. National Ballads. History

[86] For Emerson's reading in Hume and Hallam, see above, p. 8, n. 10ᵃ. Hume's account is laced with contempt for the motives and disgust at the conduct of the first Crusade. Emerson doubtless knew Gibbon's chapters on the Crusades (58 and 59) in *The Decline and Fall of the Roman Empire*, 12 vols. (London, 1821), an edition listed in his library catalogue.

[87] The last three letters of "with*out*" are doubly underlined in ink, most certainly by Emerson, but bracketed in pencil, probably by Edward Emerson. Emerson has adapted the Mother Goose rhyme "Robin and Richard."

[88] The phrase is written aslant from "said" below to "does not" above.

[89] In the bottom margin beneath "Count me out 60 merkes" is "William Rufus" circled in ink. A penciled line and arrow, probably by Edward Emerson, carry the phrase to above the poetry, as a title.

May it please my lorde there's a Jewe at the doore.
Bring him in, sayde the King, what waits he for?
I wot sir you came from Abraham's loins
Eat no porke, love no Christ, doe no good with
                                     your Coins.
My lord the King I doe as Moses bids
Eschewing all badness I shut my coffer lids.
From the law of the Mountain, ⟨J⟩God forbid I
                              should swerve
The uncircumsized Nazarite my race cannot serve
But Isaac my son to idols hathe gone over
And no man I can find my firstborn to recover,
I would give 60 merkes & my gabardine to boot
To the Rabbi that should turn him from the
                              Christn faith about
But phylactered Rabbins are far far oversea
Vouchsafe my lord the King f⟨o⟩rom the house of Magog
To send my son back to his own synagogue.
Why I'll be the Rabbi where's a fitter Pharisee
Count me out 60 merkes & go send your son to me

[84]   The King filled his mouth with arguments & gibes
To turn the lad's head to the faith of the tribes
But the young Isrealite was so hard & stiffnecked
That by no means could the King come to any effect.
So he paid back the old Jew 30 merkes of his gains
Quoth he I'll keep the other 30 for the payment
                              of my pains [90]

[No more dams I'll make for fish
Nor fetch in firing
At requiring
Nor sc[r]ape trenchering nor wash dish

[90] The poem was printed in modern spelling in *The Offering for 1829* under the
title "William Rufus and the Jew." Emerson found the story in Hume, *The History
of England*, ch. V. Ralph Thompson is wrong in his conjecture that the immediate
source is one in which William II of England (Willim Rufus) asks for three fifths
of the reward instead of half, for "fifty marks" in the printed version was "60" in
the original. See "Emerson and *The Offering for 1829*," *American Literature*, VI
(May 1934), 157.

'Ban 'Ban Ca Caliban
Has a new master Get a new man]
[Shakespeare, *The Tempest*, II, ii, 184–189]

↑Philip never saw a gate shut so tight that he could not edge in a mule laden with a bag of gold.↓

Misery acquaints a man with strange bedfellows. Most poor matters point to rich ends; grind their joints with dry convulsions[,] shorten up their sinews with aged cramps.
[*The Tempest*, II, ii, 41; III, i, 3–4; IV, i, 259–261]

Why has my motley diary no jokes? Because it is a soliloquy & every man is grave alone. I. There is no royal road to Learning. II Let not your virtue be of the written or spoken sort but of the practised. III The two chief differences among men (touching talents) ⟨are⟩ consist 1. in the different degrees of *attention* they are able to command; 2. in the ↑unlike↓ expression they give to the same ideas. IV There is time enough for every business men are really resolved to do. V Obsta principiis.[91] Take heed of getting cloyed with that honeycomb which Flattery tempts with. 'Tis apt to blunt the edge of ⟨the⟩ appetite for many wholesome viands & rob you of many days of health. X. Let no man flatter himself with the hope of true good or solid enjoyment from the *study* of Shakspeare or Scott. Enjoy them as recreation. You cannot please yourself by going to stare at the moon; 'tis beautiful when in your *course* it comes."

[85] We make great pretensions to variety; to a huge world cut into an infinite dissection, its body made of numberless unlike elements to whose shapes & hues & dissimilar properties ⟨th⟩ no science can set an end[;] to a population of this globe that defies art in its description & census in its number. Wherein the hosts of bird & beast that walk & fly in our sight are a handful to the inconcievable ↑animal↓ crowds ⟨of anim⟩ that leap & creep & glide & swim & move in unknown ways or sit still in undescribed attitudes & for unexplained purposes. High over all was said to sit the great Biscayan nobility of man, the wide family of demigods and in these was no monotony, no prosaic uniformity to give the Universe a leaden look. We thought

[91] "Resist at the start" (Ed.).

in the many & strange ways in which the connexions between the individuals of this talented race were ⟨instituted,⟩ ↑spun,↓ in the natural
& artificial leagues they make there must spring a bewildering variety
of incident. These are a solitary's thoughts out of the noise of the
world & its opportunities of observation. Doubtless, he says, there are
scenes enough in all the ↑tracts &↓ corners of the planet for those
who relish the unstable spectacle. And a motley crew it must be that
meet in the congregations of men. [86] For there are the sons of
different nations, the interest of many classes, the skill of many
trades, the lovers of virtue, the darlings of fortune, the victims of
vice, the masters of the heart, the profoundly learned, sagacious,
heroic, silly, beautiful, & unfortunate men   words; words; [92]

 Whoever regards society as a subject of improvement soon distinguishes with particular notice one class of it as that part where all
experiment & all change must commence. Young men from the age
of thirty when the individual's lot has for the most part been already
cast, down to ↑that of↓ fifteen are the only part of the huge community in which the philosopher concieves a⟨ny⟩[n] ↑deep↓ interest.
The hope he rests with them ⟨is⟩ remains his sole consolation for ↑all↓
the errors that have chased each other time out of mind, in the ⟨h⟩
uneven fortunes of the race. A qualified Perfectibility or, to drop a
suspicious word, a tendency to indefinite progress in the human species
is a lurking dogma which in the face of all that has been writ and
done to disprove it does neverthe⟨ss⟩less mu↑l↓tiply its proselytes
every day & is a logical consequence from the condition of man in
Society. Now this section of mankind is that in which the bigots to
this creed are found & [87] where, if anywhere, we must seek the
establishers of the fact. In this light, it is readily seen that these are
the proper objects to whom all the lessons of experience & genius
ought to be read.
 I shall not pretend that I mean to make no personal strictures;
for if the remarks apply to no person they can do no good & had
better be forborne. I shall not indeed call you by name nor will
my finger aid me to point my censure. But I shall aim to attack

[92] Apparently added later, the comment again expresses Emerson's dissatisfaction with his creative efforts.

living & active vices assured that it is better to cure systems that are sick than deride or condemn those that are dissolved & forgotten.

⟨Ministry⟩   Country Clergy in the Revolution. If one considers what is the history of our young men he will find that of all those hopeful spirits which our University & Colleges annually turn out amounting to about /500/⟨|| … ||⟩000/ young men in the acme of youthful ardour[,] fraught with a salutary reverence for the great of past ages, with a passion of tender regard to their country, & in common with a solemn & suitable respect for the religious institutions & the moral health of the community, and above all with a lively & unbounded personal ambition whose unsettled eye seeks it knows not what object where it may anchor [88] its immeasurable hopes. These are speedily divided in the study of the three liberal professions; another part embrace the vocation of Schoolmasters private & public; others who have already been discouraged by ill success in letters enter the Compting house and a small part retire to their homes without any object ⟨but⟩ ↑beyond↓ present ease. All are very soon ingulphed in the great vortex of a busy world, and in the encroaching interests of the temporary pursuit into which chance has thrown them have set by till a more convenient season the ripening of those intellectual projects which were ↑lately↓ so dear to their judgments. Time & the World soon put their effacing fingers on those associations which a few moons since seemed to be intertwined with life. He is astonished but he is enslaved by the ⟨pre⟩ ponder⟨ating⟩↑ous chain↓ ⟨& exclusive weight⟩ of the present and all those generous plans of life[,] outlines of future years are filtered away in today's sand heap of pitiful concerns. That golden hoop ⟨being⟩ ↑is↓ snapped asunder ⟨with⟩ ↑by means of↓ which a monastic society brought them into close literary connexion & whereby they were enabled to use the force of Sympathy which is the mightiest [89] ⟨engine⟩ of all moral engines in this cause & at the same time to confine (which is of chief effect,) their ⟨a⟩undivided thoughts to literature — the associating ties are severed & the object forgotten. Rivals are the best monitors, and the society of those who can understand your merit and assign its praise is a sharper spur in the sides of indolence than any hope can be of the vague respect arising in a mixed society from the report of your

talents & toils. The ordinary consequence of ⟨a se⟩ absolute independence in a young man's studies is an uncertain & miscellaneous
reading now roving with a bold freedom into a partial and unsupported erudition and now repenting of the caprice under the fear
of pedantry and injudicious selection,ⁿ exhibiting a melancholy fluctuation between unlike & incompatible plans. He plunges into an
adventurous attempt and when he is in the midst ⟨a⟩he is tormented
by a line, a casual word of an oracular author who disparages the end
of his labour. (Lord of himself that heritage of wo.) [93] This is the sort
that are most susceptible & of the most uneven temper. Mark the
End. Life, that no declamation could adequately [94] picture in its just
brilliancy is but a beggar's opera to them, a rotten delusion. They sow
the [90] wind & reap the whirlwind. Of all those therefore who
leave the College for solitary study only a very small minority may
reasonably expect eminent success, & these are not those who have detected in themselves early accomplishments & that facility of apprehension ↑and consciousness of being no publican↓ which is often
called Genius; but those stout & masculine minds who to distinct
notions ↑of truth↓ unite habits of indifference ⟨& apathy⟩ to those
sources of pleasure whose seduction ⟨is exquisite to⟩ ↑overmasters↓
indolent & refined minds; habits of study in the closet, temperance
at the table, self command in the street, whose judgments are stronger
than their imaginations, who can make their appointed duty surmount
the prodigious attraction which fine spirits exert to dissipation, & the
disheartening influence of dark hours or rather (which is the true
case) which has not this elevation or this fall. Where is this native
Stoic? The world never grudges him ⟨o⟩neither oak leaf nor amaranth.

August 11, 1824.

[93] Byron, *Lara*, I, ii.
[94] "V. Adam Smith" is written vertically in the left margin from "could adequately" to "midst ⟨a⟩he" above.

No. XV

1824–1826

Journal No. XV continues the sequence of regular journals. A period of eight weeks intervened between the last dated entry of Wide World XIII (August 11, 1824) and the first dated entry of this journal (October 8, 1824). This period is to be accounted for by the lost journal No. XIV, which is cited on the first page of No. XV: "Continued from p. 40, No XIV." Regular entries in this journal extend through February, 1825. The last dated entry is January 8, 1826.

The manuscript is composed of 66 leaves of folded sheets arranged in 16 gatherings of 2 sheets (8 pages) and one gathering of a single sheet (2 pages). The leaves measure 17.5 x 21 cm. The pages are numbered consecutively from 1 to 131, and a final page, the verso of leaf 66, is unnumbered. The cover, of deep blue cartridge paper on cardboard and measuring about 16 x 20 cm, originally enclosed a notebook numbered "Vol. XIII" by Emerson's father and bearing indexes in his hand on its paste-down end-leaves. All of the original pages were torn away from the covers, and the spine was repaired with a strip of brown paper glued to linen. Another gathering of sheets was then sewn to the repair strip and the remainder of the spine, as is evident from matching sewing holes in each. These sheets may well have constituted Emerson's missing journal No. XIV. They too were separated from the covers, which were finally used to enclose the sheets of No. XV. The edges of the first and the last pages, which extend beyond the cover, are considerably darker than the rest of these pages. On the repair strip, Emerson appears to have printed his name three times, canceling it twice. He printed "CANTERBURY", wrote "Test. R", and cited twice by page the account of John Adams which appears on p. 104. At some time he pasted pages inside the covers and used them for quotations. Since those on the inside front cover and the inside back cover appear upside down in relation to each other, it would appear that they belong to different periods. The back page may well have belonged with No. XIV.

[front cover verso] [1] quam parva sapientia regitur mundus! [2]

Good when sense is seconded by spirit

Emerson.
architect
faber quisque fort[unae suae] [3]

1   Ere the base laws of servitude began
     When wild in woods the noble savage [n] ran   Dryden [4]

        Thy way thou canst not miss me mine demands
             [Cf. Milton, *Paradise Lost*, III, 735]

2   No there is a Necessity in Fate
     Why still the brave bold man is fortunate. [5]

Economy not ungenerous not inelegant [6]

        Men's failings live in brass
        We write their virtues in water [7]

        'Freely they stood who stood & fell who fell.'
                 M[ilton, *Paradise Lost*, III, 102].

     — 'While Fate grew pale —
     And turned the iron leaves of his dark book
     To make new dooms or mend what it mistook.' [8]

[1] Emerson used the front cover verso almost entirely for quotations, which he wrote down in various styles of handwriting and at different times, squeezing some in between others. The order of entry being indeterminable, the quotations are printed in their physical sequence. The beginnings of quotation "2" and those by Johnson, Howell, and Cowley are struck through diagonally, probably to indicate use. The page is reproduced as plate II.

[2] "With how little wisdom is the world ruled" (Ed.). The comment has been made by Pope Julius III and Count Axel Oxenstiern, but Emerson's version comes closest to Dr. Arbuthnot's in a letter to Swift of 1732.

[3] The spacing in the manuscript suggests that Emerson was thinking of himself as the "architect of his own fortune." For the quotation, from Bacon, see pp. 112 above and 364 below.

[4] *The Conquest of Granada*, Pt. I, I, i. Quoted by Johnson in *Life of Dryden* (see *Lives of the English Poets*, ed. G. B. Hill, 1905, I, 461. This edition is cited in notes 5, 8, 9, 11, 12, and 13 below).

[5] Dryden, *The Conquest of Granada*, Pt. I, IV, ii. Quoted by Johnson in *Life of Dryden* (see *Lives of the English Poets*, I, 462).   [6] See p. 346 below.

[7] Cf. Shakespeare, *Henry VIII*, IV, ii, 45–46: "Men's evil manners live in brass; their virtues We write in water."

[8] Dryden, *Tyrannic Love*, I, i. Quoted in Johnson, *Life of Dryden* (see *Lives of the English Poets*, I, 461).

273

"He that runs against Time has an Antagonist not subject to any Casualties." Johnson.[9]

"An acre of performance is worth the whole Land of Promise" Howel[1] [10]

> Laugh all the powers that favor tyranny
> And all the standing army of the sky,[11]

Don't weave your honor of such Cobweb texture that ev'ry fly can break it.

> Men doubt because they stand so thick i' the sky
> Cowley   If those be stars which paint the Galaxy.[12]

Happiness is a suspension of disgust

> Then we upon our orb's last verge shall go
> And see the Ocean leaning on the sky. Dryden [13]

> To be no more: sad cure; for who would lose,
> Tho' full of pain, this intellectual being,
> Those thoughts that wander thro' eternity?
> Milton. [*Paradise Lost*, II, 146–148]

> "Candidus insuetum miratur limen Olympi
> Sub pedibusque videt nubes et sidera Daphnis."
> Apud Leibnitz de Bayle [14]

[1]   No XV.[15]
Oct. 8, 1824.   Continued from p. 40, No XIV

[9] *Life of Pope* (see *Lives of the English Poets*, III, 117).

[10] Though Emerson is not known to have withdrawn James Howell's *Familiar Letters* (London, 1673) from the Boston Athenaeum before April 13, 1830, he had obviously encountered Howell earlier. The quotation is in Bk. IV, Letter xxxiii. (See *Epistolae Ho-Elianae, The Familiar Letters of James Howell*, ed. Joseph Jacobs, London, 1890, p. 611.)

[11] Dryden, "Palamon and Arcite," III, 671–672. Quoted in Johnson, *Life of Dryden* (see *Lives of the English Poets*, I, 469).

[12] "Ode: Of Wit," ll. 39–40. Quoted by Johnson in *Life of Cowley* (see *Lives of the English Poets*, I, 36).

[13] "Annus Mirabilis," st. 164. Quoted by Johnson in *Life of Dryden* (see *Lives of the English Poets*, I, 460).

[14] Quoted from Stewart, *Dissertation* (see *Collected Works*, 1854, I, 322, n.3), where Leibnitz is quoting Virgil, *Eclogues*, V, 56–57: "Daphnis, in radiant beauty, marvels at Heaven's unfamiliar threshold, and beneath his feet beholds the clouds and the stars."

[15] The title is enclosed in a rectangle. No. XIV, mentioned below, is missing. See *JMN*, I, 406, n. 6.

It is a striking feature in our condition that we so hardly arrive at truth. There are very few things of which we can wisely be certain tho' we often let unfounded prejudices grow into bigoted faith. We are immersed in opposite probabilities whenever we turn our thoughts to any of those speculations that are the proper exercise of our understandings. The final cause of this is no doubt found in the doctrine that we were not sent into this world for the discovery of truth but for the education of our minds. And our faculties are best exercised by doubts not by facts. The immediate consequence of this arrangement like all other parts of human nature has its ↑ad↓mixture of evil. It is productive of that scepticism which throughout the world combats the advancement of truth. What you say is probable, says the Pyrrhonian but the interval is always infinite between the highest probability & certainty. I will not renounce my old opinion for what may be an ||e||rror. Prove it true, and I will be converted.

[2] In opposition to this scepticism, in Science, reason fights with truth; in ⟨morals⟩ religion, conscience. When a pure creed is proposed and accepted by the multitude in whom the force of truth & Conscience ordinarily overbalances the ambition of doubting, the infidelity of the Wise ⟨to⟩ who⟨m⟩ alone are privy to the full force of objections is commonly kept a secret among themselves. That the number of avowed infidels is small must not be ⟨co⟩esteemed decisive on the success of Christianity. On the contrary there are few men who cannot number in the small circle of their acquaintance one or more sceptics. There are few Christians indeed who have not nourished if they don't now nourish a latent scepticism as to some portions of their system. And in consequence of that law of our condition we noticed just now. ⟨Now we must solve all reasonable doubts and none seems to be more worthy of this rank than the questi⟩

Rom. Cor. I & II⟨,⟩ Galat. Thess I & II Ephes.

'Tis a noble language of Dryden to say of ↑the death of↓ one best & greatest

> "*his great Creator drew*
> *His Spirit, as the sun the morning dew.*"
> ["On the Death of a Very Young Gentleman," ll. 25–26]

[3] Hence arises a specious objection in an early stage of our progress. For when one considers that such is the constitution of

the human mind that physical truth even when established by experiments of invariable success, is forced to encounter innumerable obstacles from ⟨the⟩ vulgar prejudice as in the instance of vaccination, of Czar Peter's Canals,[16] of Harvey's blood-circulation, & the like & since great force is added to the apprehension that a metaphysical theological creed will not prosper but against infinite odds, a doubt may very naturally arise ⟨as⟩ whether God would leave his dispensation ⟨to stru⟩ of such immeasurable moment to his creatures to struggle against this mighty bias with so small chances of success. The more this objection is weighed the more its force will be felt. We are so much the creatures of education that we find it hard to put ourselves in the place of those who lived under the imperfect religions of paganism. Christianity is so ↑much↓ adapted to the course of human feelings [4] that it requires more discrimination than we are perhaps masters of to separate its fruits from the native promptings of humanity. There are moments in the life of every reflecting man wherein he seems to see farthest into the intellectual world ⟨and in which⟩ ↑when↓ his ⟨bel⟩ convictions of the existence of God & his own relations to him rise upon his mind with far greater force than they are accustomed to exert. But it is by no means certain that the mind of the old idolaters ached for any inspiration or accused philosophy & nature with any emphasis for their scanty revelations. And if not, the greater was the likelihood that the gospel would be rejected which came to supply wants which never had been felt. This objection it is proposed to examine.

This objection in the first place asserts that God will not leave a truth of vast importance to find its own way to the ear & heart of each man but will add some special means to command the attention of men.

[5] I would ask what ground there is in common experience for the expectation of ⟨this⟩ any extreme caution that you be informed of these truths? Providence supports but does not spoil its children. We are ↑called↓ sons not ⟨bantlings.⟩ darlings of the Deity. There is ever good in store for those who ⟨seek⟩ ↑love↓ it; knowledge for those who seek it; and if we do evil we suffer the consequences of

[16] As Emerson noted in his Encyclopedia, p. [23], the Boyars thought Peter the Great's canals impious, "for since God made the rivers run one way man ought not turn them another." See Editorial Title List, *JMN*, I, 408.

evil. Throughout the administration of the world there is the same
aspect of stern kindness; ↑of good against your will; good against
your good;↓ ten thousand channels of active beneficence, but ⟨afll⟩
all flowing with the same regard to general not particular profit.
The political revolution that puts twenty millions of abject slaves in
possession of their freedom & properties, involves the downfal of
innocent & deserving men & the loss of their properties & lives. And
to such an extent is this great statute policy of God carried, that many,
nay, most of the great blessings of humanity require cycles of a
thousand years to bring them to their height. That busy invention
which today ranks so [6] high among the capacities of men and
which makes them inhabitants of all the elements & increases their
dominion over matter a thousandfold ⟨and⟩ is in all its triumphs only
the gradual & natural developement of powers planted at the first.
The arts which so exalt & lengthen life by carrying on the old landmarks of thought to new stations make a vast difference in the existence of the 1st & the 60th Century. Yet all these truths of such vast
consequence to our improvement lay hid. The Compass, Press, Steam
Engine; Astronomy, Mathematics, Politics; have ↑scarce↓ begun to
exist ↑till↓ within a thousand years. Yet the principles of which they
are results are surely in our Nature. "Nature," said Burke, "is never
more truly herself than in her grandest forms. The Apollo Belvidere
is as much in nature as any figure from the pencil of Rembrandt or
any clown in the rustic revels of Teniers." [17] It is our nature to eat
bread yet the making of this substance is a very artificial process.
↑"Man has no natural food" but was expected to convert inedible to
edible substances.↓
Thus too God has done with the religious education of men; he has
sowed truth in the [7] world but has let them arrive at it by the slow
instrumentality of ⟨th⟩ human research.

Such is the wise remark of Origen

X X X X X X X

In the second place it ⟨may be said⟩ ↑must be remembered↓ that
God *was* willing to distinguish this system above other truth & so
announced it by miraculous agency.   family bread[?] of More

X X X X X X

[17] *Letters on a Regicide Peace*, Letter III (see *Works*, 1865–1867, V, 407).
Quoted in *JMN*, I, 348.

"And the ray of a bright sun can make sufficient holiday"
             [Byron, *Childe Harold's Pilgrimage*, IV, xxxii]

　　* The great library of books that is in the world instead of
making all mankind wiser & better is addressed ⟨to⟩ for the most part
to a very small minority of men[,] to the learned alone. In so great
a mass ↑of works↓ doubtless every appetite must be suited & so we
find a portion which seem specially inten⟨ed⟩ded for coxcombs &
deficient persons. ⟨Nor let it be deemed unreasonable severity to
assign⟩ To ⁿ this department ↑belong↓ the greatest part of Novels &
Romances & all that part of the English drama which is called Living
Plays. It would be wicked to put these works into the hands of children [8] and no man of sense could waste ⟨a⟩his time[;] they must
be evidently intended for children of a larger growth — in the childhood of the understanding. But the third class of men[,] the great
body of society who make up nations & conduct the business of the
world[,] these are least consulted in the composition of books. The
immense importance of this order of men makes them indeed the
subject of authors[;] they form the groundwork of their reasonings
& from them illustrations are quoted. But ↑the↓ books ⟨are⟩ written
on them are not written to them. Authors write to Authors. And as
this Order to use a ⟨popular⟩ ↑local↓ term[,] this Middling Interest
of mankind[,] are immersed in daily labours for daily bread they
seldom have the will or power to take up the pen in their turn. The
Consequence often is that they utter the same complaint as the Lion
in the fable that if they were painters &c[.]

　　[9] Now this ⟨partial⟩ oversight of the greatest human interests
might be excused by those political imperfections which were its cause
as long as they lasted. It cannot now be excused. That portion of the
community which all over Europe is called the Third estate, has
righted itself by God's aid in America & has absorbed into itself the
old distinctions of nobility & office. We have plucked down Fortune
& set up Nature in his room. ↑Consider who are the patrons of my
muse↓. Not a frivolous dowager queen[,] not an imbecile baby born
forsooth in a royal ⟨cra⟩ bed is now to be ⟨addressed in courtly wise⟩
↑flattered in florid prose or ⟨honied lies in⟩ ↑lying↓ rhyme↓ — then I

　　　　　[*] See Note (J) [p. 348]

had been silent. But ↑to address↓ a great nation ⟨have⟩ risen from the
dust & sit↑ting↓ ⟨as⟩ in absolute judgment on the merits of men, ready
to hear if any one offers good counsel ↑may rouse the ambition &
exercise the understanding of a *man*↓. It is fit that something besides
Newspapers should be put into the hands of the people. It were well
if short practical treatises on a hundred topics all of primary importance could make them prize what all the world covets. In the capital
of New England are many individuals who [10] both serve & adorn
their country. I have waited to hear them speak but they are silent;
the hours are passing that should complete our education[;] the
moment of instilling wholesome principles may not return. I shall
therefore attempt in a series of papers to discuss in a popular manner,
some of those ⟨daily⟩ practical questions of daily recurrence[,] moral,
political, & literary, which best deserve the attention of my countrymen.

It is now ⟨two⟩ a hundred years since the Spectator was found
duly laid on every plate in the Coffee houses & palaces of London.
It was a book daily read by near ⟨50000 t⟩ fifty thousand people of
every condition, and being a book of faultless ↑persuasive↓ morality
& a ⟨severe⟩ ↑sharp↓ censor of fashionable vices it operated with great
force on the side of virtue. The common accounts say that 14 sometimes 20,000 Spectators were sold in a day. Supposing that 4 persons
read each copy (& though some were no doubt read by less others
were read by many more) we shall have each of those moral lessons
read by ⟨50⟩more than 50,000 persons. Since, the number has been
indefinitely multiplied.

[11] Sometimes as seasons & circumstances change I shall smile;
sometimes I shall laugh, & that heartily; but my readers may expect
that my garrulous humour may get the upper hand of my moral
turn, & vent itself in anecdotes of myself & my friends living & dead
in this & every age. And that which I reckon my chief[n] recommendation is the confidence my reader ⟨will⟩ ↑may↓ entertain of finding me
his friend. ⟨Regularly⟩ Every[n] evening ↑I shall ⟨come⟩ appear↓ at his
tea table ⟨he will find me⟩ always ⟨reposing⟩ speaking to him in the
frankness of love & communicating to him my choicest observations
on men & manners. He who reflects what numbers are made miserable
by the unhappiness of missing those offices of kindness 'tis a friend's

duty to perform & who considers that the best & most consolatory use of friendship is the unreserved communication of thoughts will not lightly esteem this overture I have made in the sincere desire of soothing discontent & sweetening solitude.

[12] I have ever been noted for my fondness for children & children are always fond of me. Nature has so vigilantly provided for the care of children in the affections of parents that at a certain season of life these irrepressible feelings break forth in bachelors also & secure a thousand endearments for the child that comes in their way. 'Tis like my brother used to tell me the strong instinct of sea shells which accompany the hoarse murmur of their native Ocean though far removed from its ↑social↓ abodes[,] ↑tho' withered & dried up in cabinets↓ ⁿ and denied the ⟨exercise of their affections⟩ ↑society for which they were made↓. However this may be, my patrons will rejoice to find me /teaching/growing a favorite of/ their children in an attractive & familiar page the eternal lessons of goodness & truth.

Martial, 3d Epigram (l. IX) asserts that if the emperor should call in his debts Jupiter himself tho' he should make a general auction of Olympus would be unable to pay 2 shillings in the pound.

Gilding the Capitol cost 12000 talents = 2,500,000

battle 'tis granted not to the strong[,] race not to the swift but in the great moral universe rewards are to those that do well & punishment to those that do ill. Is it not strange then that th⟨o⟩e⟨se⟩ wise should have to bemoan their lot on earth. Milton saith "altho' divine inspiration must certainly have been sweet to those ancient prophets, yet the irksomeness of that truth which they brought was so unpleasant that everywhere they call it a burden." [18]

[13]   Bishops — 30000 £ sterling a year.

There is one question proposed to the theological student which surprises me a little by its very simplicity. It is asked whether it is credible that a revelation should be given from God to Man & whether, if given, it were susceptible of ↑proof by↓ any evidence. To

---

[18] The quotation marks are not in the manuscript. The quotation is from "The Reason of Church Government urged against Prelaty." See *The Works of John Milton*, 1931–1938, III, Pt. I, 230.

be competent to answer the first query we ought to survey the relations existing between ⟨g⟩God & his creatures from a little higher
ground than this on which we stand as part of them. We ought to
know how far God intended to make his work complete at the morning of the Creation by endowing man with latent capacities which
should satisfy by their gradual development his moral necessities, &
leave no need of his own subsequent interference. We ought to know

What more harassing than to hear men talk with the most
apparent simplicity of the sympathies of Society? They are needed it
is true to form the common ⟨herd⟩ⁿ Mind to principles of action. —
And the irritations of vanity are better concealed in a bustle ⟨since⟩
where one mortification drives [14] out the memory of another &
finally the mind loses all that vivid sensibility which nature first gave.
Tnam [19]   Many Kings Nicator, divus Augustus, & the like profane
titles of secular ambition, one even $\theta\epsilon os$, but only one Energetes[,]
only one saint Louis.

October 20. There are some questions of practical ethics (if the
phrase be just) which are so deeply involved in the roots of humanity that they may be seen recurring with novel force at successive
periods & embodying themselves in every literature from the beginning. Such especially is the question concerning the foundation of
human virtue. It is not barely a scholastic speculation whether virtue
be or be not a *fitness* ⟨of⟩ or conformity of behaviour to condition.[20]
'Tis a doctrine which numbers of nameless & obscure persons who
never heard of Woolaston but in whom misfortune has bred malignity
have adopted without any other teacher than Experience. There is
no moral sense that we know of, they will say, or men are strangely
heedless of its precepts, but the good lives we witness [15] spring
from policy, not from right feeling. —
        As long ago as Plato the question was agitated & when *Crito*
said that if two rings of Gyges should be given, one to a just, & one

[19] One of Emerson's anagrams for his aunt, Mary Moody Emerson. It apparently
indicates that what follows is taken from her, probably from one of her letters.
[20] Cf. ". . . the theory of Wollaston, in which virtue is represented to consist
in the conformity of our actions to the true nature of things, . . ." in Thomas Brown,
Lectures on the Philosophy of the Human Mind, 1822, III, 183.

to an unjust man, they would both do the same things — obey appetite. The Republic was written to refute the position. Gil Blas of Le Sage, Vestin d⟨u⟩e Pierre of Moliere,[21] Don Juan of Byron are all the fruits of the same evil tree. A rake is represented a breaker of all human & divine laws scoffing at virtue as grimace or ignorance & leading a life of pleasure in defiance of restraints. Some have contented themselves with indirect attacks by prospering the bad to the prejudice of the good or by ⟨rau⟩ pleasantries at the squeamishness of honest men; but Byron, extreme in all things, has laid hands on the everlasting foundation of human virtue,[22] he banters with indecent derision the first affections of the heart[,] "would wake wild laughter in the throat of death[,]" nay ↑if it be not impiety to write it↓ [23] the worm would laugh in the face of God. The thunder has not fallen. This extreme blasphemy has been permitted in modern genius to characterize productions of unprecedented popularity. Books stamped with these tremendous [16] traits have gone, by the ill-fame of genius through all the avenues of civil Society[;] have in palaces conversed with the great; talked with the humble in cottages; have seduced the young[;] have been tolerated by the old; an evil solace to the wearisome months of sickness &c. &c. They[n] have poisoned the vessels of moral health. They have taught men a ↑guilty↓ familiarity with language which should make every pure mind shudder & ⟨men⟩ it is ⟨a⟩within most men's experience that good citizens have already learned to hear with a smile unshocked, unastonished, what would have turned the countenance pale & brought men to their knees in a former age.

Quae fuerant Vitia mores sunt. Sen.[24]

Let it be always remembered that beyond its novelty there is no merit whatsoever in this depraved exercise of the talents. The violent inversion of all moral rules, the outrage of the sympathies, to

[21] Emerson is referring to *Don Juan, ou Le Festin de Pierre.*

[22] The clause "& loudly jeered at human accountability" that is written in the bottom margin may have been an intended insertion at this point. It is canceled in pencil.

[23] The inserted clause is in pencil but it may be by Emerson. For the quotation, cf. Shakespeare, *Love's Labour's Lost*, V, ii, 864.

[24] "Those things which once were vices have become habits." Seneca, *Ad Lucilium Epistulae Morales*, XXXIX, 6.

sing in horror, to laugh in hell, indicates no more ⟨capacity⟩ ↑superior-
ity↓ ⁿ than the ⟨poor⟩ ↑wretched↓ sailor shewed who swallowed knives
or the Italian with scaly skin. It is deformity, not excellence.

[17]²⁵ Guilt never appears first in his worst form. You may not
be uncontaminated tomorrow because you are pure now. Nevertheless
the good think that to the pure all is pure & they may listen with
impunity to vice & voluptuousness for the sake of the touching eloquence that breathes them forth. But if the face shine that has talked
with God, the heart that has consorted with demons will be unclean.
Can a pure mind hear the coarse ribaldry[,] the sly insinuation of
vice[,] ⟨th⟩ witness with impunity the inflaming signs ↑the filthy
rhetoric↓ of guilt? touch pitch & be not defiled? ⁿ When you consider
the uncomputed strength of those sympathies by which the law of
Nature has leagued your will to the wills of other men — it plainly
becomes as much a part of our duty to guard the purity of the social
bands, to abstain from vile & to affect virtuous conversation both of
books & men as ⟨to practise⟩ any known obligation[.]

> Yet know — my master God omnipotent
> Is must'ring in the clouds on our behalf.
> [Shakespeare, *Richard II*, III, iii, 85–86]

give the same scope to good feelings you permit to ill.
We have bright moments but "the weight of earth recoils upon us." ²⁶

[18]   True Epicureanism.
The best thing one can do in this world is to sidle quietly along
without any inflexible philosophy. There are in the world in all probability a vast many souls whose welfare & whose abilities rank as high
as yours & many who are a great deal better. The most absolute sway
which was ever permitted to a mortal over his fellows was necessarily
very imperfect extending to a portion of their goods & to some of
the circumstances of their lot but leaving untouched their liberty of
thought, the intrinsic sources of happiness, their means of influencing
the character of others. Nay so poor a thing is human power & so
tard⟨y⟩ily do⟨es⟩ its wheels surmount the continual impediments ⟨in⟩

---

²⁵ The phrase "as much" is enclosed between vertical lines. Written vertically beside the Shakespeare quotation are "Iroquois   fret   v."
²⁶ Paraphrased and quoted from Byron, *Childe Harold's Pilgrimage*, IV, lii.

↑that clog↓ its way that few tyrants have been sure of a prompt execution even of that part of affairs which is ↑most↓ under their control.
'Tis proverbial that between cup & lip[,] between the command & the
deed is oft a wide interval. Much more is this insignificant influence
observable in the great theatre of the world, in the vast heterogene-
ous society of ignorant & instructed[,] of mean & [19] aspiring minds.
There is no sycophant that ever beseiged the gates of a palace so
cunning or so successful ↑in his flattery↓ as every man's self conceit.
This ⟨‖ ... ‖⟩is ever at his side & threads with him the labyrinth of
life. This bloats his opinions into an imaginary consequence & sends
him out to teach them to all mankind. There is scarce a man in the
American empire so much the master of his own understanding &
so competent to a just comparison of the powers of himself & other
men as not to believe himself adequate to the first office of state who
does not secretly believe that a secret greatness inheres in his soul
which qualifies him to sit in the seat of Washington. So gross an
adulator is self. He is the father of lies. Hence it happens that each
man is born a propagandist and when nature adds a violent zeal to
his temperament ⟨&⟩ he becomes excessively uncomfortable to his
friends & himself. He is vehemently anxious to shape his course in
that straight line which the tenor of his thoughts has ⟨formed⟩ drawn.
His ardour overlooks all the towering obstacles that stand in his way.
But a thousand more ↑busy calculators↓ are making the same [20]
schemes & as no chance will make so many paths parallel they must
often encounter with violence fatal to the peace of both. I do not
praise an ignominious indolence of life & recklessness of fate which
hugs itself under the great name of Epicurus & says 'let us sleep,
for so do the gods.' I do not extenuate the fault of those who succumb to fashion & cower to strong & exalted vice. ⟨t⟩The hatred of
good men cleaves to these malefactors. I am only deprecating the
wilfulness of men & that shallow pride which thinks wisdom will die
with it & attaches a world of importance to its reveries. All that it
thinks *must be* spoken[,] all that it speaks must be done. A wise
man, therefore, is not known in the houses of men by much speaking.
He is aware of this incurable folly & he feels it to be a distinction
honourable to his feelings & *sense*, to abstain from words among so
many babblers nor hang the hope & salvation of men on any oracles

284

of his own; nor show an ungraceful pertinacity in trifles or ⟨exalt⟩ ↑magnify↓ ⟨to Hea⟩forms above [21] the moon; ⁿ as Bacon said, He was not ↑born↓ a sovereign but ⟨a fellow or⟩a subject or at best a fellow of natural events. It is therefore mad to scourge & chain the Hellespont or to weep on the margin of the Indian Ocean for more worlds to conquer. ⟨Events can't be moulded⟩ The great order & revolution of events is somewhat too huge & unweildy to be fashioned to our caprice; we must accommodate our wills to it. If the mountain won't come to Mahomet, Mahomet must go to the Mountain. 'Tis obviously an economy of wit & labor to go round large obstacles rather than from any foolish punctilio to insist on levelling them. Skill always prevails over strength. I praise those therefore who have that generosity of spirit to tolerate all philosophies & avail themselves of the advantages of all as occasion requires. And it is an observation not now made for the first time that there is oft as much sublimity in sufferance as in action. The silence of Achilles, the covered face of Agamemnon[,] are famous masterpieces of poetry & painting. The man therefore who pleases himself with his superiority to little & bestial intellects, & who is fond of making experiments on himself will often practise the selfdenial of reserve when [22]²⁷ his knowledge & situation would permit him to speak. A loftier view of the dignity becoming his nature suggests a nobler policy.

Whatever has an air of display breeds in men a suspicion of deficiency. Most branches of literature being purely ornamental & of no furtherance to the concerns of life have brought on letters a reproachful comparison with ⁿ affairs as if the first were baubles, & the second human objects. But the vulgarity & narrowness of drudges have made that character highest in common esteem which adds the elegance of liberal studies to the skilful practice of business. Pericles therefore & Caesar & Bacon have a sounder reputation than Zeno & Aristotle. ⟨The⟩ ⟨c⟩Conversation that has an air of exhibition is ⟨e⟩always in that degree offensive.   *Words; Words; breath*

1824; 4 November.
                    ↑Morality of Civilization —↓

    ²⁷ "Mor. Civilization" is centered beneath "the heart of many" at the bottom of the page.

Be not so enamoured of your own virtue as to be greedy of all possible renown. Have you not heard? [n] Hath it not been told you that virtue is its own reward? This is not a cold rhetoric of sophists[,] an unmeaning declamation[,] ↑but a blessed saying↓ worthy of all acceptation↓ it has burst from the heart of many a sufferer. [23][28] It is a sentiment known in heaven; it has led many there; it is known in whatsoever ↑uncomfortable↓ corners of the earth God's faithful servants inhabit for it constitutes their antepast of heaven. And he is but a novice in goodness who sits restless under the good he has done until it is published & praised. Must you divulge to your friends the charities of this day? Can you not avoid the tempting allusion to the triumph you ⟨g⟩ have recently gained over yourself? Because you found yourself on your knees in your closet, was it necessary to inform that holy man who takes delight in acts of devotion? [n] Are you very jealous of yourself and do you never suspect an *ambiguity* in the inspiring principle of this virtue? A happiness to which the approbation of man is essential, may peradventure be *founded* on the approbation of man.

But it may be asked if we are not commanded to let our light shine & if it /does not/has not been supposed to/ require a certain degree of heroism to avow oneself a meek & humble Christian.

The answer to this question involves a large consideration of human history.

[24][29] It is a /remarkable/significant/ trait ↑by↓ which a skilful eye detects the magnificence (if I may so speak) of Providence so infinitely removed ⟨from⟩ ↑in↓ the vastness & far-extended connexion of its works from the minute operations of human design that a longer duration ⟨rights⟩ ↑repairs↓ the errors that have grown up in a shorter. In the nascent state of God's works (& most of what we see here is in a nascent state,) there are many imperfections which instead of proving radical faults & augmenting their ⟨pernicious strength⟩ ↑evil↓ with their age, time discovers a manifest tendency to heal. One of the most beautiful of these in the moral world,[30]

---

[28] "Mor. Civilization" is written beneath "consideration of human" at the bottom of the page.

[29] "Moral Civilization" is centered beneath "known. And" at the bottom of the page.

[30] The phrase "the moral world" is underlined and followed by a subscript 1, as

is the tendency ↑of civilization↓ towards virtue. Modern science,[31] in-
credulous of that fabled patriarchal life which has descended to us
in the songs of the East & West as adorning with simple dignity the
beginnings of our race, has sent its missionaries ∧ across the Ocean
to those distant islands where the barbarous rudiments of society
are still seen, where still, no knowledge is transmitted, no knowledge
desired, no metals wrought, no institutions framed, no future explored, no God known. And what was the [25][32] result recorded in
the book of ⟨history⟩ fact? Did the sailor who circumnavigated the
globe, who passed by all the abodes in which humanity ∧ is found
from the isles that spot the South Pacific to the cold latitudes of either
pole — did ⟨Byron⟩ ↑Columbus↓ or ⟨Halley⟩ or Cook or Humboldt[n]
fall in with any Elysian fields or any Fortunate isles? In the barren
coasts of New Zealand & Vandiemen's Land did the visitor find the
solitary inhabitants respect⟨in⟩ers of mutual rights hospitably introducing the stranger to the paternal tent of their chief, yielding to
pure & spiritual religion the homage they denied to priestcraft & was
civilization ↑really↓ a contamination to the pure manners of the
children of the isles? Or was not all the terrible strength of civilization in request to defend its children from subtle fraud & unrelenting
/hostility/violence/? Man had grown no wiser in the solitude of
the Pacific. Mercy & Peace & righteousness & chastity were the
strangers of another Zone. The common brotherhood of the same race
that keeps even [26][33] beasts from devouring each other, ↑was↓ altogether forgotten in a nauseous outrage that humanity shudders to
name.   These travellers went on a munificent message of
knowledge & charity; they bore to the poor savage the Arts & im-
plements that were the overflowings of Cultivation[;] they came back
with the melancholy contradiction of the poetic *visions of the golden

[*] see, v. ⟨1⟩7

---

if to indicate an intended change in order, but Emerson did not show what it was to
precede.
      [31] Emerson drew diagonal lines from "Modern science," through "deceit;" on p.
[26], probably to indicate use.
      [32] "Civilization Moral" is written beneath "the same race that keeps" at the
bottom of the page.
      [33] "Civilization Moral" is centered beneath "patriarchs is an apparent" at the
bottom of the page.

age. They found that with the strong was violence; with the timid was ⟨fraud⟩ deceit; they found that depravity was not the consequence of refinement but was planted wherever the seed of man was sown.[n] I had not dwelt thus long on this disastrous scene but that it ⟨is⟩ ↑seemed to me↓ just to draw from it the inference I have drawn, & to pronounce the infancy of Society *generally* a state of very defective morality. The ⟨hi⟩state[n] of comparative innocence pourtrayed ⟨in⟩by the Sacred Histor⟨y⟩ians in the life of the Chald⟨aic⟩↑ean↓ patriarchs is an apparent [27][34] exception but one for which themselves account by making that purity ⟨their⟩ ↑an↓ obedience to the immediate injunctions of Heaven. And this fact adds confirmation to the remarks we have made, inasmuch as the very fact of a special interference of God to establish in the hearts of men the dominion of his moral laws indicates a speci⟨fic⟩↑al↓ evil to be counteracted; indicates that the infancy of Society is a state of defective morality.

Experience justifies a farther step & permits us to say that on the whole the advancement from the first to the second stage of civilization is attended by ↑a↓ cotemporary moral advancement. God is discerned by his children as much ⟨by⟩ ↑in↓ the minutest contrivances to produce good in his Universe as ⟨by⟩ ↑in↓ the greatest[;] & commonly greater conviction comes from those whose delicacy fits them to our optics than from those of less convenient magnitude. Yet so ambitious is the human understanding that it is ever better pleased to soar than to creep — to track the footsteps of the Invisible in those great provisions which having vast objects in view appear more agreeable to our conception of the grandeur of his employments.

[28][35] It is therefore a blessed triumph in the eyes of the Christian ⟨when he reads⟩ ↑to recognize that /universal order/principle/ in↓ the doctrine of the Modern Political ⟨O⟩Economists that the moral character of a community is mended or relaxed with the greater or less security of property and that on the same security of property Civilization depends. If the dark hours of persecution & poverty[,] if public calamity & private anguish were the only cultivators of human virtue[,] if piety were an exotic which throve only in dens of

[34] "Civ. Mor." is centered beneath "his employments." at the bottom of the page.
[35] "Civilization Moral" is centered beneath "or begotten" at the bottom of the page.

death, in mountain fastnesses, on volcanoes or in sanctuaries, ↑(in the purple testament which Spain brought to the New World)↓ — the fearful homes of faith in stormy times[,] we should indeed doubt whether that could be essential to man which only an ⟨unnatural & convulsed state⟩ ↑disorder↓ of society could produce. With reason we should call that *fanaticism* which sprung up only in agony. That could not be ↑universal↓ health which was caused by incidental disease. But now what is piety? That which is seen to be good & promote good when all the institutions of society are in prosperous action which is indispensable to their perfection & is itself seconded or begotten by them. [29][36] In vindication of this fine doctrine the Economists quote the licentiousness which debauched Europe at the era of the Plague. When God let loose on mankind that tremendous minister of his judgments instead of that ⟨silent⟩ breathless expectation of the destroyer & the intense devotion which fear should be supposed to extort, it was found that a pest as dire & as uncontrollable had broken out & was poisoning the *moral* health of mankind. Vices & Crimes ascended to a pitch[,] to a madness that had no parallel & men beheld each other with mutual astonishment to see how soon modesty & temperance & ⟨the fear of God⟩ ↑conscience↓ were become bygone words, & how ⟨the⟩ speedily a wild & prodigal iniquity & a foolhardy blasphemy had taken the place of the ↑old↓ fear of God & the regard of man. ⟨It was found that⟩ ↑It was found that ↑the↓ impulse to devotion was counteracted by a mightier impulse to disorder & that no human hand could repair the enormous mischief that had befallen society↓. ↑When↓ the destruction of 40,000 (?) people in London had left property without owners or without ⟨ot⟩protectors[n] ⟨It⟩ ↑it↓ was found [30][37] that the despair of life operated to annihilate that pruden⟨t⟩ce which in ordinary times cultivates the good opinions of men & lays up the means both of selfish & of social enjoyment & that the root of all the horrors of the time was the insecurity of property. When this was confirmed by the collateral ⟨facts⟩ examples of the immorality of new countries & of many districts of Europe under the unsettled governments of the Dark Ages

---

[36] "Civ. moral" is written beneath "without ⟨ot⟩protectors" at the bottom of the page.
[37] "Civilization moral" is centered at the bottom of the page.

& of the character of outlaws as of the Buccaneers, Robinhood & his Merrymen, ⟨(⟩and often of Camps (which classes live in the continual expectation of death & therefore feel that insecurity of property, & consequent ⟨ea⟩ relish for present intemperate enjoyment)ⁿ why then, the doctrine might be considered to be founded in fact ⟨⟨but⟩that civilization & human⟩ that the growth of Virtue was coeval with that of Civilization or with the institutions for the security of Property.

[31]³⁸ I do not intend in calling Virtue the natural fruit of Civilization to disparage that Virtue which has grown up under far other auspices. I neither wish nor dare to stigmatize that as fanaticism because it grew up in the most adverse soil of persecution — which evinced the purest principles. They who have sacrificed ease, honor, society, & life for conscience' sake have made the costliest proof of their sincerity. This giving up of the ghost for the truth is the divinest act permitted to human nature; it is a sublime heroism which dazzles the imagination & cancels all paltry imperfections &c &c &c &c[.]

I have only said that the virtue growing from persecution & suffering is an exception & not an example of the ordinary course of affairs. & that if it only throve thus we should pronounce it not essential to the soul. Men have ⟨lived⟩ wintered in the neighbourhood of the ⟨North⟩ Pole, have ascended into the atmosphere, have survived poisons. And yet it was no part of Nature's design that they should inhabit the air or the Poles or feed on venom.

[32]³⁹ In the long progress of mankind from the planting of the race in Asia & the first awkward efforts of art to the maturity of which we are so proud,ⁿ ⟨the day arrived when⟩ time was when vice *overcame* in ⟨the⟩ its eternal Contest with virtue, when the yet unpurged eye of Reason could not see the pure light of truth, & in consequence Virtue had no majesty in men's eyes.

Time is not barren of epochs when corrupt manners defiled the face of society, when the only means of rising to consideration were dishonest⟨y ambition⟩, when God seemed to have left himself with-

³⁸ "Civ Mor" is written beneath "air or" and to the right of "venom." at the bottom of the page.
³⁹ "Civ. Mor." is written beneath "Not poor" at the bottom of the page.

out witness on earth, when ⟨those who the⟩ ↑the masters of mind
were↓ foremost in libertinism, when those who were the constituted
⟨rea⟩ heads of law & state scowled on faith & holiness & denounced
religion as ungentlemanly ⁿ & poor spirited. Then not poor spirited
were they who had the courage to lean upon their own integrity &
bid defiance to the corruption & insolent unrighteousness of the great
& proud. Not poor spirited but heroic was [33]⁴⁰ the man, whether
Ebionite, Hug⟨u⟩anot, or Presbyterian in the infamy branded on
him by ⟨his foes⟩ ↑angry bigot⟨ry⟩s↓ who had the /great/large/ soul
to endure & despise the martyrdom of scorn. In that season, & it
came oft & ⟨remained⟩ ↑tarried↓ long, ↑I admit in answer to the query
that begun this discussion↓ it did require no ⟨small⟩ little fortitude to
avow one's self the meek & humble Christian. But in stating the provision for melioration of the species I have ⟨also⟩ ↑already↓ insinuated
the fact which is forced on our notice in this connexion, that altho'
it did once require heroism to be virtuous it has now, praised be
God, ceased to do so. It has ceased to require ⟨any des⟩ heroism to
avow one's self the disciple of Christ. The stake is not dressed, the
faggot is not kindled, the lean beasts of the amphitheatre are not
unchained to compel the incompellable service of your soul. A meek
& quiet temper, a due conformity of life to the relations which you
were created to ⟨f⟩bear to the Universe is not now the laughingstock
of the world. I cannot precisely date by causes & events the era of this
excellent revolution in human minds for it has been the gradual
growth of [34]⁴¹ high & distant causes, and the Kingdom of God
comes *without observation.* The great expansion of ⟨the mind⟩ ↑knowl-
edge↓ which has been the fruit of printing & Commerce in modern
times has indeed added worlds to the ⟨conquest⟩ ↑dominion↓ of the
mind. It has annexed a vast ⟨impe⟩ meaning to the ⟨words⟩ ↑⟨dis⟩↓
distinction of ancient & modern refinement, & inasmuch as knowledge
is power it has increased the ability to do mischief or good. It was
therefore an event which sages & holy men of old (whose prophetic
sagacity foresaw ⟨with⟩ this inevitable growth,) ↑might↓ anticipate⟨d⟩

⁴⁰ "Civilization Moral" is written beneath "been the gradual growth" at the
bottom of the page.
⁴¹ A faint sketch of a man's face in left profile appears below "fancy of" in the
text. "Civ Mor" is centered beneath *obligation* in the bottom margin.

with trembling interest to see if that Virtue which they held sacred & dear would subsist in immortal beauty to the superior under-stan↑ding↓ of future ages or whether it would go down to dust with other pleasing visions which the fancy of ignorance created. It has stood the test of time. What they secretly worshipped in closets & oft in dungeons the sounder sense of this age has drawn into the light & recommended to the adoration of men. In all the seats of wisdom & pure civilization that are in Christendom are found the eloquent apostles of this cause who have insisted at this day not so much on the imperative *obligation* as on the *beauty* of [35]⁴² Virtue & have invited men to recieve her not so much ⟨as⟩ ↑in the capacity of↓ accountable as of intellectual beings.* ⟨The moral effect of Milton's Comus & the⟩ It has ceased to be a sacrifice to be virtuous. You chime in with the tune o' the time. You but follow a fashion to espouse this ancient cause.

Let me not be esteemed the prophet of ⟨a⟩ lukewarm doctrines betraying my sacred cause to the desire of conciliating ease & worldli-ness. I have expanded my topic to this degree in order to illustrate ⟨the⟩ ↑certain↓ remarkable traits ⟨of ⁿ magnificent⟩ ↑not↓ of a beneficent interference ↑⟨but of a ⟩↓ in human affairs but of a beneficent order of events adapted in the beginning to be productive of a late but progressive ——— and also to form an answer to a question frequently ⟨made⟩ ⁴³ ↑put↓ by [36]⁴⁴ pretenders to Virtue & which was quoted in the beginning whether it does not require Courage to profess one'sself the disciple of such a creed. And as I have said, it seems from the aspect of the age & the propension to virtue everywhere apparent to have no claim to such merits. Let me not be thought to stand thus unworthily in the place of the Apostles. Let me be now

---

* Of this sort is the reputation of Brown & Stewart in Scotland. So of Frisbie & Norton in America. The same is the moral effect of Bishop Butler altho' chiefly a priest of *Reason*; & preeminently ⟨so⟩ of Milton's poetry & prose as the "Comus" & "Unlicensed printing" & "Reason of Ch[urch]. Government."

⁴² "Civ Mor" is centered beneath "of Ch. Government." in Emerson's footnote.
⁴³ The word "⟨made⟩" is underscored several times, probably indicating intended revision.
⁴⁴ "Civilization Moral" is centered beneath "appearance essential" at the bottom of the page.

distinctly understood to call it a perilous thing for Religion to become
a Fashion. Virtue is always to be estimated not by the effect but by the
motive; *is* always so measured [by] the Judge of Virtue. But ⟨human⟩
↑our↓ eye⟨s⟩ which cannot penetrate beyond the outward act ⟨are⟩
↑is↓ not only frequently imposed upon by false appearances of our
neighbour's virtue but (⟨by⟩thro' the strange blandishments of ego-
tism) by the false appearances of our own ⁿ ↑tho' you yourself only
know whether you be cowardly or cruel[,] faithful & devout[,] as
'tis obvious others can only hazard conjectures — See Note E↓ [45] We
accustom ourselves entirely to judge from the appearance ⟨& we⟩
untill we begin to think the appearance essential & if [37] [46] we fulfil
the expectations of mankind, flatter ourselves we have fulfilled the
demand of duty. Especially are we liable to this self deception when
the tone of feeling in society runs with any strong current towards
the natural obligations of Conscience. And now when virtue has eclat,
— and Fashion ↑itself↓ has ⟨usurped her robes & devoutly⟩ taken the
Cross there is indeed danger lest we mistake our conformity to this
prevalent correct taste for the fruits of severe & ineradicable principles. Those sacred rules of life, companions of its sorrow & its well
being, companions & elements of its eternity, the objects of its present
probation, the ties by which 'tis to be bound to the Universe of Good
beings, are not thus easily put on & off ⟨with⟩ with the succession of
insignificant opinions & the customs of high life.ⁿ They are slowly
formed by many sacrifices of self, by many victories over the rebellion
of passion, and ↑their genuineness↓ are ever to be suspected when of
hasty growth. Such is the force of sympathy over human hearts [38]
& such the accumulated temptation to adopt the opinion which is
sanctioned by all that is reputable in society that ⟨a⟩ wise man will
scrutinize his heart with unusual jealousy when its dictates conform
to the bias of the world. He will beware lest when that transitory
bias shall find a new object his rectitude also may be attracted in
its train. For the fashion of this world fast passeth away but ⟨not⟩
one jot or one tittle ⟨of this law⟩ shall in no wise pass from this *law*,
till all be fulfilled.

[45] See p. 347.
[46] "Civilization Moral" is written beneath "sympathy over human" at the bottom
of the page. "S" is written twice near "Those sacred . . . sorrow &" in the left
margin.

[It is perilous for Religion to be a fashion as it is apt to lead men to errors both in the *nature* & in the *degree* of their virtue.*]

It is to[o] humiliating to see & f⟨l⟩eel with what complaisant ease the sycophant & fashionist with a heart cold as marble ↑to the inspiration of piety↓ can assume the language & sentiments of exalted devotion,ⁿ to hear the libertine interrupt for a moment his licentious song & call on men to see how [39] skilfully he can mimic the sweet music of devotion,ⁿ & then take up again with new zeal the melodies of swine or devils. Judge not therefore by outward appearance. —

And if ever in administering to the wants of one class of my readers I should offend another I must ask their Charity beforehand for my case answering as I must such different demands & it becomes me like the old lady who worshipped the picture of St Michael ⟨to⟩ ↑while I↓ hold up one candle to the saint & ⟨one⟩ ↑to hold another↓ to the dragon.⁴⁷ I shall also allow myself such a latitude as to relate to my younger readers occasionally certain old stories which I heard in Germany touching the Troldfolk & the Elf gentry that yet lurk in some corners of that ancient empire. For I spit at the scepticism of the moderns.

↑Set down Hor. Var. Tib. Pollio. Virg. Contem in Dissert↓ ⁴⁸

I propose to write presently on the use⟨s⟩ of our powers & passions, on abstinence & action, on hermits & men of affairs.** I propose to remember that ' 'tis one thing to stifle & another to direct a propensity.' I propose to look philosophically at the conduct of life. To remember [that] to the course of the meanest all the high rules of the theor⟨e⟩ist can be applied,ⁿ & of the [40]⁴⁹ acceptance that sedulous action will find on high beside shiftless contemplation, & infer a law

* and these shall be better discriminated when the last paragraph is remodelled.

[**] See note (J) p. 130

⁴⁷ The source of the story is probably Montaigne. See *The Essays*, 1892, II, 254.

⁴⁸ Emerson seems to have meant that Horace, Varro, Tibullus, Pollio, and Virgil were all contemporaries, and that he intended to cite them in his "dissertation" or essay in contrast to "the moderns." He refers to his experimental writings as "dissertations" on p. 300 below.

⁴⁹ "On the Study of Final Causes" is centered beneath "does not understand" at the bottom of the page.

whether either life be embraced or a golden mean preserved. Admit
the exception of possibility of sublime virtue in absolute inaction,
when inaction is martyrdom but scrupulously exclude the claim of
conceited or decieved indolence. A fine train of final Causes in the
rewards attached to action[.] — ↑Eichorn — relatively & absolutely.↓ [50]

[51] We have all occasionally heard or uttered the complaint that
life was barren of interest. It is not barely an idle saying of those who
would say something or even of the melancholy or of the sick in soul
or in body. It has been made the excuse of intemperance & of squandered time. ⟨& of deeper guilt. It charges on Providence the faults
↑errors↓ of man and⟩ ⟨i⟩It is thought to argue some signal ⟨deficiency⟩
↑incompetency↓ in the means or objects of human action to ↑⟨fill⟩↓ the
Capacity employed upon them,ⁿ & charges &c. He who reads a book
in a language unknown to him[,] he who shuffles the draughtsmen in
a game he does not understand may [41] [52] easily tire of his employment,ⁿ & complain of its insupportable dulness. But ↑in the one
instance↓ [53] the practised eye that traces the well known characters
of his native tongue, recieves from those mute ⟨tokens⟩ signs the inspiration of ⟨eloquence⟩ ↑thought↓. By that dumb page his understanding is enlarged, his passions startled from their sleep, he is
moved with wonder, he is stung by remorse. The playe⟨d⟩r watches
with equal anxiety the ⟨carved⟩ chips of ↑carved↓ wood ⟨he⟩ with
which he plays his game; & the petty alterations of place which move
the scorn of the beholder have to him an eloquence passing that of
⟨song & of story⟩ ↑words↓ a⟨n⟩ ↑fatal↓ eloquence ↑often↓ which intoxi-
cates his spirit & overcomes his virtue. It is almost needless to explain
the appositeness of these illustrations. Ignorance is the cause, whence
life as well as the book & the game appear worthless & dull. We rest
in the objects of sight without extending our regard to the consequences ⟨to which they are linked⟩ ↑which they involve↓. We examine

[50] William Emerson, now in Germany, had been sending Emerson reports of
Johann Gottfried Eichhorn's lectures on the higher criticism of the Bible.
[51] From "We" to the end of the paragraph, on p. [41], is crossed through by
single diagonal lines, probably to indicate use.
[52] "FINAL CAUSES" is written beneath "be removed." at the bottom of the
page.
[53] Emerson inserted the phrase in pencil.

⟨the⟩ ↑particulars↓ letters & baubles in themselves unmeaning, & give no heed to the train of real events of which they are made arbitrary signs.

Perhaps then the same interest may be made apparent in life if our ignorance of the connexion between its events could in any degree be removed.

[42] [54] Ignorance is not a malady contracted on the earth nor an incidental defect foreign to the purposes of our existence but is an original want with which we were created & which it is a chi↑e↓f business of life to supply. As hunger stimulates us to procure the food appointed for our sustenance ignorance is but an appetite which God made us to gratify. And if it be contrary to Nature to deny our bodies food it is contrary to a higher nature[,] it violates the Order of Providence (which in its provision of final causes adapted the inquisitiveness of childhood to the wants of the mind) to bury the mind in sinful sloth & forfeit that knowledge which is its vital principle. So apparent is the duty of expelling it, of chasing from the mind this great darkness by the light of intellectual truth that the wise pagan represented wicked men as involuntary offenders, as doing what seemed to them right & profitable in the thick mist which hid from their eyes [43] [55] their real interests. In all languages, also, this easy & natural metaphor from knowledge to light & from ignorance to darkness hath gone into common use.

⟨He that looks beyond the⟩ ↑It is a↓ great & moving scene that the world offers us. The noble & unexpected trains of events, the[n] simple & untiring grandeur of the theatre whereon they pass; the number, & ⟨variety⟩ character of the agents, their forms & qualities, the apparent minuteness of their means in comparison with the ends they bring about, & the superstition or the religion men entertain touching the invisible spectators of their action — ⟨tend⟩ ↑combine↓ together ⟨tend⟩ to make a very attractive ⟨picture⟩ ↑spectacle.↓ The sciences as they are called, or the classes of facts which human investigation ↑into the laws of nature↓ has laid open have attained a

[54] "FINAL CAUSES" is centered beneath "hid from their" at the bottom of the page.
[55] "FINAL CAUSES" is centered beneath "dominion of" at the bottom of the page.

sufficient maturity & magnitude to occupy alone the best part of man's
years & deserve a great expense of time. The arts are at this day so
numerous & have made the dominion of man over na[44]⁵⁶ture so
co⟨mplete⟩↑nsiderable↓ as to add very greatly to the worth & beauty of
the spectacle. Not content with the ⟨first⟩ satisfaction of his first wants
—to be wholesomely fed & warmly clothed & lodged; & making it
his sole philosophy to reduce the number of his wants; ⟨he has⟩ &
spurning the imaginary greatness of that primitive state of society
When wild in woods the noble savage ran⁵⁷ ⟨the⟩ man has invented
new wants for the sake of new gratifications. He has emerged from the
woods where he shivered beneath storm & cold. The sheep is sheared,
the loom is contrived. & mines, vegetables, or fishes lend his raiment
their splendid dye. Granite & marble is quarried for his structures.
He descends to the margin of the sea & launches his little bark into
its unfathomable waters. A bauble, a particle on the interminable
waste, — I see it mount the ridges & sink in the vallies of the ocean;
but the understanding of him that guides it, sits sovereign of its
course. Its curious furniture of helm & sail & compass lead the little
adventurer on in safety & tho' the whirlwind from heaven sweep
across his path [45] & the tempest tear his canvass as in sport—he
contends with the elements & rides *out* the storm & comes at last over
↑nearly a straight line of↓ thousands of leagues of water to visit the
farthest corners of the world. When the message of another nation
is delivered here & the fruits of the tropics are bartered for those of
the pole[,] when the character, language, & country has been scrutin-
ized by the eyes of the stranger he sets his sail anew & flees over the
deep to enrich ↑the ⟨knowledge of⟩↓ ⟨his own city⟩ ↑science of his own
land↓ with ↑his strange tidings & its ⟨commerce⟩ ↑wealth↓ with↓ those
gifts of Providence that are denied to its soil ⟨& its science with ⟨its⟩
his tidings⟩. This is but a part of the Catalogue of his arts. ↑Nov 28↓
The manufacture of books is the art of arts that has impelled thought
& information like a torrent over the globe[,] [the art by means of
which he that sits recluse & obscure over a midnight lamp is able to

---

⁵⁶ Pages [44], [45], [46], and [47] are crossed through with single diagonal
lines, probably to indicate use. "FINAL CAUSES" is centered beneath "heaven sweep
across" at the bottom of page [44].

⁵⁷ Quoted from Dryden. See p. 273 above.

speak in thunder to societies & nations & in the exercise of a higher power ⟨laugh at⟩ /↑deride↓/↑leave behind him↓/ the impotent prerogatives of Kings] ↑(See Note D p. 129)↓. 'Tis the device by which ↑the↓ subtile creations of the intellectual power which come & go in the vision of genius but leave no trace when the soul that entertained them is extinct are invested with the permanent attributes of matter & made to speak to all countries & times. But I ⟨will⟩ desist from any attempt to enumerate the endless inventions by which Civilization is supported. The world is shaken by the enginery that [46] [58] man's wit has confided to his industry. It ploughs the deep, it lays bare the river beds or arches them with stone, it perforates mountains or climbs on their precipices into the kingdom of eternal cold & builds observatories amid A↑l↓pine avalanches & compares the purity of upland & lowland air ↑& the altitude of hills.↓ When the summits of Andes have been surmounted, ⟨it⟩ indefatigable art descends into the valleys & searches the bosom of the earth & ransacks the subterranean chambers of nature for gems & gold, for iron, silver, & coal. ↑See Note A. p. [346]↓ A thousand feet below the surface in chasms whence the sun & moon & the face of the Universe were never beheld man is immured ⟨in salt mines⟩ & wears out his cheerless years in the streets of salt mines. In short art is everywhere seen. Art dives into the sea & traverses land. Art arms man against man with chemical forces that can hardly be computed & joins men together with facilities for joint useful action which separates taught from untaught man by an ↑almost↓ infinite interval.

These sketches are taken with a design of shewing that the scene which the world offers us is not wholly void of interest & worth,[n] and that [47] [59] a spectator who turns his attention only to the occupations of men need not deplore the ↑total↓ unprofitableness of leisure devoted to these observations. It is intended to suggest that to minds so constituted as ours such a scrutiny into the works of man as is proposed can be made to lighten the intolerable burden of vacant time,[n] and enliven it by exciting a curiosity to be gratified. I praise the discretion which assigns a large portion of youth to the pursuit of

[58] "FINAL CAUSES" is centered beneath "interest & worth," at the bottom of the page
[59] "FINAL CAUSES" is centered at the bottom of the page.

these inquiries. I respect that ardor that is not quenched by mature years. But I will not disguise the fact that these also may fail of their end,[n] that the man who is best acquainted with what is known & done will sometimes sigh at the vanity of his acquisitions & the barrenness of life. The eye is dazzled at first, & tires at last of the magnificence with which it has become familiar. When this has exhausted its power to please we have yet a capacity & appetite[n] which it ⟨is⟩fails to fill, ⟨&⟩or satisfy. ↑But,↓ we[n] do not therefore recede from our first position that our unhappiness is ⟨the⟩ caused by our ignorance & our ignorance is our fault; ⟨but⟩ we only look elsewhere ⟨search another⟩ for its food.

[48] [60] We are made ⟨with⟩ ↑for↓ perception of other truth
Continued on p. ⟨4⟩50
(Here should follow an account of the moral Economy of life, an insight into the moral consequences of actions, & an enumeration more or less complete of such final causes as can be distinctly traced in the principles of human conduct. It may be remarked that Providence works cheaply; at a small expense for much fruit which order is reversed in man. Scrutiny should be made into those ↑small↓[n] primitive differences which result in infinite disparities. The analogy of all things in the Universe in one respect[,] that of motion or growth[,] should be commented on & explained; it should be remarked how manners verge into morals, how blemishes swell to monstrous size, how Virtue & Vice are but seeds which by necessity expand.) Sword law

⟨Give What are the reasons that make life so dull & barren. Is it that we have no stake in the game⟩ I undertake no easy task; things unattempted yet; for tho' the moral world & the rig⟨t⟩hteous economy manifested in the issues & events of common life be not new terms in speculation yet an outline & map of that world[,] ⟨an⟩ a[n] condensed enumeration of the particulars such as poets frequently give of the great traits of the material world hath never that I know been made.

[49] [61] Dec. 1. — I may digress, where all is digression to utter a

[60] "FINAL CAUSES" is centered at the bottom of the page.

[61] "⟨FINAL CAUSES⟩" is centered beneath "all reasonings go back" at the bottom of the page.

wish not altogether fruitless that there might be an Order introduced into the mass of reading that occupies or impends over me. It was a reasonable advice that a scholar [62] gave me to *build* in the studies of a day; to begin with solid labour as /Hebrew & Greek/Theological Criticism/ — Moral Philosophy & laborious writing should succeed; then history; then elegant letters — that species of books which is at once the most elevated amusement & the most productive suggester of thought of which the instant specimens are the bulk of Johnson's works as Lives of Poets, Rambler, &c, Pope's Moral Essays, & conspicuously Montaigne's Essays. Thus much for the day. But what arrangement in priority of subjects? When shall I read Greek, when Roman, when Austrian, when Ecclesiastical, when American history? Whil⟨e⟩st we deliberate, time escapes. A poor plan is better than none; as a poor law. I propose therefore every morning before breakfast to read a chapter in Greek Test. with its Commentary. Afterwards, if time serve Le Clerc; [63] or[n] my reading & writing for dissertations; then Mitford [64] (all history is Ecclesiastical, and all reasonings go back to Greece,) & [50] [65] the day end with Milton, Shakspeare, Cicero or Everett, Burke, Mackintosh, Playfair, Stewart, Scott. ↑Pope, Dryden↓

From p. 48 —

We will pass now to another class of facts[,] to a new scene of relations abundantly distinct & important in their character & we will sift these to ascertain if they also are dull & dreary to the hungry eye. I cannot pretend to compass the moral world & can only sketch with haste some of the prominent points of what is to every reflecting man a scene of wonders. The key to all the language of events is the knowledge that man is moral & accountable & is set in oppor-

[62] Possibly William Ellery Channing (see *Life*, 103).

[63] Probably Jean Leclerc (1657–1736), the Swiss theologian and defender of Arminianism. Emerson may have encountered him first in Stewart's *Dissertation*, where he is quoted. See *Works*, 1854, I, 33–34.

[64] William Mitford, author of *History of Greece*, 6 vols. (London, 1795–1797). Volumes 1–4 were withdrawn from the Boston Library Society Jan. 15, 1825. Volumes 1 and 2 were returned Feb. 3; 3 and 4 Jan. 29. Volume 2 was withdrawn from the Harvard College Library Feb. 14, 1825. See p. 321, n. 110, and p. 324, n. 116 below.

[65] "FINAL CAUSES" is centered beneath "himself he begins" at the bottom of the page.

tunities of doing good & ill by a benevolent being desirous of his
working out his own happiness. He is set down in a great train of
final causes which are to teach ↑him↓ in most audible accents the
nature & wishes of his maker. Scarce has he left the cradle and entered the threshold of life when he is taught the alphabet of moral
distinctions & begins to assume the responsibility of himself [—]
he begins to see the [51] [66] aspects of the Universe [—] ⟨in what respects it is uniform & where in what mutable⟩ when it is mutable, &
when it is uniform. He is to learn its tendencies & their several events.
For instance he is to learn the universal tendency that is in all things
to growth. The little rivulet that drops from a rock swells to a torrent & a sea; the seed expands to a ⟨tree⟩ ↑oak↓; the child grows to a
man. So ↑a wish advances to↓ an indulgence, ↑an in[dulgence].↓ grows
to habit, habit hardens into tyranny. So levity that smiles on vice,
turns to the tolerance that permits crime, & tolerance to the depravity
that commits crime. This is one of those great lessons of Providence
which he that will not learn by a studious application of his faculties
to the fortunes of other men must learn to his bitter cost by the experience of his own. Though the maxim be reckoned unsound that
all men are born free & equal yet the disparity of ⟨the⟩ original lot
is generally very much less than is commonly supposed by men who
↑falsely↓ compute the inequality of the ⟨cause⟩ ↑beginnings↓ from the
inequality of the event. Streams which diverge ⟨from each other⟩
thousands of miles & empty into ⟨different⟩ ↑two↓ oceans begun their
course from ⟨the selfsame⟩ ↑one↓ mountain.

[52] [67] And it is an observation of too vast weight to be a
matter of mere speculative entertainment that the most trifling dis-
similitudes in early life by the time the man has /taken/fixed/ his
station in society ha⟨s⟩ve taken a decided & indelible cast which ↑must↓
stamp the whole future existence with their good or evil characters.
Hence it is of right that wise parents ⟨should be⟩ ↑are↓ often trem-
blingly alive to the least incidents having a⟨ny⟩ moral bearing in the
lives of their children[,] anxious that each adventure which in those
days of easy impression may be a crisis of character, should impart

---

[66] "FINAL CAUSES" is centered beneath "⟨the selfsame⟩ mountain" at the bottom of the page.
[67] "Time" appears beneath "thought" at the bottom of the page.

a favourable bias. This growth is one & but one of those features in divine Providence which demand the study of reflecting men.

Dec. 10, 1824.

I confess I am a little cynical on some topics & when a whole nation is roaring Patriotism at the top of its voice I am fain to explore the cleanness of its hands & purity of its heart. I have generally found the gravest & most useful citizens are not the easiest provoked to swell the noise tho' they may be punctual at ⟨the⟩ polls. And I have sometimes thought the election an indi[53] [68] vidual makes between right & wrong more important than his choice between rival statesmen & that the loss of a novel train of thought was ill paid by ⟨the⟩ ↑a considerable pecuniary↓ gain. ⟨of a guinea⟩ It is pleasant to know what is doing in the world & why should a world go on if it does no good. The man whom your vote supports is to govern some millions— and it would be laughable not to know the issue of the naval battle. In ⟨eight⟩ ↑ten↓ years this great competition will be very stale & a few words will inform you the result which cost you so many columns of the newsprints, so many anxious conjectures. ⟨And⟩ ⟨y⟩Your soul will ⟨outlive⟩ ↑last longer than↓ the ship; & ↑will↓ value ⟨the⟩ its just & philosophical associations long after the memory has spurned ⟨its⟩ ↑all↓ obtrusive & burdensome contents. Merriment to relieve care, occupation to amuse sorrow, may be gathered in a thousand corners at a less expense tha⟨t⟩n men usually incur. There has lately been shewn to the world an economist of time who by rigid attention to his course of reading ⟨p⟩ ⟨accomplished more⟩ acquired more knowledge than others from the same number of pages. This is plainly a laudable & practicable [69] triumph over common obstacles. Such is the admirable abridgement of which knowledge is made ca- pable (by the ex[54]quisite skill of the Artificer of mind) that it is found that the human understanding can digest & command a sum of ideas which is altogether prodigious & that it contrives to become acquainted with the history of all empires in all ages with a facility which ⟨would⟩[n] could ⟨hardly⟩ scarce ⟨have⟩ be⟨en⟩ anticipated in the first periods of time. It recieves & contains without embarassment that

[68] "TIME" is centered beneath "made" at the bottom of the page.
[69] Above "practicable" is what appears to be a question mark.

inundation of facts & deductions which ↑bursts in↓ an age of inquiry
⟨accumulates⟩ from a thousand fountains. Instead of being oppressed
& buried under the mass of its acquisitions the strength & excellence
of its capacity is fed thereby. Master of all its treasures it administers
all, sans inconvenience, & swells its power to a diviner nature by
their use. A metaphysician would exhibit a work of magic who should
⟨write an accurate account of⟩ ↑describe↓ all the means in which knowledge is mastered, arranged, & ⟨reduced to convenient & useful pro-
portions⟩ ↑abridged↓. The arrival at general laws, the connexion of
associated principles, the enlargement of meaning in words which
permits the grand discovery that hundreds ↑of laborious minds↓ promoted, to be conveyed in a bare epithet, — would be a picture to astonish & delight. It would also [55] instruct ⟨& su⟩ by suggesting the
method of ⟨acquiring wisdom⟩ using time to most advantage in
accumulating wisdom.

> "To be no more; sad cure; for who would lose
> Tho' full of pain this intellectual being
> Those tho'ts that wander thro' eternity?"
>   [Milton, *Paradise Lost*, II, 146–148]

    [70] A celebrated English preacher whose praise is in your churches
closed his discourse with a⟨n eloquence⟩[n] bold appeal which the fervour of his eloquence permitted to the passions & imagination of his
hearers. He pointed their minds' eyes to the Recording Angel who
waited on the wing in the midst of the assembly to write down some
name of all that multitude in his book of Life. "And shall he wait
in vain?" he said, "and will you let him take his departure ⟨to⟩for
heaven without making him the witness of a single soul converted
from his sins?" My friends we know that his sentiment was but a
flight of oratory natural enough to ⟨the⟩ ↑a↓ fervid ⟨heat of his⟩ spirit
& which the urgency of the occasion might excuse. My friends no
Recording Angel that we know of hovers over our assembly, but a
greater than an Angel [56] [71] is here. There is one in the midst of

---

[70] Emerson struck through this paragraph with single diagonal lines on this
and the following page, probably to indicate use. The "celebrated English preacher"
is probably Phillip Doddridge (1702–1751). See *JMN*, I, 324.
    [71] "FINAL CAUSES." is centered beneath "confined personal" at the bottom of
the page.

⟨you⟩ ↑us↓ though ⟨y⟩our eyes see him not who is not a fictitious or
imaginary being but who is too great & too glorious for ⟨y⟩our eyes
to bear. There is one here imparting to ⟨yo⟩u↑s↓ the life & sense ⟨you⟩
↑we↓ at this moment exercise, whose tremendous power set yonder
sun in the firmament, & upholds him & ⟨you⟩ ↑us↓. *You* cannot discern
him by the gross orbs of sight but can you not feel the weight of his
presence sinking on your heart[?] does no conscious⟨n⟩ feeling stir
in your bosoms under the eye of your author & God who is here?[n]
What doth he here? & how shall we acknowledge the almighty mind?
He searches the hearts of his worshippers —— &c &c[.]

Wednesday Evg., Dec. 15, 1824.
The moral contrivances of Providence which we call final causes
are the next sources of honest useful & interesting inquiry. I propose
to allude to a few beautiful examples of this economy.[72] It must have
often occurred to a contemplative man that individual advantage is
inseparably linked to the general welfare so that wheresoever & whatsoever efforts are made for the most confined personal betterment
[57] [73] the same effort ⟨in the same degree⟩ ↑to its whole extent↓
ameliorates the condition of mankind. So fast are the cords of social
being drawn that its good & its evil are never insulated but penetrate
thro' vital channels to parts where the agent never meant or knew
his influences would be felt. The most ↑contracted↓ selfishness which
shuts its door on the beggar in the winter night & grudges its pittance
contribution to the necessities of the state & denies to its own frame
almost the comforts of life is nevertheless compelled to benefit⟨s⟩ its
fellowmen at a greater distance than its narrow soul ever comprehended. His house, his clothes, his medicine, his food, are products
whose price he must pay to the encouragement of honest industry.
The order of the elements does not consent to selfishness. If you make
a fire to warm your corner you must warm all those who are in the
room. If you daintily feed & delicately dress your own body you will
liberally pay the wages of labor & the more diligently you procure
your own convenience the more efficiently you contribute to that of

    [72] Emerson struck through the rest of the paragraph by single diagonal lines,
here and on pp. [57] and [58], probably to indicate use.
    [73] "FINAL CAUSES" is written beneath "and the farmer who" at the bottom
of the page.

others. It was an early discovery of political economy that in no form could labor be exerted to less advantage than in an attempt to confine its fruits to the laborer: and the farmer who strove [58]⁷⁴ to make his own shoes, weave his own cloth, build his own house, & teach his own children & ⟨save⟩ ↑prevent↓ the price of these goods enriching his neighbours very soon found himself on the road to ruin. (Whilst, on contrary, that laborer who throws himself on Society by giving up his life to a single branch of mechanical industry, as the nail, pin, paper, shoe maker, which cannot itself produce a morsel of food, thrives ⁷⁵ & lives & benefits the world.)

The further we follow this inquiry, the more exact consistence we shall discover. The love ⟨inculcated⟩ we bear to our country & the world is, except in moments of enthusiasm, very calm & cold compared to that which nature has lodged in our bosoms towards ourselves & in the next degree towards our offspring. If the service of our country was any overt & distinct action it is likely it would be ⟨ra⟩seldom & irregularly rendered. But in the wise arrangem[en]ts of Providence not only is it the means of winning advantages to individuals to [59]⁷⁶ affect the praise of patriotism but every furrow on the brow[,] every laurel on the head of toiling Ambition is a↑n↓ ⟨new⟩ index of some new acquisition bought by the genius & industry of one to the cause of humanity. In all districts of all lands[,] in all the classes of communities thousands of minds are intently occupied[,] the merchant in his compting house, the mechanist over his plans, the ⟨p⟩ statesman at his map, his treaty, & his tariff, the scholar in the skilful history & /angry/chastised/ eloquence of antiquity[,] ⟨all⟩ ↑each↓ stung to the quick with the desire of exalting himself to a hasty & yet unfound height ⟨of⟩ above the level of his peers. Each is absorbed in the prospect of good accruing to himself but each is no less contributing to the utmost of his ability to ⟨make⟩ ⟨set forward the march the human race⟩ fix & adorn human civilization. He that grows rich & respectable by his own ingenuity has ⟨helped⟩ ↑smoothed↓

⁷⁴ "FINAL CAUSES" is centered beneath "advantages to individuals" at the bottom of the page.

⁷⁵ A subscript 2 appears under "thrives", probably to indicate intended transposition with "lives", but there is no subscript 1.

⁷⁶ "FINAL CAUSES" is written beneath "influence in the minds" at the bottom of the page.

& not obstructed the way he has trodden. He that makes himself illustrious by inventions has by those same inventions added facilities to art, solaces to life. He that loves splendor & adorns his house adorns his city. He that prints a book to immortalize his name ⟨gives⟩ ↑creates↓ an immortal influence in the minds of his [60] countrymen. ⟨For if the change that takes place⟩ And the same is true of every exertion from the highest to the humblest of intellect. And this is the high characteristic of that workman whose arrangements embrace all his creatures in their provisions. (Trace the ⟨ch⟩ hand of this artist in his rain, thunder, air, &c.) And who ⟨ma⟩ delights in seeing them all augmenting each other's power & joy ⟨& extolling ⁿ his Glory⟩ as Man ⟨Makes⟩ adapts to each other the properties of substances in his machines.

I propose to write an Essay on the *Evils of imagination* which after such a panegyrick on this beautiful faculty as it easily shall admit may treat of those egregious errors that growing out of some favourite fancy have shot up into whole systems of philosophy or bodies of divinity, & have obstructed truth for thousands of years. The Essay should exemplify its statement by some of the most signal instances of this captivity in which the Imagination has held the Reason of Man.** Thus the picturesque dogma of a *ruined world* has had a most pernicious fascination over nations of [61] believers. It was an error locked with life. They gave up the ghost for the love of this lye. And it clings to this day in the high places of knowledge & refinement. Hence the avidity with which tales of wonder are caught & propagated. Hence Gibbon's remark that men of Imagination are dogmatic. See on this subject one of Stewart's Introductory Chapters in the Philosophy.⁷⁷ See Mr Hume's remarks on the agreeableness of the

* See letters in Theme book ⁷⁸
** See Note G. p. 130.

⁷⁷ Emerson may have had in mind Stewart's account of the infatuation with Luther's "supposed doctrine" that led Amsdorff "to maintain that *good works are an impediment to salvation*," of Mosheim's indictment of Melanchthon and others for their myopic adherence to doctrine, and of the addiction of various learned men, like Bodin, Erasmus, and Kepler, to superstitious beliefs or practices. See *Dissertation, Works*, 1854, I, 39, n.1, and pp. 56–57.
⁷⁸ Presumably a reference to the College Theme Book. It contains an entry by

feelings engaged — Chapter on Miracles.[79] & some of the fables anciently recounted touching Memnon's marble harp renowned of old & the oracles of Dodona & Delphos. & the histories of *enchanters, ghosts & stars.* Le Saurin called Earth scaffold of div[ine]. vengeance.*[80] Also e.g. Nature abhors a vacuum disposed.[81] On this head consult the Introductory lectures of Brown's Phil.,[82] Quietists, Essenes, Quakers, Swedenborgians

v. Prideaux[83] For Proselytism & Missions see Vattel p. 219.[84]

X[Christ] came not unforeseen by the ancient prophets whose eyes had caught a glimpse of blessed light across the cloud of futurity. A thousand years brooded over the prophecy ere the event was matured[.]

[62] Another remark which belongs to the Economy of Providence is the cheapness (if the expression may be used) with which its operations are performed. A man conversant in books of history

*Origen conforming himself to the extravagancies of his time shews the necessity of 4 Gospels, from 4 winds, 4 pillars of a house and ransacks nature & nonsense for resemblances of the Cross.

Emerson on the follies of preferring the imagination to the reasoning faculty, but this breaks off at the point where sixteen leaves are torn out. These or other torn-out pages in the Theme Book might have contained letters in which the *"Evils of imagination"* were discussed. A list of Biblical texts, quotations, and general topics includes "The evils of imagination." See *JMN*, I, 171–172, 161 and 203.

[79] Cf. "the passion of *surprize* and *wonder*, arising from miracles, being an agreeable emotion gives a sensible tendency towards the belief of those events, from which it is derived" in Hume, *Philosophical Essays*, 1817, II, 110. Volume 2 was withdrawn from the Boston Library Society, Sept. 11, 1824–Feb. 3, 1825. Section X (pp. 103–124) is concerned with miracles.

[80] See p. 225 above.

[81] Emerson may first have written "Nature abhors a vacuum" — the statement is in print writing — and then added "disposed" later. The manuscript offers few clues to Emerson's real meaning.

[82] In Lecture I, Thomas Brown recalls the concern of former theologians with such irrelevant questions as whether angels "can exist in a perfect vacuum. . . ." *Lectures on the Philosophy of the Human Mind*, 1824, I, 3. Volume 1 is listed in Emerson's library catalogue.

[83] Probably Humphrey Prideaux (1648–1724), dean of Norwich, orientalist, and author of *Old and New Testament connected in the History of the Jews.*

[84] *The Law of Nations or Principles of the Law of Nature. . .* , by M. D. [Emmerich von] Vattel (Northampton, Mass., 1820).

must often have deplored the immense expense of wit[,] of time that are incurred ↑by us↓ to promote any designs of considerable extent. If a legislator would relieve the necessities of a ⟨hund⟩ thousand paupers he has the task of life & of all his abilities & of many more lives & ⟨abilities⟩ minds than his own. Much of his labor is mere experiment & much therefore of his labor is lost. Private & public subscriptions which searched the charity & taxed the means of a whole nation may leave the evil as bad or worse than it ↑was↓ found. ⟨it⟩ Almshouses & houses of industry may rise in vain; bounties appropriated to stimulate industry; new lands converted to cultivation from heath & waste, & new plans of laying out land contrived in vain. And the required relief may not be obtained until laws have been enacted, which shall change the ↑intestine↓ relations & interests of society & these have been corrected by other laws which shall serve to connect the regulation of a petty district or a small number with the fortunes of remote /countries/colonies/ and distant [63] ages. Does Providence botch up its broken or disordered machinery with the same awkwardness, miscalculation, & prodigal expense? Look a little at its vast & serene policy & see how it answers the same end which we have seen human wisdom toiling to gain. As if to delight itself with the exhibition of its contrivance it brings all men into life paupers. Not destitute of wealth alone but in the destitution of all faculties of action & capacities of thought & enjoyment—without virtue, affection, knowledge, or passion. This deplorable poverty it is the proposed problem to relieve & it may furnish amusement to many hours of Idleness in him that once thought life wearisome, to detect the beauty & simplicity of the means whereby it is done. (Read Rousseau's Emile, Rousseau the unrivalled o⟨f⟩bserver of infantile development, & Buffon the ingenious & benevolent describer of the growth & habits of animals.)

— Faith is a telescope —

Gloss Rom. VIII c. 17 v. *And if children, then heirs.* which can expand to this; You are the child of the rich & wert bred in delicate raiment & on dainty fare & you look to inherit the ⟨magnificent⟩ princely mansion & the rich patrimony of your ancestors. *You* are the child of God & shall inherit the house of Cherubim & seraphim & all the patrimony of power & perfections omnipotent opulence can confer.

308

[64]⁸⁵   Roxbury, Jan. 4th, 1825.

I have closed my school. I have begun a new year. I have begun my studies.⁸⁶ And this day a moment of indolence engendered in me phantasms & feelings that struggled to find vent in rhyme. I thought of the passage of my years, of their even & eventless tenor and of the crisis which is but a little way before when a month will determine the dark or bright dye they must assume forever. I turn now to my lamp & my tomes. I have nothing to do with society.ⁿ ⟨nothing⟩ My unpleasing boyhood is past, my youth wanes into the age of man and what is the unsuppressed glee, the cheering games, the golden hair & shining eyes of youth unto me? I withdraw myself from their spell. A solemn voice commands me to retire. And if in those scenes my blood & brow have been cold⟨er⟩[,] if my tongue has stammered where fashion & gaiety were voluble & I have had no grace amid the influences of beauty & the festivities of Grandeur I shall not hastily conclude my soul ignobly born & its horoscope fully cast. I will not yet believe that because it has lain so tranquil, great argument could not make it stir. I will not believe because I cannot unite dignity, as many can to Folly that I am not born to fill the eye of great expecta-tion, to speak when the [65] people listens nor to cast my mite into the great treasury of morals & intellect. I will not quite despair nor quench my flambeau in the dust of Easy live & quiet die. ⁸⁶ᵃ

Those men to whom the muse has vouchsafed her inspirations, fail, when they fail, by their own fault. They have an instrument in their hands that discourses music by which the multitude cannot choose but be moved. Yet the player has sometimes so many freaks or such indolence as to waste his life. If you have found any defect in your sympathies that puts a bar between you and others go & study to find those views & feelings in which you come nearest to other men. Go & school your pride & thaw your icy benevolence & nurse somewhere in your soul a spark of pure & heroic enthusiasm. Ambi-tion & curiosity — they will pro⟨p⟩mpt you to prove by experiments the affections & faculties you possess. You will bind yourself in friend-ship; you will obey the strong necessity of Nature and knit yourself

⁸⁵ "Self" is centered beneath "expectation," at the bottom of the page.

⁸⁶ Since the spring of 1824 Emerson had been teaching in his own School for Young Ladies in Boston (which his brother William had left in 1823). He closed the school on December 31. He had begun his studies at home; it was not until February 11 (?) that he registered at Harvard Divinity School.

⁸⁶ᵃ Scott, *The Bride of Lammermoor*, ch. 3.

to woman in love.* & the exercise of these affections will open your apprehension to a more common feeling & closer ⟨connexion⟩ kindred with men. You will explore your connexion with the world of spirits & happy will you be if the flame of ardent piety towards the Infinite Spirit shall be taught to glow in your breast.

[66][87] Shall we recieve good at the hand of the Lord & shall we not recieve evil? was one of the eldest sentiments of struggling humanity — the first sentiment in the book of Job; — of whose antiquity inquire.

Affliction cometh not forth of the dust neither doth trouble spring out of the ground.[88]

It has been charged on many elaborate & exquisite productions of the human wit that they have had only local adaptation or have failed in human interest & their date has in consequence been circumscribed by narrow bounds. & the great world which won't stop its march for the convenience of any of its atoms has long outstripped[,] outlived the songs & maxims of its miscalculating boys. Now this fate of their productions indicates a defect in the understanding of their authors by whatever accomplishments they were adorned which no accomplishments can atone. For the masters of the mind have all been inspired by "the ↑sober↓ divinity of Common sense" which taught them that simplicity of thinking which ensures an immortal application to the pursuits & bosoms of men. A book commendable for this merit is the Proverbs of Solomon a work of no transitory or sectarian renown but one whose solid sense & choice of topics have improved the wise, & taught the ignorant of every age. Time in its passage & events has proved but a commentary to illustrate & point its oracles. The extraordinary character [67][89] & fortunes of its author, perhaps his inspiration, enabled him to emerge from the cloud of prejudice & barbarism that surrounded him & to speak in the assured tone of wisdom to his own & to following generations. He was no sickly student immured

* No thought infirm altered his cheek
[Cf. Milton, *Paradise Lost*, V, 384–385]

[87] "Solomon" is centered beneath "oracles. The" at the bottom of the page.
[88] Job 5:6. The question which begins page [66] is from Job 2:10.
[89] "Solomon" is written beneath "the good & wise" at the bottom of the page.

in ⟨schools⟩ ↑a↓ librar⟨ies⟩y & reading men thro' the spectacles of
books; no ⟨forced⟩ ↑cowled↓ philosopher ⟨deriding⟩ describing at awful distance the manners of Courts, & deriding the follies of which
⟨p⟩he pined to share, but a man whose curiosity & ⟨genius⟩ ↑temper↓
made him an indefatigable pursuer of ⟨pleasure⟩ happiness. Happiness he sought where it could & where it could not be found. He
acquainted himself with all the aspects of the passions and all the
degrees & varieties of ⟨life⟩ ↑lot.↓ He was a monarch on the throne
of Israel in times of peculiar felicity; and a throne is that seat in
society, which admits of the greatest tho' oftener condemned ↑from
the incapacity of its tenant↓ to the smallest prospect into the wide &
various scene of life over which it is exalted. A man of understanding
will brush away the silken ⟨curtain⟩ ↑drapery↓ which canopies his
throne the moment it ⟨obstructs⟩ ↑intercepts↓ his insight into the concerns of his extended family. For hither come, by the necessary influences of wealth & power, ⟨the genius⟩ not the fops & court fools,
those summer flies ⟨of⟩ that swarm in the warm ray *of vulgar
majesty, but valor & virtue, genius & knowledge, ⟨are⟩ the favorites
& pillars of wise ⟨Kings⟩ administrations. I speak no opprobrium to
the good & wise when I attach [68]⁹⁰ them to the palaces of power.
For it is the order of Providence which knows that kings' sons are
as the sons of other men subject to the same or greater defects of
character & intellect & must therefore ⟨be⟩ rely on ⟨st⟩ more strenuous
arms & deeper sagacity than their own, it is the order of Providence
to bring them side by side. And it therefore puts into the hand of
power these inducements which will avail ⁹¹ with wisdom & virtue
that disdain to be bought. Patkul (?) came to the Court of Sweden
not because wise counsel would find a market but because a bad law
was passed which affected himself & his province. Newton removed
to London not to be made Mintmaster to Queen Anne but because
a court collects a city & this can furnish the facilities of books & in-

* See Note K [p. 348]

⁹⁰ "Solomon" is centered beneath "procure more information" at the bottom of
the page.
    ⁹¹ " "Those who think" &c" is written vertically in the left margin from
"counsel" below to "& deeper" above. The words enclosed in Emerson's quotation
marks may have been intended for insertion at this point.

struments & above all of kindred society which science demands. Mirabeau ⟨the last hope of⟩ in whose sublime eloquence lay the last hope of France came to court as its enemy. (The three most limping instances I ever had the misfortune to meet.) But however these advantages are procured, certain it is that a ↑wise↓ King has an opportunity of making acquaintance with the best & wisest of his subjects & can commonly procure more information [69]⁹² on any measure or of any sort than other men↑.↓ ⟨commonly can.⟩ (Perhaps this long digression should be supplied by one of broader application on the connexion instituted by Providence between Mind on one hand & Power & Wealth on the other.) With these keys to the gates wherein ⟨Pleasure⟩ Happiness is ⟨by a hoary error⟩ believed to reside, the monarch explored the limits of temperate and of intemperate enjoyment. He was a man who escaped that calamit⟨y⟩ous defect incident to men of letters — whom the greatness of knowledge does not elevate to greatness of soul but while they ⟨as⟩ rule the passions & minds of others are themselves bondmen of jealousy & diseased sensibility. And I am sorry to add in my inconsequent account of the Wise Man, he was a man whose virtue bore no proportion to his understanding, a conspicuous witness to the melancholy fact that the knowledge does not always lead to the practice of ⟨go⟩ moral rules[,] that the splendor of intellectual light may sometimes shine on a hideous & baneful depravity — Seal up seal up

It were a sermon much wanted, much more than flippant essays on perfectibility, that which should bring home the probability of the constant presence & moral action of Deity, tho' the thunder does not strike transgression. ↑For it is the want of visible tokens of judgment that generates all skepticism.↓ It should speak of the opinions men have held concerning our connexion with God not on the great scale but of hourly, instant, existence. It should quote what Stewart reasons of a *machine*. It should quote what a wideworld s[ai]d. of the inspiration of certain moments.⁹³ It should borrow its conclusion from the sketch on p 55 of this book.⁹⁴

⁹² "Solomon" is centered beneath "the sketch" at the bottom of the page.

⁹³ Perhaps a reference to the last three sentences of the discussion of God in Wide World 7 (see p. 34 above).

⁹⁴ See pp. 303–304 above.

[70]⁹⁵   Sequel of p. 66

It is pleasant to trace the identity of our race at vast intervals. We are glad to be able to give the lie to the calumniators of our degeneracy[,] to the panegyrists of our fabled improvement. Those who in any age have found the true key to which the ears of nations would accord have an immortal principle in their eloquence which keeps the integrity of its effect from the beginning to the end of its course. Humanity, in its weary cycle of events — journeying on through six thousand years of good & ill; of alternate ignorance & education; of the invention, the loss, & the recovery of arts; of ⟨the⟩ war & peace; of the triumphs of the passions, & the victories of the intellect; of the sound of the shackles of Slaves ⟨&⟩ the blaze of persecuting fire, — ⟨of⟩and the silver ⟨trumpet⟩ ↑accents↓ of the Reformation & the blessed jubilees of ⟨freedom⟩ ↑liberty↓; through care & consolation; thro' times of hope & times of anxiety; — has contracted no decrepitude from the weight of ages. Her front is presented to heaven ↑serene↓ as of yore. The sorrowful mixture of life has not abated the courage of her heart, nor withered /the roses/ the bloom/ on her cheek.⁹⁶ As Adam came out of Eden, so Man still issues into the ways of life with a confiding soul; conscious of error, conscious of disappointment but sustained by hope & resolute in right. All over the world the elements of character suffer no change ↑from the soil in which they grow↓, offer no new product to the analysis of the metaphysician. ⟨The⟩ Faculties are [71]⁹⁷ developed ⟨in⟩ under the ↑/infin[ite]./countless/↓ impulses to which they are subjected but faculties are not created. There is a conservative principle in human nature which perpetuates the proportions, the dependencies, & the passions of our frame. The same laws[,] the same boundary fixes the laudable exercise of our passions & their excess *now,* as ever. The connexion between the sexes observes its ancient law, & marks the subtle difference between love & lust. All the passions that spring up between man & man in social intercourse, the emulation of each other's goodness & greatness & the imitation of what surpasses ours,

⁹⁵ "Solomon" is centered beneath "metaphysician." at the bottom of the page.
⁹⁶ The phrase "withered the roses" is enclosed in square brackets, possibly to indicate intended revision.
⁹⁷ "Solomon" is centered at the bottom of the page beneath "recognizes the" and between "to be" and "culled" in Emerson's footnote.

our self congratulation at any points of superiority in our own character or fortunes & the tendencies these feelings have ⟨to sharpen into
sterner energy⟩ on quitting their milder forms to act with stern energy ↑up↓on the social system — all these phenomena were familiar
to the eldest moralist. We use to think that we have made a prodigious
advancement on the sluggish nations of antiquity & that our arts &
arms, books & laws, manners & conversation, have got to such a pitch
as would ⟨dazzle⟩ ↑confound↓ our simple forefathers. 'But the spirits
of the wise sit in the clouds & mock us.' [98] The book that suggested
all this talking (from p. 66 till now) tho' written   years ago
is ↑not↓ cobwebbed with ⟨no⟩ ↑any↓ antiquated notions, ⟨&⟩ ↑any↓
obscure allusions to uncouth & ⟨dissimilar⟩ ↑unusual↓ customs.* He
that reads the book of Proverbs inspects a picture of the strong &
weak points of his own character[,] he recognizes the lineaments of
himself [72] [99] unseen before, in every line. He recognizes many
convictions that have been present to his mind at certain passages of
his life but which ⟨he⟩ had never formed themselves into language.
He recognizes ↑this↓ brother & ↑this↓ friend & ↑this↓ [100] enemy — the
wayfaring men that have accompanied his journey of life; the portraits of virtue & wisdom are there; the diligent & the sluggard; the
backbiter[,] the talebearer; lover & scorner; the blessed wife, & the
flaunting harlot; ragged indolence & dishonourable old age and
Folly — Folly — exposed in all parts of the drama. The ↑unerring↓
sagacity of his observation, the extent & minuteness of the judgments
in this masterly commentary on human life confirm the claims of his
youthful vision to denominate him the Wisest of men. The character
of Solomon is the more admirable to us that the lessons of his sublime
understanding are seconded by the ⟨pathetic⟩ fine sentiments of the
heart laid open to us in Ecclesiastes. Altho' Reason makes merriment
out of the tears of Nature our praise of the Reason is ↑always↓ en-
hanced by the knowledge of its connexion with sentiment. [It ↑else↓ⁿ
wants the completeness of its nature. It is man without wife.] The

* Here insert whatever is to be culled from p. 66 & seqq.

[98] Shakespeare, 2 *Henry IV*, II, ii, 155–156.
[99] "Solomon" is centered beneath "when hackneyed" at the bottom of the page.
[100] This and the first "his" are circled, possibly for correction.

sage is made amiable to us when we find no mistaken philosophy has
steeled his bosom to the sympathies of humanity. He is a man as
we are. He sighs at the ↑altered↓ aspect the ⟨hackneyed⟩ world
/presents/wears/ to him when hackneyed in its ways. [73] He[n]
breathes the melancholy eloquence of disappointment over his buried
friends, his buried hopes, the wife of his youth, the hour of his joy,
before the daughters of music were brought low & before the mourners went about the streets. We respect in these opinions the oracular
judgment of genius & experience & not the commonplaces of base
discontent. His magnificent structures, his plans of empire, his ardent
affections, his studious acquaintance with nature & man, his princely
amusements, the feast, the dance, & the song were so many experiments by which the monarch sought to satisfy the hunger of his
mind. And well has he told to all the seekers that shall follow him
in the same pursuit the failure of his experiment.

> ↑His eye had measured the cedar ⟨of⟩ ↑on↓ Lebanon
> & the hyssop of the rock[.]↓

[Pray in your multifarious reading look out for an instance to disprove Bacon's & the common opinion that the armed nation is the
prosperous one.[101] Can ye not find in the extent of time one people,
one hour, when a conquered unambitious community surpassed the
Victor in comfort, in intelligence, in real enjoyment? It concerns the
weal of mankind that the position be denied. Dies delet commenta
opiniorum, etc.[102]] Whoever was the author of the pleasant biography
of John Horner must have had in his eye the insipid lives & language
of thousands of mankind

> "Little Jack Horner
> Sat in a corner
> Eating his Christmas pie

[101] An apparent inference from Bacon's statement in "Of the Greatness of Kingdoms and Estates": "But, above all, for empire and greatness, it importeth most,
that a nation do profess arms as their principal honour, study, and occupation."

[102] Cicero, *De Natura Deorum*, II, 2, 5. The full and exact quotation is
"Opinionis enim commenta delet dies, naturae iudicia confirmat" — "The years
obliterate the inventions of the imagination, but confirm the judgements of nature."

He put in his thumb
He pulled out a plum
Says What a great man am I!"

[74] When some fifty pages back my communicative mood[n] was on me & I was fain to take captive in print ⟨the⟩ not as before, one or two compassionate eyes whom accident brought to my page but the whole world of hearts I attempted to bespeak some kindness for my fortunes by promising to make the reader acquainted with my friends, my habits & my worldly lot. I frankly told him that I spurned the vanity of external greatness & had no sympathy with the effeminate soul that was cheated by the unmeaning names of Grace & majesty. ⟨That,⟩ ⟨f⟩For me, I had as lief be the Simple Cobler of Agawam [103] as the lineal Bourbon of the house of Capet; and a thousand times rather recieve my immortal life from Sophroniscus [104] the stone-cutter & his plain spouse the midwife so that I should be to future times the godlike mind, the Liberator of the Understanding who sprung from them, — than be any Porphyrogenet of them all. I shall have future occasion to give a reason of my dissent from the universal prejudice to which no man can succumb & be wise. I return to my purpose of describing my connexions. . .

It is my own humor to despise pedigree. I was educated to prize it. The kind Aunt whose cares instructed my youth (& whom may God reward) [75] told me oft the virtues of her & mine ancestors. They have been clergymen for many generations & the piety of all & the eloquence of many is yet praised in the Churches. But the dead sleep in their moonless night; my business is with the living. The Genius that keeps me, to correct the inequalities of my understanding did not make me brother to clods of the same shape & texture as myself but to my Contraries. ↑Thus↓ one[n] of my house ⟨there⟩ is a person of squared & methodical conduct. Another on whose virtues I shall chiefly insist is an accomplished gentleman of a restless worldly ambition who will not let me dream out my fine spun reveries but ever and anon jogs me and laughs aloud at my metaphysical sloth.[105]

[103] Cf. Nathaniel Ward, *The Simple Cobler of Aggawam*, first published in 1647.
[104] The father of Socrates.
[105] Edward Emerson identifies "a person of squared & methodical conduct" as

In the acquaintance I propose to form with my readers I shall insist
on my brother's opinions as often as my own and without knowing
or caring whence spring the differences in character between equals
in ⟨condition &⟩ education or whence falls the seed of virtues & abilities into the child which were not seen in the sire. I shall yet try to
clothe him to the reader's eye in those attractions & dignities wherein
he appears to my own. The day is gone by with me, — such are the
connexions into which Providence has thrown [76] me, — the day has
gone by, when the useless & the frivolous should command my respect. ↑I know very well that↓ the ⁿ great brotherhood of folly in
the world, the idlers, the maniacs, & the fools in society exercise an
influence over the daily course of events as vast and intimate as that
of men of study & soul. Since it is not truth but bread that men seek;
& when bread is ⟨easily⟩ procured, ⟨not so much⟩ the exercise of their
faculties delights them not so much as love & pride it follows that
very different agents enter into the offices of life from those of which
wise men would compose their ideal commonwealths. A fair skin, a
bank note, a fashionable dress, a tapestried parlor, a granite house,
⟨cost⟩ ↑cause↓ more steps and acts each day & keep more eyelids open
by night than all the theories of the French Academy or all the lofty
images of Paradise lost. If one of those silly angels that writers sometimes feign, to help them out of their difficulties, [77] should be
stationed at the corner of Court Street to inquire of every passenger
the business he was upon, no doubt he would marvel much for what
ends this world was made. For, not one in a thousand could inform
him of any mental or moral concern he had in hand. Every one[,]
whatever bait attract him[,] whatsoever associates accompany him[,]
picks out his own course ⟨& lives as if th⟩ forgets in his own engrossing
occupations the infinite multitude that bustles round him. It slips his
memory that there are six hundred times ten hundred thousand persons on the planet; and set aside the score of people with whom he
has habits of ⟨close⟩ familiar connexion & the one or two hundred
more with whom he has occasional intercourse & the rest are of as
little consequence to his life & his death as if they were the tenants
of another globe. No information transmitted from one man to an-

---

William Emerson, "an accomplished gentleman" as Edward Bliss Emerson (*J*, II, 42,
notes 1 and 2).

other can be more interesting than the accurate description of this
little world in which he lies. & I shall deserve the thanks of ⟨my⟩
every knowing [78] reader, if I shall shew him the colour, orbit, &
composition of my particular star.

Jack Cade was not more inclined to proscribe grammar from
his domains than I method from mine. I had a freak three days ago
to describe Tom, Dick, & Harry but my freak is clean gone by. I
have been at an Ordination ⟨&⟩ hearing maxims on eloquence till I
burned to speak. I have been ↑reading↓ Everett's rich strains at
Plymouth,[106] — gazing at the Sun till my eyes are blurred. This
consenting declamation from every quarter on the auspicious promise
of the times; this anxious and affectionate watching of the elder
brothers over the painful birth of new nations in South America,
Asia, Africa, (this "transfusion of youthful blood into aged veins"
in Greece) is an authentic testimony to the reality of the good, or
at least to a degree of it. It is infinitely better than that ill omened cry
of warning & fear that in the Middle age bemoaned an enormous
present degeneracy and the destruction of the world ↑drawing↓ nigh
⟨at hand⟩. Men congregated together in processions, fasts, penances,
[79] miseracordias ⟨to express⟩ ↑impelled by↓ the sympathies of fear.
The tremblers saw nothing in nature but symptoms of decay; nothing
in the heavens but the torches that should light the conflagration.
Nation shouted to nation the melancholy elegy which was the natural
language of depraved manners, deformed institutions, raging vice in
public & in private, when their bitter fruit was apparent in the world
& the eye of conscience was suddenly turned to the hideous ruin. It
is better to go to the house of feasting than to such a house of mourning as that. Sympathy with the wassailers is twice as easy & clever.
But for my part I am sorry that they could not have remembered
the only thing worth remembering in those pallholders, namely, their
devotion. In their tribulation they kneeled to God, and acknowledged
him as the sender of the adversity which overshadowed them. But
⟨in⟩when as the Hebrew bard would say God repented of the evil

---

[106] Emerson may have read Everett's speech in pamphlet form — *An Oration De-*
livered at Plymouth, December 22, 1824 (Boston, 1825). This is listed in his library
catalogue.

which he thought to do, men in their prosperity forget the salutary
lessons of an uniform & ancient experience[,] forget how the ↑heart↓
has always grown giddy & proud & blasphemous with what ought
to make it thankful [80] ⟨I mourn⟩ & now forsooth in congratulating
each other on their prosperity they pronounce themselves *fortunate*;
the advancement of knowledge[,] the acknowledgement of popular
rights *fortunate*; & the settlement at Plymouth (the most ⟨remar⟩
conspicuous interposition of God's Providence in these latter days)
fortunate.* I mourn at the scepticism of prosperity,ⁿ the scepticism
of knowledge, the darkness of light. I love to trace the unambiguous
workings of a greater hand than ours. Poetry had better drink at
immortal fountains. Eloquence is best inspired by an Infinite Cause.
It is always an agreeable picture to the human imagination, ⟨to⟩the
allusions to ⟨a⟩the strength of seeming weakness. No ⟨mind⟩ ↑eye↓
was ever offended at the tiny violet peeping out in fresh bloom on
cold autumnal days when the leaves are fallen & the oak is bare.
⟨naked of his leaves⟩ None are dis⟨pl⟩gusted at the fable of the
↑bending↓ willow which ⟨bent t⟩ outlived the storm that tore down
the monarchs of the forest. Yet such a power of meek sublimity is
detected all along the course of human events, ⟨among men, not of
men⟩ impelling & immortalizing the salutary principles of nature.
Who that witnes[81]¹⁰⁷sed the feeble development of human principles in the morning of Time and compared the weakness of man
with the armed might of beasts ↑the tiger in the wood, the snake
in the grass, the leviathan on shore↓ and contrasted the tenderness of
man, unclothed, unhoused, with the ⟨violent power⟩ ↑stupendous
force↓ of those elements ↑not from which he must escape but↓ with
which he must contend ⟨not for comfort but for life⟩; ⟨looking⟩
aghast whil⟨st⟩e the volcano ⟨vented its ch⟩ ↑illuminated the night
with a↓ cataract⟨s⟩ of fire from which he must shield his hut & his
harvest & the Ocean heaving on high its tempestuous surges which
he must confine to ⟨its vast abyss⟩ ↑their↓ bed ⁿ ("barbarians driving
him to the sea, the sea casts him back on the shore.") or admitting
what can scarce be avoided[,] some garden of Eden, some protected
Paradise, in which his ignorance might be instructed, his strength &

* See Note F. p. 129

¹⁰⁷ "Infant Arts —" is written beneath "The fire" at the bottom of the page.

spirits nourished to /qualify/educate/ him to bear the ills of life, yet who that considered the subtlety & peacefulness of Reason & the sense of Right in relation to the boisterous ungovernable nature of the Passions; the faint articulations of Conscience to the loud command of Interest; & the fatal ease with which men (even when educated & refined) can be brought to hate & destroy each other — who in sight of this would not ⟨devote⟩ ↑compassionate↓ that slender stock in its pitiful beginnings ↑& devote it↓ to a brief & miserable existence[,] to a sure and untimely end? — Yet has that tender unprovided race struggled silently up to maturity & strength. The inundations of the deep have not swallowed it; nay, it has contrived & builded bulwarks to set bounds to the mighty waves. ⟨T⟩ ↑It has planted & peopled a Country abounding in arts & arms lower than the level of the sea.↓ *The fire has not consumed it but is its [82]¹⁰⁸ minister and engine. Earthquake, winter, famine, pestilence, war, tempest, have thinned the numbers but never prostrated the spirit or extirpated the race of men. And whilst speculators consider the steady growth from savage need to the wealth & strength & joys of civilized society & remember the fearful odds against which they have succeeded & the apparent aid of an omnipotent Providence so often ⟨propping⟩ rescuing or fortifying their littleness — in the view of it all, they ⟨s⟩ blot out the sweet harmony & tint of the picture in the mind, ⟨&⟩ thrust in the blank & shapeless agency ⟨energy⟩ of Chance instead, and behold, say they how *fortunate* is man!

Jan. 23, 1825. Poetry, wise women have said, hath a noble inutility & is loved as the flowers of the field, because not the necessaries but the luxuries of life; yet I observe it has sometimes deigned to mix in the most important influences that act on society. The revolutionary spirit in this cold & prudential country it is said was kept alive & energized ↑in 1776↓ by the seasonable aid of patriotic songs [83]¹⁰⁹ and satirical ballads pointing at well-known names & acts. Of Tyrtaeus & his conquering elegies who has not heard? And Greek history has another more ⟨remark⟩ extraordinary instance to

* See Note A p. 129

¹⁰⁸ "Practical poetry" is centered beneath "aid of" at the bottom of the page.
¹⁰⁹ "Keeping" is written beneath "were" at the bottom of the page.

the purpose. When Lycurgus meditated the introduction ⟨o⟩into Sparta of his unprecedented political model, he prevailed on Thales, whom he met as he travelled in Asia Minor to pass to Laconia & ⟨write &⟩ compose poems there of such a character as to prepare the minds of his countrymen for the novel schemes of the Reformer.[110] ↑of *Swift* — see note D.↓ [p.346]

He that searches analogies in arts & life will discern something akin to what in painting is called *keeping,* in many corners where 'tis unlooked for. For tho' mine ear is untaught by nature or art in the mysteries of music yet I have found my guess that such performance was good or bad, on more than one occasion borne out by competent hearers when my only means of forming a judgment was the observation that there were abrupt transitions from [84][111] loud to soft sounds without the just degrees which might be termed the *keeping* of music. A skilful critic will readily see the justice of the application of this figure to any composition also ⟨in⟩whether in verse or prose. (Tho' I admit the propriety of certain exceptions in all the applications of the rule; as when in ⟨Handel's⟩ ↑Haydn's↓ "Creation," an explosion of sound announces the change from darkness to light; or in Dryden's Ode on St Cecilia's day ⟨abrupt⟩ violent transition of subject and manner is permitted.) But I should not have tattled on this topic if I had not conceived it capable of one final application which alone concerns me, viz to ↑human↓ character. I will say then that the influences of sympathy are so strong that man never was or can be insulated in his feelings in the midst of society,[n] can never present an absolute contrast to those who surround him. The reveller who falls into the company of mourners will find himself struck with the sudden infection of sadness and the mourner at a festival will borrow a tinge of cheerfulness. The proud man will [85] be disappointed who expects that ⟨his⟩ the expression of his self conceit in an indifferent crowd will excite anything else than a retorted expression of pride. Much more perfect is this levelling of opposite peculiarities

---

[110] Emerson undoubtedly found the story of Lycurgus in Mitford's *History of Greece,* 1795–1797, I, 311. For the record of his withdrawals of Mitford, see p. 300, n. 64 above.
[111] "Keeping" is written beneath "cheerfulness." at the bottom of the page.

&ⁿ ⟨conciliation⟩ assimilation of feelings in the case of individuals than in that of crowds. Two men who converse together will not only rapidly find an equilibrium of the ↑different↓ passions that may have agitated the bosom of each but they will make their accordance yet more complete (tho' never so much strangers) by feeling round on the ordinary topics of conversation until they are able to find some topic of common interest to both. And ⟨each will⟩ the proportion of his own feelings which each introduces into their intercourse will depend on the intensity of those emotions which each brought to the conference. The ⟨very⟩ angry man will more excite the spirit of his calm friend than he will be pacified by hi⟨m⟩s ↑calmness↓. And wherever there is any considerable force of feeling exhibited it always calls out from those who come into its influence the thoughts & expressions within them most nearly allied to that state of mind * — most agreeable to the expectations that are felt to exist. And hence frequently follows an evil consequence, that men out of a spirit of kindness are betrayed [86] into compliances of speech & action — compliances to the present passion of a companion which they will lament, ↑unavailing regrets, "those spectres whom no exorcism can bind"↓,[112] the moment they are past as ↑profuse↓ sacrifices of the freedom of Opinion and the Consistency of Character to the base fear of offence.

These thoughts ⟨give an insight⟩ furnish adequate explanation of a fact of considerable notoriety & great practical importance. I allude to the different lights in which the same character is presented in the different reports of spectators. For few stay in discussing the character of one they have met to collate the accounts which many render & ↑thence↓ infer carefully what are & what are not the distinctions of his understanding & heart; he is described in the aspect he bore when subjected to such influences as the describer could exert over him and with such exaggeration of those peculiar qualities that endeared him to this person as might be supposed to flow from predominant passion. A man is therefore often surprised to hear his

* There is an exorcism[,] an energy in passion that *commands* the spirit to come out. [R. W. E.]

[112] Byron, *Childe Harold's Pilgrimage*, IV, xxiv.

friend praised by unlike humourists for unlike & opposite & incompatible virtues & to be unable to recognize in the warm eulogy [87] any of those qualities which he is accustomed to regard as the best distinction of his friend. * See Note H. p. 130[.]

Beware then how you put yourself irretrievably into the power of any one who in anxious & affectionate desire to applaud you, actually promulgates an ill fame of you to the community. Be not so mad as to be thoughtless. The past is wholly unalterable. You can't change or efface the least act[,] the least indiscretion from the faithful memory of those who will count it to your cost & who may commit it to every wind that blows. Besides it is inscribed in one Memory which will shew it to you in judgment.

[113] It is observable & passing strange (I may say it in this connexion as well as in any other) to ↑see↓ how short an arm man extends to propel the great revolution of events[,] how a little matter enkindleth a ↑so↓ great fire. 'Tis like the infant's hand which plays with the pin of an engine till he has ignorantly set in motion ⟨powers⟩ wheels that astonish him with their acti⟨f⟩vity & deafen him with their thunder. So do men habitually begin actions which in their influences have immortal duration & immeasurable magnitude. We daily behold consequences proceeding to a greatness ⟨altogether disproportionate to⟩ ↑out of all proportion to↓ the insignificancy of the things that [88] gave them birth. Kings & Counsellors whom Oceans part will league together in the prosecution of magnificent schemes which after a parade of embassies & panegyric that send its fame everywhere ends in smoke. At the same moment in an obscure corner, a peasant[,] a beggar raises his finger from the dust, or in the train of thoughts an idea darts into his soul, which action or thought is the parent impulse which numbers ages & nations among its coadjutors & ⟨the⟩ all the after history of mankind ⟨i⟩as its effect. And no man can reach that foresight which shall say to this event, prosper, and to another, go in vain. You cannot discriminate the seed that shall rot in the soil from that which shall multiply ↑itself↓ a thousand ⟨times⟩ ↑fold↓. ⟨If⟩ No necessary genius is inherited by the statesman's or

[113] From "It" to "thousand ⟨times⟩ ↑fold↓." is struck through by single diagonal lines here and on p. [88], probably to indicate use. (The line was inadvertently extended to "the statesman's" in the next sentence.)

the poet's child. No prophetic light is shed over the infant's head who is to /touch/move/thrill/ the hearts or educate the understandings or point the swords of millions to separate between him & vulgar cradles. The present moment is in your power; but the past is unalterable; the future is inscrutable. Nor do you know when you give utterance to an idle or an evil word whether its poison is [89] to be lost in instant oblivion, or whether it is to be the accursed occasion of prodigious & eternal calamities. (I have not thought proper to fortify this talk by its ordinary examples. Good instances of great events flowing from petty causes may be found catalogued in Byron's Preface to Marino Faliero. But I had in my eye still slighter & subtler causes than the spilling water on a favourite's gown. Those who know how minds are affected will see that a word, a tone, a smile, or less, may be one event in a train that ends in prodigies.) Judge not therefore by the outward appearance.

Perhaps all morality is only well defended on grounds of Expediency. To beings who could only smell, the finding that certain smells tho' grateful to the sense were in the end pernicious to their noses it would soon become the point of virtue to ⟨a⟩overcome the temptation to use such odours. The strong-points of barbarian virtue were ever the useful. As hospitality & valor. The nature of man was the preacher who made known their rights & interest & obligations. And before philosophy was born and where scripture & tradition were dumb as you wandered in barbarous tracts of the Peloponnessus you might meet rude pillars [90][114] of stone which registered the infamy of a breach of faith & denounced the vengeance of the Gods on the perfidy of Kings. ↑(So also Pisistratus inscribed moral maxims on Stones by public ways)↓.[115] (See Mitford Vol. I p. 371 — de Arcadia — slaying King Art [Aristocrates]) [116]

↑Note L↓ [p. 349] [117]

[114] "SOLITUDE" is written beneath "barren meditations" at the bottom of the page.

[115] Emerson wrote the additional statement in the bottom margin of p. [89], apparently because there was no room at the point where it logically belonged.

[116] The reference is to the story of the traitor Aristocrates, slain by his people, the Arcadians, in William Mitford's *History of Greece*, 1795–1797.

[117] Emerson wrote "See Note L" in the bottom margin but later inserted the reference in the text.

JAN. 29, 1825. Roxbury

*They will make fair theories concerning the conduct of life
& by putting them familiarly into men's mouths you are likely to
take what is plausible for what is true. But if you so dislike to lead,
and love to be guided, as that you will not use that keen understanding
God gave you for this very purpose, that you might steer clear of
rocks & quicksands, you may as well go sleep and spend it in dreams.
You will be told that it is wholly a fanciful scheme, such as boys all
have in their turn and all sound minds outgrow — thus to talk of
divorcing yourself from Society and making yourself a haughty alien
from flesh & blood & its vulgar concerns in the conceit of giving your
life to books, prayers, & barren meditations and when [91][118] you
have been taunted as a friar grave sophists will accost you and tell
you under the sanction of great names that man is born by the side
of his father and *therefore* should remain a social being; [n] that it is
deducible from the laws of political economy that we should be social
and that many of the human faculties have no use in solitude which
i⟨t⟩s the strong voice of nature pronouncing you fool. They will tell
you that **Newton & Bacon & Shakspeare were nursed & bred in
crowds. Nay, veteran reasoners may go a step or two beyond and
tell you in a learned whisper that Religion has been mere Reason
of State ever since Numa's time, and always will be; that tho' men
of sense & spirit are seen in *public* worship 'tis merely as they countenance the Constables and that by no accident did any eye in earth
or Heaven ever detect them in *private*. So 'twere better you did not
set your judgment against the whole world's, and so ⟨lose⟩ ruin a
promising youth by falling into disesteem & opprobrium. Against this
consenting witness, or more, against this lofty derision what stoic
can stand? You judge it best to leave the ground you took and rather
than [92][119] be persuaded twice, O son of the ill advised Adam,
pluck the fruit that others have plucked and rush into the great
↑foolish↓ procession that goes thro' the world drawing all men into

*Take Galat. I C. 15, 16, 17 verses.
　**By putting in these instances you sacrifice your cause, my
muse. These cultivated the solitude I treat[.]

[118] "SOLITUDE" is centered at the bottom of the page.
[119] "SOLITUDE" is written beneath "has mistaken" at the bottom of the page.

its train & none know whence they come or where they go. "O for
a warning voice which He that saw the Apocalypse heard cry in
heaven aloud[,] woe to the inhabitants of Earth."[120] And you too
will enter[,] you who should have been prophet & rescuer to a thousand of your brothers. You will submit that hopeful character to
these depraved influences & be ground down to the same base level.
Meantime tho' you have let it go, there *is* a good, solid and eternal[,]
in casting off the dishonest fetters of opinion and nursing your solitary faculties into a self existence ⟨which may give⟩ ↑so that↓ your
thoughts & action shall be in a degree your own. I commend no
absurd sacrifices. I praise no wolfish misanthropy that retreats to
thickets from cheerful towns and scrapes the ground for roots and
acorns either ⟨from⟩ ↑out of a↓ grovelling soul or a hunger for glory
that has mistaken grimace for phi[93][121]losophy. It is not the solitude
of place but the solitude of soul which ⟨I⟩ is so inestimable to us.
It is the vice of society that you are leaning on the deceptive judgements of other men, that you are *flattered* by interest or pity, that in
the great press of conflicting & conspiring opinions your own mind
has no room to expand itself to those dimensions which its divine
Architect designed. It is not that you should avoid men, but that
you should not be hurt by them. Not to break the brotherhood of
the race but to enable you to contribute to it a greater good. ⟨"⟩It is
solitude or a divesting yourself from the inordinate (& pernicious)
influences of others that must "teach you how to die. It hath no
flatterer⟨e⟩s⟨rs⟩. Vanity can give no hollow aid; man with his God
must strive."[122] If this be thought an appeal to the ⟨ro⟩imagination
partaking of the romantic & chivalrous spirit that prompts boys to
sally into the meadows on May day, I am content it be disregarded.
⟨I⟩ ↑You should↓ despise the understanding that can be cheated into
sedulous pursuit of wrong by the frolicsome tricks of the fancy. But
I appeal to your coldest maturest judgments whether you [94][123]
have not often been, whether you are not daily a sufferer from bad

[120] From Milton, *Paradise Lost*, IV, 1-2, 5.
[121] "SOLITUDE" is written beneath "maturest judgments" at the bottom of the
page.
[122] From Byron, *Childe Harold's Pilgrimage*, IV, xxxiii.
[123] "SOLITUDE" is written beneath "more careless of" at the bottom of the
page.

influences of Society. In all your intercourse with it, has it never been false to your cause? never once seduced you from what your reason approved? ↑Reduce the speculation to the practical history of every day & I suppose↓ youⁿ eat & drink for the sustentation of nature, & never (from ill example) for gluttonous delight. You buy & sell, to surround with comforts those whom you love and honour & to acquire for yourself only more refined means of education & enjoyment[,] only more extended ⟨means of⟩ usefulness, only as one experiment of the ↑ever-↓active mind in its study of the nature of itself & outward things; and ⟨so purely benevolent is the⟩ so *reluctantly* is this profane turmoil of the world entered by your ⟨heavenly⟩ heavenborn & heavenward mind, & so purely is the pursuit begotten of curiosity & benevolence, that no sinister feelings are ever known to violate its angelic serenity; you are observed as you grow rich, ⟨to⟩ in the same or a faster proportion to become ben⟨f⟩eficent & wise, more & more careless of perishable vanities, [95][124] more and more enamoured of your intellectual being, inquisitive of the nature of man, inquisitive of the revelations of God. It is the rich conspicuously who in the martyrdom of self, in the incessant study of *other's* good, in *charity*, to *men*, in habitual intercourse with the Divinity hold themselves ever in the perfectest preparation which imperfect mortals can ⟨acquire⟩ ↑make↓[,] impatient to dissolve this wretched clay and enter on the world of spirits? And this is one of the specious defences of the superior expediency of social nurture! ↑And solitude would be detriment & shipwreck of the soul whilst↓ theseⁿ are ⟨the⟩ virtues incident to the cares of commerce and affairs ⟨and it must be clear how plainly love of money, love of pleasure, extortion, avarice,[125] and purse pride are the vices of some other altogether separate class of the community⟩ and who does not see that lovers of money, winebibbers, /lovers/seekers/ of low pleasure, extortioners, misers, & the *purseproud* are sinners in some other and quite different class of men. I shall be excused if I persist in applying to ⟨the⟩ other occupations of social life, the same indirect style of rebuke. In society ⟨it is reckoned a chief advantage⟩ 'tis enumerated among its first essential advantages that an open intercourse of conversation is ever acting on

[124] "SOLITUDE" is written beneath "on men's" at the bottom of the page.
[125] The word "avarice" is encircled, perhaps for revision.

men's minds. Solitude is [96]¹²⁶ travestied. Men scoff at solitude as
dumpish & moping[,] as selfishly ⟨conv⟩ exhausting in dumb contemplation the powers ⟨that⟩ ↑by which men↓ in social life ↑mutually↓
encourage and instruct each other. And so you talk in society, at your
table and to all that throng whom you daily meet. And is that conversation inspired ⟨ever⟩ ↑invariably↓ by the desire of knowledge? Is
it guarded and sweetened by kindness? Do the studies of day & night
point to it? and from its impulse do all the moral and intellectual
eras of your advancing /greatness/life/ date themselves? Speech,
said a wise Athenian, ⟨h⟩ is like cloth of Arras opened and its in-
wrought embroidery displayed which in the mind are folded together
& shut up.¹²⁷ And did the Athenian only describe the grave & instructive intercourse that fills ⟨the⟩ so many hours of our days? ⁿ You
are convinced ⟨of⟩ the important service it renders compensates for
the time it consumes. ↑You are quite sure↓ it ⁿ never departs /a/one/
moment from its dignity or wit to ⟨fo⟩ unprofitable chat and buffoon-
ery, much less to flippant slander & backbiting and least of all to be
the organ of base ⟨vile⟩ passions, obscenity, blasphemy, or lyes. ↑No↓[,]
God forbid. In all places and times among the small and great[,] in
confidential ⟨co⟩ whispers and in salutations in the market place —
conversation — this grand element of social life, is made by you and
by most men to [97]¹²⁸ contribute to the vast moral ⟨ends⟩ purposes
of life? Surely then the sin we have heard lamented, of time
/squandered/murdered/ in what is termed small talk, or abused in
bickering or calumny can be no sin of social life. On the contrary,
blessed are they who abide under this perpetual and benignant stim-
ulus to action, and he only of all men most miserable who secludes
himself from it. But it is time to conclude this account whose irony
it may be is too violent for the desk[.]

It cannot be ⟨disguis⟩ concealed[,] it is too gross to be disguised
that in that counterpoise of good & evil which Providence has instituted in all the relations of man a great amount of moral evil accrues
to individuals ↑out of their union↓ which is ↑almost↓ inseparable from
the high advantages of social life. It is palpable that whilst men be-

---

¹²⁶ "SOLITUDE" is written beneath "made by you" at the bottom of the page.
¹²⁷ Paraphrased from Bacon, "Of Friendship."
¹²⁸ "SOLITUDE" is written beneath "the strong" at the bottom of the page.

wail the shortness of time, they do daily swerve aside from the labours
for which it was lent ⟨bestowed⟩ against their better convictions under
the shallow but availing consolation that what they do, they do ⟨in
company⟩ in a crowd and that others have done worse. It is clear
that the attention of men in society does not rest where it ought to
rest[,] that it is withdrawn from the deepseated sentiments and
sources of action to ⟨the⟩ superficial modes & customs, from the strong
self application of the notions [98] of personal accountability & ↑per-
sonal↓ immortality to ⟨a regard⟩ an idolatrous re⟨spect⟩↑gard↓ for
forms and opinions, to a slavish love of bodily pleasure, in the pursuit of which the only things worth living for diminish in our distempered judgments till they wear a fantastic visionary form and at
last cease to disturb our fatal lethargy. It is also apparent that it
requires much more selfdenial than most men are masters of to resist
the strong contagion of example in practising ⟨the⟩ what the understanding enjoins in enforcing ↑on↓ themselves the salutary discipline
of frequent silence, of invariable temperance, of self-withdrawal
from free & jocund society, of stated abstractions of the soul from
earthly converse to her sublimer soarings from her native to her
adoptive land[,] to the care of her active duties to men & of prayers
to the Father of Spirits. Hence is argued the reasonableness of Solitude as a part of ⟨th⟩ every man's education to whom his mind & his
destiny are dear. Because it gives a breathing space, a leisure, out of
the influence of ⟨the⟩ dazzling delusions, the pomp, & vanity of this
wicked world; [n] because ⟨from⟩ by removing these outer attractions
it sends the soul back on himself —— X X X The Parnassian nag I
rode I percieve has thrown me, and I have been bestriding a hobby.
It was my design & must be the topic of a [99] true discussion of
this nature to commend Study, meditation, the preference of moral
& intellectual things to appetites for outward things; and as far as
Solitude can be a generalization of these things it may be admitted
as the cardinal topic. But in this light, 'twere foolish to admit Newton,
Bacon, & Shakspear as counter instances or ↑at all↓ as exceptions. For
all that made them great, is my very argument, the very stuff I praise;
and all that subtracted from their respective worth is the very object
of my invective, sarcasm, admonition, rebuke, irony, satire, derision,
assault. O ye words, I have no breath to utter 'em. The philanthropist

329

will perchance throw in the teeth of the anchorite the verse of Milton

> The Mind is its own place & in itself
> Can make a Heaven of hell a hell of heaven
> What matter where if I be still the same?
> [Milton, *Paradise Lost*, I, 254–256]

I only propose to let that mind be unswaddled[,] unchained and there is no danger of any excess in the practice of this doctrine "so forcible within our hearts we feel ⁿ The bond of nature draw us to our own." [129] Nature vindicates her rights & society is more delicious to the occasional absentee. Besides tho' I recommend the wilderness I only enforce the doctrine of stated or frequent and habitual closetings. v. p. 102.

> Men may be read as well as books too much.
> [Pope, *Moral Essays*, I, 10]

[100] Old in sin[,] every honest and natural virtue being festered and eaten out[,] you keep a fair outside & go down reputably to the dust. Your eyes are decently closed by your kindred. "They ⟨m⟩Maintain a mourning ostentation, And on your family's old monument, ⟨h⟩Hang mournful epitaphs, and do all rites ⟨t⟩That appertain unto a burial." [130] But here the curtain falls, & hides from the eyes of mortals ⟨the subsequent⟩ the unutterable history of the following hour.

⟨Jan⟩ ↑Feb↓ not Jan for he is gone over the flood.

February 6. And if Henry Clay is dead, another great spirit has gone like Byron's over the unvoyageable gulf, another contemner of moral distinctions to the award of the Divinity who set those distinctions, and not the less created the genius which defied them. Man feels a property in the eloquence as in the poetry of his fellows or rather owes ⟨them⟩ allegiance ⟨and exercise⟩ to those who exercise lordship over ⟨their⟩ ↑this↓ noblest & dearest capacities & so the public loss is mourned as when a sovereign dies. But it is a paradox that is again ↑& again↓ forced on ⟨th⟩ our wonder how those who act ⟨p⟩ a part so important in its influences on the world should be permitted to give their genius to the worst passions, to cast the children's bread

[129] Slightly altered from Milton, *Paradise Lost*, IX, 955–956.
[130] Shakespeare, *Much Ado about Nothing*, IV, i, 206–209. "They" is added by Emerson.

before the dogs. That [101] ancient doctrine that a human soul is but a larger or less emanation from the Infinite Soul is so agreeable to our imagination that something like this has always been a cherished part of popular belief. He who brings home to his daily convictions the events of life as the functions of Providence and men tho' scornful & proud as limitary beings, — in each extraordinary effort of human intelligence reverently sees a new bestowment of high & gorgeous revelations of an unutterable agency he sees that what the true poet miscalls his Muse is the secret suggestion of an illimitable mind; that the torrent of eloquence which prostrates the understanding of a multitude; the thought, the ex[c]lamation, that strikes with ↑sudden↓ ghastliness an armed throng & casts down with invincible persuasion the sword & lance is the ⟨dread⟩ inspiration of the dread Spirit who *made* the *clay creatures on whom he acts.* Man is but the poor organ thro' which the breath of Him is blown.[131] A pipe on which stops are sounded of strange music. A ⁿ torch not lighted for itself. Yet these, such is the mystery of Free Will, turn on ↑the↓ hand that feeds them, dishonour the energy that inspires them, blaspheme the spirit that ↑in them↓ blasphemes. Byron, who partook richest of Divinity, foully ridicules the virtues practised to obey ⟨h⟩Him. *Clay* scorns the laws which bind all God's creatures.

Feb. 8. He is not dead. The story of the duel was false. Alas! for mine ejaculations.[132] ——

[102]   Continued from p. 99.

Let it be understood that I have no ambition to broach new doctrines by preaching up a Crusade against Society. I have not created an imaginary nor detected a recondite evil. It is an old, it is a *historical* regret of thinking men to which I give utterance, when I lament the unavoidable mischiefs of social life. As far as history reaches, ↑deep

---

[131] Cf. Emerson's quotation from George Bancroft on p. 221 above.

[132] On January 28, an anonymous Jacksonian had attacked Clay in *The Columbia Observer*. In *The National Intelligencer* of January 31 Clay denounced his unknown detractor as a "calumniator, a dastard and a liar" and made the affair a matter of honor. On February 3, George Kremer, an eccentric who went about in a bearskin, acknowledged authorship of the attack but backed away from the threat of a duel. Nevertheless the New York papers soon printed the dreadful news that Kremer had killed Clay in a duel. What was probably a newspaper hoax was revealed in *The National Intelligencer* on February 8.

into antiquity↓ the curious student can recognize the operations of this feeling. It weighed heavily on ⟨the⟩ ↑many↓ minds, and oft wrought out mistaken attempts at deliverance. In India, the Gymnosophist. In Magna Graecia, the ⟨Scholars of⟩ wise Pythagoras.[n] In Britain the Druid[.] In the Christian age an army of hermits and subsequently the Monasteries — all evidently grew out of this same sentiment when it recurred with unusual force to any prepared mind. But all these are signal examples of ⟨injudicious⟩ ↑overweening↓ zeal — which led to an error ↑quite↓ as fatal as that which it sought to shun. The sottish world was ever cheated into some extravagancies in the pursuit of novel hypotheses. But the great minds who reduced to practice in other ages the theories I treat, the true evangelists of this obliterated ⟨testament⟩ law were those to whose pious history fame & fate were [103] partial, were those great lights whose pure splendours are continually attracting our eyes from their distant eminences.

(Roxbury)
[February 8,] 1825. It is the evening of February eighth,[n] which was never renowned that I know. But be that as it may 'tis the last evening I spend in Canterbury. I go to my College Chamber tomorrow a little changed for better or worse since I left it in 1821. I have learned a few more names & dates, ⟨a fe⟩ additional facility of expression, the gage of my own ignorance, its sounding places, & bottomless depths. I have inverted my inquiries two or three times on myself, and have learned what a sinner & a saint I am. My cardinal vice of intellectual dissipation — sinful strolling from book to book[,] ⟨&⟩ ↑from↓ care to idleness[,] is ⟨a⟩ my cardinal vice still; is ⟨th⟩ a malady that belongs to the Chapter of Incurables. ⟨I have found⟩ I have written two or three hundred pages that will be of use to me. I have earned two or three thousand dollars which have paid my debts & obligated my neighbours so that I thank Heaven I can say none of my house is the worse for me. In short, I have grown older and have seen something of the vanity & something of the value of existence[,] have seen what shallow things men are & how independent of external circumstances may be the states of mind called good & ill.

332

[104][133] Cambridge, Feb. 1825. Today I went to Quincy to see its Patriarch. The old President sat in a large stuffed arm chair, dressed in a blue coat, black small-clothes, white stockings. And a cotton cap covered his bald head. When we were introduced he held out his hand & welcomed us. We told him he must let us come & join our Congratulations to those of the nation on the happiness of his house. He thanked us & said "I am rejoiced because the nation is happy. The time of gratulations & congratulations is ⟨ov⟩ nearly over with me. I am astonished that I have lived to see & know of this event. I have lived now nearly a century (He will be ninety next October) a long harrassed & distracted life." I said, the world thinks a good deal of joy has been mixed with it. "The world does not know" he said "how much toil anxiety & sorrow I have suffered." I asked if ⟨he⟩ Mr Adams' letter of acceptance had been read to him. Yes, he said, and then added, My son has more political prudence than any man that I know who has existed in my time. He never was put off his guard. And I hope he will continue so. But what effect age may [105] work in diminishing the power of his mind, I do not know; it[n] has been very much on the stretch ever since he was born. He has always been laborious child & man from infancy. When Mr J. Q. Adams' age was mentioned he said he was 58, or would be in July, and mentioned that all the Presidents were of the same age. Gen Washington was about 58, and I was about 58, ↑& Mr Jefferson↓ & Mr Madison, & Mr Monroe. ⟨When⟩ ⟨w⟩We asked him when he expected to see Mr Adams, he said, "never; Mr Adams will not come to Quincy but to my funeral. It would be a great satisfaction to me to see him but I don't wish him to come on my account." He spoke of Mr Lechmere whom he well remembered "to come down daily at ⟨the⟩ ⟨a⟩ great age to walk in the old townhouse, and I wish I could walk as well as he. He was collector of the customs for many years under the royal government." Edward said, "I suppose, Sir, you wouldn't have taken his place even to walk as well as he." "No,"

---

[133] This and pp. [105], [106], and [107] as far as "the late Plymouth oration" are struck through with single or double vertical lines to indicate use. In *J*, II, 56, Edward Emerson omitted the passage on the visit to Adams because "Mr. Emerson printed it in full" in "Old Age," *Society and Solitude* (*W*, VII, 332–335). The passage was considerably improved in the printed version, and the sentences on p. [107], "We were told . . . to excel." " do not appear in the essay.

he said, "*that* was not what I wanted." He talked of ⟨w⟩Whit[e]field
and remembered when he was Freshman in College to have come in
to the Old South (I think) to hear him, but could not get in; he
however saw him thro' a window & distinctly heard all. "He had a
voice ⟨wh⟩ such as I never heard before or since. He *cast* it out so
that you might hear it at the meeting house (pointing towards
Quincy Meeting h[ou]s[e]) and had the grace of [106] a dancing
master, of an actor of plays. His voice & his manner helped him more
than his sermons. I went with Jonathan Sewall." And you were
pleased with him, Sir? "Pleased, I was delighted beyond measure."
We asked if at Whit[e]field's return the same popularity continued,
"Not the same fury," he said, "not the same wild enthusiasm, as
before but a greater esteem as he became more known. He did not
terrify, ⟨he said⟩ but was ⟨mor⟩ admired."

We spent about an hour in his room. He talks very distinctly
for so old a man — enters bravely into long sentences which are interrupted by want of breath but carries them invariably to a conclusion without every correcting a word. ⟨We wer⟩ He spoke of the new
novels of Cooper, & Peep at the Pilgrims & Saratoga with approbation & named with accuracy the characters in them. He likes to have
⟨rea⟩ a person always reading to him ⟨&⟩ or company talking in his
chamber,[n] and is better the next day we were told after having visi-
tors in his chamber from morning till night. He received a premature
report of his son's election on Sunday afternoon without any excitement and calmly told the reporter ⟨it⟩ he had been hoaxed for ⟨the⟩
it was not yet time for any news to arrive. The informer however
[107] something damped in his heart insisted on repairing to the
Meetinghouse & the Congregation in the midst of service were so
overjoyed that they rose in their seats & cheered thrice. Mr. Whitney
dismissed them immediately. We were told that his son Judge Adams
can at any time excite him in a moment to great indignation. He mentioned to us that he had spoken to the President of the late Plymouth
oration & said Mr Everett had ambition enough to publish it doubtless. The old gentleman exclaimed with great vehemence "I would
to God there ↑were↓ more ambition in the country, ambition of that
laudable kind to excel."

Cambridge, Feb. 1825.

I have a mind to try if my muse hath not lost a whit of her nim-
bleness; if the damps of this new region[,] its prescribed & formal
study haven't chilled a little her prurient & prolific heat. I would
boldly take down a topic and enter the lists were there not reason to remember & fear the old orthodoxy concerning fortune (& I think I have
heard it whispered of fairies too & of Wit even) that when the hu-
moursome jealous Coquet is presumed on she withdraweth straight
her smiles & leaves the [108] audacious votary to curse his sel⟨c⟩fcon-
ceit in the dark. Nevertheless I am fain to solicit of the Muse some
revelations on the matter of Solitude on which heretofore we held
some sweet counsel together. I am anxious to gage the doctrine that
was propounded, doubtless, o Muse! with oracular darkness. And I
would gladly know how far the same should be accounted grave doctrine & how far fanciful. It is submitted whether a matter like this
intimately concerning the education & daily habits of men be visionary & unfit for discussion & whether a decision on the expediency of
seclusion, *that is,* by no means absolute & perpetual but habitual &
stated seclusion, a decision fortified by the precept & the practice of the
wisest men, strongly confirmed by the observations we can make on
the present condition of society & impugned by the uniform immemorial habits of the majority of men — whether this decision be unsubstantial & false.

[109] I propose to sketch a sermon soon or late on the daily
habits, the outward observances of life, on the moral of manners. I
will praise temperance in meats & drinks, early rising, cautious conversation, the hour perhaps & the frequency of prayer, etc. It is hard
to preserve bold & true conceptions of this life as altogether a relative
condition, as a mere school, entry, introduction to the Enlarged life.
But assuredly things of such ⟨daily⟩ hourly recurrence & things woven
by their nature into the texture of moral ⟨events⟩ condition, deserve
exact consideration. I insert here that there seems to me a fine moral
in the passage of the ancient hist[orian]. who says the Lacedemonians
were in the habit of rising up very early to pray[,] that so they might
be beforehand of their enemies & preoccupy the ear of the Gods.[134]

[134] The ancient historian is Xenophon, but Emerson found the story in Hume,

335

Yes but the world will be sadly changed to you when these novelties have grown old & dull & disgusting to you. When there are no more praises to be earned, no more offices for you to discharge, no more books for you to read;[n] when your eyes are quenched & the Eye of your understanding is dim; when your heart has ⟨felt the ice of age⟩ ↑⟨gr⟩ become cold↓ & the hearts of your friends are grown cold toward *you*, when the obstruction & decay that attend your spirit down to the dust scare men with the suggestion that [110] no ↑morn[in]g of↓ resurrection will awaken it again[,] will that dismal season be cheered by the memory of a brilliant & voluptuous imagination[,] of profuse leisure dedicated to amusement &c.[?] Alas I fear these accusing recollections will cleave unto you living, will cleave unto you dying, will not be left behind with [the] carcass they pampered in its hour of bloom.

> "But to sit idle on the household hearth
> A burdenous drone; to visitants a gaze
> Or pitied object"   [Milton,] Samson Agonistes [ll. 566–568]

> "Short is the date of all immoderate fame
> It looks as heav'n our ruin had designed
> And durst not trust thy fortune & thy mind"
>   [Dryden,] Abs[olom] & Ach[itophel, ll. 847–849]
>   [To Ossory] [135]

> "Dim as the borrowed beams of moon & stars
> To lonely weary wandering travellers
> Is reason to the soul; & as on high
> Those rolling fires discover but the sky
> Not light us here; so reason's glimmering ray
> Was lent not to assure our doubtful way
> But guide us upward to a better day.
> And as," &c [Dryden,] Religio Laici [ll. 1–8]. ⟨Religio⟩

> "This only doctrine does our lusts oppose   (Bible)
> *Unfed by nature's soil in wh. it grows.*" Reli La. [ll. 158–159]

Philosophical Essays, 1817, II, 382. Significantly, Hume was using the practice as one of many examples of absurdity in the worship of polytheists.

[135] The phrase appears in the margin beside a bracket enclosing the quotation. Ossory was the eldest son of the Duke of Ormond.

> "Scripture was scarce & as the market went
> Poor laymen took salvation on content
> As needy men take money good or bad
> God's word they had not but the pr⟨e⟩iests they had"
>   Rel. La. [ll. 380–383]

As much as you men of the world acknowledge good & noble is all derived from religion; from those principles of nature to which I appeal, as your honor, &c [R.W.E.] —

[111] What have we to say worth the attention of men when we put on in these latter days the profession of the sacred teacher? We remember with pride & gratitude the venerable men who in all past time have instructed humanity from those oriental sages who gave the first direction to the understanding down to the accomplished orators whose accents yet ring in the ear of this generation. And have they left anything unsaid? Is this a science of discoveries? What contribution in your hand[,] what hope have you in heart? Theology which in pagan lands was only one part of Ethics the revolution of events has enriched with noble parts. Theology, since Revelation, has become the great science of man[,] the only object here known worth the sole engagement of the intellect. Ethics is a secondary — a branch of this first philosophy. A correspondent change affects its professors. To be the curious speculators on the contradictory phenomena of thought, to be the humble advisers to courses of conduct least dark where all was doubtful [—] this was the ambition[,] this the merit of the heathen sages. The ordinations of the Divinity respecting this world have put that office on different foundations. Those men who assume the charge of directing the devotions & duties of society are now the immediate representatives of the Deity, the organs thro' which he speaks to his creatures, the vicars, as the ambitious have said with a profane secular import of God. Ah! what? Has Nature broke her marble silence?

[112] Has the spell of weary centuries dissolved & the Deity disclosed himself to men? Has the most high opened his sublime abodes & come down on his sorrowing children with healing in his wings? Speak! How came he? What is he? what said he? & what is to come? Here we sat in the world, waiting; admiring what could be the design of the appointments we seemed to be fulfilling, enduring as we could

337

the pangs we met, desiring joy, but embracing evil with heavy hearts, sickening and alway[s] dying, to the eve of our short day, which went down in darkness and especially moved with a sad curiosity & foreboding as to what should befal us after death. We saw in the world that some Mind has wrought or now perchance consummated its active will with ⟨transcendant⟩ inexpressible might & we waited when at last he should break out into audible declaration of himself to our ears. But in vain we waited who died before the sight. Say what he ⟨s⟩hath said. This is the language the eager Stoic should utter to us when restored to consciousness.

[113] There can be no doubt that ⟨as⟩ in the disposition of human affairs which Providence has made, there are great natural advantages proper to the Social state. But it is equally conformable to divine dispensations that these should be blended & balanced by disadvantages. It is the part of wisdom therefore to chuse that safe middle path which shall avail itself of the good & escape as much of the evil as is possible. It is true of all our affections that they may be indulged to the point of weakness. In our ⟨cautious recommendation of seclusion⟩ ↑animadversions upon soc[iety]↓ therefore we are to be understood only as combating this weakness. The attractions of Society are very great, because whilst they are urged by the strong voice of nature they are ↑also↓ seconded by our observation of their innocent & beneficial tendencies; no ⁿ man can examine the connexions & dependencies of men in society without being struck with the harmony & value of the whole design.

That infinity of relationships which spring from parentage[,] from marriage is a singular advantage of the present order of things. If the world should be conceived to be peopled in any other ⟨manner⟩ mode the innumerable connexions that tie society together being taken away would take ⟨aw⟩ off a mighty check from the bad passions. It is pleasant to see in society two strangers introduced. True to the social principles of nature they begin to feel round on the ordinary topics of conversation until they find where they can nearest meet & sympathize. And you can hardly make two countrymen ac[114]quainted who will not presently find some name with which both are ⟨acquainted⟩ connected by nature, affection or acquaintance; so far do the roots of families extend.

It is an ignoble & ungrateful part in a man who rightly considers the goods of existence to submit to be only born to this heritage, to be passive recipient ⟨to⟩ of life or to lay a light & sloven hand on the generous bequests of Nature & Providence. It manifests a noble spirit in harmony with the liberal Giver to come eagerly ↑in↓to the enjoyment to which we are invited instead of sculking to a mouthful in the dark. We would not be the parasites of God's bounty[,] hungry for the good but too mean & selfish to be capable of gratitude. We would rather be forgiven for a noble daring, for an ambition to see all, to know all, to use all. We would fain try the virtue of these powers, we would grapple with what is great, we would follow what flies, take hold on truth & imprison pleasure. We would go boldly on our adventurous quest & risque something to acquire a light on the nature, extent, & end of our condition. In short we would feel that it is action which exalts our nature above the slothful clod.

There is reason in Action. The good that is borne to us is not sharpened by our sluggishness. There is no indication in the fearful whirl of the rolling [115] Universe that we should squat down unprofitable quietists in its lap. Besides[,] the strong presumption there is that by pushing these energies to their utmost we may even *deserve* something, may earn *merit*, instead of being a charge on the Universe.

> Hae ye seen the caterpillar
>   Foully warking in his nest
>   'Tis the puir man getting siller —
>   Without cleanness without rest
>
> Hae ye seen the butterfly
>   In brae claithing drest
>   'Tis the puir man gotten rich
>   With rings & painted vest
>
> The puir man crawls in web of rags
>   And sair beset with woes
>   But when he flees on riches' wings
>   He laugheth at his foes

339

[116] Jan. 8, 182⟨5⟩6.[136]

I come with mended eyes to my ancient friend & consoler. Has the interval of silence made the writer wiser? Does his mind teem with well weighed judgments? The moral & intellectual universe has not halted because the eye of the observer was closed. Compensation has been woven to want, loss to gain, good to evil, & good to good, with the same industry, & the same concealment of an intelligent Cause. And in my joy to write & read again I will not pester my imagination with what is done unseen, with the burden that is put in the contrary scale, with the sowing of the death-seed in the place of the nettle that was rooted up. I am a more cheerful philosopher and am rather anxious to thank Oromasdes ⟨for his boon⟩ than ↑to fear↓ Ahriman.

Since I wrote before, I know something more of the grounds of hope & fear for what is to come. But if my knowledge is greater so is my courage. I know that I *know* next to nothing [117] but I know ↑too↓ that the amount of probabilities is vast, both in mind & in morals. It is not certain that God exists but that he does not is a most bewildering & improbable ⟨& wild⟩ chimera.

I rejoice that I live when the world is so old. There is the same difference between living with Adam & living with me as in going into a new house unfinished ↑damp↓ & empty, & going into ⟨an old⟩ ↑a long occupied↓ house where the time & taste of its inhabitants has accumulated a thousand ↑useful↓ contrivances ⟨for comfort⟩ has furnished ⟨its⟩ ↑the↓ chambers ⟨has⟩ ↑stocked the cellars and↓ filled ⟨its⟩ ↑the↓ library. In the ⟨old⟩ ⟨h⟩new house every comer must do all for himself. In the old mansion there ⟨is⟩are ⟨a⟩ butlers, cooks, grooms, & valets. In the new house all must work & work with the hands. In the old one there are poets who sing, actors who play & ladies who dress & smile. O ye lovers of the past, judge between my houses. I would not be elsewhere than I am.

[118][137] All things are double one against another said Solo-

[136] During the long interval since the preceding entry, Emerson had suffered severe eye trouble. Although he appears to have continued light study at the Harvard Divinity School, he was unable to read very much. From September to the end of December, 1825, he maintained a boys' school in Chelmsford. Shortly before this entry, he had opened another boys' school in Roxbury.

[137] "COMPENSATION" is centered beneath "rank earth" at the bottom of the

mon.[138] The whole of what we know is a system of Compensations.
Every defect in one manner is made up in another. Every suffering
is rewarded; every[n] sacrifice is made up; every debt is paid.

The history of retributions is a strange & awful story; it will
confirm the faith that wavers & more than any other moral feature is
perhaps susceptible of examination & analysis & more than any other
↑fit↓ to establish the doctrine of Divine Providence[.]

In the outset it must be conceded to me that wealth, aye, and
honor are not happiness. For I will not undertake to prove that the
seed of the righteous never begged bread. Neither will I deny that
riches can⟨not⟩ add to the comfort of a ↑⟨healthy⟩↓ man which I consider undeniable. But it is as undeniable that there are ⟨d⟩ stamped
damned victims going up & down in the world whom no external
splendour can adorn, no comfort can warm, no riches satisfy; men
who have fixed their hopes in rank earth & are late [119] in learning
their miserable mistake. There is no poetry in this. There is no poetry
in *them*. Descriptions of this cast are apt ↑I know↓ to fall coldly &
unregarded on the ear but ⟨because⟩ it is because they are so much the
commonplace of life that they have been quoted out of it & become
the commonplace of the moralist. I have seen, all men in the common
circumstances of society may see the thrift[,] coldblooded & hard-
hearted ⟨that⟩ thrift, that has wrought out for itself its own reward[,]
↑men & women↓ that set out to be rich, that sold their bod⟨ie⟩y⟨s⟩[,]
its strength, its grace, its health, its sleep, yea and sold their soul,
its peace, its affections, its time, its education, its religion, its eternity
for gold. They have paid the price & by the laws of Providence they
shall recieve their purchase. But by the laws of Providence they shall
recieve nothing more. They have not bought any immunity from
bodily pain, any grace from the elements, any courtesy from the diseases.[n] They made no mention with their dealers of gentle affections
and asked no more of the Intellectual Principle than how to cast
their [120] [139] drivelling balances of loss & gain. Health, Knowledge,

---

page. Pages [118] through [121] are struck through, each by a diagonal line or
lines, probably to indicate use. Page [118] is reproduced as plate III.

[138] Ecclesiasticus 42:24.

[139] "COMPENSATION" is written beneath "on every side & adding" at the
bottom of the page.

Friendship, God, these were no parties to their contract[,] no guarantees ⟨for its fulfilment⟩ against disaster. These were defrauded of the just debt which each human being owes them to scrape together the means by which wealth was to be bought. But these are Creditors that will not let them pass unchallenged. They have asked no protection against the evils of life & God has left them naked to them. There is not a corner that does not swarm with enemies to our peace & ⟨existen⟩ to our very nature[,] & the design of our being is to ↑teach us how some may be↓ overcome ⟨many co⟩ ↑some may be↓ neutralized ⟨many⟩ ↑some↓ to contemn many to encounter some on equal ground.[140] But these have neglected the designs of their Maker. — Ignorance shall curse them with a leaden cloud on their understandings[,] their hours shall drag by in stupid darkness unvisited by Thought[,] the daughter of God denounced, forgot, unrecognized by the great brotherhood of intelligent minds who are penetrating into the obscure on every side & adding new provinces [121][141] to the kingdom of knowledge. But these poor parrots unmindful of these consolatory triumphs, cold to these hopes shall sit by their firesides in chambers that many climates perchance have contributed to adorn & shall prate to each other their stale gossip smelling of corruption & folly, shall feel the sad inefficacy of things without to mend the error or deficiency within. The maladies whose seeds are sown in all our frames, shall plague them; shall fasten on their souls, when they torment their bodies. When these visit the instructed philosopher, he freely bids them try their worst on his body, for ↑he↓ knows it is clay, he knows it is not himself. He exults in the harmony & health of his inner existence when the outer is torn by pain or broken by age. The Stoic[,] the Christian gathers himself unhurt within. But these have no divine antidote to the poison of mortality. Their "soul can scarce ferment its mass of clay."[142] They say to the worm thou art my brother[,]

---

[140] Had Emerson finished the revision, the planned sentence would presumably have read: "There is not a corner that does not swarm with enemies to our peace & to our very nature, & the design of our being is to teach us how some may be overcome, some may be neutralized, some contemned, some encountered on equal ground."

[141] "COMPENSATION" is written beneath "brother to Corruption," at the bottom of the page.

[142] Dryden, *The Hind and the Panther*, I, 318.

to Corruption, my sister [122][143] and my Mother. The approach therefore of these ghastly ministers is with reason dreadful to them & we know not but in the economy of God's Providence, whoso puts his talent in the earth, whoso neglects his soul shall lose it. The spark of existence that was never fanned to flame may be quenched.

But all who sell themselves ⟨are⟩ ↑do↓ not sell for wealth. There are many dupes of many passions. Nor are the compensations that God ordains confined to a single class of moral agents. To come nearer to my design I will venture to assert that whilst all moral reasonings of necessity refer to a *whole* existence[,] to a vaster system of things than is here disclosed[,] there are nevertheless strong presumptions here exhibited ⟨of⟩ that perfect Compensations do hold,[n] that very much is done in this world to adjust the uneven balance of condition & character.

[123][144] There are certain great and obvious illustrations of this doctrine which lie on the outside of life & have therefore been always noted. That prodigality makes haste to want; that riot introduces disease; that fearful crimes are hunted by fearful remorse; that the love of money is punished by the care of money; that honest indigence is cheerful; that in fertile climates the air breathes pestilence & in healthy zones there is an iron soil; that whilst the mind is ↑in↓ ignorant ↑infancy↓ the body is supple & strong[;] when the mind is informed & powerful the body decays;[n] these and all this most important class of facts ⟨a⟩lie at the foundation of our faith in God's being & providence. And they will readily suggest themselves with all the force that belongs to them to every mind. There is a class of observations of as powerful influence on this subject but less known or less quoted to which I shall devote a few words.

[124][145] I proceed to say then that sin is ignorance[,] that the thief steals from himself; that he who practices fraud is himself the

---

[143] "COMPENSATION" is centered beneath "character." at the bottom of the page. From the line beginning "reasonings of necessity" to the end of the paragraph is struck through with a single diagonal line, probably to indicate use.

[144] "COMPENSATION" is centered at the bottom of the page. Pages [123] through [128] are struck through, completely or nearly completely, each with a single diagonal line, probably to indicate use.

[145] "COMPENSATION" is centered beneath "richer that I have" at the bottom of the page.

dupe of the fraud he practises;[n] that whoso borrows, runs in his own debt; & whoso ⟨len⟩ gives to another, benefits himself to the same amount.

Our nature has a twofold aspect[,] towards self & towards society[,] and the good or evil[,] the riches or poverty of a man is to be measured of course by its relation to these two.

And in the view of individual unconnected character as a moral being having duties to fulfil and a character to earn in the sight of God am I impoverished that I have given my goods to feed the poor[,] that I have hazarded half my estate in the hands of my friend in yielding to calls of moral sentiment which made a part of my highest nature? Am I the richer in my own just estimation that I have unjustly taken or withheld from my fellow man his good name, his rights, or his property? Am I the richer that I have tied up my [125][146] own purse & borrowed for my needs of the treasure of my friend? Shall I count myself richer that I have recieved an hundred favours & rendered none? Myself, the man within the breast am the sole judge of this question and there is no appeal from the decisive negative. The daily mistake of thousands & tens of thousands who jump to make any pitiful advantage of their neighbour must not be quoted against this tribunal. For they err by taking the representative for the principal, the picture for the substance, the false for the true. It is not ⟨a⟩the true estimate of a man's actual value that is made from the balance of figures that[n] stands in his favor on his le⟨g⟩dger. This is to be corrected from the book of Life within him, by an appeal to his sense of how the pelf was obtained. If it was acquired by clandestine fraud which has yet escaped disclosure it is clearly a false estimate. If it was obtained by arts at which the eye of the law connives but which still are in substance frauds it is clearly a false estimate. If it is the reward of honest industry & skill to which said the ancient philosopher [146a] the gods have sold all things, his [126][147] estimate is correct, his doings are respected in heaven & in earth. ⟨He k⟩ Each man knows whatever language his ⟨ac⟩ neighbours or his journals

[146] "COMPENSATION" is written beneath "gods have sold all" at the bottom of the page.
[146a] Epicharmus (see Young, *Emerson's Montaigne*, p. 97).
[147] "COMPENSATION" is written beneath "[. . .]nt of benefit on his" at the bottom of the page.

may speak, knows what is his ⟨J⟩just standing[,] whether he is indebted or whether he has rendered others rich & happy. We mistake
in ⟨ta⟩ assuming the outward property[,] the mass of plate & stamped
paper that men can shew for their ⟨prop⟩ real possessions; these are
but representatives of real value & where real value is not, these
may often be counterfeited. We have, we trust, made it apparent,
that in the aspect of *Self*, our doctrine that nothing in the intercourse
of men can be *given*, is sound.

The doctrine is no less true[,] no less important in its respect
⟨of⟩ ↑to↓ our *social* nature. If a man steals, is it not known? If he
borrows, is it not known? If[n] he recieve gifts, is it not known? If I
accept important benefits from another in secret or in public there
arises of course from the deed a secret acknowledgement of benefit
on his part & of debt on [127] mine or in other words of superiority
& of inferiority. Of course, whatever be the extent of his obligations
or the number of his connexions the record of each transaction is
faithfully transcribed in the bosom of himself & of his brother man.
And it matters not tho' he should strive to hide his obligations to
other men & make none privy to his dependence. The impression that
is stamped on my mind of any character is readily transferred with
exactness to other minds & he who is conscious of uncommon liberality
or who expects returns that are not rendered, is seldom slow to speak
of the tardiness of gratitude. He is stupid who has succeeded in obtaining many loans which he knows his inability to pay & imagines
his credit to be firm. He has got the sorry reputation of a borrower,
& he will soon learn that the reputation will defeat the ends for which
it was borne. Further, suppose a man on the e↑x↓pectation that his
frauds will be unknown to all[,] perchance on the distrust of the Providence of God [128][148] takes a clandestine advantage of his neighbour
& repeats the crime on others and guards the fact with such scrupu-
lous & profound deception that mortal wit cannot uncover his iniquity;
↑see p. 132.↓ is there any reasonable man who can fear that such an
offender will maintain the standing of upright principle in society?[n]
Whoso labours under such apprehensions mistakes strangely his own
nature & has scanned with but incurious eyes the enginery of the

[148] "COMPENSATION" is written beneath "hope, every affection," at the
bottom of the page.

moral universe. When I have swallowed arsenic I have not only
tasted a bitter drug[,] I have done a fatal mischi⟨f⟩ef to my constitution & ⟨the⟩ time will soon betray not what potion or what quantity
I have taken but that I have poisoned myself. He who breaks over
the virginity of his virtue will soon make it felt that his moral health
has been assailed & disordered. The insidious sin will infect every
avenue of life, every hope, every affection, every thought.

[129]¹⁴⁹ *A* # Your Earthquake is the first chemist. He is a rare
ironmonger, Goldsmith, & Brazier & ⟨work⟩ wrought to some purpose
in his great laboratories long before poor mortals borrowed the hint
of him & melted metals in their crucibles.

(B)
Economy is neither ungenerous or inelegant.¹⁵⁰ It is not felt to be
such when you witness it in liberal minds. But when the soul was born
with hereditary or accidental contractedness it finds it no easy task
to mimic the independent air with which a noble mind submits to
parsimony. Though the instance be not unexceptionable yet there
are few who could do gracefully what Pope records of Swift.¹⁵¹

(C)
It would be good if a minister should institute weekly lectures for
the discussion of collateral subjects for the illustration of his Sabbath
discourses. For example if Paley should call his congregation together
on secular days to hear his Natural Theology.

D. The most remarkable instance of the *power* of mere literature
is Dean Swift, ↑a modern Tyrtaeus,↓ ⟨|| ... ||⟩who turned the tide of

---

¹⁴⁹ The notes on pp. [129]–[131] are keyed in the text as follows: A, pp.
298 and 320; D, pp. 298 and 311; E, p. 293; F, p. 319; G, p. 306; H, p. 323; J,
pp. 278 and 294; K, p. 311; and L, p. 324. Notes B, C, and I are not keyed on any
page.
¹⁵⁰ See p. 273 above.
¹⁵¹ Emerson presumably had in mind the story he must have found in Johnson's
Life of Swift — how Pope and Gay were forced by Swift to accept compensation
for a dinner they wouldn't accept from him because they had already eaten. See
Lives of the English Poets, 1905, III, 58–59.

political opinions and the British nation, ruined Marlborough, & denounced Wood's halfpence by pamphlets. Nothing fell from his pen in vain, says Johnson. Idolized by the Irish & proud of his influence. See Lives of the Poets.

E a very good sermon on self government & private life is Montaigne's chapter on Repentance.[152]

F That anything happens by Chance, said B[isho]p. Butler, ever‖y‖ thinking man knows is absurd.

[130] [G] Man, says Brown, loves what is simple much but he loves what is mysterious more. X X X X "I am persuaded," said Fontenelle, "that if the majority of mankind could be made to see the order of the universe such as it is as they would not remark in it any virtues attached to certain numbers nor any properties inherent in certain planets nor fatalities in certain times & revolutions of these they would not be able to restrain themselves on the sight of this admirable regularity & beauty from crying out with astonishment 'What! ⟨&⟩ is this all?'"—apud Brown's Phil. Vol. I p. 92.[153]

Ex↑c↓ess of simplification & love of ultimate principles

(H) For a most remarkable instance analogous to these, of *keeping*, (if it be not to refine too subtilly on the term) see Pensees de Pascal. Preface—"Un artisan qui parle des richesses, un procureur qui parle de la guerre, de la royauté, etc. Mais le riche parle bien des richesses, le roi parle froidement d'un grand don qu'il vient de faire, et Dieu

[152] Emerson refers to *Essays*, Book III, ch. 2, "Of Repentance." He had inherited one volume of the *Essays* from his father — probably the second volume of the third edition, "Made English by Charles Cotton," published in London, 1700, and listed in his library catalogue. When "newly escaped from college," he read this and "procured the remaining volumes" (*W*, IV, 162). Volumes 1 and 3 of the second edition, London, 1693, translated by Cotton, also appear in his library catalogue, and would seem to be "the remaining volumes."

[153] Thomas Brown, *Lectures on the Philosophy of the Human Mind*, 3 vols. (Phila., 1824). Volume 1 is listed in Emerson's library catalogue. Emerson's paraphrase of Brown's comment on man's love for the mysterious is based on a passage which immediately precedes Brown's quotation from Fontenelle.

parle bien de Dieu." [154] If there were many more such ⟨fine⟩ ↑grand↓ fragments in the sweepings of his study 'tis pity the editor did not print them all; they are seeds for sermons, for Epics, for Civilization.

(I) Newton was for a time the fool of astrology. Butler could stoop his giant understanding to the doctrine contained in V. Serm. p 98.[155] (See a collection of wondrous instances in Warton's Edit of Pope Vol. [III] p. [186n.]) [156]

(J) L'étendue des connoissances dans les temps modernes ne fait qu'affoibli⟨e⟩r le caractère quand il n'est pas fortifié par l'habitude des affaires et l'exercice de la volonté. Tout voir et tout comprendre est une grande raison d'incertitude; et l'energie de l'action ne se développe que dans ces contrées libres et puissantes ou les sentiments patriotiques sont dans l'ame comme ⟨dans⟩ le sang dans les veines et ne se glacent ⟨a⟩qu'avec la vie. Mme de Stael's Germany [157]

[131] K Simonides was asked why wise men followed the rich & not the rich the wise. Because s[ai]d he the former know their interest & the latter do not.[158]

[154] See Pensées, section XII, #799, in Oeuvres de Blaise Pascal, 14 vols. (Paris, 1904–1929), XIV, 237.

[155] Of the various editions of Joseph Butler's sermons, the one Emerson seems to be citing is Fifteen Sermons Preached at the Rolls Chapel . . . , To which are added, Six Sermons Preached on Publick Occasions, 4th ed. (London, 1749). The "doctrine" is apparently that of "over-great Refinements; of going besides or beyond the plain, obvious, first Appearances of Things, upon the Subject of Morals and Religion." Given the low capacity of ordinary men for speculation, Butler argues that "Morality and Religion must be somewhat plain and easy to be understood: It must appeal to what we call plain common Sense, as distinguished from superiour Capacity and Improvement, because it appeals to Mankind" (pp. 98–99).

[156] The Works of Alexander Pope, . . . with Notes and Illustrations, by Joseph Warton, 9 vols. (London, 1797). In annotating Pope's line "Unthought-of Frailties cheat us in the Wise" (Moral Essays, I, 69), Warton mentions inter alia Newton's study of astrology, Augustus' alarm if he put his left slipper on his right foot, Roger Ascham's love of cock-fighting, Bayle's love of mountebanks, and Bishop Hoadley's dread of thunder.

[157] De L'Allemagne, Première Partie, ch. II, last two sentences. There is no record of Emerson's reading in the work near the supposed period of the entry. Volumes 1 and 2 of De L'Allemagne, 2e éd., 3 vols. (Paris, 1814), had been withdrawn from the Boston Library Society March 21–May 23, 1822, and May 1(?)–June 7, 1823.

[158] Cf. Diogenes Laertius, "Aristippus," Lives of Eminent Philosophers, II, 69: "When Dionysius inquired what was the reason that philosophers go to rich

L A vicious person like the basest sort of beasts never enjoys ⟨‖ . . . ‖⟩ himself but in the herd. South [159]

A good action from a good motive is worth all external observances, is something which all the sacrifices & synods & canons & creeds & missions that ever were cannot weigh down. — [R. W. E.]

———

Him[?]

[132][160] p. 128
This will seldom be possible perhaps never; * for mortal wit can undo what mortal wit can do. The ingenuity of honesty can devise no cipher ↑can engrave no plate↓ which the ingenuity of dishonesty cannot counterfeit. The system that has been combined can be analyzed by an equal understanding. —— In short ⟨what⟩ the hist. of the world ↑may↓ testify that whatever ⟨performance⟩ ↑truth↓ the wit of man has ever been sufficient [160a] to shroud the wit of man has been found sufficient to reveal.

*Insert the two following sent.t.
On account of the stern equality that pervades the intellectual endowments of men in all nations ——
No mind was ever created of such towering greatness but that it can easily be matched by a level mind. ——
Yet granting that it were possible

---

men's houses, while rich men no longer visit philosophers, his reply was that 'the one know what they need while the other do not.' " Another version of the story appears in Bacon, *The Advancement of Learning* (see *The Works*, 1860–1864, VI, 116).

[159] Possibly Robert South (1634–1716), English court preacher of clear and vigorous sermons.

[160] The page is unnumbered. It appears to have been used at one time for a geometry exercise, since two faint geometrical figures appear upside down, in pencil. The text consists of planned additions to p. [128] at the point marked "see p. 132"; however, the additions were not adequately revised, and slash lines from "This will" through "mortal" and from "the two" through "ever created" suggest that Emerson abandoned the additions. Some random ampersands and a canceled "No" which have no apparent relation to their context in Emerson's footnote are omitted.

[160a] The ms. reads "been a sufficient". Emerson may have intended a noun to follow the adjective.

[inside back cover] [161]   ⟨Though[ts?]⟩
                    [R.W.E.] signifies *original*.

          Si le roi m'avoit donné
                 Paris sa grand ville
          Et qu'il me fallut quitter
                 L'amour de ma mie
          Je dirois au roi Henri
                 Reprenez votre Paris

          J'aime mieux ma mie, oh gay!
               J'aime mieux ma mie [162]

          For the true laurel wreath that Glory weaves
          Is of the tree no bolt of thunder cleaves. BYRON
                      [*Childe Harold's Pilgrimage*, IV, xli]

          Figure de savant, sur les bancs du theatre;
          Y decider en chef, et faire du fracas
          A tous les beaux endroits qui meritent des Ah.'
                           Misantrope [III, i, 794–796]
               l'on loue aujourd hui tout le monde
                           [*Le Misanthrope*, III, v, 1069]
          _____
                 D'éloges on regorge, à la tête on les jette
                 Et mon valet de chambre est mis dans la gazette
                           [*Le Misanthrope*, III, v, 1073–1074]

On peut etre honnete homme et faire mal des vers.
                           [*Le Misanthrope*, IV, i, 1144]

          Save just at dinner; then prefers no doubt
          A rogue with Venison to a saint without
                           [Pope, *Moral Essays*, I, 79–80]

[161] "⟨Though⟩" and "[R. W. E.] signifies original" are written right side up at the top of the page. Except for a circled "14" in pencil in the bottom left-hand corner, not by Emerson, the rest of the matter appears upside down on the page. Emerson apparently entered the quotations as though this were an inside front cover (see p. 272 above). The page contains no original material. From "Si le roi" to "BYRON" is crowded into the space at the upper left, from "Y decider" to "Save just at dinner;" below. In the line "Figure . . . theatre;" the tops of some letters and most of "theatre;" appear on the paste-down end leaf.

[162] Quoted from Molière from Antoine de Navarre in *Le Misanthrope*, I, ii, 393–400. Modern editions properly give "au gé!" in the refrain, but "oh gay!" appears in a 1734 edition. See *Oeuvres de Molière*, 13 vols. (Paris, 1873–1900), V, 468, n.1.

'Tis Use alone that sanctifies expence
And Splendor borrows all her rays from sense
                    P[ope]. [*Moral Essays*, IV, 179–180]

"And thus we play the fool with time
And the spirits of the wise sit on the
Clouds & mock us."
                    [Shakespeare, 2] *Henry IV* [II, ii, 156–157]

'Glory is like a circle in the water
Which never ceases to enlarge itself
Till by wide spreading it disperse to nought'
                    [Shakespeare, *1 Henry VI*, I, ii, 133–135]

'As gardeners do with ordure hide those roots
That shall first spring & be most delicate'
                    [Shakespeare, *Henry V*, II, iv, 39–40]

And how or why we know not nor can trace
Home to its cloud this lightning of the mind [163]
                    [Byron, *Childe Harold's Pilgrimage*, IV, xxiv]

Sometimes we are devils to ourselves
When we will tempt the frailty of our powers
Presuming on their changeful potency.
                    [Shakespeare, *Troilus and Cressida*, IV, iv, 97–99]

Le Misanthrope appears near the end of "Catalogue of Books Read, 1819–1824"
(see *JMN*, I, 399). The quotations from the play, and probably all the others on the
page, were doubtless entered in 1824.

[163] A diagonal slash line through "And" and "Home" is perhaps a use mark,
like those on the inside front cover.

Who is he that shall controul me? Why may not I act
& speak & write & think with entire freedom? What
am I to the Universe, or, the Universe, what is it to me?
Who hath forged the chains of Wrong & Right, of Opinion
& Custom? And must I wear them? Has Society a sceptre &
is it my King? Or is there any Community or any man
or more than man, whose slave I am? I am solitary
in the vast society of beings. I consort with no species. I indulge no sympathies. I see the world, human, brute & inanimate nature; I am in the midst of them, but not of them;
I hear the song of the storm, — the Winds & warring Elements sweep by me — but they mix not with my being.
I see cities & nations & witness passions, — the roar of
their laughter, — but I partake it not; — the yell of their
grief — it touches no chord in me; their fellowships of ashions
lusts & virtues, the words & deeds they call glory & shame,
— I disclaim them all. I say to the Universe, Mighty one!
thou art not my mother; Return to chaos, if thou
wilt, I shall still exist. I live. If I owe my being,
it is to a destiny greater than thine. Star by star,
world by world, system by system shall be crushed, —
but I shall live. Dec. 21. 'Animasque in vulnere ponunt'
Virgil
It is an ancient question which Mr Alison
has helped to settle, whether there be an ultimate standard of Taste. Is there in Nature any final test
by which all tastes may be tried, & to the authority of
which tribunal all will submit. In matters of

PRIDE   TASTE.

Plate I   Wide World 12, page 5   Text, pages 189–190
An expression of self-reliance, later indexed "PRIDE"

quam parva sapientia regitur mundus!

good when Sense, is seconded by think

Emerson.

architect

1 Ere the base laws of servitude began   faber quisque fort
   When wild in woods the noble savage ran

            Thy way thou canst not miss me mine demands   Dryden

2 No there is a Necessity in Fate
   Why still the brave bold man is fortunate.

Economy not ungenerous not inelegant
            Mens factisque live in brass

            We write their virtues in water
      ' freely they stood who stood & fell who fell.'

— While Fate grew pale —
And turned the iron leaves of his dark book
To make new dooms or mend what it mistook

      ' He that runs against Time has an Antagonist
         not subject to any Casualties." Johnson.

" An acre of performance is worth the whole land of promise
                                                      Hamel
            Laugh all the ... favor tyranny
            And all the standing army of the sky.
Doubt weave your honor of such Coward Orders ...
         doubt because they stand so thick i' the sky
   Cowley If those letters which paint the galaxy. go
Happiness is a suspension of disgust Then we upon our orbs last verge slide
            and see the Ocean leaning on y' sky
         To be no more; sad cure; for who would lose (Dryden
         Tho full of pain, this intellectual being,
         Those thoughts that wander thro eternity?
                                 Milton.
   " Candidus insuetum miratur limen Olympi
     Sub pedibusque videt nubes et sidera Daphnis."
         Apud Leibnitz de Bayle

Plate II   No. XV, *front cover verso*   Text, *pages 273–274*
A typical page of quotations

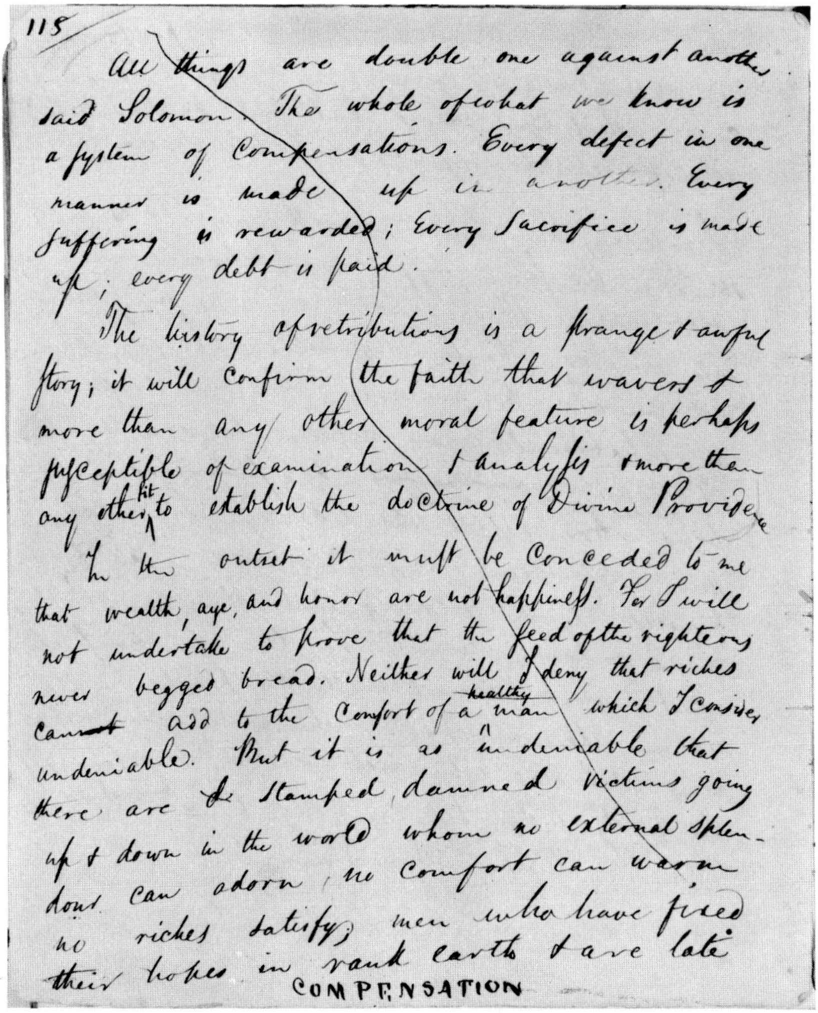

115

All things are double one against another, said Solomon. The whole of what we know is a system of Compensations. Every defect in one manner is made up in another. Every suffering is rewarded; Every Sacrifice is made up; every debt is paid.

The history of retributions is a strange & awful story; it will confirm the faith that wavers & more than any other moral feature is perhaps susceptible of examination & analysis & more than any other, to establish the doctrine of Divine Providence.

In the outset it must be conceded to me that wealth, aye, and honor are not happiness. For I will not undertake to prove that the seed of the righteous never begged bread. Neither will I deny that riches cannot add to the comfort of a healthy man which I consider undeniable. But it is as undeniable that there are stamped, damned victims going up & down in the world whom no external splendour can adorn, no comfort can warm no riches satisfy, men who have fixed their hopes in rank earth & are late

COMPENSATION

Plate III   No. XV, page 118   Text, pages 340–341
Part of an early "essay" on compensation, with a use mark

in of burch in their greatest concernment; nor
swallow such fables as to admit the firmness with
which I see society amid all her institutions stand
without ascribing to men's Conscience of some
wholesome & sublime authority it possesses now
"a single house will shew whatever is done or
suffered in the world. Juvenal.

But our Author should
remember if there are some things absolutely impossible as
to be found by the
most curious & microscopic
eye "for what never
was will not easily
be found not even by
the most curious."
Public Prosperity was Content
in old times in old nations
with very gradual advances

Plate IV   No. XVIII[A], page 47   Text, page 386
An entry in large script, at the time of Emerson's eye trouble

PART TWO

Miscellaneous Notebooks

No. XVIII [A]

1821?–1829

Entitled by Emerson "No. XVIII," this notebook is designated No. XVIII[A] to distinguish it from an earlier notebook also entitled "No. XVIII" which was published in volume I. The notebook occupies one half of a hard-covered copybook, the reverse of that part of the book published as College Theme Book in volume I. Some few materials are not later than 1821, but the notebook really begins in January, 1823, when Emerson started using it for quotations, miscellaneous notes, and copies of letters. In most instances the year dates of the letters are taken as the year dates of entry, but these must be regarded as partly conjectural. Entries continue sporadically until 1829. Eight leaves are missing. Ink pagination extends into the reverse sequence of the College Theme Book and an index appears on pages that are paginated for both the College Theme Book and No. XVIII[A]. Since Emerson cited this ink pagination in two entries made earlier in the College Theme Book (see *JMN*, I, 189, n. 42), the pagination would appear to have been inserted some time before Emerson actually began entries in No. XVIII[A].

The copybook originally consisted of 144 leaves, measuring 17.3 x 21 cm. What has been published as College Theme Book in volume I comprises 39 of the original 72 leaves of the first half of the copybook. The part occupied by No. XVIII[A] contains 64 leaves, what remains of the original 72 leaves of the second half of the copybook. Entries begin on the front cover verso. Six of the first eight leaves have been torn out; five of the stubs bear evidence of writing in Emerson's hand. The two remaining leaves (4 pages) are not paginated but have been numbered ix–xii by the editors. Pagination in ink begins on leaf 9. Two leaves between the pages numbered 32 and 33 were torn out before the pagination was inserted. Two other leaves, one between pages numbered 24 and 25 and the other between pages numbered 26 and 27, have been ignored by the manuscript pagination and this fact has been indicated in the text by the use of subscript numbers. Except for these variations, pagination continues from 1 to 120 in the 72 leaves of the copybook occupied by No. XVIII[A]. The pagination extends, however, through the page numbered 155 into the pages occupied by CTB, so that these pages have a double pagination with numbers running both front to back and back to front. The pages numbered 121, 126–131, and 137–155 carry entries for CTB, upside down and back to front (numbered 130, 125–120, and 114–96 respectively in the reverse pagination of CTB); pages numbered 122–125 (in the reverse pagination numbered 129–126) are blank. On the pages numbered 132–136 (but numbered 119–115 in the reverse pagination) appears an index for both No. XVIII[A] and Wide World 9 (see p. 395, n. 100).

355

[front cover verso][1] [1824?] Why has the moon little or no atmosphere? Why not form one as Lavoisier says the earth has done?

Can any known natural power produce out of the diminished quantity of sun's rays at Saturn or ♅ a temperature as high as the Earth's?

[1821?]   Bad & stiff
                                                   Penmanship

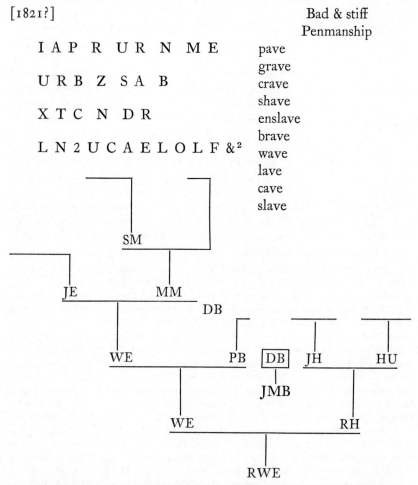

I A P R U R N M E   pave
                             grave
U R B Z S A B   crave
                             shave
X T C N D R   enslave
                             brave
L N 2 U C A E L O L F &[2]   wave
                             lave
                             cave
                             slave

SM

JE   MM

DB

WE   PB   DB   JH   HU

JMB

WE   RH

RWE

[1] The list of rhyme words appears upside down on the page. In the center of the page, to the left of the list and below the capital letters, is a penciled sketch of the bust of a man. "Bad . . . Penmanship" is in an ornate hand. A bracketed date indicates the probable year of all entries which follow it.

[2] Although the letters are spaced irregularly, their meaning is fairly clear.

[ix]³   grand irregularity

Εις οιωνος αριστος αμυνεσθαι περι πατρης ⁴

No XVIII
               Irregularity
Emulative   Ah is this
               ↑You↓ Dandy
               Jack
               bless us ⁵
irregularity
               dogmas of Epicurus
Andover
     Andover Penmanship Penmanship
[x]⁶ [1822?] Kant's 3 Editions ⁷

Lines 1, 2, and 4 seem conventional, line 3 experimental:
              I appear your enemy
              You are busy as a bee
              Ecstasy and dear
              Ellen do you see a yellow elephant
In line 4 Emerson deliberately made the "2" to look like a capital script "Q."
Lines 1, 2, and 4, apparently printed by Emerson, appear on the verso of a letter
from Mary Moody Emerson endorsed "1824" (in Houghton Library).

    ³ Four leaves have been torn out between the front cover verso and p. [ix].
Besides arithmetic and practice penmanship, the page contains numerous sketches
in pen or ink, of a building and of male heads, profiles, and full figures. Some of the
words or phrases are written vertically on the page. "WHP. fecit" appears on the
largest and best of the sketches, that of a young dandy, with a tall hat and a
monocle. The artist may well be William H. Pope, a senior who was listed with
Emerson and Amos Goodwin in the Harvard Commencement program for 1821
as a participant in "A Conference, 'On the Character of John Knox, William Penn,
and John Wesley.' "

    ⁴ "One omen is best, to fight for one's country." Homer, *Iliad*, XII, 243.

    ⁵ "Ah . . . us" is written inside the lines formed by the drawing of the hat
mentioned in n. 3 above.

    ⁶ "Book" is written large in pencil in the upper middle section of the page.

    ⁷ There were no three "editions" of Kant at this time; Emerson apparently
meant the three critiques. His most likely source of information was de Staël's *Germany*, in which the critiques are discussed at length. Emerson read *Germany* periodically from 1822 on, sometimes in French, more often in English translation. The discussion of Kant is in Part Three, ch. VI. See *Germany*, ed. O. W. Wright, 2 vols. in
1 (Boston, 1887), II, 157–180.

[1821?]   consilia
Scipio Africanus narrans
                      proposita [8]

      Britain withdraw her legions from the land
      Her thirsty despots & their fierce command
      And Hindoo heroes rule their native shore
      And heaven the long lost boon of Peace restore

           Duchess d'Aut̂vergne↓ — 144 yrs. after her socer [9]

[1824?]
Banian tree — 3000 yrs old
2000 ft circumf. shelter 7000 men,
in India by the Nureddah.
Bamboo — rises 60 ft. in 5 months.
India

[1821?]

      And he the godlike bard of Caledon
      A double wreath thy honoured brows have won
      And I'll tread on the neck of the proudest he
      That

"Un Serpent mordit Jean Freron — Eh bien? Le Serpent en mourut." [10]

      When Fortune decks old Learning's nak̂te↓d shrine
      And bids his cobwebbed libraries be fine
      Young merit smooths his aspect to a smile
      And fated Genius deigns to live awhile——

[8] "Scipio . . . proposita" is in pencil and not certainly in Emerson's hand. The intended meaning may be "Scipio Africanus relating the proposed plans."

[9] The reference may be to Madeleine de La Tour d'Auvergne (1501–1519), wife of Lorenzo de' Medici and mother of Catherine de' Medici. The note is obscure, since "socer" means "father-in-law."

[10] The saying is derived from Voltaire's famous epigram against his critic Élie Catherine Fréron:

      "L'autre jour, au fond d'un vallon,
      Un serpent piqua Jean Fréron.
      Que pensez-vous qu'il arriva?
      Ce fut le serpent qui creva."

[1826] Ship Clematis 300 tons — 105 ft long, deck mast about
100 ft [11] high from deck, 25 sails Cost — $26,000.[12] —
Capt Baldwin crossed Atlantic 135 times

[xi][13] [1821?]   CAIUS MARIUS.

"Tu ne homo audes occidere Caium Marium" [14]

[xii][15] ab impari ⟨pugna⟩ ↑certamine↓ⁿ indignabundus necessit.[16]

⟨Emerson & John[?] of Wine[?]⟩
May they have a pleasant time.

There is within the noble frame of man
A thing which men call Genius 'tis a thing
As indescribable as heaven; nor plan
Nor

Why the 10 millionth ⟨part⟩
Is lower than a foetus is.

[11] "GOW" follows here.

[12] In November, 1826, Emerson sailed from Boston on the *Clematis*, Captain Low, for Charleston, S. C.

[13] Most of the page is taken up by a figure of a man in Roman dress seated on a cushioned bench, with what appears to be a book on the floor before him. The penciled sketch has been partly traced over in ink. "CAIUS MARIUS.", in pencil, is near the top margin; the Latin is near the bottom.

[14] Despite the separation of "tu" and the enclitic "ne," and the lack of a question mark, the intended meaning may be: "Do you indeed, man, dare to strike down Caius Marius?" Emerson may not be quoting.

[15] Most of the page is taken up with the signed doggerel of John L. Gardner, a classmate of Emerson's at Boston Latin school and Harvard. Sketches of three men's heads, a rifle butt, and a rifle are also apparently his. Sketches of a building, a man sitting in a chair, a table, two men's heads, and a man's face may be Emerson's or Gardner's. "⟨Emerson . . . time." is by Gardner. "There is . . . plan Nor", by Emerson, is written small at the right of the page, from "foetus is." to "⟨half a fart)" below. Conjecturally, it was written first, and Gardner's stanza is an answer to it; "Vilest . . . rhyme", from the different handwriting, is the comment of some other wit on Gardner's wretched verse; and the last two lines of verse are Gardner's brilliant riposte. In the middle and at the end of "Ceres . . . pounds" appears Gardner's name in Emerson's hand.

[16] The intention is obscure, since Latin has no form "necessit." The rest may be translated "enraged by the unequal struggle" — perhaps in reference to the crude poetic contest in which Emerson and Gardner and a third friend appear to have engaged.

359

It wouldn't be worth a ⟨half a fart⟩
It scarce would cause the smallest ⟨ov‖ ... ‖⟩[17]

    Vilest of the vile
    Is this attempt at rhyme

But you would it spoil
By adding on your ⟨chime.⟩   John L. Gardner

   [1824] Ceres and Pallas are not either so large as a good Scotch estate nor should we weigh there more than a few pounds[.] [18]
   S   Solidity

[1][19]   Seeds ——   Jan. 28th, 1823.
"The Pigmies (27 inches high) every spring mounted on rams & goats marched in battle array to destroy the crane's eggs, aliter, says Pliny, futuris gregibus non resisti." [20] Gibbon.[21]

   Be moral Pigmies equally wise.

X   "Sixty thousand blacks are annually embarked from the coast of Guinea never to return to their native country: but they are embarked in Chains: and this constant emigration, which in the space of two centuries might have furnished armies to overrun the globe, accuses the guilt of Europe & the weakness of Africa" Gibbon V. iv, p. 309 [22]

   I presume the fact would be no less striking if I knew the amount of the *present chained emigration*. Ans 67.000

[17] Only the last letter is canceled beyond recovery. The best conjecture is "ova".

[18] Paraphrased from Edward T. W. Polehampton and John M. Good, *The Gallery of Nature and Art . . . ,* 6 vols. (London, 1821), I, 193. Emerson recorded "2 Vols" of this in his "Catalogue of Books Read, 1819–1824 (see *JMN,* I, 399); the date of reading is undoubtedly 1824 (see "Early Reading List"). Reading in Polehampton, I, 192 and 194, may have given rise to his questions on the front cover verso, and most of the information about the banian tree on p. [x] is in Polehampton, V, 46–47, though Emerson has "Nureddah" for "Nerbedda."

[19] Between pp. [xii] and [1] two leaves have been torn out. "Patriotism" is written in the bottom margin directly under "which I still" and is partially circled. It is an index heading to the note beginning "In ⟨the⟩ 378," above.

[20] "Otherwise they could not protect themselves against the flocks of cranes that would grow up" (*Natural History,* VII, ii, 26).

[21] *The History of the Decline and Fall of the Roman Empire.* Emerson omits parts of Gibbon's text. See *The Works of Edward Gibbon,* ed. J. B. Bury, 15 vols. (New York, 1907), IV, 238, n. 134. This edition is cited in the notes to this journal, and where Emerson supplies volume numbers, the edition he used is also cited.

[22] *The History of the Decline and Fall of the Roman Empire,* 12 vols. (London, 1821), which is listed in Emerson's library catalogue. See *The Works,* IV, 238–239.

X "What authority surfeits on, would relieve us"[23] is the cry of poor men in all the world. Just?

X   "He was a thing of blood whose every motion
          Was timed with dying cries" Coriolanus [II, ii, 113–114]
X   "And with a sudden reenforcement struck Corioli like a planet."
                                              [*Ibid.*, 117–118]

X In ⟨the⟩ 378, the invasion of the Goths made the number dangerous of the Gothic youth who had been distributed in the cities of Asia. They were accordingly collected by promises of lands & money in the capitals; — "At the same hour, in all the cities of the East, the signal was given of indiscriminate slaughter; and the provinces of Asia were delivered, by the cruel prudence of Julius, from a domestic enemy, who, in a few months, might have carried fire and sword from the Hellespont to the Euphrates. The urgent consideration of the public safety may undoubtedly authorise the violation of every positive law. How far that, or any other consideration may operate to dissolve the natural obligations of humanity & justice, is a doctrine of which I still desire [2][24] to remain ignorant." Gibbon Vol. IV. p. 416[25] — The question is very formidable. The number of victims is not mentioned or probably known, but twelve years had increased them in the places to which they had been originally sent.

X   "The *Cyropaedia* is vague and languid; the *Anabasis* circumstantial & animated. Such is the eternal difference between fiction & truth." Gib.
       note[26]   ↑Truth. Xen.↓

X Julian's *fortuna*, in Bacon's peculiar use of the term, was remarkable. No instance better than Constantius' death at the moment when Julian prepared to attack him. His own death, considering the difficulties wherein he was involved, was *fortunate*.[27]
                                              ↑Fortune↓

[23] Shakespeare, *Coriolanus*, I, i, 16–17.
[24] "Fanaticism" is centered beneath "their places at the" at the bottom of the page. Like the insertions after the quotations, it is, of course, an index heading to the note above it.
[25] *The History of the Decline and Fall of the Roman Empire*, 1821. The story begins on p. 414, and the quotation on p. 415. See *The Works*, IV, 321.
[26] *The History of the Decline and Fall of the Roman Empire*. See *The Works*, IV, 163, n. 119.
[27] *Ibid.*, IV, 25–26.

X 'A naked scimetar, fixed in the ground, was the only object of the religious worship of the Alani.' This tribe dwelt between the Tanais & Wolga, where the Russians now are; but their manners & laws penetrated into Siberia & India & Persia.[28] It would be curious to ⟨compare⟩ contrast the old & present creeds of these climes. Mammon, Venus, & Fashion, and in some places still, the naked sword dispute with God the allegiance of the Russians & Orientals. ↑(Idolatry.)↓

X The Prophet speaking of the Egyptians, says — "Their strength is to sit still." [29] This is a profound remark in its application to certain states, and the characters of individuals. It may be added in confirmation of the prophet's assertion, that it was proverbially impossible (in the III century) to extort a secret from an Egyptian by torture.[30]

↑(Policy)↓

X ⟨P⟩Fanaticism, in all ages, makes a disgusting perversion of holy phrases & names. "Praised be God" was the mob-cry of the savage Cir↑cum↓cellion⟨e⟩s in the churches of Africa ⟨i⟩of the III century; and Praise-God Barebones ↑was↓ the Regicide Englishman of the XVIIth. The Cir↑cum↓cellion⟨e⟩s fought with a club called an "Israelite"; and the Britons with the "sword of Gideon." The complaint of Ammianus is true — "Nullas infestas hominibus [n] bestias, ut sunt sibi ferales plerique christianorum expertus." [31]

In fanatical seasons as in times of civil war, for obvious reasons, the best & wisest men will be cast in the background of the state. After the wholesome lesson of a tremendous political convulsion, when society begins to recover its equilibrium, these will naturally resume their places at the head. Happy, if [3][32] order returns soon, before the ancient leaders of public opinion have been replaced by that dangerous set of men ⟨that⟩ ↑who↓ frequently blaze in the front of stormy times, & who possess energy & activity without principle, ⟨&⟩

---

[28] *Ibid.*, IV, 286 and 285.

[29] Isaiah 30:7.

[30] Gibbon observes this in *The History of the Decline and Fall of the Roman Empire.* See *The Works*, III, 394.

[31] "No wild beasts are such enemies to mankind as are most of the Christians in their deadly hatred of one another." Emerson got the story of the Circumcellions and the quotation from Ammianus from Gibbon, *The History of the Decline and Fall of the Roman Empire* (see *The Works*, III, 404–409, and 408, n. 164).

[32] "Burial" is centered beneath "to its channel" at the bottom of the page as an index heading to the note above it.

who can command all the world but themselves. Contemplative men stand no chance in troubles, bold men win all; in peace, ↑both↓ courageous & contemplative men stand midway; practical sages rise to the top.

"We may talk what we please of lilies & lions rampant, & spread eagles in fields *d'or*, or *d'argent*; but if heraldry were guided by reason, a plough in a field arable, would be the most noble & ancient arms." Cowley.[33] Agriculture is the venerable mother of all the arts and compared with the pastoral or the hunting ⟨age⟩ life is certainly friendly to the mind; it is next to commerce in this respect, but must necessarily precede commerce in the growth of society. Virtue & good sense, and a contemplative turn are universally characteristic of an agricultural people. In the city, "those who think must govern those who toil,"[34] in the country, the labourers both toil & govern.

Nothing can better illustrate the character of Honori⟨s⟩us (who by a most undeserved fortune retained quiet possession of his luxurious royalty for 28 years in the time of Alaric) than the *false* report, that, he was abundantly alarmed by the loss of *Rome*, till he understood that it was not a favourite chicken of that name, but *only* the capital of the world. V[ide]. V. Vol of Gibbon for his insignificant character & for the greatness & virtues of Stilicho.[35]

Of Monuments none could be more magnificent than the unseen one made to Alaric, who was buried in the bed of a river with the spoils of Rome, which river had been turned out of its course, & was then returned to its channel to flow over his grave & conceal it [4] forever from the Romans. The slaves who had been employed were then killed. Of a similar character was the ingenious cruelty of Periander, Tyrant of Corinth, who ordered two young men to go to a certain road & kill the first person whom they met & bury him instantly. He then ordered four to go out to meet & kill & bury these

[33] "Of Agriculture." See Abraham Cowley, *The Essays and Other Prose Writings*, ed. A. B. Gough (Oxford, 1915), p. 146.
[34] Goldsmith, *The Traveller*, l. 372.
[35] *The History of the Decline and Fall of the Roman Empire*, 1821, V, ch. 29, especially pp. 150 and 173–175. See *The Works*, V, ch. 29, especially pp. 118 and 135–136. Gibbon declines to repeat the "improbable tale" about the chicken. Emerson presumably found it in the source Gibbon cites, Procopius, *De Bello Gothico*, Bk. I, ch. 2.

two; & then eight to despatch the four. When these orders were issued, he went out at night to meet the first messengers, and hid his grave forever from the vengeance of his countrymen.[36] The Buccaneers killed a slave where they buried their treasures that his ghost might scare away curious intruders. A ⟨Roman⟩ lady, of cannibal or conjugal memory, one Mrs Artemisia, eat up the ashes of her dead husband in her meals; having heard perchance ↑of↓ a patriot buried in the hearts of his countrymen.

"But chiefly the mould of a man's fortune is in his own hands" said the Lord Verulam, & ⟨I believe⟩ added "Faber quisque fortunae suae." [37] Plainly this is a question which can never be ⟨answered⟩ determined, any more than whether Genius is innate or acquired.

National good fortune once ran so high in Switzerland, that ⟨a⟩ ↑this↓ blasphemy became proverbial, ⟨|| ... ||⟩[n] "God has been recieved a burgher of Berne." "There is a tide in the affairs of men." [38] Fortune moreover in the opinion of the English philosopher rather demands a moderate than an excessive share of intellectual attainments. 'The diseases,' said the Idol, 'the elements and Fortune, they nourish no aristocracy.' It is greatly to be doubted whether good accidents ⟨happen⟩ fall mostly to those who are on the lookout for them, or to the indifferent.   ↑Fortune↓

Charles I forced on the introduction of the liturgy. "In his whole conduct of this affair," says Hume, "there appear no marks of the good sense with which he was endowed: a lively instance of that species of character, so frequently to be met with; where there are found parts & judgement in every discourse & opinion: in ⟨every⟩ ↑many↓ actions, indiscretion & imprudence. Men's views of things are the result of their understanding alone; their conduct is regulated by their understanding, their temper, & their ⟨fr⟩passions." [39] (Charles I.) ↑Character↓

[36] The story of Alaric is told in Gibbon, *The History of the Decline and Fall of the Roman Empire* (see *The Works*, V, 256). The story of Periander is in Diogenes Laertius, *Lives of Eminent Philosophers*, I, 96.

[37] Bacon, "Of Fortune." See above, pp. 112 and 273.

[38] Shakespeare, *Julius Caesar*, IV, iii, 218.

[39] See *The History of England*, 1850, V, 100.

"And wonder with a foolish face of praise" [40]

[5]   Philosophic Imagination

Buckminster was remarkable for a 'philosophic imagination.' It is the most popular & useful quality which a modern scholar can possess — to become a favourite in society. It imports a spirit of liberal philosophy which can impress itself by the applying of beautiful images. Its advantage is owing to the ⟨fo⟩ circumstance that moral reflections are ⟨to⟩ vague & fugitive whereas the most vulgar mind can readily retain a striking image from the material world. Many men might say 'that the labours of the mind must be occasionally relaxed,' and it was easily forgotten, but when one said 'Non semper arcum tendit ⟨a⟩Apollo,' [41] — it served to imprint the truth & is ever remembered. That, 'great minds are unlike each other & do⟨e⟩ not appear twice in the world,' — men might hear & forget, until it was established by the adage that 'Nature has broken the mould in which she made them.' It is better for popularity than scientific sagacity, for it is more easily appreciated. One is at a loss to say if Ba⟨con⟩ had it or no; he is not precisely the mind at which the term points, because he had *more* of the philosopher than the poet, which is the reverse of Everett, Buckminster, Bancroft — and is superior to them. X

Of Rochester, Dryden, & other licentious wits of Charles' days Hume says There is as much difference between the freedom of the ancients & the indecency of these as between the nakedness of an Indian & that of a common prostitute. [42] X

X My lord Bacon thinks it better to be the second than the first of a family; for, Men seldom rise except by a mixture of good & evil deeds. This is less true (thank Heaven) in a Republic. X

X Of good resolutions, Young saith

> The world's infectious; few bring back at eve
> Immaculate the manners of the morn. [43] X

[40] Pope, "Epistle to Dr. Arbuthnot," l. 212. See above, p. 239.

[41] "Apollo does not always stretch the bow." Horace, *Odes*, II, x, 19–20. Quoted by Bacon, *The Advancement of Learning* (see *The Works*, 1860–1864, VI, 147).

[42] Emerson is partly paraphrasing, partly quoting. See *The History of England*, VI, 375–376.

[43] *Night Thoughts*, "Night V," ll. 142–143.

X Saw you ever Luxury? He is not attired in gold but in *green* and his diadem is not of gems, but of *wild flowers*.   [R. W. E.]

[6] Hume often remarks, that, where religious influence is introduced into the state, all the known laws of the human mind are at fault in accounting for consequences. This is an indirect but forcible argument for the reality & greatness of the *Cause* which has been ill applied. — Madness cannot subsist without Mind; nor Fanaticism without Religion.

X   Gibbon's fascinating Chapter on Monachism, & its Notes indicate the unequalled wealth of his mind in knowledge, imagination, & force of language. A good guess at the causes which filled the desart with monks may be gathered from the frank confession of a Benedictine abbot — "My vow of poverty has given me an hundred thousand crowns a year; my vow of obedience has raised me to the rank of a sovereign prince."[44] Interest is the commandment that outweighs all the law & the prophets upon earth. In the corrupt manners of the old countries, divines complain that fraud in every abominable form is familiar to men, that the paths of hell are[45] trodden as the paths of interest & earlier observation proclaims that when Interest walked in the paths of Heaven they too were frequented. X   Venice is in a state of complete decay and Englishmen buy splendid marble palaces for 1200 dollars & then take them down to transport the⟨m⟩ ↑marble↓ to England to build their houses there. $100 is an ample rent for a palace in this city. There are not more than four or five ships in its harbour. The Austrian government lay discouragements upon its commerce in order to favour Trieste — duties heavy enow to amount to a prohibition. When a man crosses the Alps he is but one day's ride from Milan, Milan but one day's ride from Bologna, Bologna one day's ride from Florence, Florence two days' ride from Rome, Rome *two* days' ride from Naples.

[7]   Σ   Canterbury Nov. 11, 1823.
[7]–[8] [Letter omitted][46]

[44] Emerson has been reading ch. XXXVII of *The History of the Decline and Fall of the Roman Empire*. For the quotation, see *The Works*, VI, 173, n. 58.

[45] "Alaric" appears above "hell are" and beneath "abominable" above.

[46] The letter is from Emerson to Mary Moody Emerson, apparently of some date in 1822. It is partially printed in *J*, I, 324–327, with the omitted passages in

[8]⁴⁷ ⟨*La Place*⟩ⁿ ↑A French philosopher↓ said We may now anticipate the time when the whole world will all be united under the same laws, the same religion, & *the same system of weights & measures.*

[9] English noblemen are the most imposing body of men in the world. Their unconquerable pride does not admit American travellers to their Company; nor do literary claims avail as in France to break down this barrier. Their enormous revenues enable them to live in a ⟨style⟩ grandeur of which we have no conception. Many of them spend 5, 6, or 7 00 000, dollars a year. Prince Esterhazy, the Austrian, spends among them 10,00,000 dollars per ann. The nobility are all provided with the most perfect education the age can afford; & become, by birthright, members of the Imperial Parliament. They are also remarkable, it is said, for noble *persons.* X
NOBILITY ⁴⁸   "I was born where men are proud to be." ⁴⁹

Biscay

Weights & measures are made interesting by the philosophical radicalism with which the French Revolutionary authorities took up

---

L, I, 139. Both Edward Emerson and Rusk date the letter Nov. 11, 1823, but the date is at best dubious; it seems to be the date of entry, not the date of composition. Headed "Σ," it praises Newton, asserts that a "diligent devotion to earth and its pleasures" is one way of avoiding scepticism, cites Bacon's view of a wife and children as hostages to fortune, and questions whether people lose or gain faith as they grow older — "Do they realize . . . life is a smoke, a dream, a bubble?" Mary Moody Emerson takes up all these and other points, often echoing the very language, in a letter labeled "(Answer to *your* 3)" which Emerson entered in his College Theme Book between her letters of July 25–26, 1822, and June 14, 1822 (see *JMN*, I, 198–199, where Emerson's reversal of "Σ" is printed as "3"). Neither the original letter nor the answer is in the Houghton Library collection. Why Emerson should have waited until 1823 to enter a letter whose answer he had entered in 1822 is not clear, but on pp. 373–376 below he enters other letters of 1822.

On p. [8] in the left margin beside "because he continually discerns new connexions" (see *J*, I, 326) is an asterisk; another asterisk and "V. Stewart — SCEPTICISM" are written at the bottom of the page. It is not clear whether the words are a reference to discussions of the subject in Dugald Stewart or a reference to Stewart and an index heading to the letter, which deals in part with scepticism, but the second alternative seems more likely.

⁴⁷ "Transfer" is written upward in the left margin beside the note on the "French philosopher".
⁴⁸ An index heading for the paragraph above.
⁴⁹ Byron, *Childe Harold's Pilgrimage*, IV, viii.

the subject, and by Mr. Adams's ⟨Essay upon the matter.⟩ ↑Report.↓
After inspecting a decimal system, the mere recitation of one of the
vulgar tables (of Long Measure for example) is ridiculous. The
French adopted the 1/40,000000 of a quadrant of ⟨the earth's ⟨cir-
cum⟩ meridian⟩ a meridian as the invariable standard, about a yard,
and called it a *metre.* A less measure they called by Greek [10]⁵⁰
⟨as⟩names as decametre, ekametre, chilometre, &c. Larger measures
they designated by Latin terms as centimeter &c. To measure the
Capacity of vessels they gaged them with these rods, & called them
litres, decalitres, &c. with corresponding names. If this system could
be adopted all over the world it would put an end to the cumbrous
inconvenience of the thousand tables in use. It would infinitely facili-
tate the intercourse of nations.

The ancient systems which were arbitrary like ours, cannot be
now accurately ascertained. But if such an order were once established
as this, it would be easy ⟨for⟩ to perpetuate it through any ↑political↓
convulsions, & to recover it if lost. But so inveterate ⁿ is men's prejudice for a pound, & so shocking is the innovation of a barbarous
kilometre, that this philanthropic plan is premature.

A Salem merchant who traded with the natives of one of the
East Indi⟨e⟩a islands for spices is said to have made some thousands
in [11] this manner. The ⟨simp⟩ natives ⟨co⟩ had no pound weight to
measure their spices with. "Oh" said the American, "my foot weighs
just a pound," & put it on the scale. As may be supposed, he got 56
weight, or more at the price of each pound. X

Time is ⟨long⟩ short; art is long. Chill penury repressed his
noble rage. Charles II never said a foolish thing & never did a wise
one.⁵¹ Earl [Carnarvon's] speech is a curious piece of English history. "My lords I do not understand Latin. I am an unlettered man
but am acquainted with the details of English history, & I know
the fortune of impeachments. I will not however go farther back
than Elizabeth's time. At that time the Earl of Essex ran down

⁵⁰ "WEIGHTS" is centered beneath "to have made" at the bottom of the page.
⁵¹ Emerson took his three "quotations" from Hippocrates(?), Gray (*Elegy in a Country Churchyard*), and John Wilmot, Earl of Rochester.

and your lordships very well know what became
of the Earl of Essex; Chancellor Bacon ran down the Earl of Essex
and your lordships very well know what became of Chancellor Bacon;
the duke of Buckingham ran down my lord chan[12]cellor Bacon
& your lordships know well what became of the duke of Buckingham. — Sir Edward Hyde ran down the duke of Buckingham &
your lordships know what became of Sr E. Hyde. The earl of Danby
ran down Sir E. Hyde & what may become of Earl Danby your lordships best can tell. But let the man stand up who dares run down
the E. Danby & we shall soon see what will become of ⟨him.⟩ ↑that
man.↓[52]

Sire, said the Duke of Buckingham ↑to Charles 2,↓ I should
like to know if the Duke of Ormond be out of favour with your
Majesty or your Majesty with the duke of Ormond; for of the two,
you seem the most out of countenance.[53]

Good morning ⟨y⟩my Lord Mayor Good morng to your excellency[.]

In India the *shadow* of a Pariah [n] passing over meat, milk, or other
food, defiles it for the higher castes.

"Where are you going Mr. Whit[e]field?" said Dr. Chauncy.[54] "I'm
going to Boston, sir." — "I'm very sorry for it," said Dr C. "So is
the Devil" replied the eloquent preacher.

Not so much matter *what* as *how* men do & speak.

"I hate war, for it spoils conversation," said the witty Fontenelle.[55]

[52] Emerson is said to have found this speech, his version of which is highly in-
accurate, in *The Parliamentary History of England*, ed. W. Cobbett and J. Wright,
12 vols. (London, 1806–1812), IV, 1073 (J, I, 329, n. 1). Edward Emerson prints
a more accurate version from a later journal, T.

[53] See Hume, *The History of England*, 1850, VI, 246. Emerson's version has
some changes and omissions.

[54] Reverend Charles Chauncy (1705–1787) was an enemy of the religious emo-
tionalism represented by George Whitefield (1714–1770), the English evangelist
and enthusiastic leader in the Great Awakening.

[55] Quoted by Stewart, *Dissertation* (see *Works*, 1854, I, 332, n. 1).

[13]⁵⁶   —— Mete↑o↓rology ——

Snow. When the snow falls in a quiet still air, each flake if carefully examined will appear a regular ⟨five sided crystal,⟩ ↑figure; for the most part a little star or rowel of 6 points, being perfect & transparent ice↓ⁿ or a twelvesided one, or sometimes a flat round surface. The angles of this little icicle are invariably the same. If it be windy, the flakes are found to be composed of a lump of broken crystals of this form. In the London Phil[osophical]. Transactions is noticed a fall of snow which had none of the ordinary figures, but was made up of little pillars whereof some were tetragonal, some hexagonal with a neat ⟨basis.⟩ ↑pedestal.↓ On the top they were somewhat larger as the heads of columns are. Considering the whole shape, the name of Nix Columnaris was given to it.⁵⁷

Before a fall of snow it has been observed that the wind always changes; and in England (⟨for⟩ ↑during↓ one winter) the wind previous to the snow always blew from some point between the South & West, and afterwards from some point between the East & N. West. Now those winds coming from S & W proceed from warm Climates & pass over vast quantity of water in a state of powerful evaporation, & must therefore possess a great [14]⁵⁸ degree of humidity & are commonly of the temp. of from 45° to 60° of Fahrenheit. But the winds coming from E. & N.W. come from high latitudes & pass over immense fields of ice, and contain little water & great cold,ⁿ and are ⟨of⟩ from 32° down to 0°.

Now suppose this northern wind meets this southern, the intense cold of the one will convert the water of the other to ice. And the instantaneous application of the cold produces the flakes, because it has not time to ⟨f⟩ concentrate itself into drops. This is a beautiful chemical phenomenon; for the warmer air having a strong affinity for the colder air than for the water it holds in solution, the water

⁵⁶ To the right of and below the title "Meteorology" is a rough cartoon of a man's face with an exaggerated nose.

⁵⁷ The paragraph is partly quoted and partly paraphrased from Edward T. W. Polehampton and John M. Good, *The Gallery of Nature and Art . . .* , IV, 167–168 and note. The article is reprinted from *The Philosophical Transactions of the Royal Society of London*, 1809, II, 54, with a footnote added about "Nix Columnaris."

⁵⁸ "METEOROLOGY" is centered beneath "from the different" at the bottom of the page.

is disengaged, crystallised by cold & precipitated in form of snow.[59]

The curious fact that storms commonly begin at the point to which they blow appears to have been observed first by Dr Franklin. In 1740 that phil[osopher]. was prevented from observing an eclipse of the moon ↑at Philadelphia↓ by a North E. storm which begun at seven o'clock P.M. He was surprised to learn ⟨the next day⟩ ↑soon after↓ that the storm did not begin at Boston till 11 o'clock P.M. and by comparing the accounts from the different colonies [15] of the same storm he found it to be always an hour later the farther N. East for every 100 miles. He explains his idea of the course of the storm by a long canal of water stopped at the end by a gate. The water is at rest till the gate is opened, then it begins to move out & the water nearest the gate is first in motion & moves on towards the gate; & so on each portion successively till the water at the head of the canal is in motion, which it is, last of all. — So to produce a N.E. storm he supposes a great rarefaction of air in or near the G. of Mexico; the air thence arising has its place supplied by the next more northern & denser air; a successive current is formed to which our coast & inland mountains give a N.E. direction. Dr Mitchell noticed a similar storm in 1802. It began at Charleston S. C. 21 Feb. at 2 o'c. P.M. ⟨a⟩At Washington several hundred miles to the N.E. it was not observed till 5, P.M.; at N. York it began at 10 P.M. and at Albany at daybreak on the 22d. Its motion therefore was 1100 mls in 11 hours, or 100 mls pr hour.[60] (Of the fall of avalanches & particularly of one which buried for 36 days under the snow 3 women, who escaped at last — see a fine account in Polehampton's Gallery of Nature & Art. p. 177 Vol IV) [61]

[16] Hurricane. "The last of these hurricanes on the coast of Coromandel is that which happened ⟨i⟩on 29 Oct 1768. Of this sufficient notice was given, but the officers of the Chatham Indiaman, then in the road, did not avail themselves of it; for, on the preceding evening the sea was violently agitated, the sun set in a haze deeply tinged with red, with every

[59] The preceding two paragraphs are partly quoted and partly paraphrased from Polehampton and Good, The Gallery of Nature and Art . . . , IV, 170–171.
[60] The preceding account of storms is taken almost verbatim from The Gallery of Nature and Art, IV, 203–204.
[61] The account continues through p. 180.

other prognostic of a gale of wind. But, unfortunately there had been a misunderstanding between the captain & officers & the former being on shore, the latter probably waiting for orders remained at anchor, notwithstanding they might have put to sea with the N.W. wind which as usual at the commencement of these hurricanes blew off the land. The governor & council who foresaw the danger even time enough to have prevented the loss of the ship, ordered signal guns to be fired with shot, by way of directing the officers to weigh anchor & stand out to sea. But either they did not ⟨wait⟩ hear the guns or were too punctilious in waiting for orders, & in consequence of this inflexibility were lost, for the ship was never seen or heard of after the evening of the 29th. It is possible they were not able to distinguish the signal guns, for many of the inhabitants of the fort during the violence of the hurricane did not hear them & the flashes of the guns might be mistaken by the officers for those of lightning. [17] Vessels lying at this time at anchor in open road of Pondicherry were not in the least disturbed by it, & ships that put to sea in due time very soon get beyond their influence to the Eastward; & they never extend far inland; — all which prove them to be whirlwinds whose diameter can't be more than 120 mls & the vortex is generally near Madras or Pulicat, where a branch of the Ballagat mts. extends towards the sea." [62]

[18] [blank]
[19] [63] Letters

When a spirit of liberal theology prevails it is seldom of partial application but pervades all speculative science natural & moral. What is the end of it & how far will ⟨in⟩ it go? After Greece had recieved Epicurus' lax philosophy, which was a pleasant covert atheism & had gloried awhile in its liberality, Aristotle bound men down with his dogmatic law, for a thousand years. And this seems to be the common course. Men go free awhile, & strut to the end of their tether, & then a dark age chains the mind in sleep & makes a weary atonement for the boasted light & liberty. It may be ⟨said⟩ that the philosophical spirit may hold once more (which Heaven avert) the wild Bacchanalia it held in France; may abolish the Sabbath, & deny God. But France has got back into her old traces. Romish Superstition & Bourbon monarchy are as strong as before, & human perfectibility has failed. Man's fortunes in this way seem to obey the laws of natural bodies, which do not move ⟨i⟩on in a line, but revolve in orbits. We go a little way & hold a jubilee because we have got so far, & are

---

[62] The account is taken almost *verbatim* from *The Gallery of Art and Nature,* IV, 241.

[63] "LIBERALISM" is centered beneath "appetite or passion who" at the bottom of the page.

straightway mortified to find we are only returning to our old position. There is nothing new, said Solomon, under the sun. Dec. 20, 1823.

↑Tnamurya↓ [64]

"Savages who act by blind impulse of appetite or passion who have only a glimmering [20] [65] of moral sense & but ill qualified to discover Deity in his works. In the savage state man multiplies his invisible malevolent powers without entertaining any notion of a superior being. They who are most possessed with the opinion of evil spirits have least idea of God." Essays

Does not this militate with some of *your* essay? (See Wideworld No 4(?)) It seems the very instinct which leads the savage to multiply invisibles was the principle which was designed to lead to the perception & belief of a first Cause, & may not the miseries the savage feels lead him to the idea of a bad spirit? Tnam. [66] X X X [67]Is the Muse become faint & mean? Ah well she may, & better far better leave you wholly than weave a garland for one whose destiny leads to sensation rather than to sentiment. Whose intervals of mentality seem rather spent in collecting facts than energising itself — in unfolding in operating [?] its budding powers after

[64] One of Emerson's anagrams for his aunt, Mary Moody Emerson, author of the letter. The original letter is not in the Houghton Library collection. The letter is presumed to have been entered after Emerson began reading and quoting *The Gallery of Nature and Art* in 1824.

[65] "SUI" is written beneath "&" at the bottom of the page.

[66] Another anagram for Aunt Mary. The letter is not in the Houghton Library collection, but it must be subsequent to March 10, 1822, when Wide World 4 was completed, and before July 26, 1822, when Aunt Mary wrote that she was returning the Wide Worlds, which Emerson had sent her. The reference is not to Wide World 4 but apparently to Wide World 3 (see *JMN*, I, 72 and 75).

[67] The following copy, ending with "earthly dramas" on p. [24₁], contains most of Mary Moody Emerson's letter of June 26, 1822 (in Houghton Library). A major omission is the shrewd comment, following "into eclat": "tho' like Cicero perhaps, your poetry will not be valued because your prose is so much better." *Complete* words inserted in the text in square brackets are supplied from the original letter. Emerson has inserted a few unimportant words of his own. Bracketed dots mark a passage he omitted without the usual "X's". He noted on the letter that it was "a most beautiful monument of kindness and highminded but partial affection. Would I were worthy of it. Reread Dec. 1822   R. Waldo E   Cop[y]".

It appears that this letter answers a lost letter of Emerson's — one not listed in *Letters*. In an omitted passage Aunt Mary writes, "I began with the last sentence of your letter . . . ," and she refers to a speech of Caesar's which Emerson "quotes" and which appears in no other letter. She also laments Emerson's plans for a "reform in drama." He had evidently written her about the series of corrective "essays" on the drama which he began on June 10 in Wide World 6 (see *JMN*, I, 139–156, *passim*). As late as October, he was still "proposing . . . reformation in . . . the Drama . . ." (see p. 22 above).

the sure yet far distant glories of what Plato, Plotinus, & such godlike
worthies, who in the language of St Austin showed that none could
be a true philosopher that was not abstracted in spirit from all the effects
of the body. &c &c more than I dare to impose. Yet it is verily [most]
valuable to find the principles of the human Constitution the same when
developed by philosophy in all ages & nations — to find that after all
its *dissections*,(?) at bottom is an insatiable thirst for what they [well]
denominate "a state of mind being unable to stay after its highest flights
till it arrive at a being of ⟨undoubted⟩ unbounded ⟨goodness⟩ ↑greatness↓
& worth!" O would the Muse [21] forever leave you till you had prepared for her a celestial abode. Poetry that soul of all that pleases — the
philosophy of the world of Sense — yet the Iris — the bearer of the resemblances of uncreated beauty! Yet with these gifts you flag — your muse
is mean because the breath of fashion has not puffed her. You are not
inspired in heart, with a gift for immortality, because you are the nursling
of surrounding circumstances. You become yourself a part of the events
which make up ordinary life — even that part of the economy of living
which relates ⟨to⟩ ↑in↓ the order of things necessarily to private & social
affections rather than to public & disinterested. Still there is an approaching
period I dread worse than this sweet stagnation, when your muse shall be
dragged into eclat X X Then will be the time when your guardian Angel
will tremble. In case of failing of becoming decieved & vain there will yet
remain a hope that your fall may call down some uncommon effort of
mercy & you may rise from the love of deceitful good to that of [the]
real. Had you been placed in circumstances of hard fare for the belly —
labour & solitude it does seem — you would have been training for those
most insidious enemies which will beset your public life on every hand.
How little you will be armed with the saying of a French divine of highest
order 'that it is safest for a popular character to know but part of what is
said.' You provoke me to prose by eulogising Caesar & Cicero. True the
speech you quote (— I believe — "You bear Caesar & his fortune") [68]
is sublime & instanced by Christians but for him for that tyrant (whose
only charm the love of letters was not accompanied by enthusiasm) it
[22] was mere rant or he was thinking of the egg from which *Venus*
sprung which was preserved by fishes & hatched by doves — to whom he
was a most de⟨voted⟩↑bauched↓ devotee. As to Cicero one wants to admire
him but different accounts forbid — tho' none are favourable enow ever

[68] The words in parentheses are Emerson's. He might have remembered the
phrase from Plutarch's life of Caesar (xxxviii, 3); or he could have translated a quotation from Bacon, probably in "Of Fortune," though "Caesarem portas et fortunam
ejus" is also quoted in *The Advancement of Learning* and in "Of the Colors of
Good and Evil." See *The Works*, 1860–1864, XII, 217, VI, 362, and XIII, 286.
The "eulogizing" of Cicero may have been directed to *De Senectute*, XXIII, 84
(see *L*, VI, 333).

to place him one moment beyond the imperious controul of passing events. Dejected in adversity & without any respite from age or experience — pursuing begging other people to let him be praised. Is not this enough to neutralize those effects for the public as we know not their motive to be beyond emulation? His eloquence it is true is glorious but himself remains an object of pity & the only apology for becoming the meanest of scavengers, is that in company with genius is the love of fame, & he knew of no object hereafter to feed it. Such are the men you are more excited by than by your [noble &] heroic Ancestor! "Pomp of circumstance" Merciful Creator! this child so young so well born & bred, yet so wedded to sounds & places where human passions triumphed! When he knows that spots the most famous even by thine own appearances are swept out of record! X X X Whoever wants power must pay for it. How unnatural — one man asks another to give him up his rights; this is the nakedness of the traffic & if there be ever so much fraud & violence, after ages produce slaves enow to celebrate their conquerors. As to words or languages being so important I'll have nothing of it. The images, the sweet immortal images are within us — born there ↑our↓ native right & sometimes one [23] kind of sounding word or s⟨il⟩yllable awakens the instrument of our souls & sometimes another. But we are not slaves to sense any more than to political usurpers, but by fashion & imbecillity; Aye if I understand you, so you think.[. . .] Sorry you meditate a reform in drama which will oblige you to go thro' such bogs & fens & sloughs of passion & crime. True one ought to sacrifice himself to the public but how long & poisonous the execution compared to that of other martyrs. Still if by plucking up those principles of human nature which have made dramas agreeable to the populace & which have been sometimes considered as drains to human vices, or preventatives to worse places, — if you pull down old establishments which have found place in almost every age & nation of cultivated or semibarbarous life — why may you not undertake it? To men in general, it would seem gigantic. And to me who am, if possible, more ignorant on the hist[ory]. & charac[teristics] of [the] drama than on any other subject seems a less useful exercise as [it] respects the Reformer, than any scientific or literary pursuit. Mathematics &[or] languages remain with one for use & ornament & all the universe of facts which are collecting will some time or other prove something; & if they don't they are apologies for higher [exercises]. The picture of a bud[bird] is better than the idle jokes & saturnine gossip of ordinary society. There is one idea ⟨that⟩ of dramatic representation interesting, that of Eichorn respecting the Apocalypse of St John. The learned German you know believes all passed in Patmos in scenic [24₁][69] ⟨a⟩order. And why may not this be a key to many revelations. In the infancy of the world men were taught by signs. It would

[69] "EVIDENCES" is centered beneath "That portion" at the bottom of the page. The following leaf, omitted in the original pagination, is numbered [24₂] and [25₁].

seem that the higher & last made [of] instructions from Heaven applied to Reason as well as Sentiment. And I am glad to escape from all sorts of earthly dramas.

Oct. 24, 1823.[70] You surely don't insinuate that mysteries were *designed* 'to puzzle all analysis.' The ordinary effect of an inexplicable enigma can do no hurt for while it remains inexp. it tells no bad tales of any operations of Nature illusory or contradictory. Is it not wholly satisfactory to reason that all it discovers & *knows* indicate design & good ends? Were not the laws Newton discovered inexplicable before his day? And did he ever complain that he remained as ignorant ⟨of⟩ as the vulgar of any connection between what he called gravitation and solidity, or motion & thought or where the power resided? The bible theist exults in the secrets of what is called *nature*, for after finding a God tho' it were only such as the wise heathen had he is satisfied for the present with the immutable limits of his own understanding, & finds every thing to invite hope & curiosity. Besides he worships with new ardor at every new proof that the God of nature & the bible are the same as this never offers to explain metaphysical difficulties, but the consequences of those evils which have arisen from these difficulties are no more to be charged on the bible than the bigotry & scepticism of the Infidel on the book of nature. That portion of misery which ap[24₂]pears in slavery involves some of the most difficult questions and by the old Xian have been quieted somehow or other. One thing seems certain, that the state of a negro slave is not so despicable as that of the one of Court favor. — Tnam.

Men are so essentially alike, ⟨in all ages⟩ that if you do not radically alter their institutions you will find the same habits recurring monotonously from century to century. Friars & Monks of the Roman priesthood very closely resembled the country clergy of N. England ⟨though⟩ notwithstanding the very considerable progress of public opinion thro' ⟨half⟩ a score of generations. The town clergy no doubt are a vast many degrees higher but they may perhaps fitly represent the eminent abbots whom public admiration elevated to the episcopal & archiepiscopal thrones[n] of Rome, Constantinople, Paris & London. If one be curious enough to notice the topics & turn of conversation & the ability wherewith 'tis managed by clergymen in mixed or chosen company I think he will not be struck with any distinct marks of excellence or see that thoughts are broached today

[70] The original letter, in Houghton Library, is so dated, and is in answer to Emerson's letter of Oct. 16, from which Mary Moody Emerson quotes (see *L*, I, 137).

which might not have been [71] suggested in the ↑tea↓ table talk of
⟨the 1st or 2d Century.⟩ a thousand years ago.

[251] [72] Whit[e]field was as good & as bad as Peter the Hermit;
Mr Channing, & Mr Norton, & Mr Buckminster make good the
place of Athanasius, St Cyril, & Bernard (the name I think of the
hermit of Abelard's time) & Mr Everett will serve for many a polite
& dignified Archbishop who staid at home & kept his choice rhetoric
for the ear of kings. As for the plebeian & rustic clergy whom want
of sense or cash or consequence sent into the comfortable & ignoble
stalls of the villages & mountains, who covered round bellies with
the cassock & foolish faces with the cowl, who illuminated missals
at the expense of years of time, & gave the sweat of their brows to
the construction of puns & anagrams & rhyme, who *whistled* as they
went thro' the world for want of thought, & who borrowed from
the wretched mask of hypocrisy that consideration which their own
weight of character could never gain, as[n] for them I wish society
afforded no image of their mould, but the country, *this* country
does not blush to shew hundreds of them. Men who shun light &
find sin & ruin in the bed of indolence & who are no nearer akin to
the soaring spirits who have [252] [73] opened their eyes to the sunlight
of Truth than are the mole & the lion among the beasts of the field.

⟨H⟩ Let me not be thought to charge man foolishly & to forget
the amount of good wrought by the gentle but incessant zeal of piety
in every age. No doubt beneficent & devout hearts have in humble
spheres regenerated generations & the world. But I complain of the
great multitude of the laxer sort, whose profane feet some filthy interest drew into the high places. But all the world complains. "Let
each," said Franklin, "take care to mend one." I add, 'tis worth
while to notice how the black coats wind their way into the foremost
ranks of the proudest company.

What can the reason be why a priest of whatever god under
whatever form should in every clime & age be open to such liberal
abuse, & to ineradicable suspicion? Is the reason to be found in Eccle-

[71] "Have" and "en" in "been" are circled, perhaps to indicate that the phrase
should read "might not be".
[72] "PRIESTCRAFT" is centered beneath "akin to the soaring" at the bottom of
the page.
[73] "PRIESTCRAFT" is centered beneath "profession?" at the bottom of the page.

siastical History? Questionless this has been very bad. The pious professors have been outrageous rogues in a thousand temples from Memphis to Boston. Or is its origin deeper fixed in the nature of the profession?

[26₁][74] Dr Johnson was so poor when he first came to London, that he was obliged to live for weeks on four pence half penny pr day—and to walk with Savage the streets all night, for want of lodging.

⟨Diamonds⟩

Letters.[75] [April 6, 1824] Does a bold eye never grow impatient of the ill-starred monotony of history nor ask *to what end* (cui bono) this everlasting recurrence of the same sin & the same sorrow? Why does the same dull current of ignoble blood creep through a thousand generations in China without any provision for its own purification, without the mixture of one drop from the fountains of goodness & glory? Does the secret ⟨a⟩Agent who pours the tide of existence hope any new result of this ancient experiment?[n] In our feeble vision, it would seem that the immoveable institutions of the yellow men, will disappoint for 50 centuries more all expectations of a change. Or is their cheerless (because hopeless) stupidity, thus embalmed for immortali⟨zed⟩ty on account of any faith or philosophy or science of which they are depositaries & which they keep for other members of the family of nations? No, they worship crockery Gods which in Europe & ⟨a⟩America our babies are wise enough to put in baby houses; the summit of their phi[26₂]losophy & science is how to make tea. Indeed, the light of Confucius goes out in translation into the language of Shakespear & Bacon. The closer contemplation we condescend to bestow the more disgustful is that booby nation. The Chinese Empire ⟨h⟩ enjoys precisely a Mummy's reputation, that

[74] The following leaf, omitted in the original pagination, is numbered [26₂] and [27₁].
[75] Rusk does not print the following excerpts as parts of an Emerson letter but quotes and summarizes some of them, observing that they may be "material for an epistolary filler," or matter from an actual letter of Emerson to Mary Moody Emerson, Feb. 1, 1824, or, less likely, from his aunt to Emerson (*L*, I, 140). The nature of the revisions suggests that this may be an Emerson letter, but since it is only partially printed in *Letters*, it is printed here in its full journal-entry form. For similar thoughts of Emerson on China, see pp. 228–229 above.

of having preserved to a hair for 3 or 4,000 years the ugliest features
in the world. I have no gift to see a meaning in the venerable vegetation of this extraordinary ⟨nation⟩ people. They are not tools for
other nations to use. Even miserable Africa can say I have hewn the
wood & drawn the water to promote the wealth & civilization of other
lands. But, China, reverend dulness! hoary ideot!, all she can say at
the convocation of nations must be — 'I made the tea.' Egypt, Assyria, Persia, Palestine, polished Greece & haughty Rome have bequeathed us arts & instit[utions]., the memory & books of great men,
& the least legacy that has been left is the moral & argument deducible
from the outlines of a history. These nations have left ruins of
noble cities as the skeleton & monument of themselves. China is her
own monument. ⟨If⟩ For myself if such inexplicable doubts (as this
Cui Bono) chance to obtrude themselves, they are entertained as a
raree shew a little time & then dismissed from the prodigal Memory.
But I know & revere some whose life is th[ei]r. thought, who zealously pursue all those inquiries that promise to make a little light in
the Cimmerian shade of man's state & relations, [27₁] who encounter
doubts & scowl on ⟨s⟩Sceptics & whose impatience won't let a cloud
lie on the ways of Providence. I very much wonder how the pages
of history are viewed by such. X X X Are God's blessings geographi-
cally circumscribed? ⁿ No lesson is taught, no good that we know is
done by Asia's miserable immense population. And the kindling of
a new star, in the abysses of space to hold for a myriad of years the
same unmixed unrighteousness & ignorance would shock all our
notions of heaven. "What can we reason but from what we know." [76]
Calvinism is one hypothesis to solve the prob[lem] but as bad itself.
Apr. 6, 1824.

I shall transcribe a passage from Gibbon —

The Caliph Abdalrahman left this memorial in his closet at his decease
— ' "I have now reigned 50 yrs in victory ⟨&⟩or peace: beloved by my
subjects, dreaded by my enemies, & respected by my allies. Riches and
honours, power & pleasures have waited on my call nor does any earthly
blessing appear to have been wanting to my felicity. In this situation I have
diligently numbered the days of pure & genuine ⟨felicity⟩ happiness which
have fallen to my lot: they amount to 14. O man! place not thy confi-

[76] Pope, *Essay on Man*, I, 18.

379

dence in this present world!" ' Gibbon notes — 'If I may speak of myself (the only person of whom I can speak with certainty) *my* happy hours have far exceeded & far exceed the scanty numbers of the Caliph of Spain.'

Vol X. I subjoin a monument of fanaticism. After Mahomet arose Cufa[,] a fanatic who set up his own authority as superior to Mahomet & [272] his Caliph. Abu Jaher embraced his party & succeeded to his power. Having one day advanced with only 500 men against [a] ↑lieutenant of↓ the Caliph, he was advised by the ⟨C⟩Vizier to retire as the bridges were broken down & the ways beset.

'Your master,' said the intrepid Carmathian to the messenger, 'is at the head of 30,000 soldiers[;]   three such men as these are wanting in his host.' At the same instant turning to three of his companions, he commanded the first to plunge a dagger into his breast, the second to leap into the Tigris, the third to cast himself headlong down a precipice. They obeyed without a murmur. 'Relate,' continued the imam, 'what you have seen: — before the evening your general shall be chained among my dogs.' Before the ev.g. the camp was surprized & the menace was executed.[77]

Tnam[78]   ⟨Boston, April 25, 1824⟩

"Imagination will always revolt at the ⟨sight⟩ ↑loss↓ of the butterfly's beauty, & the rude waste of the rich dew of the welkin from its own azure cups, — but be patient. There are many who are forced to creep thro' the entrails of reptiles & roots to find an infinite Designer. Never dislike their little lobes & [livers] and all their capacities to enjoy the raptures of sense, for they afford so much comfort to those who seek for analogies, & who are otherwise related to the amiable instincts of animals than [28] to the lofty relations of reason & principle in the higher orders. The longer you live, the more you will have to endure the elementary existence of society, & your premature wisdom will distaste quiescence, when the old become gay & the young grave at the portraiture of a fly & the Galen dissection of a flower. Then you find no necessary sacredness in the country. Nor did Milton but his mind & his spirits were their own place & came when he called them in the solitude of darkness. Solitude, which to people not talented to deviate from the beaten track, is the safe ground of mediocrity, without offending, is to learning & genius the only

[77] *The Decline and Fall of the Roman Empire,* 1821, X, 39–40, 40, note d, and 74–77. See *The Works,* IX, 268, 268, n. 60, and 297–299. The "fanatic" was not Cufa (a city) but Carmath, and his successor was Abu Taher.

[78] The original of the following letter, in Houghton Library, is dated April 13, 1824. The canceled date is undoubtedly the date of entry. Editorial treatment of the letter follows that described in footnote 67 above.

sure labyrinth, tho' sometimes gloomy, to form the eagle wing ⟨of⟩ that will bear one farther than suns & stars. Byron & Wordsworth have there best & only *intensely* burnished their pens. Would to Providence your unfoldings might be there — that it were not a wild & fruitless wish that you could be disunited from travelling with the souls of other men of living & breathing, reading & writing with one vital time-sated idea — *their opinions*. So close was this conjunction that a certain pilgrim lived for some months in an eclipse [29] so monotonous as scarcely to discern ↑the disk of↓ her own particular ⟨d⟩star. Could a mind return to its first fortunate seclusion where it opened with its own peculiar colours & spread them out on its own rhymy pallette with its added stock & spread them beneath the Cross, what a mercy to the age. That religion so poetical, so philosophical, so adapted to unfold the understanding, when studied "where sublime sentiments & actions spring from the desire which Genius always possesses of breaking those bounds which circumscribe the imagination. The heroism of morals, the enthusiasm of eloquence, the love of an eternal fame are supernatural enjoyments allotted only to minds which are at once exalted & ⟨wearied⟩ melancholy, and wearied & disgusted with everything transitory & bounded. This disposition of mind is the source of every generous passion & philosophical discovery." Would this description of character which I have copied from a glorious author suit even our boasted Everett? Is he not completely enveloped in foreign matters & an artificial character? I am glad that his notice has fallen on Edw. who will be for flinging his light on a civil profession than on another destiny. If Virgil's shades still lingered in curiosity about their old world, I may have it about those "gospels of thought & wisdom" which you find so gossamer, when two or three old books contain everything grand for me. Yet you call this age the ripest. [30] Where are its Martyrs? Where was an age since Christianity, when the public mind had less hold of the strongest of all truths? The mass will ever be in swaddlings & there ever have been great minds, so I cannot see clearly the comparison between infancy & age. The arts not equalled. And even Milton casting an eye toward Ovid & Virgil which seems less bearable than towards Homer. ⟨Your⟩ — — X X X. I would remind your ⟨g⟩Grace — tho' but an Abbess of a humble Vale — that the triple bow was never seen before the Deluge nor is it a legend. There were no rains in those regions or none heavy enow to give the binding of that flowery verge before the alteration the flood caused. St Pierre favours this. Rich as is the triple bow of promise (and it has been seen ⟨reflecting⟩ ↑bending↓ on the grave of long buried friendship) it would lose its best beauty, even if the Commentat⟨e⟩ors restoring it as a *Covenant bow* were just. I am glad to shew out a scrap of learning to your science-ship in revenge for your speaking of my moral scrawls & sybilline scraps. In truth I have nothing of the old Eld but as many sands ⟨i⟩which I fear. The better part of the flattering letter I re[c]ieve as a token of kindness. It was ingeniously done to write so well on my old almanacks. And I never reject handsome compliment for the only thing would occur to you what possible interest would any one have in flattering me. Yet in solitude it is not necessary as in society, where even the oars of life can hardly be kept in motion without. But if you tax me with any payment [31] in the course of this letter, why take it as debt or due to merit for it is always passable in the best society. April 13, — 1824.

[31]–[36] [Letters omitted] [79]
[36]   From Waterford [80]

"He talks of the holy Ghost. God of Mercy what a subject! Holy Ghost given to every man in Eden; it was lost in the great contest going on in the vast universe; it was lost, stifled; it was regiven embodied in the assumed humanity of the son of God; [n] and since — the reward of prayer, agony, self immolation! Dost not like the faith & the means? Take thy own — or rather the dictates of fashion. — Let those who [37] love the voice of uncorrupt nature seek for supernal aid — for an alliance with the most powerful of spirits — the holy Ghost. Such was the ambition of Paul — of holy martyrs — it burnt up every earthly element & would not stoop to ask an angel's record nor an angel's wreath. Would to God thou wert more ambitious — respected thyself more & the world less. Thou wouldst not to Cambridge. True they use the name *Christo* but that venerable institution it is thought has become but a feeble ornamented arch in the great temple which the Christian world maintains to the honor of his name. It is but a garnished sepulchre where may be found some relics of the body of Jesus — some grosser parts which he took not at his ascent & which will be forgotten & buried forever beneath the flowerets of genius & learning if the master spirits of such as Appleton, Chalmers & Stewart and the consecrated Channing do not rescue it by a crusade of

[79] The letters, from Emerson to Mary Moody Emerson, none of which seem to be complete copies, are as follows: (1) April 30, 1824, printed in *J*, I, 374–377, with "fame of the influence" (p. 377) for "fame or the influence," and omitting the cancellation "which was eminently practical & useful" which originally followed "with like felicity and ease" (p. 375); (2) July 26, 1824, printed in *J*, II, 4–5, with "the admiration" (p. 4) for "this[?] admiration"; (3) Dec. 17, 1824, printed in J. E. Cabot, *A Memoir of Ralph Waldo Emerson*, 2 vols. (Boston, 1888), I, 105–106, with some omissions, and in *J*, II, 32–33, with "[ages]" (p. 33) for "s. c. g. s." and "first" for "just".

Two leaves are torn out between pp. [32] and [33].

[80] The original letter of Mary Moody Emerson's, in Houghton Library, is dated Dec. 6, 1824, but the section from "He talks of the Holy Ghost" through "earthly emolument" does not appear there. It was presumably an enclosure, for the letter begins "The enclosed was written", for which Emerson substituted "This was written". Editorial treatment of the letter follows that described in footnote 67 above.

faith & lofty devotion. The nature & limits of human virtue, its dangers,
its origin — "questions answered at Cambridge — easily" — God forgive
thy child his levity — subjects veiled with something of thine own awful
incomprehensibility, soothed only by the faith which reason loves but can
never describe which rests in solemn delight on [38] Him who not once
calculated it for any earthly emolument. — This [the enclosed] was written
with the pen taken for the old almanacks at the moment of reading yours
of antediluvian date. Then you do not go to Stewart. You might like him
tho' he makes mouths at the heartless   of kindnesses which tickle, not
benefit the weak world. He thinks a man in pursuit of greatness feels no
little wants. Why did you not study under the wing of Channing which
was never pruned at Cambridge. If he advised Cam. [he did not know
your capacity to think for yourself]; ↑X X X X or↓ he is not able or good
enow to [be willing to] set out alone tho' he avows dissent in some points.
Alas that you are there. There is a tide in the affairs of men who connect
the soul to the future which taken at the moment ⟨leads⟩⟨beats⟩[n] bears on
to fortune; omitted, the rest may be shallows. Do we repine that so much
is dependant on mortal life? The reason we can't determine yet that this
dread responsibility is not extended is not lengthened to the unknown world
is matter of constant gratitude to those who find terrors in the divine law⟨s⟩
& govt. & in His natural attributes. Were this protection to be extended as
the liberal believe to those who have heard of the gospel — of what reason
was that [39] astonishing apparatus given? Did ↑not↓ Christianity even as
much as the good Ware allows (which seems to leave more difficulties
tho' not so frightful as Calvin & the improvements of Woods) imply much
war with human nature? Why do its professed disciples run into Atheism
so often rather than deism. Diluted as it is it demands too much lofty &
serious virtue & as humanitarianism opens [gave] the door to conclusions
most forbidden they make them. Price, so eminent yet so flouted says Christianity cannot be credible on Lardner's scheme rather does it seem more
so if necessarily connected with the Trinitarian. Blessed be God for the
history whether its penmen were inspired or not of primitive religion in the
Old & New T. A descended being the Companion of God before time
living & suffering as he did — giving not an intimation that he provided
for any earthly comfort to his disciples,[n] leaving if but a few of the precepts & engagements which he did contains enow to demand constant
martyrdom of speculation or interest — gives & does enable its devoted
children to look at death & hell with sovereignty,[n] to call God tho' so
tremendously holy to witness that while he sustains their fulfilment of his
conditions, [40] while they love him thus He himself can do nothing against
them. This deep & high theology will prevail & German madness may be
cured — The public ⟨are⟩ ear weary of the artifices of eloquence will ask
for the wants of the soul to be satisfied. May you [dear youth] be among
others who will prove a Pharos to your country & times. But I wander,

because it is a penance, from the design of writing. It is to say that the years of levity & pride &c &c (which [...] render me unworthy to speak of the heights of religion) I cannot but think were in some measure owing to the atmosphere of theology; to my own speculation to what is worse & certain the sore of human nature — could years of penitence restore me the last ⟨1⟩20 years. It was pretty — it seemed best to tell children how good they were — the time of illusion & childhood is past & you will find mysteries in man which baffle genius. x x May the God of your fathers bless you beyond your progenitors to the utmost bounds of your undying existence." Dec. 6, 1824.

[41] I copy a part of a note to G. B. E.[81] from my great Correspondent wh↑ich↓ has been, I know not whence or why in my possession a year or two. —

"But seriously dear Coz., these fine Cambridge folks whom I do well respect, may forget you, or ↑even↓ dislike you before the long & wayward paths of versatile life are ended. I shall not, but from my palsied bed may be reaching to my attendants for their Newsprint which they say has your name,[n] whether a record of some honor or his death I know not — if the last, the curiosity & affection of   will be up in arms and, age like, many vague recollections & indistinct perspectives will flit through the mind. Yet it will hold most tenaciously on a few indissoluble ties between this life & advance in another. Old fashioned piety, benevolence contempt of transient things — Then she may vapour about the crude notions he used to have of the old Testament, its morality & design. And that tho' he loved & honoured the 5th Command he seemed to have little respect for the 4th. But memory under this new excitement will return to favourite visions of the other world, especially that described by Milton in the flight of Abdiel to the throne of retribution.

And Newton came & bowed his laurelled head at the foot of the X[.][82]

[42] x x[83] "In my view you should have scorned to shine. Again on the

[81] George B. Emerson (1797–1881), Emerson's second cousin, tutor at Harvard 1819–1821, and at this time principal of a school for young ladies in Boston. The note is not in the Houghton Library collection.

[82] Possibly a quotation from Mary Moody Emerson.

[83] Of the three following excerpts of letters from Mary Moody Emerson, of which the originals are in Houghton Library, the first is from a letter to Emerson dated 1824 by him, the second from a letter to Charles C. Emerson written at the end of the first, and the third a letter to Emerson misdated 1825 by him on the letter and correctly dated Sept. 15, 1824, at the end of the journal entry. The initial and terminal phrases of the excerpts are, in order, "In my view . . . guns firing",

score of fortune, that capricious & blind deity was by the very heathen
thought that that man was greatest who contested with her frowns. They
preferred the noble vessel too late for the tide & contending with winds
& waves dismantled and unrigged to her companions borne into harbour
with colors flying and guns firing."

x x As to the Scholarship — "Confusion of languages was a punishment and paucity of ideas the need of learning many. That excelling in
them has little to do with the broad & deep foundations of literature is
certain. See Montaigne & Rousseau & Shakspeare & Pope & others."
x x Yet the very waters of the tarn waved pleasanter at the approach of
La Fayette one of the few living monuments of another race — of other
palms — which like those same waves succeed each other & are forgotten
forever in the mighty immensity. You have not had time to feel that this
huge globe was but a web drawn round us that the light the skies the
mountains are but the painted vicissitudes of the soul. But it is the happier
power of bodiless souls perhaps to estimate the beauty of such a description
& to love the offerings of a mortal imagination. x x x To my dim sense
human perfectibility is among human institutions the dreams of enthusiasts with Godwin & De Stael. If the divine law, if that scheme (in which
you find a mixture of [43] clay — but which has ⟨done⟩ none any more
than the original law) so perfect, fails & becomes weak thro' the corruption of the means to which 'tis committed, — what can human institutions do? What have they done in our blessed land to keep Adams from
calumny & the people from intestine war? x x x The eclat of name of
fame is often present to my thought when I see some beauteous cloud
impress its image on the tranquil lake and as it passes to mingle in the
vast vault its shadow climbs the sides of the mountain over bog & brake
& tree and suddenly disappears at the instant of arriving at its summit.
But if shadows add to the beauty of fleeting scenes how much more the
aspirants of other mounts to the interest of life. Where were some of the
present joys of solitude had not genius spoke & wrote? This richly laden
season whose every leaf begins its own mystic story, which soothes the
soul & dwells ⟨o⟩upon the soul & blends itself into the soul derives a zest
from the tale of other days & from the prophecy of those who are rising
into honor. Sept. 15, 1824."

"Do good *when, where,* and *as,* you can" —

"He that can elate you with his praise, can distress you by his ridicule and
⟨ra⟩ instead of adulation being construed the tribute of respect it seems
rather to be an expression of superiority in him that offers it" Palfrey.[84]

"Confusion of languages . . . & others", and "Yet the very waters . . . into honor."
   [84] John Gorham Palfrey (1796–1881), Boston Unitarian minister and later
editor of *The North American Review* (1835–1843).

Dr Channing used *'sheathed* spirit' as the description of affected preaching.

[44]–[47] [Letter omitted] [85]

[47][86] [R.W.E.] But our author should remember that there are some things so absolutely impossible as not to be found by the most curious & microscopic eye "For what never was will not easily be found not even by the most curious."

Public prosperity was content in old times in old nations with very gradual advances. [48] She made many pauses & some retrocessions but latterly she has mended her pace & has called in art to her aid[;] she travels the land in rail roads & steam coaches[;] she sweeps the sea with a pressure of a thousand lb & all sails spread & sends her parachute thro' the air like a cloud.

There are some men whose minds misgive them when they see the prodigious rate at which they are borne in the public vessel. They cannot help [49] but be giddy & out of breath [at the] accelerated velocity of their motion. A Sabbath⟨s⟩ day's journey would be a safer jog[.]

"He knew not what to say, & so, he swore." [87]

Choose a sensible man to a responsible place rather than a man versed in the particular art, which is to be taught, inasmuch as a method of acquiring truths is better than the truths it has ⟨acquired⟩ already ascertained.[88] Let your discipline liberalize the mind of a boy rather than teach him sciences, that he may have means more than results. 1825.

[85] The letter, apparently incomplete, is to Mary Moody Emerson, March 1825, and is partially printed in *J*, II, 63–66, with "strongest" (p. 64) for "strangest" and "all mighty" for "all the mighty". The omissions are printed in *L*, I, 162.

[86] The following entry, which runs through "a safer jog" on p. [49], is scrawled in a large hand, indicating, as Edward Emerson notes in pencil on p. [47], that Emerson's eyes were weak. Presumably the entries occurred sometime after March, 1825, when according to his manuscript Autobiography, he "lost the use of [his] eye[s?] for study." The book list on p. [50] is in the same large hand. The three entries on p. [49], however, are in Emerson's regular hand, with no hint of eye trouble, and the second is dated "1825." It seems clear that in making these series of entries, Emerson skipped pages and then wrote on them later, but the exact order of writing is indeterminable. "[R.W.E.]", from its position, could refer to what follows or to the letter above. See plate IV.

[87] Cf. Byron, *The Island*, III, v, "and as he knew not what to say, he swore."

[88] Cf. " 'A method of discovering truths is more valuable than the truths it has discovered.' Playfair" (*JMN*, I, 192).

The Indian will give his bow for the knife with which it was made.

[50]   Books to be read.[89]

Philippe de Commines
Machiavel
Cardinal de Retz
Montaigne Essays.
Plato's Dialogues
Isocrates' Panegyric
Constitution of U. S.
Adam Smith, Works.

[51][90] Excess of feast, dress, gold, intemperate riot in the Cabinet, high blasphemy in the mouth, atheism in the heart of a state are the warning notes that strike for a country's ruin. The knell they beat is heard from nation to nation tho' mountains rise & oceans roar between. It vibrates in the mountain air[,] it is heard above the voice of the storm. It finds out somewhere the appointed avengers & calls them with irresistible command to the slaughter & the spoil[.]

I pursue my speculations with confidence & tho' I can discern no remoter conclusion I doubt not the train I commence extends farther than I see as the first artificer of glass did not know he was instructing men in astronomy & restoring sight to those from [52] whom nature had taken it. There is no thought which is not seed as well as fruit.   It spawns like fish.

When success exalts thy lot
God for thy virtue lays a plot;
And all thy life is for thy own
Then for mankind's instruction shewn;

---

[89] The only positive record of Emerson's reading in this list near the time of this entry is that from Nov. 26, 1825–March 4, 1826, he had on loan from the Boston Library Society volume 2 of M. Dacier's *The Works of Plato Abridg'd*, 2 vols. (London, 1772). He apparently owned a set of Montaigne's *Essays* (see above p. 347, n. 152).

[90] Edward Emerson's penciled speculation at the top of the page — "(1826) Apparently a year's interval with bad eyes & health" — is probably correct within a few months.

And, tho' thy knees were never bent,
To heaven thy hourly prayers are sent,
And whether formed for good or ill,
Are registered & answered still.[91]

Prov. Ch 2. V. 18 The Jewish philosopher did not know that the soul survived the body yet there seemed to him a peculiar sympathy & conjunction between vice & death and the idea was natural & suggests the evidence we have from nature of the immortality of the soul. The intellections [53] of the mind are scarcely discriminated from the sensations which occasion them. They end in themselves & do not imply the notions of merit & reward. But moral actions seem not a mere bundle of facts but of relations,[n] relations to something unseen & because thus related to something to which the body was not, possess for themselves a principle of life in which the body had no share. Since virtue was imperishable every act contrary to it would seem to tend to the destruction of the agent. ——

Vice is the soul's suicide.

[54]–[79] [Letters omitted] [92]

[91] According to Edward Emerson, the last four lines arose from a remark made to Emerson by "a Methodist laborer, named Tarbox" in the summer of 1825 when they were working in a hayfield on the farm of Emerson's uncle William Ladd in Newton. Tarbox observed that *"men were always praying,* and that *their prayers were answered"* (J, II, 98, n. 1). Rusk questions whether the date was 1825 or 1826 (*Life,* 117).

[92] Inserted before the first letter is "Letters to M. M. E." The letters, none of which seem to be complete copies, are as follows: (1) Emerson — Mary Moody Emerson, June 15, 1826, printed in J, II, 99–105; (2) Emerson — Mary Moody Emerson, June 30, 1826, printed in J, II, 105–110, with "propose" (p. 106) for "pursue" and the following paragraph omitted at the end: "⟦The aphorism of Bacon shd. never be forgotten ⟨All greatness come of place is by a winding stair,⟩ which is hardly truer in the corrupt govts. of the old world than in the corrupting govt. of the New, All greatness &c."⟧ Rusk misplaces this at the end of the letter of April 10 (L, I, 169). Emerson is misquoting Bacon, "Of Great Place"; (3) Emerson — Mary Moody Emerson, Aug. 1, 1826. The original letter is printed in full in L, I, 169–171. The journal excerpts are printed in J, II, 111–113, with "exigencies" (p. 112) for "exigences"; (4) Emerson — Edward B. Emerson, Aug. 12, 1826, printed in J, II, 113–114; (5) Emerson — Mary Moody Emerson, Sept. 28, 1826, printed in J, II, 121–123. The passage indicated as omitted on p. 123 is also omitted in the journal copy; (6) Emerson — Mary Moody Emerson, Oct. 1826, printed in J, II, 124–125.

[79] Dec. 13, [1826.] Charleston, S. C.[93] ⟨Ther⟩ I have for a ⟨week⟩ fortnight past writ nothing. My bosom's lord sits somewhat drowsily on his throne.[93a] It is because I think not at all that I write not at all. There is to me something alarming in these *periods* of mentality. One day I am a doctor, & the next I am a dunce, that is so far as relates to my own resources. An educated man who thinks for himself can of course at any time by contact with a powerful mind ↑whether↓ by conversation or by book, be easily wrought upon & go into action. But put away these foreign impulses & the mind will be treacherous to its alleged immortality, inasmuch as suspended action independent of the [80] waking & sleep of the body assaults the notion of spiritual life. The true account of the scarecrow is this. At sea a fortnight elapses in which I always remember myself to have been in times past a channel thro' which flowed bright & lofty thought. But I find in me no disposition[,] no power to recreate for myself the same brilliant entertainment. I come to land & the weary days succeed each other as on the desolate sea, but this coveted power does not return, & every attempt to force the soul is heavily baffled. Now suppose it should never return; the causes are concealed, the sun & the moon are hidden which affect the ebbs & flowings of the intellectual tides. They are determined by something out of me & higher than me. If the virtue that is gone out of me be withheld I have parted with what in life was best, & eternity will lose its dread attractions. Eternity is only desireable when regarded as the career of an inquisitive mind. It would be a disappointment[,] a prolonged [81] sorrow to him who mourned the loss of the sense, which only could unlock[n] its treasures. Yet during the days of this eclipse, the notice of the loss of light sometimes rises into apprehension lest it might not return. This is our boasted human dignity & majesty & so forth. We are such bubbles that when we mount, we see not how; and when we grow great we cannot commend ourselves. Much less can we discern the secret of life (I speak of the ⟨body⟩ soul) or confide with the approbation of reason in its continuance. Peace then to the

---

The reproduction of the letter excerpts in *J* does not include cancellations, but none of these are important. For excerpts printed in Cabot, see *L*, I, 169.

[93] Since Emerson's health had failed again in the fall of 1826, he had gone to Charleston in November.

[93a] Cf. Shakespeare, *Romeo and Juliet*, V, i, 3.

pride of man—there are states of feeling in which it must appear
either laughable or disgusting. And yet the cinders will live in its
ashes & make the man glad with a foolish gladness, that they are not
utterly extinct. It is the leading idea of Pascal's Relig[ious]. Meditations to contrast what is grand & pitiful in hum[an]. nature. And I
can't write a page in one tone of sentiment tho' that tone be grounded
in truth without doing injustice to the *whole* of Man. God has balanced us. And you remember Luther's comparison of hum[an]. nature
to a drunkard on horseback; put it up on one side it falls on t'other.
'Tis a lobsided thing. Therefore tho' humility be a most appro-
pri[82]ate & worshipful virtue, who so mean as to part with pride?
And tho' we know nothing of the future & nothing of the tenure
by which life & identity stand, who would doubt of his immortality
or the permanence & improvement of his powers? —

[82]–[94] [Letters omitted] [94]
[95] M. M. E. To X X X -p-y [95]

[94] The letters, none of which seem to be complete copies, are as follows: (1)
Emerson — Charles C. Emerson, Jan. 27, 1827, printed in full in L, I, 187–188.
The journal excerpt includes only "I place before my eye . . . regeneration of
man." and "It is not to be denied . . . Everlasting beauty." There are a few minor
differences in the wording; (2) Emerson — Edward B. Emerson, Feb.? c. 23?
1827, printed in J, II, 170, and tentatively dated in L, I, 192. The journal excerpt
is but one short paragraph of what was probably a letter of some length; (3)
Emerson — Charles C. Emerson, Feb. 23, 1827. The original letter is printed in
full in L, I, 190–192. The journal excerpts are printed in J, II, 170–172, with
"greatness" (p. 170) for "great men" and "spouting" (p. 171) for "shouting"
and "is it consecrated?" for "it is consecrated."; (4) Emerson — Mary Moody Emerson, Feb. c. 23? 1827, printed in J, II, 173–175 and tentatively dated in L, I, 192.
J has "the extremes" (p. 173) for "these extremes" and "how large" (p. 174) may
be "how huge". The passage indicated as omitted on p. 175 is also omitted in the
journal copy; (5) Emerson — Mary Moody Emerson, March c. 25? 1827, partially printed in J, II, 179–181. The missing passages are printed in L, I, 195, where
the letter is tentatively dated; (6) Emerson — Mary Moody Emerson, April 10,
1827, partially printed in J, II, 183–185, with "part of a gentleman" (p. 184) for
"port of a gentleman" and "all her electrical" (p. 185) for "her electrical". The
omissions are printed in L, I, 195.
The reproduction of the letter excerpts in J does not include cancellations, but
none of these are important. For excerpts printed in Cabot, *A Memoir of Ralph Waldo
Emerson*, see L, I, 187–195, *passim*.
[95] Edward Emerson identifies the recipient as Sarah Alden Bradford Ripley,
wife of Emerson's uncle the Reverend Samuel Ripley of Waltham, and explains that
Mary Moody Emerson was sharply criticizing the decline in faith which Mrs. Ripley

"Yes from my epicurean leisure if it so please you I scarcely peep out — but let the mutation go on which is one day to be lost in the fine elements. 'Struggle for existence' — what a phrase for one like you about the bubble life! How much better the ease of Mr Horse & Mrs Cow & Miss Sparrow. — & these might fill the earth with much more comfort to themselves if Mr Man & Woman were not in company — & would prove to other spectators that there was a designing & good creator. One surely as good as the Deity of old & late skeptics, who refer not only all the powers of our mind but God also to the fortuitous concourse of atoms, that such a being *must* necessarily have resulted from these operating from eternity. Well such a being (which leaves us it is said all as before for nat[ural]. & revealed religion) is better than none. Were atheism the order of the universe would it be better to take part in active life? Would not death be indeed terrible then. To have loved & been loved would indeed be death to die! How much better to be a quiet dreamer; to [96] lose by little the breath; to contract the sails of life; to despise honor & patriotism & friendship for indeed they would be but phantoms to embitter the grave. But then where could be this thing — this wondrous substance which loves & hates & prophecies & reasons a priori or was able to? But I know this is begging the question & I had lain all to sleep & it seemed so natural for my neighbors; but without any logic in me upstarted such a mind as S. A. R. & overset the theory. Any thing the whole of — Calvinism is nothing so absurd as that her spirit her any thing that acts should slumber & by the work of ages again chance in the form of a lily or a lobster.

'Can't believe.' Commit a crime — form an intrigue such as Queens & great outlaws do; blot the fair fabric of your fame quench the torch which has been light for others & you will have faith enough. Conscience will do an [97] office which reason seems slow in doing. Early education ⟨will⟩ would then react like a penal Angel. And is it thus is human nature in its best estate so ungracious a thing that fear will influence where love is useless? Oh no the budding of the trees the gentle breezes will dispel the demon. Alas! their buds wither & the Morng soon clouds. But man has an invincible appetite for sorrow & apprehension of some kind which increases with his years & it is only the old book which can quiet & sublime them

Well you'll say what a canting old Maid this has become. She has forgotten how many bright thoughts I gave her callous brain on the subject of faith. Oh these afterbirths — the bible believer don't like them don't respect them since the glory of Socrates & such like have given place to a

acknowledged after reading the new science and philosophy of England, Germany, and France (*J*, II, 191, n. 1). The original letter is not in the Houghton Library collection.

higher Prophet. Your would be faith is stumbled at a gibbet. A gibbet. He never had any education. Has gone where he who hung on a cross will procure means to instruct him. Besides what's his crime? Some sudden theft or rash murder nought of ambition which don't [98] wash out look not at him but at some long faced hypocrite some cruel slave holder some lying office seeker or some carnivorous man that feeds on human character & grows fat on the entrails of human defects.

How little can we recapitulate without vomiting at mortal condition & resigning that the knot should be cut if it cannot be untied by the revelation. Adieu. You speak of those who dream about future influence & knowledge. It is natural that the active should. They can hardly imagine an existence where they are not efficient & why should not this part of the constitution go forward. The Mystics I believe think a higher order of virtue attainable and I admire the Mystics without knowing them." 26 May 1827 Lost lost lost! [Scott, *The Lay of the Last Minstrel*, III, xiii] [96]

[98]–[100] [Letter omitted] [97]

[100] From MME [98] Oct., 1827. Would I could die today that this aching sense of immortality might be satisfied or cease to ache. The difficulty remains the same when I struggle with the extension of never, never, never — just as I repeated the exercise in childhood — Can't form an idea can't stretch myself to that which has no end it may be owing to the limits of childhood repeating the idea & wishing to come at an end in vain. If so unhappy instructions which have bound my intellect fated to be always small. This smallness is the will of God & the most absolute resignation is with it. But this inexplicable eternity! Oh how vanish⟨es⟩[n] the difficulties of a Deity simple or complex — no matter — of the madness of the understanding in fanaticism of bigotry & persecution of dungeons & racks. Is it because of these lumps of matter which move with us & above us of their perpetual changes & influences that we can't form an idea of the identical immortal substance which is to remain [101] essentially & absolutely the same. Without end, had it a beginning? or was it always an idea of God like Plato's ⟨system⟩ notion. After ages of individuality will it be reabsorbed? New orders rise. In those orders will transmigrate this immortal (but what is immortal?) essence principle within this coffined case — these excrements of the inhabitant. I'll go to the woods — but there I shall see a sort of immortal matter — a reproduction of seeds. Well but I shall not think [—] don't think [—] only feel pleasantly

---

[96] Emerson may have added this comment on the letter at a later time.

[97] The letter, apparently incomplete, is to Mary Moody Emerson, June 1827, partly printed in Cabot, *A Memoir*, I, 130, and more fully in *J*, II, 210–212, with "falsified" (p. 212) for "satisfied".

[98] The original letter is not in the Houghton Library collection.

abroad [—] rather don't try — Can't ⟨n⟩ever think — there's this crazy
yeast[-]like matter which makes the bark unwholesome. — It is this
impossibility of losing oneself tho' ages pass over the change that argues
immortality — yet clouds & darkness rest upon its nature i.e. endlessness.
Again "Philosophy in Germany has defended by abstract reasonings all
the fine affections of the soul." De Stael throws a rich halo of sentiment
round the words 'infinite feeling' — but it don't explain anything. She
felt the subject of an indefinite future with enthusiasm — but had no leisure
to travel with it in untravelled depths for she never sacrificed the charms
of fame & pleasure to obscure motives. She was heroic & noble in sacrificing
to friendship. But none should dispute but forever respect her faith in the
succeeding chap. on Protestant. That the 'feeling infinite' is an attribute
of mind is certain & like ⟨all⟩ the principles of all the Sciences which are
there but seldom developed.

[102] Were not God whether simple or complex personal how much
more vague & terrific mt. be this never ending necessity of existing. Perhaps not — ⟨a⟩if his influence is certain as it does appear on our otherwise
inexplicable existence & delights — what matters — tho' we are now incapable of finding any links to attach our faith to? *Jesus* the emanated
created (or what polemics please) ⟨G⟩god has a tangible visible ↑personal↓
existence — loves — angers — knows what virtue & glory mean — pursued them as perhaps none other could? Of these things reason can be
only acquiescent? not revolted? Her instruments are experience — & of
that world she can have none — the intuition⟨s⟩ of the soul supersedes
those & more readily link themselves to what are only objects of faith.
Priestley & Belsham have no soul & they tame away ⟨life⟩ revelation till
it's not worth accepting. For if it reveals nought beyond our every day
reason what is it? Did the tragedy or something like it in Eden give type
to the whole world of tragic poets? To the terrible mythologies of barbarous ages not yet exploded? Did not these become more bloody & dark
after the antediluvian revelations were lost — or Noahic? Did not the confusion of languages multiply pernicious idolatries? Yet it was it seems a
design of utility to mankind? To prevent an overwhelming monarchy?
One language will never absorb others. What a strange notion of Everett's
about a national lit. promoted by one lang. Burke says none can aspire to
act &c. & my Burke &c — — & if he ⟨ask⟩ say I ask why night is night,
day day, time time, why those questions can be answered speculated on
as Shakspear could not.

[103] Let all the angels laugh if so pure beings can be frivolous at
"the days of epic if there are those episodes to high & soft recollections."
"Periods when the soul feels as tho' it were an epoch when some revelation is about to be made. They may shew a Newton as an ape of their
knowledge but those sublime feelings are of their very *nature*. 'Tis then
the mind perceives the harmony of the works & word of God. No fear —

no apprehension of those errors & interpretations which surely exist but of no importance except to the mere caviller of words — to the digging mole. His eyes are designed for their place & that is of use in the great whole. Indeed it is the very office of these worthy ants who bring their grain to the heap of erudition to confirm the faith of the Xn world. On the very authority of their contentions we may rest assured that disputed texts have an antiquity of indisputable authority. & they were early begun & have stood the test of almost the whole age of Xnty. Such as refer to the nature of the mission of Jesus of an expiatory kind. The pride of philosophy was as much opposed to any thing in the way of implicit faith of anything inexplicable as the modern monopolizers of knowledge. Yet their heresies were not able to expunge those texts from the early records which represent the death of Xt as something more than martyr & teacher. But it were credulity to take insulated texts as guides. It is the whole history of man as described in the revelations the types of which appear under every form of worship instituted by Patriarchs & Prophets. The divine oracles of prediction which are styled the testimony of Jesus, of a [104] suffering Messiah. Now if he were no more than man & his sufferings only of the short continuance of his ministry & crucifixion & of no more meaning than a great inspired prophet what fitness is there between the apparatus & the end? If we attend only to his institution of the supper (believing its authority acc[ording]. to our theory) & the exact but more full repetition of St Paul, is there not strong evidence to believe that the voice which proclaimed in the infancy of man respecting his ceremonial sins that without shedding of blood there was no remission was typical of that same voice which proclaimed the same to man in his fuller growth? Was not the world prepared for the development which the fulness of time gave by the first acts in the great drama & by the exhibition of Judaism exposed to all nations? And is it not the succession of the acts & scenes of Providence which are connected thro' the whole series that gives the very "portion of truth bright & sublime" (brighter & sublimer for every improvement of individual genius) "that lives in every moment." But here we verge by this series to necessarianism. Well on the absolute conclusions of that there is no other resource than "the public" (to the whole universe) "execution of a god," of the creator & governor of the fallen beings. If it revolts the sense of the eternal fitness of things if indeed imputation satisfaction in your full bearings appear [105] absolutely impossible & the Calvinist & humanitarian ⟨&⟩ necessarian give us a scheme that can't stand, must we not adopt the middle one of Butler & Price? The extremes of the others meet. Channing talks most eloquently of nature in the N. Y. & Gannett sermon. But how /lo⟨s⟩ose/lose/ a term. Moral nature retains as many secrets as at the advent of him who commanded the physical. The Hottentot, the savage, the tyrant born to a mitre or a crown cultivate the seeds of every vice which comes to advantage — & those of every virtue are likewise indigenous yet in the whole race how few spring & are less cultured? Now what analogy to use his word has the pure, forbearing, selfdenying spirit of the gospel with moral nature of man? With Plato & Socrates & Aristides it would have assorted with little difficulty — but it came to call sinners — adapted to their wants & here we get back to something of a *fall*. Xty appears, as ⟨when⟩ⁿ we have often talked like a regimen a compensation to the original plan which was disturbed by the greatest of all secrets the freedom of moral agents (higher than man probably & man himself) & the prescience of God. If the text which represents the angels as beholding the wisdom of God in a newer & higher light by the ministry of Jesus be genuine & authentic there must be something [106] then teaching & bringing futurity to clearer light & to the Germ[an]. Divines who believe nothing of inspiration (so besotted) the meaning of the old & new testament to some of them is clearly that of a certain indefinite expiation. So says Stewart. — M. M. E.

[106]–[116] [Letters omitted] ⁹⁹
[117]–[155]¹⁰⁰

⁹⁹ The letters, from Emerson to Mary Moody Emerson, none of which seem to be complete copies, are as follows: (1) Nov. 20, 1827, printed in *J*, II, 220–223; (2) Dec. 17, 1827, printed in *J*, II, 223–225, where the elision marks indicate omissions in the manuscript; (3) Jan. 6, 1829, partially printed in Cabot, *A Memoir*, I, 147–148, and more fully in *J*, II, 258–260, where "MY DEAR AUNT" is supplied and "on what" (p. 258) is given for "in what", and the full hymn is given on p. 259 (see *L*, I, 258, for the original reading); (4) Nov. 15, 1829?, mostly printed in *J*, II, 272–274, with an omission printed in *L*, I, 287.

¹⁰⁰ For a description of the remaining pages of this journal see p. 355, above. Pages [132]–[136] contain the beginning of an index similar to that used for Wide World 1 (see *JMN*, I, 26, n. 53). Topics are indexed according to their initial letter and first subsequent vowel. Numbers indicate the pages in the two journals indexed, No. XVIII[A] and Wide World 9. Of the two sets of numbers, each of the first is preceded by "s.", each of the second by "i." It is obvious that Emerson was using the nineteenth letter of the alphabet to refer to No. XVIII[A], his nineteenth numbered journal, after Wide Worlds 1 through XIII and Nos. XIV–XVIII. He used the ninth letter to refer to Wide World 9.

The topics indexed by page in No. XVIII[A] are "agriculture" (3), "Burial" (3), "Fanaticism" (2), "Fortune" (2), "heraldry" (?) (3), "Honorius" (3), "Imagination" (5), "Patriotism" (1), "Pigmies" (1), "Policy" (?) (2), "Xenophon" (2), "slave trade" (1), and "Truth" (2). The topics indexed in Wide World 9 are "Alfred" (5), "animals" (40), "company" (23), "Depravity" (22), "Domestic Manners" (30), "Enthusiasm" (14), "Equality" (38), "Grave" (9), "Greatness" (49), "Hermit" (44), "History" (20), "Moral Sense" (12), "past" (1), "Prayer" (15), "Saracens" (48), "Social" (47), and "Temperance" (42).

No. XVI

1824–1828?

Although No. XVI has an initial sequence of entries from October 1, 1824, to December 22, 1824, its remaining pages were used mostly for poetry of the years 1825, 1826, and 1828(?). It also contains a few quotations. It is a miscellaneous notebook rather than a regular journal.

The manuscript was originally composed of 22 folded sheets arranged in one gathering and sewn through at the center leaves. The cover, of the same blue cartridge paper on cardboard as that on the cover used for No. XV, also measures about 16 x 20 cm. It was originally numbered "Vol. XI" by Emerson's father, and its paste-down end-leaves contain indexes in his hand. All of the original pages were torn away from the covers, the spine was destroyed, and a new one created by joining the covers with a strip of printed paper reinforced by heavy linen. The 44 gathered and sewn leaves were then cropped at the right and bottom margins to a size of about 16.2 x 19.8 cm and sewn to this strip. On the front of the strip Emerson printed "R. W. Emerson No. XVI", and "18" in pencil also appears on the strip. On the backstrip appears "Robinhood's Barn.", "FAR" (twice), and miscellaneous markings. A page bearing on its verso the beginning of an address in an unknown hand was used to cover the front paste-down end-leaf, and a page bearing on its verso a letter, probably of late 1823 from Mrs. Hannah Lee to Emerson's brother William, was used to cover the back paste-down end-leaf. The economically homemade notebook was apparently first used by Charles C. Emerson. His name and "Jan. 1824" in his hand appear upside down on the inside back cover, and most of the stubs of the last 19 leaves, which were torn or cut away, bear what seems to be matter in his hand, written from back to front. The inside front cover was used by Emerson for quotations, presumably contemporary with early entries on the sewed-in sheets. Of these, the first 10, the stubs of which bear matter in Emerson's hand, were cut or torn away, leaving 19. Some of the pages are unnumbered and some are blank; most are numbered in pencil.

[spine strip]   R. W. EMERSON   No. XVI.
[front cover verso][1] 1 So bad were laws that it was suggested as censure upon Socrates, Pythag[oras]., & Diog[enes]. that they were
great men every way but in too subject obedience to the laws
⟨which⟩ to second & authorize which true virtue must abate a good
deal of its vigor. — [2]

2   Nothing useless has insinuated itself into the Universe. Our being
is cemented even by our vices. Take away from us the seeds of
revenge, ambition, jealousy, envy, superstition, & you will de-
compose the whole. Mont[aigne].[3]

3   All moral philosophy may as well be applied to a private life
as to one of greatest employment.

> Who shames a scribbler[?] break one cobweb thr⟨u⟩o'
> He spins the slight selfpleasing web anew
> Destroy his fib or sophistry, in vain,
> The creature's at his dirty work ⟨in vain⟩ again [n]
>
> That Flattery ev'n to Kings he held a shame
> And tho't a lye in verse or prose the same [4]

4   "I think there is reason for questioning whether the body & mind are
not so proportioned that the one can bear all that can be inflicted on the
other, whether virtue cannot stand its ground as long as life & whether a
soul well principled will not be separated sooner than subdued." Johnson.[5]

5
6
7
8
9

[1] Beneath the quotation from Johnson is a small sketch of a woman's face enclosed in a double hexagon.

[2] Although what seems to be a quotation mark appears over the dash, the passage
sounds less like a quotation than a paraphrase.

[3] "Of Profit and Honesty." Emerson is paraphrasing. See *The Essays*, 1892, II,
252.

[4] In order, the lines are 89–92 and 338–339 of Pope's *Epistle to Dr. Arbuthnot*.

[5] *The Rambler*, No. 32, in *The Works of Samuel Johnson*, 12 vols. (London,
1806), IV, 211–212. This edition is listed in Emerson's library catalogue.

[1] History.   H[6]   EMERSON
Oct. 1.   What higher & really more honourable distinction
has this busy human mind than that extensive knowledge of trains
of events in distant periods, in lands remote from each other which
is called History. An intelligent man would scornfully reject the
proffer of changing state with a boy. He percieves it to be silly for
he would exchange a vast existence for a very narrow one. ⟨By⟩ In
the exercise of a rational nature for many years he has come in connexion with many hundred men & has hence acquired a various knowledge of the habits, character, & modes of thinking of so many, & the
events that have befallen them whether of forecast or unexpected.
These characters & fortunes[n] he compares with ⟨his ow⟩ each other
& with his own. Out of these comparisons arise infinite inferences of
his understanding about which his thoughts are incessantly occupied
& which are related to each other by a thousand connexions which
make the substance of his intel[2]lectual life. He has ascertained many
of the laws of mind. He has percieved the consent of mankind in
moral rules. He has observed the consequences of actions. He has
observed analogies & has judged of the future. He feels the new
superiority of his present to his ancient existence when he remembers
the unambitious blank of his infant mind. This is obvious that in
comparing minds, that life is most worth which lives for most; that
soul which has the greatest compass & abundance of thought. ⟨Now⟩
    History "proves by events the reasonableness of opinions." John-
son

"History with all her volumes vast hath but one page" Byron.
        [*Childe Harold's Pilgrimage*, IV, cviii]

Now History is an art (⟨arranged⟩ ↑devised↓ in correspondence
with th⟨at⟩e faculty of Memóry,) — which multiplies a thousandfold
these riches of the soul. Instead of strolling into the world's great
fair like ignorant boys wondering at all we see, we are already behind
the curtain[;] we have seen the great series of individuals & nations
whose wars & ⟨ac⟩ compacts have brought the world [3] into the
state we see. We have not ⟨s⟩ owed all our information to the small

[6] Though large and ornate, the "H" appears to have no special significance. It
does not, for example, indicate any connection between this journal and Wide Worlds
9–12, which were re-designated I, K, L, and M, for No. XVI is later than Wide
World 9 (see *JMN*, I, 404, n. 1).

company of associates into which God has cast us but have made some acquaintance with all in every country & age who have borne the human shape. Jew & Gentile, Roman & Barbarian, France, Spain, Austria, America, the South Sea, have entered into our copious comparison & made our inductions larger & juster.

"By books," says the Gentle Shepherd, "I crack with kings." [7] 'Tis a godlike invention which thus annihilates to all purposes of mental improvement both space & time & suffers the solitary scholar by these silent interpreters to converse with minds who illuminated the beginnings of the world. My memory goes back to a past immortality, and I almost realize the perfection of a spiritual intercourse ⟨by⟩ which gains all the good & lacks all the inconvenience & disgust of close society,ⁿ of imperfect beings. We are then likest to the image of God for ⟨a th⟩ in this grateful rapidity of thought a thousand years become one day. Providence has equitably distributed the highest order of minds along successive periods [4] of time & not clustered them all into one fortunate ⟨society⟩ age. Hereby their potent influence enlightens the dark & cheers the gloom of barbarism. But an evil ⟨is⟩consequence ensues that they are deprived of that splendid enjoyment which their equal society would afford them. But as they every where rise above the sinking mass in which they stand the eye of the distant historian associates them together as in a distant prospect the vast ↑intervening↓ lowlands vanish and the mountains tower above them seeming to come together in solemn & sublime society.

All pictures of life are true, grave or gay; for they are copies of sentiments in the mind which are creations of the mind albeit suggested by external events. When I call men wise I describe an image present to my soul; when I say, man is fond or vile I ↑but↓ describe another sentiment. In neither do I accurately depict human nature for the moral history of the species must be general to be true.

[5] Let who will think well of it, I am a little ashamed of the last paragraph. I am partial to one sort of portrait. I like the line

> That one small head could carry all he knew.
> [Goldsmith, *The Deserted Village*, l. 215]

[7] See Allan Ramsay, *The Gentle Shepherd* (New York, 1852), p. 52. "By books" is not in the text.

I like the image my fancy presents me of a wise man well bred to a vast variety of sound learning carrying thro' ⟨wind & storm⟩ sun & rain, through his rambles & business, and animal[8] refections & filthy occupations, thro' visits of ceremony and all the attitudes into which the versatile scene of life may throw him — his *soul*, that rich world of thought; that subtle & elegant arrangement of conceptions ripe for communication so soon as another spirit is presented. I like an unity of purpose in a man like the oft repeated warning of Cato[,] It[n] is also my opinion that Carthage should be destroyed. Scipio also. Mr Wilberforce never speaks in Brit. Parliament but for Slaves. Mr Everett is the expounder of a certain practical philosophy which always breaks forth ⟨acc⟩↑inc↓identally or in the plan of all his productions. In Voltaire they ↑who↓ have vainly sought for any unity [6] of character or object have been reduced to fix it in the absolute disregard of all character, object, & truth. ⟨Byron⟩ Anacreon tried to sing of heroes but his lyre responded only Love; Byron's lyre returned but one sublime note & it was *hatred*. He dreamed by day & by night ⟨of⟩ but one ⟨image⟩ ↑dream↓, himself. He hated all others & also himself.

> Come from the banquet leave the merry dance
> Stop music's tone & shut the gay romance
> Seal up thy ear to comely Flattery's wile
> Nor let yon mirror see thy passing smile.
> For not to Fortune's minions, bards like me
> Should grate their ears with our harsh minstrelsy
> The viol tinkles in the light saloon
> And lovers warble odes beneath the moon
> And feverish Fashion in his vine-clad bower
> Hath a new pleasure ripe for every hour
> Content with these if thou a worldling be
> Go, amble in yon silken company
> Let Moore the laureate bard of lust & wine
> Write devil-melodies & songs for swine
> And lull in luxury the charmed soul
> And sop seared conscience in the poisoned bowl

[8] "See v. 3" is interlineated between "sun &" and "animal" and a double line in the margin marks the insertion.

[7]   Let Byron's fame on false foundations built
             Search its sublimity in awful guilt
             For me, for me, 'tis blameless to be proud
             And scorn to mix with the besotted crowd
             I scorn to make fair Poesy a curse
             To man; & marry Vice to Verse.
             But in the earth's vast family are some
             Not yet are branded with the common doom
             ⟨Nor set the world as elephants are⟩
             ⟨Acme ‖ ... ‖ feverish & naked[?] ‖ ... ‖⟩
             Men live who ——

Charity
    The philosophical account of charity in its largest sense seems to be something like Massillon's idea that 'tis ↑no ⟨after⟩ evil accident but↓ an essential part of the system that there should be objects of Charity, — objects for the legitimate ⟨workings⟩ exercise of powers & feelings within others. The great & wise are the representative governors of the mass of men. They stand in the stead of Providence to dispense bread to the hungry, cheerful encouragement to the sick at heart, wise advice to the ignorant.
    And 'tis remarkable, we note, the simplicity & beauty of the divine arrangements are such that where man succeeds best 'tis ever some imitation of an order of ⟨nature⟩ providence. We applaud, & with cause, [8] the beautiful invention of representative government as the nearest approximation to perfection our institutions have made. Yet 'tis but an imperfect imitation of this relation in which rich & powerful men under God's Administration ↑stand↓, to others. But here that which we seek in vain is fully compassed. We aim to make the power delegated to one in some manner the gift of all but such are the impediments that obstruct our enginery, that, in practice, no government parts from *all* but ever from a busy *portion* of the people. In God's system the virtue pervades the whole world & none so poor as not to partake: if not opulent he may impart ↑of his↓ wisdom, if foolish of his strength & so thoroughly *social* is our constitution that scarce an infant or ideot exists who can not ⟨in⟩ somehow or other contribute to the well being of the Universe. ⟨a⟩All are in-

evitably amenable to the Author [9] of their power for the right use of it & chiefly or in the highest degree those who have most liberally recieved. Are you then chief among ten thousand in the rarest endowments of genius, of wealth, of power, of accomplishments? You are but the wider channels thro' which ⟨his⟩ the streams of his goodness flow.[9] It was a noble saying of a Stoic that wise men are the perpetual priests of the gods.

⟨priv tal help⟩ pub . . ↑Provid[idence]. works cheap↓

Tiberius forbade they should consult the Sybilline books about the Inundation perinde divina humanaque obtegens:[10]——

A. E. I. O. U.[11]   ut callidum ejus ingenium ita anxium judicium.[12] The Spanish Philips have been Tiberii. Austria today is Tiberian. 'Tis so true & common & so bad a combination of ⟨pure⟩ ↑real↓ human elements that Tacitus might have wrought it up, as Xenophon did the character of Cyrus. *exempli causa* [13]——

A man is known by his companion so was Hannibal ruined & therein Antiochus by P. Villius the Roman Ambass[ador]. Prideaux [14]

Men may live on weeds[,] men may live by gnawing leather as Pizzaro's men on their saddles when left by Orellana. Of late a fashionist may dine almost any where since ashes & steel filings & chalk & charcoal have become diet. Mummy was better than these.

[10]   Nov. 19, 1824.

From Brown I learn that Hume was right in saying that ⟨the⟩ our faith in testimony consisted in the less improbability of the facts reported than of the falsehood of the /witness/reporter/. & that Hume's error rests in what has not been attacked by theologians[,] his definition of a miracle⟨s⟩ as "a violation of ⟨th⟩ a law of nature."

---

[9] Cf. the quotation from Bancroft, p. 221 above.

[10] "Preferring secrecy as in earth so in heaven." Tacitus, *Annals*, I, lxxvi.

[11] Why the five vowels should appear here is a mystery. They appear to have nothing to do with the context.

[12] ". . . as his [Tiberius'] intellect was shrewd so his judgment was hesitant." Tacitus, *Annals*, I, lxxx.

[13] "As an example" (Ed.).

[14] For the story, see Humphrey Prideaux, *The Old and New Testament Connected in the History of the Jews. . .* , 2 vols. (New York, 1850), II, 93.

We are formed with a principle of inevitable belief in the uniformity of these laws & on this belief depends our faith in the existence of God. That these laws should be violated is a thing monstrous involving a physical contradiction as to say triangle of two sides. — Therefore if a miracle were this, — testimony could not prove it; could only suspend the judgment between the miracle of such an evidence & the miracle of such violation.

Instead of a violation — the miracle is nothing but the proper consequent of a new antecedent[,] namely the will of God. Because God is the greatest of all Powers, his Will is not the less ⟨a⟩ ↑one of the↓ Powers of Nature & on occasions worthy of its introduction into the series of causes & effects it may be philosophically admitted. [11] It is ⟨kne⟩ new & unknown but not for that a violation any more than a shock of electricity which an ignorant man recieves is violation.[15]

[December 22] Whose is this bark that comes over the deep
    And ⟨leans⟩ ↑flags↓ on ⟨as⟩the waters while winds are asleep
    The ⟨foa⟩ saltfoam scarce whitens the wake of its keel
    Scarce a motion of air can its loose sail reveal
    No gay streamers aloft on its maintop are hung
    No ensign declares whence its mariners sprung
    Unconvoyed the dull vessel sails and forlorn
    Her masts have been racked & her canvass is torn
    Whose is this bark & what doth she here
    By this winterbound coast in the night of the year.
    War is not the errand this traveller brings
    For her sides are not ⟨lined⟩ ↑armed↓ with the thunders
        of Kings
    Nor for Commerce she visits yon barbarous shore
    Which the ship of the stranger ne'er greeted before
    Heave gently, dark Ocean! thou bear'st on thy breast
    The hope of mankind to its home in the West
    If the tempest should bury that ship in the deep

[15] Emerson found Brown's commentary on Hume and the substance of his own conclusions in *Inquiry into the Relation of Cause and Effect*, 1822, Note E, especially pp. 219–221 and 224–225.

The fortunes of nations beside it should sleep
For she brings thro' the vast solitudes of the sea
The pride of old England, the
The pilgrims of England

                                                    Dec. 22d.

[12]   1   ¹⁶ O What have I to do ⟨with⟩
        2   With merr⟨y⟩iment & jollities
        4   And deafening games that children prize
        3   Youths ⟨With⟩ golden hair & sparkling eyes?

I am not made to tune a lute
Nor amble in a soft saloon
Nor mine the grace of kind salute
To mien of pride & heart of stone

My pulse is slow my blood is cold
My stammering tongue is rudely tuned

I care not who shall kiss the cup
That Fashion holds to Beauty up
Nor who shall slip thro' the smiling throng
With honied lyes upon his tongue
The swift hours that go singing by
Tell not the triflers they must die

Man to his work the merry to their wine
Friend to his friend folly to festivals
All hopes & humors to their several ends
Sages to schools, young Passion to its love
Ambition to its task and me to mine.
I am not charged with dallying messages

---

[16] The verse on pp. [12] and [13] might belong to the last few days of 1824, but it is probably the expression of Emerson's relief at closing his school for young ladies ("the silken troop") in January, 1825, and enrolling in Harvard Divinity School in February. Edward Emerson printed "A sterner errand . . . ambassador" (ll. 28–50) under the title of "The Summons" and dated it 1826 (*Poems*, *W*, IX, 384–385), but later he printed these lines and nearly all of the rest of the poem under the date 1825 (*J*, II, 38–40).

That thus I mingle in this glittering crowd
Seeing with strange eyes their buffooneries
I am not tangled in the cobweb net

[13]   That wanton Beauty weaves for youth so knit
To ⟨the⟩ some fair maid he follows with his eye
A sterner errand to the silken troop
Has quenched the uneasy blush that warmed
    my cheek
I am commissioned in my day of joy ⟨sin⟩
To leave my woods & streams & the sweet sloth
Of prayer⟨s⟩ & song that were my dear delight
To leave the rudeness of my woodland life
Sweet twilight walks and midnight solitude
And kind acquaintance with the morning stars
↑&↓ The /smooth passage/glad heyday/ of my house-
    hold hours
The innocent mirth which sweetens daily bread
Railing in love at those who rail again
    ↑by mind's industry sharpening the love
    of life↓
Books, Muses, study, fireside, friends, & love,
I loved ye with true love, so fare ye well.

I was a boy; boyhood slid gaily by
⟨a⟩And the impatient years that trod on ⟨these⟩ it
Taught me new lessons in the lore of life.

I've learned the /burthen/sum/purport/ of that
    /sad/heavy/ history
All woman[-]born do know, that hoped for days
Days that come dancing on fraught with delights
Dash our blown hopes as they limp heavily by
But I — the bantling of a country Muse
Abandon all those toys with speed to obey
The ⟨lofty⟩King whose meek ambassador I go.

[14] I shall set down perhaps as I meet them the particulars

which ought to belong to the ordinary proud enumerations of what man has done in the world worth doing. "The Ocean hath its chart, the Stars their map";   (Byron) [*Childe Harold's Pilgrimage,* IV, lxxi] "We see under the influence of legislative wisdom insurmountable multitudes obeying in opposition to their strongest passions the restraints of a power which they scarcely percieve, & the crimes of a single individual marked & punished at the distance of half the earth." (Brown) [17]

The province of Holland once the most populous in Europe is below the level of the sea; [18] (?)

[15] [blank]

[16] [1825]   ?[Prose run mad.]↓ [18a]

    The panoply of Paradise is mine
    No armourer wrought ⟨to⟩it on Eteian forge
    No dear luxurious maiden brought the gift
    By lying bards profanely deemed divine
    I ⟨boast⟩ am clad in mail of ⟨une⟩ celestial proof
    I brandish Michael's sword of flame
    And I come to quell the pride of the world
    But avaunt these toys of poesy Why wrap
    The fiery truths in riddles dark
    Truth treads on the pride of Plato
    Truth ⟨c⟩treads on lovesick rhymes
    The fashion of riddling priests
    The trick of Delphos & Dodona
    The cunning of Homer & Hesiod
    Mischievous polytheists who /deceived/betrayed the
      cause of/mankind
    These delusions are overpast.
    The altar of the Capitoline god is crushed
    The spindle of ancient Fate is broken

---

[17] The source may be *Lectures on the Philosophy of the Human Mind.*

[18] If Emerson did not find the information in a secondary source he may have encountered it in Baron Georges Cuvier, *Essay on the Theory of the Earth,* transl. Robert Kerr (Edinburgh, 1813), p. 139. He was later to re-use the information as he found it extended by Cuvier in *A Discourse on the Revolutions of the Surface of the Globe* . . . (Phila., 1831). See *Lectures,* I, 43, and p. 320 above.

[18a] Pope, "Epistle to Dr. Arbuthnot," l. 188.

The sisters do not spin the eternal thread
There is no fire glowing on Persic mountains
↑Where↓ The sun (is not) ↑was↓ greeted with fragrant
    spikenard
The Nile breeds crocodiles in his slime
And the pyramids are by great Alcairo
But the swarthy votary will not adore the reptile
And the dead oppressor is not entombed in the piles
The immortal Gods are deceased
Go let your fabled muses chant their obituary.
    Do you see how the world slides away

[17]   How its huge pomps dwindle to unsubstantial things
Tho' they were dear to the heart & solid to the eye
There is a sentence on the lip of Tully
That Truth ↑shall↓ last tho' the fabrics of imagination
    decay.
Many incidents up & down in the world shall verify
The simple oracle.
The proud hieroglyphic shall be the child's bauble
    alphabet
The spectral tale that blanched the forefather's cheek
Makes merriment for vermillion maids.
Fools judge by outside show, for while
The champion vanquishes in vain
And armed kings are met unprofitably
(Great things that have no harvest home)
⟨Un⟩The unconscious wit scratches his paper in a corner
And ⟨what is writ,⟩ the ⟨lines⟩ ↑words↓ that are writ
⟨Rankle⟩ ↑⟨Burn⟩↓ like ⟨adders⟩ ↑⟨pains⟩↓ in ten thousand
    memories
And are chanted in thunder to the four winds.

1825 [19]   And the pillars of social fabrics are shaken ↑at the sound↓
    like bulrushes.

    [20] ⟨Ah   Fate   Cannot a Man⟩

---

[19] The date was added at some later time. The word "Till" appears above it
and to the right, but there is no apparent grammatical connection.
[20] This seems to be the first version of stanza 1 of "Fame." A revised version

⟨Be wise without a beard?⟩
⟨Or through the tribes from Beersheba to Dan⟩
⟨Pray was it never heard⟩
⟨That wisdom might with youth be gotten⟩
⟨Or wit be ripe before 'twas rotten⟩

[18] ↑1826↓   The spirits of the wise, sit on the clouds
And mock the ambition of man[20a]
For his breath is vapour; his beauty the colour of a cloud
And his body & soul are parted by a sun, a storm
Or the feeble fork of a poor worm
And who shall tell his household
Whither the soul of the dead man is gone.
Is it gone to live in torture
Enduring a dread resurrection into pain
And perce⟨e⟩ive mortal plagues in ↑an↓ immortal body
Sighing to the heavy centuries, that bring
No light no hope in their immeasurable train?
Is it gone to farther regions of unequal lot
To a land where the colours of love & disgust
Are blended anew in the texture of the web
And the web is stained with black & bloody clouds.
Is it gone to harmonies of joy
To the ardour of virtue & the wealth of truth
Is it gone to blank oblivion
The mockery of hope & virtue & the death of God.
[↑?]Alas! Alas! Alas!
Wo is me! for the sad survivor [↓?]

[19]   Tho' Fortune threw good not evil in his way
Showering the roses of pleasure & the laurel of Fame

---

and three more stanzas appear in Journal 1826, p. [18]. Edward Emerson dated the completed poem 1824 (*Poems, W,* IX, 383–384), but printed it under the date 1826 in *J,* II, 80–81. This first stanza, however, most certainly belongs to 1825. It is written in the same large scrawling hand as an apparently concurrent entry in No. XVIII[A], and was undoubtedly composed during the period of Emerson's severe eye trouble in 1825 (see p. 386, n. 86 above).

[20a] Emerson borrowed most of these two lines from Shakespeare (see pp. 314 and 351 above).

Whilst his brother breasted the driving snows
Alas for the sad survivor.
He walks the long streets of his native City
But the peopled street is like the desolate sea.
Men study his face and its lofty lines
And love the graceful tones of pride & power
Rolled with rich thunder of eloquent words.
In the bosom of his own land.
They love him and they honour him
And they think his heart leaps at the voice of their praise.
But their thoughts are dark & their eyes are dim
And they cannot see that a noble nature
Must pine or be matched with noble things.
It is ill with the living, it is well with the dead.
It is better with the dead who live
Than it is with the living who die daily.
Oh Life, thou art a house wherein Fears inhabit
And when Man, poor pilgrim, enters the doors
They flock unto him with icy hands
They lead him in their shivering company
And if he come to a shining room
They tell him it leads to a dungeon tower.

[20] ↑Animula↓ 21

Tho' Beauty's skin deep yet it sends its dart
Thro' skin blood & bone to the core of the heart.

What lends thy cheek a bloom so bright
When merry bells chime on gay Twelfth Night?

And tho' my heart ⟨is conscious it is⟩ ↑repents it is too↓
        kind
I am deemed churlish by the fickle world

What is life? a running stream
And man? a mote; and dames? a dream.

21 "Little soul" (Ed.).

409

Thro' life & love poor mortal plunge on
For breaking my sweet sugar dungeon.

↑Animula blandula↓[22]

Skip skip little spirit
Skip skip thro' the world
Big thy body little spirit
Which the dust must soon inherit;
Save the mischief & the merit,
All the rest to ruin hurled.
[↑?]Bow, wow, wow.[↓?]

[21]   [23] This cup of life is not so shallow
That we have drained the best
That all the wine at once we swallow
And lees make all the rest.

Maids of as soft a bloom shall marry
As Hymen yet hath blessed
And finer forms are in the quarry
Than Phidias e'er released.

And Time will yet reveal such treasures
[22] [blank]
[23]   All that thy virgin soul can ask be thine
Beautiful Ellen [24] ⟨a⟩Let this prayer be mine
The first devotion that my soul has paid
To mortal grace it pays to thee fair maid
I am enamoured of thy loveliness
Lovesick with thy sweet beauty which shall bless
With its glad light my path of life around

[22] "Gentle little soul" (Ed.). The phrase is written aslant beside line 2 of the verse. Emerson seems to be recalling "Animula, vagula, blandula," the first line of the Emperor Hadrian's well-known lyric, "Morientis, Ad Animam Suam."

[23] The two quatrains are printed under the date 1826 in J, II, 132, and 1827 in J, II, 219–220 and Poems, W, IX, 387.

[24] Ellen Louisa Tucker, whom Emerson met December 25, 1827, and to whom he became engaged on December 17, 1828. The verse would seem to have been written in the latter month.

Which now is joyless where thou art not found
⟨I was a hermit whom the lone muse cheers⟩
⟨I sped apart my solitary years⟩
Now am I stricken with the sympathy
That binds the whole world in electric tie [25]
I hail love's birth within my hermit breast
And welcome the bright ordinance to be blest
I was a hermit whom the lone Muse cheers,
I sped apart my solitary years,
I found no joy in woman's meaning eye
When Fashion's merry mob were dancing by;
Yet had I read the law all laws above,
— Great Nature hath ordained the heart to love —
Yet had I heard that in this mortal state
To every mind exists its natural mate,
That God at first did marry soul to soul
Tho' lands divide & seas between ⟨us[?]⟩them roll.
Then eagerly I searched each circle round
I panted for my mate, but no mate found
I saw bright eyes, fair forms, complexions fine,
But not a single soul that spoke to mine.
At last the star broke thro' the hiding cloud,
At last I found thee in the silken crowd
I found thee, Ellen, born to love & shine,
And I who found am blessed to call thee mine.

[24–36] [blank]
[37] [26] [...]

[38] For versatility of Genius see Livy de Cato the Elder[,] Shakspeare de Henry V — "Hear him debate of Commonwea[l]th affairs" &c &c,[27] Aubrey de Bacon, Byron de Caesar, Plutarch de Themistocles. Milton de Education, & Stewart, Fred. III's bottle in cellar; jack of all trades good at none — What's worth doing worth doing well.

---

[25] Emerson is echoing Byron. See above, p. 254, n. 72.
[26] The lower part of the page is torn out. The page bears only a repetition of the first stanza on p. [21].
[27] Shakespeare, *Henry V*, I, i, 41 ff.

No profit comes where is no pleasure ta'en
In brief Sir study what you most affect.[28]

Nature /cuts/notches/ the edge of the ⟨daisy⟩ ↑petal↓ leaf &
hurls the globes in orbits[.]
[inside back cover [29]]   Alcoran

[28] Shakespeare, *The Taming of the Shrew*, I, i, 39–40. Emerson gives "comes"
for "grows."
[29] Several leaves are torn out between p. [38] and the cover. Besides the single
word, the inside back cover has a penciled sketch of a man's face in left profile upside down in the lower left corner, probably by Emerson. "C. C. Emerson, Jan.
1824." also appears upside down, in Charles Emerson's hand. A circled "15" in pencil
is of recent date. For further details, see the headnote, p. 396 above.

No. II

1825

Dated "March 1, 1825," No. II is a remnant, not a complete note-book. It contains only the outline and the partial development of an essay entitled "Unity of God." Though apparently written shortly before Emerson's eyes failed, it is in a clear, firm hand. It may well have been an abortive exercise for the Harvard Theological School, which Emerson entered in February. Since the first page is numbered 45, the manuscript must have been at one time a part of a complete notebook or journal. "No. II" may, of course, imply another notebook or journal, "No. I," but there is no positive evidence of this. It may also imply a prior essay, either on the "Unity of God," or on some related subject.

The manuscript is composed of 12 leaves of folded sheets which were laid one on top of the other and sewed into one gathering and then enclosed in a cover of coarse paper. The leaves measure 15.2 x 19.1 cm, and the top leaves of each sheet are marked in pencil from "a" through "f," indicating that the essay was written before the leaves were sewed together. Emerson numbered leaf 1ʳ 45 and continued the pagination on every odd page through 67, though the essay ends on p. 65. Pages 46, 48, 55, 59, 61, 63, 66, 67, and 68, the last, are blank.

[45][1]   No. II. ⟨Feb⟩ March 1, 1825.
"   Unity of God.
        What Arguments from Reason
                        from Scripture
        What objections to it from the Constitution of Nature
                                the course of events &
                        from Scripture
                and how are they removed
What opinions have been maintained inconsistent with the divine
Unity?"

It is an opinion as old as Theism, tho' not as universal, that God

[1] The page bears some scrawls which may be practice penmanship with some effort to turn it into sketches.

413

is ONE. Apart from sacred history, the oldest records in the world of human opinions, conspire in this tradition. ↑Homer &↓ Hesiod ↑bear witness↓ & Herodotus ⟨bear⟩ ↑very↓ [2] explicit witness to this fact in very curious passages. And Plato & Aristotle are not only Unitarians themselves but affirm the antiquity of their faith. On the other hand it is certain that a gross polytheism has in all ages prevailed & now prevails over a large portion of mankind.[3] It cannot therefore be now known how far the doctrine of the ↑divine↓ Unity is a deduction of the human understanding [47] or how far it is indebted for this conception to primitive Revelation. There is undoubtedly much solid ground for the latter supposition and particularly from Hume's suggestion that if men by reasoning found out this doctrine ⟨they⟩ it would ⟨not⟩ ↑never↓ have ↑been↓ lost.[4] ↑But there is no doubt that our doctrine is not new↓. ⟨the⟩ It is a remark of Mitford⟨'s⟩ the historian of Greece ⟨"⟩ that "all the Greek philosophers were aware of the recent origin of that religion which in their time was popular."[5] It has been supposed that Plato whose whole philosophy involves the idea of the divine Unity did never declare his own belief being intimidated by the fate of his master Socrates. "One God," he says "it was reported once governed the Universe but a great & extraordinary change taking place in the nature of men & things infinitely

[2] All the insertions and the cancellation are in pencil, probably by Emerson. For the antiquity of the idea of a single God, Emerson has drawn in part upon William Mitford, *History of Greece*, 1795–1797, I, 99–125, *passim*, where the religion of the Greeks is discussed.

[3] The conclusion and some of the words are Hume's. Cf. "and thus polytheism has prevailed, and still prevails among the greatest part of uninstructed mankind" in "The Natural History of Religion," *Philosophical Essays*, 1817, II, 377–378. Emerson had withdrawn this volume from the Boston Library Society, Sept. 11, 1824–Feb. 3, 1825. He would also have been using *Essays and Treatises on Various Subjects* in the two-volume London edition of 1768, for on Feb. 20, 1825, he borrowed volume 2, which contains the same essay, from the Harvard College Library.

[4] Emerson is referring to the following passage in "The Natural History of Religion": "But farther, if men were at first led into the belief of one Supreme Being, by reasoning from the frame of nature, they could never possibly leave that belief, in order to embrace polytheism; but the same principles of reason, which at first produced and diffused over mankind, so magnificent an opinion, must be able, with greater facility to preserve it. The first invention and proof of any doctrine is much more difficult than the supporting and retaining of it." *Philosophical Essays*, 1817, II, 371.

[5] Mitford, *History of Greece*, 1795–1797, I, 107.

for the worse, (for originally there was perfect virtue & happiness on earth,) the command then devolved upon Jupiter with many inferior deities to preside over different de⟨ities⟩partments under him." [6] Without adverting to the strong incidental testimony borne by such passages to the Mosaic history, it seems proper to observe that what is called polytheism in Plato[,] his ascribing divine power to many limitary beings as [49] to demigods & heroes is a polytheism perfectly consistent with a common opinion among Christians which imparts a portion of divine power to Angels. So true is a noted saying of St Austin that Plato with the change of a few terms, is a Christian.[7] Besides the pure theology which is found in the Orphic poems this opinion is most distinctly declared by Aristotle. "It is a tradition," he says, "received from of old among all men that God is the Creator of & preserver of all things; & that nothing in nature is sufficient to its own existence, without his superintending protection. Hence some of the ancients have held that all things are full of gods; obvious to sight, to hearing & to all the senses; an opinion consonant enough to the power but not to the Nature of the deity. *God* being ONE has thus received many names according to the variety of effects of which he is the cause." [8]

Such is the remarkable purity & adequateness of the opinion anciently held by men of sense in the midst of polytheism. It is clear that the opinion must ⟨have remai⟩ find very strong support in human reason to be so faithfully kept. It is usually defended only on two grounds. In my humble judgment only one is tenable & that is sufficient to content [50] a candid mind. Whatever shews uniformity in [9] execution we refer to unity of design. We only know the Deity by his works & the *one*ness of these makes us think him *one*. It is difficult to believe the modern critic who makes the Iliad the work of

---

[6] *Ibid.* Emerson's learned source reference, "Polit. 269 t 2.", which appears in the left margin near "his master", is also taken from Mitford.

[7] The source reference "V[ide]. Op[era]. om[nia]. of Plato p." is in the left margin near "So true is". Like the reference to Plato above, it is doubtless from a secondary source.

[8] Mitford, *History of Greece*, 1795–1797, I, 109. Mitford cites "Aristot. de Mundo, c. 6" as the source.

[9] On p. [51] opposite the line "a candid mind . . . uniformity in" is a cross-mark, as though Emerson planned a note or an extension of the text.

many authors. It is difficult to believe the ⟨L⟩Statue of Laocoon the
work of 3 artists.[10] ⟨Yet⟩ ↑And yet there are 2 circumstances making
against this analogy 1.↓ we have known men working jointly a thousand times and, ↑2.↓ the unity of design in these productions is infinitely less than in the works of nature. The Uniformity in the creation & Providence of God is marked by majestic traits in the connexion
of the remotest parts of a stupendous whole. Whether the habits of
the inquirer lead him to trace the Divinity in the structure of the
earth, the organization of the mineral & vegetable kingdom, or in
the exquisite adaptation disclosed in animal bodies or whether he
prefer to ⟨d⟩scrutinize the intellect & pursue to their concealed principles those beautiful evasive phenomena, the separate dependance of
faculty on faculty, the separate functions but inseparable union of all,
the fitness of mind to mind as designed for social life — or whether
he chuse to draw more general results from the history of a portion
or the whole of these beings & explore [52] the pervading laws which
bind together the widest sundered parts, whatever branch of ⟨stud⟩
inquiry m⟨i⟩ay invite his study or whether in turn he grasp them
all, in all he discerns the same plan & the same workmanship. He
finds no perplexed & abrupt, no unfinished or incongruous parts. He
finds that whoever the Maker was he has made of one blood all
the nations of the earth[,] that he has fixed the most exact analogies
& perfect relations between limb & limb, species & species, part &
whole. Millions & millions of instances there are of this system which
can never come into the mind of one observer but as fast as they are
detected corroborate the general conclusion.

    Tho' we discover a new continent we find the same animals[,]
the same natural laws;[n] we never[,] says Paley[,] get into the dominion of another God. ⟨No⟩And when man's proud science soars to the
firmament and enquires the orbit of the planets he recognizes the same
laws prevailing in the same force, (a force he can compute to a frac-
tion.) The moon falls to the earth & Saturn falls to the Sun by the
selfsame law whereby ⟨the⟩ an apple descends to the ground. In the
revolution of ages they have remained unaltered & have given no

---

[10] In both the argument from design and the reference to the statue of Laocoön,
Emerson is following Hume in "The Natural History of Religion," *Philosophical
Essays*, 1817, II, 372–373.

sign of a divided obedience. [53] ⟨These Cavils at Dr Clarke & the priori crew may be found in Hume's Dialogue on Nat Rel.⟩

⟨These passages are all adduced in Clarke's Sermon II.⟩[11]

[54] With more ambition divines have attempted to prove the Unity of the Deity from *a priori* argumentation. To the fact of bare Existence in the Deity another fact is added to anticipate the question how he came to be. God is said to be necessarily existent & it is asserted that if we knew his whole essence or nature we should perceive it to be as impossible for him not to exist as for twice two not to be four. And then it is alleged that ⟨no⟩ Unity must be his attribute because Necessity is uniform, absolute, & universal. Now besides that such arguing is incomprehensible it has also the misfortune to be unsound. For it may be quite as reasonably urged that if We knew all the qualities of matter we should perceive its non-existence to be as impossible as for twice 2 not to be 4. The argument of Clarke to prove the material world not necessarily existent can be wholly retorted against the ↑necessary↓[n] existence of Deity. The material world says he is not necessarily existent because we can conceive it to be other than it is without any contradiction. But precisely the same thing can be said of the Necessary existence of the Deity since we can conceive any of his attributes altered or conceive [56_1] him nonexistent. If this be all that Necessity of which we hear so much it is a weak foundation to prove his unity from the ⟨absoluteness⟩ simplicity, Universality, & uniformity of the same.
[57_1] These cavils against Dr Clarke & his priori crew are all found in Hume Dial. on Nat. Rel.[12]
  [56_2] The third part of our subject is the evidence it derives from Revelation. Nothing can be more explicit, than the language of the

----

[11] By error Emerson added these comments on Hume and Clarke, then canceled them and entered them on p. [57].
  [12] "These cavils . . . Rel." is written opposite "him nonexistent . . . the same." The paragraph on p. [54] is mostly a close paraphrase of Hume, and two passages are direct quotations: "if we knew . . . to be four." and "the material world not necessarily existent" (p. 233). In the course of his argument at this point Hume identifies a quotation as by "Dr. Clarke." See *Dialogues concerning Natural Religion*, ed. N. K. Smith (Oxford, 1935), pp. 232–234.

following passages. ↑Deut vi. 4,↓ Hear o Israel The Lord our God is one Lord. iv. 39 He is God in Heaven above ⟨i⟩upon the Earth beneath there is none else. Is. 44.6 I am the first and I am the Last & besides me there is no God.

And in N. T. ↑I Cor. viii. 4.↓ We know that there is none other God but one for tho' there be that are called gods whether in Heaven or in Earth (as there be many Gods) yet to us there is but one God, the father, of whom are all things, & we in him. & one Lord J. C. [57₂] These texts adduced in Clarke Serm II p. 30 [13]

[56₃] With regard in the next place to those objections which spring from the Constitution of nature & the course of events in seeming repugnance to this doctrine, they seem to have great force in misleading men in the infancy of society. A man untaught to discern that uniformity in the works of nature of which we have already spoken and who only remarks the ⟨un⟩ operations of [58] unknown power intruding into the events of human life would be very naturally led into ⟨the⟩ polytheism. "Storm & tempests often ruin" says Mr Hume "what is nourished by the Sun. The Sun destroys what is fostered by the moisture of dews & rains. War may be favorable to a nation whom the inclemency of the seasons afflicts with famine. Sickness & pestilence may depopulate a kingdom amid the most profuse plenty. The same ⟨king⟩ nation is not at the same ↑time↓ equally successful by land & sea∧. In short the conduct of events or what we call the plan of a particular providence is full of variety & uncertainty" — . [14] When we have elsewhere found the notion of Divine Unity, reason teaches us to reconcile to it, this diversity of

---

[13] "These texts . . . p. 30" is written opposite "And in . . . other God" as a note to the two paragraphs on the evidence from Revelation; from "The third part" to "Lord J. C." "Deut vi. 4, . . . Lord J. C." is quoted practically verbatim from Samuel Clarke, *Sermons on Several Subjects.* See the 8th edition, 8 vols. (London, 1756), I, 24.

[14] "The Natural History of Religion," *Philosophical Essays,* 1817, II, 373. Emerson's caret presumably means that he intended to insert the omitted sentence "And a nation, which now triumphs over its enemies, may anon submit to their more prosperous arms." In the last sentence Emerson has altered the meaning of the original, which reads: "In short, the conduct of events, or what we call the plan of a particular providence, is so full of variety and uncertainty, that, if we suppose it immediately ordered by any intelligent beings, we must acknowledge a contrariety in their designs and intentions, a constant combat of opposite powers, and a repentance or change of intention in the same power, from impotence or levity."

event by just sense of the in⟨equ⟩adequateness of our faculties to the magnitude of the scene; teaches us to believe "All Chance, Direction which we cannot see".[15] It is certainly reasonable to beleive that the Being who placed men here in a discipline of which he alone knows the design & end directs that discipline by laws & in a consistence which we in our ignorance cannot ascertain.

[60] What objections there may be in scripture apart from verbal criticism on the names of the Deity, and apart ⟨the⟩from the passages supposed to involve the doctrine of the Trinity I am ignorant. For those which imply the agency of angels of course do not conclude anything against that Primary Being who delegates his power.

But lastly there remain certain opinions which have been defended inconsistent with the doctrine we maintain which we have not yet touched. It is objected that the heresy that has borne many names as Manicheism, Paulician, Marcionite and which is yet ⟨conta⟩ earlier contained in the old ⟨doc⟩ interrogatories of Epicurus[,] the opinion of two principles[,] strikes at the foundation of this doctrine & has never been satisfactorily refuted. Epicurus said if there be a God[,] Is he willing to prevent evil but not able? then is he impotent. Is he able but not willing? then is he male[62]volent.[16] Is he both able & willing? Whence then is evil? [17] Hence it was afterwards argued that there cannot be *One* independent First Cause. The existence of evil is inconsistent with Unity. All the contrivances of good we behold bear the appearance of imperfect remedies applied to the evils of our state. Now if there be good reason for this the consolation of religion must be given up, we are bitterly betrayed, and our faith is also vain. But there are some considerations by which we think it appears that there is no necessity in nature for this monstrous supposition.

In the first place the manner in which evil makes its appearance in the world is not as if it were the work of a separate Artist but everywhere in strictest connexion with good so as to appear rather gradation of enjoyment than exception [or?] thwarting anomaly which must be the case from the jarring of discordant gods. In the second

---

[15] Cf. Pope, *Essay on Man*, I, 290.

[16] A canceled "volent" appears upside down in the lower right corner of the page, indicating that Emerson started the page upside down.

[17] "Is he willing . . . evil?" is quoted from Hume. See *Dialogues concerning Natural Religion*, 1935, p. 244.

hNOTEBOOKS OF RALPH WALDO EMERSON 11

place a ready account can always be given of each particular evil so as to make it not incredible that a good spirit originated it. Thus the pain of the eyes in watching is to warn us [64] of the mischief that will accrue to the organ if we persist in using it. The pain of a fall is to teach us what care is necessary to keep that system sound which we possess — and an infinity of the like instances. But here the objector intrudes to say that 'tis no account of the matter to pretend this use to warn us of danger for ⟨th⟩He made the danger. Why did he make the eye weak & the body frail if as you say he is infinitely good & strong?

I answer that if the object of this life be as we believe a discipline to exercise us to virtue, we have an account of evil. For it may not be possible in the nature of things that virtue should exist without discipline. The human mind cannot conceive — which is one not inconsiderable presumption that the thing cannot exist — that virtue conferred should ever be good & great as Virtue acquired. A sufficient reason is furnished for all the toils, dangers, & disasters of life when they are seen to be the seed[,] the occasion of all the manly[,] the godlike virtues of zeal, intrepidity, fortitude, resignation — adjusted to engraft a moral strength [65] on the soul that could no otherwise be got. Lastly whilst we suppose God omnipotent it does not entrench on his Unity to suppose him sending evil as punishment any more than it casts a doubt on the Unity of the human soul that sometimes it does good & sometimes evil. There is no doubt much metaphysical difficulty too hard & high for our faculties concerning the origin of evil. But the question is as perplexing to the Manichee as to his antagonist[,] Whether the soul that does a good action was created by the good principle or by the evil? If by the ⟨good⟩ evil it follows that good may arise from the fountain of all evil. If it was created by the good principle it follows that evil may rise from the fountain of all good.

420

Textual Notes
Index

Textual Notes

Wide World 7

4 ⟨as[?]⟩ **5** outdone. **6** to man,₂ already₁ | We **11** That **13** unfairly, **14** It **15** This, | All **16** a⟩↑I↓n **17** ourselv[es] ["es" blotted] **18** After **19** heavens. | pi[ti]able ["ti" blotted] **20** The | Beneath | dead; | where **21** finished.. ¶This | That | The **23** of⟩ the **24** Education₂ and taste | ⟨t[?]⟩ over **25** superior₂ knowl- edge₁ | So **26** the⟨m[?]ir **27** If **29** Il **30** melody. **31** will find₂ not₁ **32** But | my hopes₂ ⟨s⟩Should₁ **35** This **38** [Emerson changed "Avalion" to "Ajalon"]

Wide World 8

42 ⟨[?]that)[?] **43** races. **54** democracy. **55** There **58** then **60** taste⟨,⟩↑?↓ | (Innumerable | frightful.) | *Hope.* **63** And **65** place. **66** be⟨e[?]⟩ | And | ⟨G[?]⟩Lord **68** institutions,₂ laws.₁ **69** You | ⟨&[?]⟩ feelings,

Wide World 9

78 ships. **81** vanity₂ & nothing₁ **82** ⟨l⟩multi⟨[?]⟩tude **83** And | ⟨in[?]⟩to- gether **84** ⟨rank abundance) [canceled in pencil] | ⟨they⟩ **86** petitions, ⟨t⟩The **90** this; **91** ⟨I[?]⟩Will | gone. | Will **93** by the Rhine₂ in his tent₁ **94** ⟨learn⟩ [canceled in pencil] ↑get↓ [in pencil] | trees, | ⟨sla[?]⟩ **96** In **97** The **98** Sodom & Gomorrah₂ the active contamination₁ | The | exenplary **99** stripes₂ & abstinence.₁ **100** hearts. | linked₂ inseparably₁

Wide World 10

105 [The following "My" is written over "⟨This[?]⟩"] **110** he give⟨s⟩ | combat. **112** interval. | ⟨ap[?]⟩prone **113** Forfeit **115** there. | The **116** The | In **117** not₂ for that₁ | is is **119** pleasure. | ↑& . . . with↓ [added in pencil] ⟨&⟩ [canceled in pencil] | ⟨[?]⟩was **120** Nevertheless | It **121** We | Can | We **123** seasons, ↓; | .— which **124** Turning | pleasure. | government. | virtue. | In | Man . . . nature₂ to . . . protest₁ **127** Hundreds | With | The | Without **128** can . . . Him,₂ containing . . . decay;₁ — One | ⟨hom⟩↑patr↓icide. **129** die. | could. **130** ⟨[?]⟩gives | Annihilates | survive. | good. **131** feelings —. **133** force. **135** Ah! Red Men are few [encircled in pencil and directed by a penciled arrow to follow "And . . . heads" in previous line] | Red men are feeble [canceled in pencil] | Seer. —— [encircled in ink] | ↑with↓ me [canceled subscript "2"] . . . wrestle [canceled subscript "1"] **136** instead, | ⟨[?]⟩majestic | food. **137** Ardour **138** A **139** And | When **140** And **141** What, | When **142** God . . . pure₂ — if . . . salvation↑,↓.₁ | ↑from↓ opportunity & knowledge₂ ⟨are⟩ ↑he is↓ not kept aloof₁ | And | And | ⟨i[?]⟩once **143** Peradventure

Wide World 11

149 ↑waters . . . rolled↓ [in pencil] | exemption. **150** inhabit. | And **151** ⟨U[?]⟩the **153** day. | Judging | *vanity* **154** ↑i↓⟨a⟩↑n↓⟨t⟩tentions | virtue. **155** dinn | men;[?] | if | and | how | what **156** fi⟨re[?]⟩ercest | When [no paragraph] | Corners. . . . yourself. . . . loneliness. **157** he **158** instincts$_2$ of$_3$ infinite$_1$ | the **160** ⟨is⟩ ↑they have seen↓ marked$_2$ among their fellow men$_1$ | reform$_2$ & awake.$_1$ **161** album, | pulse. **162** promise. | accomplishment. **163** goodness. | The **164** passions. | ⟨Why⟩ **165** so strenuously$_2$ & so often complain$_1$ | a⟨ll[?]p-pointed **166** directed- | asked:[?] | enough. **168** Vol.) **169** convenient, [penciled comma] **170** ripe⟨ness of⟩ ↑excellence↓ . . . ↑being↓. | And | W⟨|| . . . ||⟩ar's **171** wisdom. | friends. **172** But **176** them. | profit.

Walk to the Connecticut

181 Western. | pudding. **182** ⟨ot[?]|| . . . ||o[?]⟩of **184** *granite;'* **185** eloquence. **186** At

Wide World 12

188 It **190** is | the⟨s[?]e⟩ne [or] the⟨e[?]⟩ne [with a dot added over the first "e"] | submit. **193** covet. **194** Greece, had many; | their's **195** Greece. **198** for. | fortunes. **199** whose fer⟨vent⟩ **200** ⟨fo[?]⟩ **201** th⟨ese⟩at[?] [or] th⟨eir⟩at[?] | ⟨wor[?]⟩ | down, | wont, [penciled comma] **202** though one **203** seen. **204** Affection | there [with a dot added over the "r"] **205** poetry. **206** Example, [penciled comma] | while, . . . read, [penciled commas] | with. | men **208** invents | to chew . . . shade,$_2$ & leave . . . awhile.$_1$ **209** Inquisition, [penciled comma] | free$_2$ & bold & skilful$_1$ | Rights. | rapid$_2$ & sudden$_1$ | in character$_2$ their posterity$_1$ **210** Tho' great ↑common↓ objects | revealed. **211** wit.' | the | laws,

Wide World XIII

216 Other | ⟨or[?]⟩than | inflammable. **218** ↑deemed↓ [in pencil] **219** or. | originality. **220** I[?] | The | ⟨carr[?]⟩ | A **221** ⟨vic[?]⟩ttu⟩ rectitude **222** vehemence. **223** imitation., | Galileo$_3$ Columbus$_2$ Socrates$_1$ **224** ⟨t⟩h⟨e⟩is | The **225** Justice'. **226** rest. **227** ⟨by th⟩ ↑by the↓ ["by" inserted in pencil] **228** True **230** Good | ↑so↓ obvious or just$_2$ advantage$_1$ **231** decisive. **232** For | metropol⟨e⟩is↑es↓ **234** contemporary. **236** ⟨busy⟩ [3⟨2⟩3] ⟨schemes⟩ ↑money getting of the miser,$_2$ the profligacy of libertines$_1$ **240** defends. **241** out;" **242** these **244** cont⟨ained⟩↑veyed↓ **245** Locke$_2$ & Cudworth$_1$ **248** ridicule. **249** ↑to be, &c.↓ easy to assign . . . claim;$_2$ to be . . . Time$_1$ **252** God, [penciled comma] **253** ↑that↓ [canceled in pencil] ⟨has no⟩ | an **254** Memory | γα⟨r⟩ρ φρονειν$_1$ | it. **256** speculation. **257** ⟨De⟩rision's | obloquy. **259** win . . . nature.$_2$ distinguish . . . ↑& so↓$_1$ **261** murder. **262** prayer; | such. | charm. **263** state. | a ⟨great **264** by ⟨inflexible . . . ill m⟩ | Epicureans. **265** Books . . . record [80] the . . . mention⟩$_2$ ↑Apart from↓ . . . elicit.$_1$ | world.↓ **266** designated **268** comes, **269** a⟨n⟩y **271** selection.

No. XV

273 s⟨o [or] u⟩av⟨e [or] o⟩as⟨[?]⟩↑g↓e **278** ⟨Nor . . . assign⟩ [canceled in pencil] To ["t" changed to "T" in pencil] **279** chief, | every **280** cabinets.↓ **281** ⟨herd[?]⟩ **282** &c. &c they **283** superiority.↓ | defiled. **285** moon, | with. **286** heard. | Must . . . day. Can . . . yourself. Because . . . devotion. **287** Humboldt$_2$ or Cook$_1$ **288** age;.↑(2)↓ they found . . . sown. ⟨I had not dwelt thus long on this disastrous⟩ ↑(1)↓They found . . . deceit; | ⟨hi[?]⟩state **289** ⟨ot⟩protectors. **290** enjoyment.) | proud. **291** ungentlemanly. **292** of [uncanceled] **293** own. |

& the . . . life.₂ with . . . opinions₁   294 devotion. | devotion. | applied   295 them. | employment.   296 The   298 worth. | time.   299 end. | an appetite₂ & capacity₁ | We | ↑small↓₂ those₁ | A   300 Or   302 ⟨would⟩ [canceled in pencil]   303 an ⟨eloquence⟩   304 here.   306 and who . . . & ⟨extolling   309 society;   314 ↑Else↓ 315 ways [73] he   316 ↑m↓⟨|| . . . ||⟩ood | One   317 The   319 prosperity. | bed. 321 society.   322 ⟨&⟩   325 being.   327 You | These   328 days. | It   329 world. 330 we⟨e⟩feel   331 a   332 Pythagoras; | eighth.   333 It   334 chamber.   336 read. 338 No   341 Every | diseases;   343 hold. | decays.   344 practises. | thet   345 if | society.

No. XVIII[A]

359 ↑certamine↓ [inserted in pencil, by Emerson?]   362 hominibus₂ infestas₁ 364 ⟨||...||⟩.   367 ⟨La Place⟩ ["a." appears beneath the name]   368 invet⟨r₂⟩e⟨e₁⟩rate 369 Parian   370 ice.↓ | cold.   376 thrones₃ archiepiscopal₂ & episcopal,₁   377 As 378 experiment.   379 circumscribed.   382 God.   383 ⟨⟨le⟩↑be↓a⟨ds⟩↑ts↓⟩ | disciples. | sovereignty.   384 name.   388 of relations.   389 unlock⟨ed[?]⟩its   392 vanishe⟨s⟩ ["e" canceled in pencil]   395 ⟨w↑e↓he↑a↓n↑ve↓

No. XVI

397 ⟨in⟩↑a↓⟨v⟩gain   398 ⟨w[?]⟩fortunes   399 society.   400 ⟨L[?]⟩It

No. II

416 laws,   417 ↑nec.↓ ["essary" added in pencil]

Index

438